Interviewing Experts

Research Methods Series

General Editors: **Bernhard Kittel,** Professor of Social Science Methodology, Department of Social Sciences, **Carl von Ossietzky** Universität Oldenburg, Germany and **Benoît Rihoux,** Professor of Political Science, Université catholique de Louvain (UCL), Belgium.

In association with the European Consortium for Political Research (ECPR), Palgrave Macmillan is delighted to announce the launch of a new book series dedicated to producing cutting-edge titles in Research Methods. While political science currently tends to import methods developed in neighbouring disciplines, the series contributes to developing a methodological apparatus focusing on those methods which are appropriate in dealing with the specific research problems of the discipline.

The series provides students and scholars with state-of-the-art scholarship on methodology, methods and techniques. It comprises innovative and intellectually rigorous monographs and edited collections which bridge schools of thought and cross the boundaries of conventional approaches. The series covers both empirical-analytical and interpretive approaches, micro and macro studies, and quantitative and qualitative methods.

Titles include:

Alexander Bogner, Beate Littig and Wolfgang Menz *(editors)*
INTERVIEWING EXPERTS

Audie Klotz and Deepa Prakash *(editors)*
QUALITATIVE METHODS IN INTERNATIONAL RELATIONS
A Pluralist Guide

Lane Kenworthy and Alexander Hicks *(editors)*
METHOD AND SUBSTANCE IN MACROCOMPARATIVE ANALYSIS

Research Methods Series
Series Standing Order ISBN   978–0230–20679–3 hardcover
Series Standing Order ISBN   978–0230–20680–9 paperback
(outside North America only)

You can receive future titles in this series as they are published by placing a standing order. Please contact your bookseller or, in case of difficulty, write to us at the address below with your name and address, the title of the series and one of the ISBNs quoted above.

Customer Services Department, Macmillan Distribution Ltd, Houndmills, Basingstoke, Hampshire RG21 6XS, England

Interviewing Experts

Edited by

Alexander Bogner
Austrian Academy of Sciences, Austria

Beate Littig
Institute of Advanced Studies, Austria

and

Wolfgang Menz
Institute for Social Science Research, Germany

First published 2009 by
PALGRAVE MACMILLAN

Palgrave Macmillan in the UK is an imprint of Macmillan Publishers Limited,
registered in England, company number 785998, of Houndmills, Basingstoke,
Hampshire RG21 6XS.

Palgrave Macmillan in the US is a division of St Martin's Press LLC,
175 Fifth Avenue, New York, NY 10010.

Palgrave Macmillan is the global academic imprint of the above companies
and has companies and representatives throughout the world.

Palgrave® and Macmillan® are registered trademarks in the United States,
the United Kingdom, Europe and other countries.

ISBN: 978–0–230–22019–5 hardback
ISBN: 0–230–22019–3 hardback

This book is printed on paper suitable for recycling and made from fully
managed and sustained forest sources. Logging, pulping and manufacturing
processes are expected to conform to the environmental regulations of the
country of origin.

A catalogue record for this book is available from the British Library.

Library of Congress Cataloging-in-Publication Data

Interviewing experts / edited by Alexander Bogner, Beate Littig, and
Wolfgang Menz.
p. cm.—(Research methods series)
Includes bibliographical references and index.
ISBN 978–0–230–22019–5 (alk. paper)
1. Interviewing. 2. Specialists – Interviews – Methodology. I. Bogner,
Alexander. II. Littig, Beate. III. Menz, W. (Wolfgang)

BF637.I5I57 2009
001.4'32—dc22   2009013661

10 9 8 7 6 5 4 3 2 1
18 17 16 15 14 13 12 11 10 09

Printed and bound in Great Britain by
CPI Antony Rowe, Chippenham and Eastbourne

Contents

Part III Fields of Application:
Applications of Expert Interviews in
Different Fields of Research

Illustrations

Tables

Figures

Contributors

Gabriele Abels is a professor for comparative politics and European integration at the Institute of Political Science, University of Tübingen. Her research interests are European integration, political participation, biotechnology policy, gender studies. She is the co-editior of "femina politica: Zeitschrift für feministische Politik-Wissenschaft."

Her most recent publications include: Abels, G. and Lepperhoff, J. (forthcoming 2009) "Frauen-, Geschlechter- und Intersektionalitätsforschung. Methodologische Entwicklungen und offene Fragen" in Barbara Friebertshäuser et al. (eds) *Handbuch Qualitative Forschungsmethoden in der Erziehungswissenschaft*, 2nd edn (Weinheim, München: Juventa) and Abels, G. (2007) "Trade and Human Rights: Inter- and Supranational Regulation of GMOs and ART" in Montpetit, E. et al. (eds) *The Politics of Biotechnology in North America and Europe: Policy Networks, Institutions and Internationalization* (Lanham, MD: Lexington Books), pp. 35–59.

Georg Aichholzer is project director and senior researcher at the Institute of Technology Assessment (ITA) of the Austrian Academy of Sciences and senior lecturer at Vienna University of Economics and Business Administration. Trained in Social Sciences (PhD in Sociology) his research interests focus on technology assessment, interrelations of information technology and society, and related policies. A major field of study are technological innovations in government and governance (electronic public services, electronic participation).

Among his publications are: Aichholzer, G. and Burkert, H. (eds) (2004) *Public Sector Information in the Digital Age. Between Markets, Public Management and Citizens?* (Rights, Cheltenham, UK, and Northampton, MA: Edward Elgar Publishing) and Aichholzer, G. (2007) "Opening the Black Box: Economic and Organisational Effects of e-Government" in Remenyi, D. (ed.) *Proceedings of the 3rd International Conference on e-Government, University of Quebec at Montreal, Canada, 26–28 September 2007* (Dublin: Academic Conferences International), pp. 1–10.

Maria Behrens is professor at the Department of Political Science at the University Wuppertal (Germany). Research Areas: political coordination and regulation of conflicts in international politics (global governance); the relationship of intergovernmental and transnational forms of political decision-making (private governance).

Publications: Behrens, M. (forthcoming 2009) "Beyond the competitive race: US and EU foreign trade policy" in Wynn, N. (ed.) *Conflict and*

Consensus: Transatlantic Perspectives (Cambridge: Cambridge University Press); Behrens, M. (2007) "Global Governance" in Benz, A. et al. (eds) *Handbuch Governance* (Wiesbaden: VS-Verlag), pp. 311–24 and Behrens, M. (2005) *Globalisierung als politische Herausforderung, Global Governance zwischen Utopie und Realität* (Wiesbaden: VS-Verlag).

Alexander Bogner is a sociologist by training and researcher at the Institute for Technology Assessment of the Austrian Academy of Sciences in Vienna. His main research interests are science and technology studies, sociology of expertise and methods of empirical research.

His publications include: Bogner, A. (2005) "How Experts Draw Boundaries. Dealing with non-knowledge and uncertainty in prenatal testing" in *Science, Technology and Innovation Studies 1*, 17–37 and Bogner, A. and Menz, W. (2006) "Science crime. The Korean cloning scandal and the role of ethics" in *Science and Public Policy 33*, 601–12.

Gabriela B. Christmann is head of the research department "Dynamics of Communication, Knowledge and Spatial Development" at the Leibniz Institute for Regional Development and Structural Planning (IRS) in Erkner (near Berlin). Her main research interests include the sociology of knowledge and culture, urban sociology, communication analysis, and methods of qualitative research.

Recent publication: Christmann, G. (2008) "The Power of Photographs of Buildings in the Dresden Urban Discourse. Towards a Visual Discourse Analysis" in *Forum Qualitative Sozialforschung / Forum: Qualitative Social Research 9(3)*, Art. 11, http://nbnresolving.de/urn:nbn:de:0114-fqs0803115 (accessed on 16 May 2009).

Ulrike Froschauer is Assistant Professor at the Institute of Sociology, University of Vienna, Austria. Her main research interests are in the field of the sociology of organisations, sociology of organisational consulting, methodology and methods of qualitative research and evaluation.

Among her publications are: Froschauer, U. (2006) "Veränderungsdynamik in Organisationen" in Tänzler, D., Knoblauch, H., Soeffner, H.-G. (eds) *Zur Kritik der Wissensgesellschaft* (Konstanz: UVK), pp. 157–83 and Froschauer, U., Lueger, M. (2003) *Das qualitative Interview. Zur Praxis Interpretativer Analyse sozialer Systeme* (Wien: WUV-UTB).

Jochen Gläser, PD (Free University Berlin) Dr (Humboldt-University Berlin) is a senior researcher at the Technical University of Berlin's Center for Technology and Society. His major research interests are in the sociology of science, sociological theory and qualitative methods.

Recent publications include: Gläser, J. and Whitley, R. (eds) (2007) *The Changing Governance of the Sciences: The Advent of Research Evaluation Systems* (Berlin: Springer); Gläser, J. and Laudel, G. (2007) "Interviewing Scientists" in *STI-Studies 3/2* and Gläser, J. and Laudel, G. (2008) "Creating

Competing Constructions by Re-Analysing Qualitative Data" in *Historical Social Research 33/3.*

Grit Laudel, Dr (University of Bielefeld) is a senior researcher at the Rathenau Institute in The Hague, Netherlands. She is interested in the sociology of science and the methodology and methods of qualitative research.

Recent publications are: Gläser, J. and Laudel, G. (2008) "From apprentice to colleague: the metamorphosis of Early Career Researchers" in *Higher Education 56/3;* Gläser, J. and Laudel, G. (2007) "Interviewing Scientists" in *STI-Studies 3/2;* and Gläser, J. and Laudel, G. (2008) "Creating Competing Constructions by Re-Analysing Qualitative Data" in *Historical Social Research 33/3.*

Andrea Leitner is a member of the academic staff at the Institute for Advanced Studies in Vienna. Her main research interests are labour market processes, especially interfaces between paid and unpaid work as well as between labour market and education, gender studies and evaluation research.

Her publications include: Leitner, A. (2007) *Frauenförderung im Wandel. Gender Mainstreaming in der österreichischen Arbeitsmarktpolitik* (Frankfurt/ New York: Campus) and Leitner, A. and Wroblewski, A. (June, 2006) "Welfare States and Work-Life Balance. Can Good Practices Be Transferred from the Nordic Countries to Conservative Welfare States?" in *European Societies 8(2),* 295–317.

Beate Littig is a sociologist, head of the Sociology Department at the Institute for Advanced Studies (IHS) in Vienna and a permanent lecturer at the University of Vienna. Her research interests include qualitative methodology, gender studies, sociology of practice and sustainable work.

Recent publications include: Littig, B. (2006) Book review: Lewis A. Dexter (2006). "Elite and Specialized Interviewing." With a New Introduction by Alan Ware and Martín Sánchez-Jankowski (16 Paragraphs) in *Forum Qualitative Sozialforschung / Forum: Qualitative Social Research 9(1),* Art. 5, http://nbn-resolving.de/urn:nbn:de:0114-fqs080151 (accessed on 16 May 2009) and Hildebrandt, E. and Littig, B. (eds) (2006) "Concepts, Approaches and Problems of Work-Life-Balance," *European Societies 8/2,* Special Issue.

Manfred Lueger is Associate Professor at the Institute for Sociology and Social Research, Vienna University of Economics and Business Administration. His research has focused on methodology and methods of interpretative social research, the analysis of organisations, and entrepreneurship education.

Publications include: Lueger, M. (2001) *Auf den Spuren der sozialen Welt. Methodologie und Organisierung interpretativer Sozialforschung* (Frankfurt, Berlin, Bern, Bruxelles, New York, Oxford, Wien: Peter Lang Verlag) and Hammerschmid, G., Lueger, M., Meyer R., Sandner, K. (2005) "Contextualizing Influence Activities. An Objective Hermeneutical Approach" in *Organization Studies 2005/8 (26),* 1145–68.

Wolfgang Menz, Dr, a researcher at the Institute for Social Science Research, ISF München. He studied Sociology und Political Sciences at the Universities of Marburg/Germany, Frankfurt/Germany and Edinburgh/UK. Holder of a PhD-Scolarship of the Hans-Böckler-Stiftung (2003–2006), Researcher at the Johann Wolfgang Goethe-Universität, Frankfurt (2001–2003) and the Institut für Sozialforschung, Frankfurt (2003–2007), lecturer at the Universities of Vienna/Austria and Frankfurt/Germany. His research interests include the sociology of work and organisation, science studies and methods of qualitative research.

Michael Meuser is professor for the sociology of gender relations at the University of Dortmund, Germany. His research interests are: sociology of gender, sociology of knowledge, qualitative methods, political sociology, sociology of the body.

Recent publications: Meuser, M. (forthcoming) "Gender Competence? Gender Mainstreaming, Managing Diversity and the Professionalisation of Gender Politics in Germany" in Mustafa Özbilgin (ed.) *Diversity, Equalitiy and Inclusion at Work: a Research Companion* (Cheltenham/New York: Edward Egar Press) and Klein, G. and Meuser, M. (eds) *Ernste Spiele. Zur politischen Soziologie des Fußballs* (Bielefeld: transcript 2008).

Ulrike Nagel, Dr. phil. habil., Senior Lecturer of Microsociology, Otto-von-Guericke-Universität Magdeburg, Department of Sociology. Research interests: micro-sociology, sociology of professions, European identity, biography analysis, qualitative methods of social research.

Publications include: Nagel, U., Teipen, Ch. and Velez, A. (2005) "Die Macht der Verhältnisse und die Stärke des Subjekts. Eine Studie über Ostdeutsche Manager vor und nach 1989. Zugleich eine biographietheoretische Erklärung für Stabilität und Instabilität der DDR" in *ZBBS 2/2005*, pp. 277–302 and Nagel, U. (1997) *Engagierte Rollendistanz. Professionalität in biographischer Perspektive* (Opladen: Leske & Budrich, Reihe Biographie und Gesellschaft).

Vaida Obelené, a sociologist by training, works on social stratification in post-communist Europe. Currently she is a PhD researcher at the European University Institute (Florence) in the department of Social and Political Sciences. Her thesis is entitled: "Discontinuity in Elite Formation: Former Komsomol Functionaries in the Period of Post-communist Transition in Lithuania and Belarus."

Publications: Jasiukaityte, Vaida and Reiter, H. (2004) "Jugendpolitik in Ländern des Übergangs – welchen Beitrag kann sie zur Zivilgesellschaft in Europa leisten?" in Lauritzen, P. and Otten, H. (eds) *Jugendarbeit und Jugendpolitik in Europa* (Wiesbaden: Verlag für Sozialwissenschaften), pp. 181–93 and Jasiukaityte, Vaida (2004) *Making a difference with minority youth in Europe* (Strasbourg: Council of Europe).

Michaela Pfadenhauer is Professor for Sociology at Karlsruhe University. Diplom at Bamberg University (Sociology and Political Science); PhD at Dortmund University (Sociology). She is Coordinator of the German Sociological Association research network Sociology of Profession. Her work domains are Sociology of Knowledge, Sociology of Everyday Culture (Posttraditional Communities), Consumerism and Professionalism.

Publications: Pfadenhauer, M. (2006) "Crisis or Decline? Problems of legitimation and loss of confidence of modern professionalism" in *Current Sociology 54* (4/2006), 565–78 and Pfadenhauer, M. "Ethnography of Scenes. Towards a Sociological Life-world Analysis of (Post-traditional) Community-building" (31 paragraphs) in *Forum: Qualitative Social Research [On-line Journal] 6(3), Art. 43*. Available at: http://www.qualitative-research.net/fqs-texte/3–05/05–3-43-e.htm (Date of Access: 09 23, 2005).

Rainer Trinczek is now professor at the Friedrich-Alexander-Universität Nürnberg-Erlangen. His main research interests are industrial relations, sociology of management, sociology of work, and qualitative research methods.

His publications include: Trinczek, R. (2006) "Work-Life Balance and Flexible Working Hours – The German Experience" in Blunsdon, B., Blyton, P., Dastmalchian, A. and Reed, K. (eds) *Work-Life Integration. International Perspectives on the Balancing of Multiple Roles* (Basingstoke/New York: Palgrave MacMillan), pp. 113–34, and Artus, I., Böhm, S., Lücking, S., Trinczek, R. (eds) (2006) *Betriebe ohne Betriebsrat. Informelle Interessenvertretung in Unternehmen* (Frankfurt/New York: Campus).

Angela Wroblewski studied Sociology in Vienna, since 1998 member of the academic staff at the HIS, lecturer at the Vienna University of Economics and Business Administration and the University of Vienna. Research interests: evaluation of social programmes, gender and education research.

Recent publication: Cook, T.D., Steiner, P.M. and Wroblewski, A. (forthcoming) "Randomised experiments and quasi-experimental designs in educational research" in Cousins, B., Ryan, K. (eds) *International Handbook of Educational Evaluation* (Thousand Oaks, CA: Sage).

Introduction: Expert Interviews – An Introduction to a New Methodological Debate

Alexander Bogner, Beate Littig and Wolfgang Menz

Before we go any further, we would like to begin by providing the reader with a step-by-step introduction to the methodological debate surrounding expert interviews. In doing so, we will start with a brief discussion of the generally accepted advantages and risks of expert interviews in research practice (1). We will follow this by outlining current trends in the sociological debate regarding experts and expertise, since expert interviews are – at least on the surface – defined by their object, namely the expert (2). We will then conclude with a look at the current methodological debate regarding expert interviews, an overview of the layout and structure of this book, as well as summaries of the 12 articles it contains (3).

I.1 Expert interviews: easy to manage?

The debate surrounding expert interviews is a recent one. The article published in 1991 by Meuser and Nagel was instrumental in launching an initial systematic debate on expert interviews in Germany. But it would be another ten years before the debate actually gained significant momentum, in an upward trend that is also reflected in current methodology handbooks (for example Flick, 2006, Przyborski and Wohlrab-Sahr, 2008).[1] The focus of this interest lies primarily on issues of what constitutes an expert, the differences between the various forms of expert interviews and their role in research design, as well as the specifics of interviewing and interaction in comparison to other qualitative interview forms.

The use of expert interviews has long been popular in social research. The actual role of the expert interviews in individual research design, their form and the methods used to analyse the results might vary from case to case, but there are still a number of common, practical reasons for their popularity in research.

1

Firstly, in relative terms, talking to experts in the exploratory phase of a project is a more efficient and concentrated method of gathering data than, for instance, participatory observation or systematic quantitative surveys. Conducting expert interviews can serve to shorten time-consuming data gathering processes, particularly if the experts are seen as "crystallization points" for practical insider knowledge and are interviewed as surrogates for a wider circle of players. Expert interviews also lend themselves to those kinds of situations in which it might prove difficult or impossible to gain access to a particular social field (as is the case, for instance, with taboo subjects).

The economic aspect also extends to the broad, practical matter of initiating and conducting such interviews. The organizational structures behind the experts in institutions (for example their secretaries or press offices) can often serve as an easy point of entry to the field of research. Furthermore, if the targeted expert is not only willing to participate, but also holds a key position in the organization, opportunities for expanding the researcher's access to the field may well also be unearthed in the interview. Sometimes, the expert will even indicate additional potential interviewees with expertise in a particular field during the interview itself. Equipped with the added bonus of the support of an expert in a key position, the researcher may then often find it easier to gain access to an extended circle of experts.

Beyond the direct benefits, it is also evident that expert interviews offer researchers an effective means of quickly obtaining results and, indeed, of quickly obtaining good results. Frequently, the fact that the interviewer and the interviewee share a common scientific background or relevance system can increase the level of motivation on the part of the expert to participate in an interview. A shared understanding of the social relevance of the research can then often be assumed, largely eliminating the need for further justification. A number of secondary motivating factors also make it comparatively easy to encourage and motivate experts to participate in such interviews: the professionalism of people familiar with being in the public eye; silent awareness of the scientific and/or political relevance of their field of activity or personal achievements; the desire to help "make a difference" – no matter how small; professional curiosity about the topic and field of research; an interest in sharing one's thoughts and ideas with an external expert.

Regardless of what might be myth and what is reality, the anticipated promise of rapid and unproblematic access to objective data makes expert interviews an extremely appealing option for empirical social researchers. But is the expert interview method really quite so simple and uncomplicated? If so, does this then render methodological considerations superfluous? Or are expert interviews in some ways just too tempting? Do they not – in their naïve belief in the totality of expert knowledge – harbour the danger of advocating a pre-reflexive definition of what constitutes an expert? Or the risk of granting the undisputed relevance of expert knowledge a standing that would ultimately constitute the non-validated confirmation and, thus, the legitimization of social hierarchies? A critical look at the current social science debate on experts and expertise could have a corrective effect here, and we will examine these questions in more detail in the following section.

I.2   Trends in social science research into expertise

As far as the expert and expertise are concerned, recent social science research trends have proved relatively stable. The "expert" has edged into the centre of theoretical interest from both a theory of society and a democratic theory perspective as well as from the sociology of knowledge, scientific or technical research standpoints (cf. Jasanoff and others, 1995, Bogner and Torgersen, 2005). Yet the literature on expert interview methods remains largely unmoved by this trend.

In scientific and technical circles, researchers are currently rethinking what really constitutes an expert and where the "relevant" knowledge for political decisions actually lies. In this context, Collins and Evans (2002) maintain that the sociology of expertise is currently entering a third wave. Based on their timeline, the first wave is embodied in the golden age of the expert with its clear and recognized horizontal division between experts and lay people. The expert as agent of truth and authority encounters a political system that uses its power to enforce expertise ("truth speaks to power"). The second wave is characterized by social constructivism in its prime, with its focus on demystifying science: knowledge is deciphered as a social activity and the validity of expert knowledge as a construction process is decoded. Likewise, challenging the boundary between experts and lay people accelerates the debate on the democratization of expertise (cf. Maasen and Weingart, 2005). To counter the constructivist breaking of the expert's spell – which it is ultimately claimed would lead to epistemic anarchy – Collins and Evans (2007) propose a "realist approach" as the third wave. "The realist approach (...) starts from the view that expertise is the real and substantive possession of groups of experts and that individuals acquire real and substantive expertise through their membership of those groups" (Collins and Evans, 2007, p. 3). If some form of institutionalized and autonomous area of science is to remain, Collins and Evans maintain that there is a need for genuine expertise based on expert knowledge and, thus, participation limits. The fact that they only consider "technical expertise" contributes to the suggestiveness of their ideas and, at the same time, reveals the cognitivistic constraints of their analysis of expertise. Specific problem framing is used to tailor questions in a way that makes this "technical expertise," that is the expert's factual knowledge (and not some form of lay practical knowledge), relevant. Expertise is relevant not (solely) by virtue of its own intrinsic quality, but also as a result of external conditions.

From the political science and democratic theory perspectives, expertise is viewed primarily as a challenge for democracy. Is it not the case – as is commonly feared – that the worldviews of experts and the things they see as relevant preform parliamentary decisions because they are – by virtue of their authority – considered to be the factual basis behind the political debate? The tension between expertise as necessary basis and ideological preformation of political decisions was already a point of discussion in the technocratic debate of the 1960s. Stephen Turner (2002) was the latest to question whether expertise represents a fundamental threat to liberal democracy. He bases his own trust in the democratic compatibility of expertise on the basic dubitability of the latter, realized not least in public protests and scientific self-criticism – effectively turning scientific criticism into an empirical sign of a functioning democracy.

Similar positions regarding the democratizing side effects of the expertise boom can also be found in the theory of society debate. For example, in the "reflexive modernization" debate – with its explicit socio-critical emphasis – expert knowledge is seen as the driving force and crystallization point for social conflict and as the stimulus and medium for an emancipated battle for the conditions of definition. Seen from this perspective, the side effects of the modernization process (for example global warming, ecological devastation, genetic manipulation) turn enforcement of the Enlightenment ideal of perfect control over society through expert knowledge into a moment of social self-enlightenment (cf. Beck, 1992). Since these risks and dangers are abstract in nature, scientific knowledge (that is critical experts) is required to turn them into social fact. In this regard, the expert is becoming more diversified. A new actor is taking to the stage in the battle for rationality – in the form of the counter- or anti-expert who advises critical NGOs in risk controversies. However, experts as agents of different rationality models will only be effective insofar as they actually succeed in influencing public awareness through the media. Consequently, an ability to put specific knowledge to use for political gain is a constitutive characteristic of this type of "post-traditional" expert. The key from this perspective is to interpret the world in a high-profile and influential (but not necessarily new) manner and thus – as (counter-)expert – become a powerful voice in the battle for the conditions of definition.

Expert knowledge is also accorded a central role in Giddens' modernization theory. He discusses the changes in the modern world from the point of view of knowledge dynamics (not the side effects). Expert knowledge is part of the "institutional reflexivity" (Giddens, 1991, p. 20) which supposes that all premises of individual and organizational activity will be routinely examined in the light of new information about such practices. Furthermore, experts become important when people find themselves having to deal with abstract systems (whose internal workings they do not understand). It is up to the expert here to convince them to trust such (primarily technical) abstract systems, for example by means of appropriate self-staging strategies (Giddens, 1990). This is by no means an easy task, because in late modernity the growth in relevance of expert knowledge is paradoxically accompanied by a crisis of recognition on the part of the experts. Even though progressive detraditionalization in many areas pushes us to base our decisions on expert knowledge, we are nonetheless also experts at always getting a "second opinion." Particularly in cases where problems are categorized and handled as issues of values not knowledge (for example in genetic counselling), the previously rigid hierarchy between experts and lay people tends to give way to more flexible and situative structures of interaction (Bogner, 2005).

Giddens does not, however, relate this trend to the problem framing aspect; instead he puts it in the context of an ambivalent attitude to specialization: specialization might well safeguard the continued existence of the expert and the development of new forms of expertise, but it also reduces experts to mere representatives of specialized knowledge, knowledge they find increasingly difficult to keep abreast of. The expert becomes, in many aspects, increasingly the lay person. This "laicization" of the expert changes the relationship of trust between lay people and experts: expertise must be increasingly stage-managed to gain acceptance. Beck places greater emphasis on the aspect of the acceptance or validity of knowledge claims than Giddens, because his focus on risk controversies (which are characterized by expert dissent and rivalry between kindred forms of knowledge), causes him to think more in terms of the expert/counter-expert distinction than that of the expert/lay person. This sensitizes us to the fact that something must come into play as far as the acceptance of expert knowledge is concerned, a point that will be discussed later in the context of political efficacy and practical effectiveness (cf. Bogner and Menz, in this volume).

I.3   The articles in this book:
methodology and method in expert interviews

What lessons can we draw from this brief foray into social science research into expertise for our own methodological debate? First and foremost the realization that the naïve image of the expert as source of objective information – on which one or the other simplified notion of successful expert interviews is based – has long become problematic. In our context, this confirms a need for increased reflection on expert interviews and on methodology behind them. Expert interviews are by no means simply just "information gathering meetings" used primarily for collecting facts and knowledge. To clarify any misunderstandings here: expert interviews are, of course, not only a popular way of gathering information, they are also a totally legitimate method for some forms of research. But as Gläser and Laudel's article in this book clearly shows, some basic methodological rules still apply when conducting and evaluating such information gathering expert interviews. However, the level of consideration that must be given to the methodology increases proportionally when such interviews are not intended primarily to establish a sound factual basis, but instead follow the goal that lies at the heart of qualitative research: the reconstruction of latent content of meaning. Expert interviews intended for this purpose – like all other accepted methods of gathering data – require careful validation and a solid theoretical basis. By now it should be quite clear that there is no such thing as *the* expert interview. The spectrum ranges from quantitative measures through to the use of experts as a form of information source (for example as in Schmid, 1995; frequently also encountered in text books, for example Lamnek, 2005) and the theoretically demanding, resolutely qualitative approach taken by Michael Meuser and Ulrike Nagel (1991, also in this volume).

So it is with good reason that the contributing authors in this book also seek plausible answers in their own specific contexts to the basic questions that offer justification for the existence of expert interviews as an independent research method: What constitutes an expert? What distinguishes expert knowledge from other forms of knowledge? What are the different types of expert knowledge? Which type of interview is best (for the actual goal of the research and purpose of the expert interview)? What strategies are available for analyzing the results (again in light of the form and function of the expert interview in the actual research design)?

All these questions have arisen since the dawn of the debate on the methodology of expert interviews (cf. the article by Bogner and Menz, in this volume), and we view the collection of articles included in this book as a study and continuation of this methodological debate.

The book itself is divided into three parts. The theoretical or conceptual articles in the first part examine what lies behind the methodology of expert interviews. Our aim with these articles is to offer a more precise outline of the purpose and form of such interviews and examine what actually constitutes an expert interview. The key question that must first be answered here is: What special characteristics does a person have to have to constitute an "expert?" How is "expert knowledge" obtained? What types of information and knowledge should be gathered? Can the expert interview be justifiably singled out as a separate form of interview and clearly differentiated from other forms of qualitative and quantitative interviews? What is the difference between expert interviews and the elite interviews encountered in English-speaking countries? And finally: What effect do such considerations have on data gathering methods, interaction strategies and the analysis of results?

Michael Meuser and *Ulrike Nagel*'s methodological concept of the expert interview goes far beyond their earlier groundbreaking articles in the expert interview debate (cf. Meuser and Nagel, 1991). This can be attributed not least to their reformulation of the definition of the expert, which draws on the reception of both sociology of knowledge and modernization theory approaches. In this regard, Meuser and Nagel incorporate, in particular, current thinking on the changes in knowledge production, which can, in part, be seen as an indication of a new relationship between science, politics and the general public. This refers, in essence, to the emergence of a new type of research that is characterized by its practical relevance, project-like nature and transdisciplinarity, that is the inclusion of the knowledge spread across a range of very different actors ("Mode 2"). These considerations prompted Meuser and Nagel to extend their definition of the expert. Whereas their previous publications restricted the circle of experts to members of the professional functional elite, they now extend it in light of new (global) network-like negotiation processes of knowledge production to include the people actively involved in shaping public affairs. These include, for example, NGO representatives who have (often) acquired their expertise outside their professional role. In the course of their voluntary or professional activities, these people have acquired specialized problem-solving and analytical knowledge that is of relevance in expert interviews. As far as the analysis of expert interviews is concerned, Meuser and Nagel advocate a six-step process that (in contrast to earlier concepts) should also examine the possible influence of experience gained outside the professional realm.

In their article, *Alexander Bogner* and *Wolfgang Menz* contribute to shaping the debate by differentiating between various forms of expert interview. Their typology identifies three different types of expert interview each intended for a different purpose: the exploratory expert interview used primarily to provide orientation, the systematizing expert interview targeted at the systematic retrieval of information and the theory-generating expert interview aimed – in the spirit of qualitative social research – at reconstructing social interpretative patterns and subjective action orientation criteria. They follow this by presenting a detailed definition of what constitutes an expert. Based on a classification of various dimensions of expert knowledge (technical knowledge, process knowledge, interpretive knowledge/"know-why"), they propose a reformulation of the sociology of knowledge based definition of the expert. This redefinition sees expert knowledge as an "analytical construction" and, at the same time, incorporates the expert's "formative power": expert interviews are neither characterized by an interest in limited special or specialized knowledge (as suggested in the sociology of knowledge debate), nor can they be adequately defined by separating the private sphere from the (generally occupational) functional context. Experts are generally of research interest above all because they are in a position to actually put their own interpretations into practice. Drawing on this, Bogner and Menz call for an expert interview "interaction model" in which the so-called interaction effects (normally considered as interfering variables) are seen as constitutive and productive elements in the data production process.

Michaela Pfadenhauer presents her theoretical support for the expert interview as independent qualitative method from an ethnographic design perspective. In her opinion, expert interviews are a particularly appropriate method in research aimed at reconstructing explicit expert knowledge. She also points out that an extraordinary level of prior knowledge of the subject matter – obtained essentially through an ethnographic "inventory" of the field of research – is required to guarantee their productiveness. Since the expert's impression of the interviewer influences the type of knowledge he/she will communicate in the interview, relevant expert knowledge can only be obtained through professional reference to the expert's actual relevance system. Pfadenhauer considers this specificity of the interaction, which requires that the interviewer become a "quasi expert" to successfully carry out an expert interview, as a central constitutive element of such interviews. She also advises strongly against mistaking expert interviews to be a comparatively unproblematic and "economic" way of obtaining data or "shortcut strategy."

If we compare the predominantly German-language literature on expert interviews with international articles on interviewing the elite as *Beate Littig* does in her first article in this book, more commonalities than differences are revealed. Similar issues are discussed in both, such as the problems of gaining access to these groups and the specifics of interaction and interviewing. Although not identical, even the respective target group definitions (experts and the elite) for such interviews overlap. This article discusses the commonalities and differences in these two methodological approaches, thereby contributing to a more detailed specification of the methodology of expert interviews. It concludes with a sociology of knowledge based appeal that the (professional) functional elite – given their positions of power – be considered as a specific group of experts. From a methodological perspective and as a result of their specific interpretive knowledge ("know-why") and procedural knowledge ("know-how"), experts (and thus also the elite) are of interest to social and political sciences research. Consequently, interviews with the elite aimed at generating explicit, tacit, professional or occupational knowledge should be seen as expert interviews.

The second part of the book focuses on methodological practices and the considerations that accompany them. What kind of data can be gathered from expert interviews above and beyond that obtained from the customary qualitative, guideline based individual interviews? How can the quality of the data be guaranteed? What determines and characterizes communication in expert interviews? Which personal skills, competences and attributes are beneficial in this form of interaction? What role does "gender" play here? How can the particular interaction structures be used to benefit the data gathering process? And, last but not least: Which research ethics issues have to be considered?

Jochen Gläser and *Grit Laudel* examine an issue hitherto largely ignored in the expert interview debate, namely the "quality" of the interview partner and the information and knowledge he/she provides in the course of the interview. In their opinion, neither the methodological debate nor, indeed, sociological studies take into consideration the fact that different experts with different levels of knowledge and different quality requirements in their work can be expected to provide correspondingly different information. Using their own research into the influence of institutional research conditions on the production of scientific knowledge as an example, they illustrate that, depending on the "quality" of the expert, not only can the same social phenomena be described in the interview in different ways, but it is also possible for diverging descriptions to conceal similar phenomena. To reconstruct this information and draw benefit from it in the data gathering and analysis processes, additional information above and beyond the factual information provided in the interviews must be gathered on the interview subjects. Gläser and Laudel advocate the systematic inclusion of the "expert quality" issue in the individual research steps – from the selection of the experts through to the interviewing method and the analysis of the results. In this respect, Gläser and Laudel's article can be seen as an impulse for an (overdue) debate on the validation criteria of expert interviews in general.

In their article, *Gabriele Abels* and *Maria Behrens* demonstrate the advantages of analyzing gender-specific interaction effects in expert interviews and putting them to productive use in the interview setting for the collection of practical and factual knowledge. In doing so, they make the assumption that the person of both the expert and the researcher (in their case, a female researcher) are also always present in the interview. Correspondingly, the interaction is influenced by various non-circumventable subject-related factors of influence. Abels and Behrens single out the category "gender" and analyze its implications for interviewing experts and for the success of expert interviews. They draw on their own empirical research to demonstrate that different "interaction effects" in the interview can be attributed to gender-related assumptions and prejudices. The results show – and this is their central hypothesis – that, for all intents and purposes, both positive and discriminating effects can serve to generate productive data. At the same time, the authors add two constraints: firstly that not all interaction effects are of the same use in producing relevant data and, secondly that certain interaction effects can significantly impair the validity of the data. In a second step, they verify their gender-related conclusions by means of a secondary analysis of their own interview notes from the associated research projects. This analysis reveals that subjective postscripts relating to interview situations can provide insightful material for a subsequent reflection on one's own self-reflexivity in the data production phase.

Gabriela B. Christmann discusses telephone-based interviews, a variation on the expert interview theme in which the possibilities and limitations are determined by technology. Although telephone interviews with experts have long become established research practice (not least for economic reasons), little reflection has been given to the methodology behind them. Christmann refers in her methodological considerations to experience drawn from a methodologically diverse German university project. Fourteen of the interviewed experts in leading university positions were interviewed in a face-to-face setting, while eight were interviewed by telephone for economic reasons. Based on a comparison of the two approaches and a review of the relevant methodological literature, Christmann's assessment of telephone-based expert interviews is sceptical. Even if the telephone interviews in her example research project did produce important information, methodological concerns prevail. Telephone interviews are neither easier to organize, nor is there any guarantee that the expert will be able to devote his/her full attention to the interview: since there is no face-to-face contact, the interviewer cannot predict or control distractions, lapses in concentration or interruptions by third parties. Reducing the interaction to a purely linguistic level makes it more difficult to interpret, and the interviewee has far less room for development – an aspect that perhaps carries less weight in information gathering expert interviews than in those intended for reconstructive social research theory building purposes. All in all, telephone-based expert interviews prove a difficult and taxing undertaking – both for the interviewee and for the interviewer.

Vaida Obelenė addresses the question of research ethics in the context of the expert interview. In this context she discusses the extent to which the propositions of the literature on democratic research practices are relevant for an expert researcher. By drawing on her research experiences of studying former communist functionaries, who established themselves in relation to new forms of knowledge and power in a post-communist society, Obelenė reflects such practices in terms of choices that may undermine the researcher's purposes including his/her commitment to the ethicalness of the study. Furthermore, this chapter aims to explore the tension between, on the one hand, the need of assertiveness on the part of the researcher in defending the study's purpose vis-à-vis the powerful expert, and the need of the researcher's sensitivity to the interests and vulnerabilities of the expert on the other. Against this background expert interviews can be understood as a form of 'bargained research' where the interests of both parties have to be considered.

The third part of the book contains a selection of articles that deal with the importance of expert interviews, the way they are conducted and the particular specifics of interaction in such interviews in concrete fields of application and social science sub-disciplines (industrial sociology, interpretative organizational research, labour market research and technology foresight). One particular question comes to the fore here, namely the methodological consequences that result from the structures peculiar to each respective field of research and their consequences for the success of the interviewing techniques used in an expert interview setting.

Rainer Trinczek uses an industrial sociology case study to illustrate that such interviews must by no means generally – as is a common preconception in qualitative research – adhere to the principles of neutrality and restraint. Although appropriate interviewing strategies can be found in methodological suppositions, the actual structure of such an interview has to follow the rules of normal communication, interpreting these everyday communication rules in line with the actual situation and the purpose of the interview. In the case study analysed by Trinczek (interviews with managers), the rules of communication and, thus, the expectations of the interviewees, are based on their everyday work situation; in general, the interviewees expect the interview to follow the question and answer structure predominantly encountered in everyday work situations. However, the researcher also has to take the actual subject matter into consideration when deciding whether to orient the entire interview on these expectations. Trinczek illustrates this using two thematically heterogeneous research projects as examples. An argumentative/discursive interview approach is suitable if the subject matter addresses a work-related topic. But the situation is different in research projects that deal with the "private world," where (and in line with the various communication structures encountered in everyday life) a narrative-based interview structure is appropriate.

In their article, *Manfred Lueger* and *Ulrike Froschauer* illustrate the importance of expert interviews in interpretative social research based organizational analysis. By distinguishing different levels of observation (first and second order), they propose the reconstruction of analytically different types of knowledge based on a heuristic of distinct arenas and expertise reflection levels. The interviewees (as experts in the organizational lifeworld) have internal organizational experience and know-how. From an expanded observation perspective, they are in a position to provide qualified information on internal knowledge structures and constructions. To ensure the different knowledge forms are contrasted with appropriate complexity, those persons whose professional profile qualifies them as relevant internal or external from the point of view of the actual research should ultimately be integrated into the research. Pursuant to their analytical perspective, Froschauer and Lueger illustrate the specific individual data gathering and interpretation requirements raised by the different types of contrasting expertise in organizational action.

Andrea Leitner and *Angela Wroblewski* deal in their article with the standing and specifics of expert interviews in an evaluation research context. They begin by providing an overview of the development of this branch of research and then go on to examine the possibilities and prerequisites of the use of expert interviews in a "responsive evaluation" approach. They consider the role of experts as "stakeholders" with a specific interest in the results of the evaluation to be a central characteristic of expert interviews aimed at evaluating socio-political measures. According to Leitner and

Wroblewski, this "stakeholder" problem needs to be assessed from a methodology perspective. In the approach they describe, this validity problem is counteracted by references to information from other data sources during the interview. Examples from labour market policy evaluation research are used to present the determining factors in the expert interview interaction process and discuss the possibilities available for dealing with this bias.

The Expert Delphi method presented by *Georg Aichholzer* plays an important role in the rapidly growing field of technology foresight. Against the background of some serious uncertainties in modern societies, this relatively tightly structured group communication process basically aims to "rationalize the future" through a methodologically controlled generation of expert knowledge. In many cases, foresight processes also aspire to offer social networking, voting and consensus building functions that improve the performance of innovation systems. Aichholzer's article looks at the methodology modifications and combinations that have accompanied the growing use of the Expert Delphi and illustrates them using international examples. Following an introduction to the basic elements of the Delphi method, Aichholzer explains its use in the innovative Austrian Technology Delphi, which incorporates a number of modifications to the classic Delphi. The different strategies used to capture expert knowledge in a further example – an international foresight process on the future of European transport systems – allows an interesting comparison between the Expert Delphi and cross-impact analysis. The subsequent applications discussed in the article, such as a Finnish approach geared towards balancing consensus and diversity and the use of internet assistant Expert Delphis, demonstrate other application-specific adaptations to and combinations of this method.

This book should not, of course, be seen as an exclusive compendium and the final word on a fully sanctioned research method. Far more, it is an invitation to others to reflect on and examine the different forms of expert interview in more detail. Indeed, we expect and hope that an intensified, critical debate on this topic will further increase the practical benefits of this method. The internationalization of the debate is an important step in this direction. Consequently, our intention with this book is to build a stable platform on which "experts" from different research traditions, scientific and language cultures can participate in an intensified and fertile debate on expert interviews. This would ultimately benefit not only a small community of expert researchers, but also qualitative social research as a whole.

Note

1. For a long time even representatives of the qualitative paradigm were undecided as to whether expert interviews actually did represent a discrete method of data collection that could be differentiated from other interview forms. No reference is

made, for example, to expert interviews in "A Companion to Qualitative Research" (Flick and others, 2004), the English edition of a key German handbook.

References

Beck, U. (1992) *Risk Society. Towards a New Modernity.* (London: Sage Publications).
Bogner, A. (2005) "How Experts Draw Boundaries. Dealing with Non-Knowledge and Uncertainty in Prenatal Testing" in *Science, Technology and Innovation Studies 1*, pp. 17–37, <www.sti-studies.de/articles/2005–01/bogner.htm>
Bogner, A., Torgersen, H. (eds) (2005) *Wozu Experten? Ambivalenzen der Beziehung von Wissenschaft und Politik.* (Wiesbaden: Verlag für Sozialwissenschaften).
Collins, H. M., Evans, R. (2002) "The Third Wave of Science Studies: Studies of Expertise and Experience" in *Social Studies of Science 32*, pp. 235–96.
Collins, H. M., Evans, R. (2007) *Rethinking Expertise* (Chicago and London: University of Chicago Press).
Flick, U. (2006) *Introduction to Qualitative Research*, 3rd edn (London: Sage Publications).
Flick, U., Kardorff, E. von and Steinke, I. (eds) (2004) *A Companion to Qualitative Research* (London and Thousand Oaks/CA: Sage Publications).
Giddens, A. (1990) *The Consequences of Modernity* (Cambridge: Polity Press).
Giddens, A. (1991) *Modernity and Self-Identity – Self and Society in the Late Modern Age* (Stanford/CA: Stanford University Press).
Jasanoff, S., Markle, G. E., Petersen, J. C. and Pinch, T. (eds) (1995) *Handbook of Science and Technology Studies* (Thousand Oaks/CA: Sage Publications).
Lamnek, S. (2005) *Qualitative Sozialforschung: Lehrbuch*, 4th edn (Weinheim: Beltz).
Maasen, S. and Weingart, P. (eds) (2005) *Democratization of Expertise? Exploring Novel Forms of Scientific Advice in Political Decision-Making* (Dordrecht: Springer).
Meuser, M. and Nagel, U. (1991) "ExpertInneninterviews – vielfach erprobt, wenig bedacht. Ein Beitrag zur qualitativen Methodendiskussion" in Garz, D. and Kraimer, K. (eds) *Qualitativ-empirische Sozialforschung. Konzepte, Methoden, Analysen* (Opladen: Westdeutscher Verlag), pp. 441–71.
Przyborski, A. and Wohlrab-Sahr, M. (2008) *Qualitative Sozialforschung. Ein Arbeitsbuch* (München: Oldenbourg).
Schmid, J. (1995) "Expertenbefragung und Informationsgespräch in der Parteienforschung: Wie föderalistisch ist die CDU?" in Alemann, U. v. (ed.) *Politikwissenschaftliche Methoden. Grundriss für Studium und Forschung* (Opladen: Westdeutscher Verlag), pp. 293–325.
Turner, S. (2002) "What is the Problem with Experts?" in *Social Studies of Science 31*, pp. 123–49.

Part I

Theoretical Concepts: Methodology of Expert Interviews

1
The Expert Interview and Changes in Knowledge Production

Michael Meuser and Ulrike Nagel

1.1 Introduction

The expert interview as a method of qualitative empirical research, designed to explore expert knowledge, has been developed considerably since the early 1990s. A number of readers has been published[1] and thus a gap in the methods' literature has been dealt with, much to the benefit of many disciplines and fields of research in the social sciences. It can be assumed that through increased reflection on methodical issues research into experts' knowledge has gained in professionalism and quality.[2]

At the same time, the expert interview has become very popular as a "streamlined" method (Bogner and Menz, 2002a, pp. 9–10, see also Bogner, Littig and Menz, in this volume): recruiting informants does not seem to cause any difficulties, as a method the expert interview appears to be "quick, easy, and safe" in its application, and it promises to be of good practical value. However, the authors continue, it is easily overlooked that the expert interview is an ambitious method which cannot be considered to be on a sound footing either in terms of modernization theory or methodologically.[3]

In this article we shall deal with the notion of expert and expert knowledge as outlined in the sociology of knowledge, reflecting on expert knowledge as embedded in processes of modernization, and hence in the light of modernization theory. We shall argue that expert knowledge is a knowledge sui generis with its own characteristic traits necessitating a particular methodological approach. We shall outline the distinctive features of this approach taking a closer look both at data collection and interpretation of data.[4]

Furthermore, we shall discuss the concept of knowledge in the context of changes in the production of knowledge or rather new forms of knowledge production as they are being reflected in the debates on post-modernity and the Knowledge Society. Set forth by the regime of accumulation inherent in globalization, modern societies are facing changing conditions of the production of knowledge in general and more so of knowledge-based expert systems. Following Welsch (1993), these conditions can be described as constituting a basic plurality, a plurality which cannot simply be dealt with as an intensified coexistence of spheres of knowledge and points of view of experts, but – besides the diversification of knowledge – must also be understood as a trend towards transgressing the borderlines between spheres of knowledge. Some of these characteristics of societal change shall be discussed with a view to their impact on the expert and expert systems, highlighting the difficulties and dilemmas imposed on the expert's action and interaction processes. Against the background of modernization theory and a diagnosis of our time we shall ask if and to what extent the changing forms of knowledge production will have to be taken into account when analysing expert knowledge, and to what new foci the researcher's attention is drawn.[5]

1.2   Expert, expert knowledge and societal change

1.2.1   Sociology of knowledge as frame of reference

In a pragmatic perspective – focusing on the local context of knowledge production, the status of expert could be understood as ascribed by the researcher: a person is attributed as expert by virtue of his role as informant (Walter, 1994, p. 271). Who is identified as expert and who not depends on the researcher's judgement. However, this definition remains insufficient since it does not provide the researcher with criteria to distinguish between experts and non-experts. The term "expert" might end up being used inflationarily and finally anybody might be seen as an expert – at least as an "expert of her or his own life." Following this line the expert interview would no longer be distinguishable from other techniques of interviewing, like, for example, the narrative or ethnographic interview.[6]

A definition of the term expert can best be arrived at by reviewing the features distinguishing expert knowledge from other forms of knowledge like everyday knowledge and common-sense knowledge. In scientific research an individual is addressed as an expert because the researcher assumes – for whatever reason – that she or he has knowledge, which she or he may not necessarily possess alone, but which is not accessible to anybody in the field of action under study. It is this advantage of knowledge which the expert interview is designed to discover, and it is an exclusive realm of knowledge which is highly potential because and in as far as it is linked with the power of defining the situation. What comes into sight when we combine the pragmatic definition of the expert interview with the sociology of knowledge-perspective, is the distinction between expert and lay person.

It is the researcher who according to his research objective decides who she or he wants to interview as an expert; but we have to add that this is not an arbitrary choice but is related to the recognition of an expert as expert within his own field of action. At the same time not every person recognized as an expert in a particular setting is necessarily addressed as a potential informant. We would like to conclude that a person is considered an expert if she or he possesses an "institutionalized authority to construct reality" (Hitzler, Honer and Maeder, 1994). Expert knowledge is characterized by the chance "to become hegemonial in a certain organizational and functional context within a field of practice" and, thus, "to be influential in structuring the conditions of action for other actors [....] in a relevant way" (Bogner and Menz, 2002b, p. 46, our translation, cf. also Liebold and Trinczek, 2002, p. 36).

This definition starts from the distinction between three ideal types of knowledge given by Alfred Schütz (1964): the "expert," the "man on the street," and the "well-informed citizen." The distinguishing feature for Schütz is the extent of the person's "readiness to take things for granted" (p. 123). While the "man on the street" "lives...naively in his own and his in-group's intrinsic relevances" (p. 129), the expert is at home in a system of relevances "imposed...by the problems pre-established within his field" (p. 130). These relevances to him, however, are not like a fate he blindly resigns himself to, "but by his decision to become an expert he has accepted the relevances imposed within his field as the intrinsic, and the only intrinsic, relevances of his acting and thinking" (p. 130).

The discussion within the sociology of knowledge referring to Schütz mainly focuses on the distinction between expert and layperson. This distinction is based on the specialized knowledge of the expert. Not every special knowledge, however, already is expert knowledge, as Sprondel (1979, p. 141) has shown, but only that one which can be grasped as a "socially institutionalized expertise." In a society where division of labour is an organizing principle, expert knowledge, Sprondel continues, is "special knowledge considered necessary" (p. 148) in relation to problems, which are defined as special problems. Sprondel views this knowledge as linked to the role of the professional. Defining the term expert with reference to the professions does make sense in so far as expertise – seen historically – has become differentiated in the context of the professions, and until today and to a large extent is basically acquired on this basis.

Yet more recent analyses of societal change convincingly show that new forms of knowledge production have developed. It is argued that these new forms of knowledge production do not replace the traditional specific relevances established within the various fields of action (disciplines, professions, and so on) but, rather, complement them. It seems that with these new forms of knowledge production the link between expert knowledge and professional role is loosened, the sharp distinction between expert and lay person weakened, and the professional's claim of exclusiveness for the relevances of her or his discipline, is fading. In the following chapter we will deal with these processes as implying some more characteristics of expert knowledge.

1.2.2   Societal change and new forms of knowledge production

The definition of expert and expert knowledge proposed by Schütz and Sprondel is an apt representation of the form of knowledge production dominant in modernity. In modernization theory, this form is referred to as Mode 1 (Gibbons and others, 1994). In Mode 1, knowledge is generated according to the cognitive and social norms of a disciplinary context and, in so far, is autonomous (Gibbons and others, 1994, p. 1). These norms are the relevances "imposed" upon the expert, and it is them – and them alone – which, following Schütz, determine her or his behaviour. In the expert's practice, these norms can and have to be interpreted in such a way that the requirements of situation and context are taken into account in each case. Mode 1 serves as a point of reference for the analysis of changes in knowledge production towards Mode 2. In this process the characteristics of Mode 1 – for example, disciplinarity and the distinction between expert and lay person – lose their discriminating power, and knowledge production is observed as taking place within wider, transdisciplinary contexts (ibid.). It is commonly agreed that with the emergence of Mode 2, the form of knowledge production characteristic of modernity, Mode 1, has not disappeared, but "has continued, come to a head and transformed itself. It has hardly reached its own objectives; its aporia have become even clearer, if not more incontestable, and this is exactly why in dealing with modernity shifts of perspective can be seen to be emerging" (Bonss, 1998, p. 969).

In a historical perspective, the beginnings of the changes from Mode 1 to new forms of knowledge production – as in Mode 2 – can be located in the 1960s. This decade reflects the onset of a process in which the problematic, ambivalent consequences of modernization of industrial society and of the belief in the logics of progress (as defined by functional differentiation, scientification, and disciplinarity) are clearly becoming visible. The logics of progress are increasingly criticized, accompanied by a growing scepticism towards progress, particularly towards solutions in the fields of science/technology and social engineering. The indisputability of the ambivalent side-effects of modernization in the 1970s, as exemplified by the problems related to the civil use of atomic energy, speeds up the establishment of a reflexive attitude towards the plausibility structures of modernity, and in the 1980s this leads to novel – globalized – perceptions of problems: to the emergence of new authorities of interpretation, new systems of knowledge, new concepts of production, new ways of life and so on, the situation being difficult to read and the future development still concealed, Habermas (1985) coins it as a new "Unübersichtlichkeit" (concealment).

There are two ways of looking at societal change crystallizing from this process. On the one hand, there is the discourse on risks which addresses the risks and uncertainties of contemporary society (Beck, 1992; Beck, Giddens and Lash, 1994), and "which is centered on how to control the new side-effects and the power of the side-effects" (Bonss, 1998, p. 973). On the other hand, expressing the ambivalences of modernity (Baumann, 1991) the constructionist and postmodern discourse is taking shape emphasizing the pluralization of knowledge and reason gone plural (Welsch, 1993).

In this context of complex and concealed problems of societal change expert knowledge is confronted with the following dilemma: on the one hand, due to an increasing demand of expert knowledge and growing expectations for interpretation and orientation, expert knowledge and expert systems multiply and proliferate. On the other hand, however, being the source of the risks claimed to be under control, the "conservative" – Mode 1 – scientific expert knowledge itself slides into a legitimation crisis. Various trends mixing together are making up a paradoxical situation: the questioning of Model-knowledge production; the emergence of innovative trandsdisciplinary arrangements of knowledge production in large parts of society; and the development of new authorities of interpretation with their new relevances, network-based communication cultures, and integrated forms of knowledge production which take into account local knowledge and knowledge of lay people, thereby establishing a world of counter-experts, counter-expertise, and alternative publics.[7] In the course of time the latter do not lose their impact but undergo a process of institution building of their own, and very often their personal is found in positions of power. This can be illustrated by the new social movements, NGOs, and networks of civil society – whose members when advancing in years tend to take over positions in the political, social, or cultural system, that is in the institutions of society.

It is of interest for our discussion that in the course of modernity becoming reflexive, and due to the criticism of the expertocrization of society, expert knowledge is also generated outside professional contexts. But it should not be mistaken with lay people's knowledge or the knowledge of the well-informed citizen, but has to be understood as linking up with scientific expertise, thus developing hybrids and producing knowledge differently from Mode 1; it is generated in pluralized networks, negotiated by experts and publics of lay people, and applied to concrete societal problems (and possibly organized as counter-power). As it is, the criticism of the expertocrization of modernity itself and of its side-effects is seen to be initiating the development of integrated counter-expert systems which combine non-scientific and scientific knowledge, different knowledge cultures, counter-publics, and alternative structures of participation.

The emergence of new knowledge systems and knowledge cultures; of uncommon commentators of deficits of modernization and responses to problems; of new (collective) actors and publics and their network-based negotiations in the process of knowledge production, has consequences: The superior problem-solving rationale (Mode 1) as claimed by the scientific system is exposed to systematic doubt and put into competition with the expertise originating from heterogeneous knowledge systems and spheres of interest. The latter themselves, of course, are science-based, but instead of being disciplinary they are transdisciplinary and heterogeneous with regard to the actors and their relevances, that is incorporating also local knowledge, experiential knowledge, viewpoints of lay people and others concerned. In marking their belongingness to an alternative culture some of these knowledge systems are surfacing even a new type of aesthetic, new symbols (sneakers, rainbow, sunflower). The new mode of knowledge production by negotiating relevances in pluralistic and transdisciplinary networks is more and more acknowledged as "socially acceptable." What is more, while problems and imperatives of innovation are globalized and novel in many cases – expert knowledge as created in the plural worlds of counter-experts turns into a demanded source. Mode 1-knowledge production does not become outdated. It is, as is stated time and again, indispensable as to some of its characteristics, but it is complemented by Mode 2.

> Mode 1 problems are set and solved in a context governed by the, largely academic, interests of a specific community. By contrast, Mode 2 knowledge is carried out in a context of application. Mode 1 is diciplinary while Mode 2 is transdiciplinary. Mode 1 is characterised by homogenity, Mode 2 by heterogenity. Originally, Mode 1 is hierarchical and tends to preserve its form, while Mode 2 is more heterarchical and transient. Each employs a different kind of quality control. In comparison with Mode 1, Mode 2 is more socially accountable and reflexive. It includes a wider, more temporary and heterogeneous set of practitioners, collaborating on a problem defined in a specific and localized context. (Gibbons and others, 1994, p. 3)

The universities, too, are affected by these developments. Nowotny (1997) states that with the changes in knowledge production the universities lose their privileged status as legitimate sites of the production of knowledge. The increasing number of academically trained individuals can be held responsible for this process since it is their research competence, which is influencing a variety of institutions. It is stated that this, on the other hand, was having repercussions on the "largely disciplinary organized system of knowledge production." In the case of Mode 2 knowledge production already "the definition of the scientific problem" were "carried out in the context of concrete and therefore changing applications." Mode 2 was open to societal demands and expectations. Disciplinarity as a characteristic feature of Mode 1-knowledge production was more and more complemented and also partially replaced by transdicipinarity, that is an integration not only of other scientific disciplines, but of institutions and organizations beyond the field of the sciences as well (cf. Gibbons and others, 1994). As to further development of Mode 2-theory, this aspect of opening-up the process of knowledge production for new circles of experts from the public realm, of "the closer and closer interaction of science and society," becomes a central issue and is discussed as an "indicator of the emergence of a new kind of science" (Nowotny, Scott and Gibbons, 2004, p. 7).

The new knowledge regime is interpreted by Rammert (2003, p. 483) as "the *regime of heterogeneity in the distribution of knowledge production*" (emphasis in original). According to Rammert, knowledge production is carried out in a "fragmentary" way. Knorr-Cetina (2002, pp. 12–13, 18) speaks of "epistemic cultures" which she conceives of as a structural feature of Knowledge Societies, and which, fragmented as they are, can no longer be grouped in a homogeneous model of science. Rammert, quite like Nowotny, states an extension of the circle of producers of "legitimate" knowledge. "The quality (of knowledge; MM/UN) is no longer assessed by colleagues within a discipline, the 'peers' only but by heterogeneous groups of experts, a mixture of epistemic cultures" (Rammert, 2003, p. 488). Rammert asserts that also non-scientific, political and moral, aspects play a role here, and that alternative groups such as environmental activists, NGOs, and for instance the "Chaos Computer Club" are being integrated into the process of knowledge production.[8]

1.2.3 Relevances of expert knowledge revisited

Even though the analysis of the changes in knowledge production towards Mode 2 is not at all undisputed (Bender, 2001; Hettlage, 2004), it is nevertheless supported by the debate to a great extent. We assume that today expertise both within and outside the professions is constituted in a more complex way than described in "classical" works of the sociology of knowledge. In defining the term expert this recent development should be taken into account, much to the benefit of the method of expert interview as well. What is needed is a definition of the status of expert going beyond the traditional understanding of the professional role, and linking it with a widened perspective on the "relevances imposed upon" the expert. At issue here are new forms of knowledge production and their conditions inside and outside the professions, as well as the newly emerging relevances which have to be taken into account as important aspects while analysing expert knowledge. The new conditions of knowledge production reflect the intricate demands impinged upon processes of defining and solving problems by the late-modern Complex Societies (Schütze, 2002), Knowledge Societies and the Global Risk Society (Beck, 1998), conditions, which transform the ambivalences of modernity (Baumann, 1991).

Gibbons and others (1994) and other Mode 2-theorists have derived their hypotheses from the analysis of new, pluralistic ways of knowledge production in cooperation between different spheres of society (science and its disciplines, industry, politics, public administration). In comparison with this approach our starting point is the sociology of knowledge-perspective which we have reviewed in the light of the constructionist-postmodernist or Knowledge Society brand of modernization on the one hand, and with a view to the process of differentiation of extra-professional fields of expert knowledge as illustrated by the new social movements and publics on the other hand. It is not surprising that both approaches, even though within different language games, lead to quite similar findings regarding the trans-formation of expert knowledge. It must be pointed out again, however, that the Mode 2-phenomenon is not at all unanimously confirmed by the debate on modernization; much to the contrary, empirical researchers have expressed considerable doubt about the mode of transformation as claimed by Gibbons and others.[9]

Regarding the analysis of expert knowledge it has to be ascertained that not only professional knowledge is treated as expert knowledge. We are following Gordon (1975, p. 199) who – referring to research on local politics – understands experts ("special respondents") as individuals "who are active in community affairs regardless of their position in the social status system." Active participants in community affairs, for example, are members of citizens' groups, relief organizations, and self-help groups, as well as volun-teers in welfare, social work, and similar fields. The activities of these types of actors are not restricted to local (municipal or regional) contexts. Some of them are active at the global level, for example within the scope of NGOs. All of these actors acquire a special knowledge through their activity – and not necessarily through their training – because they have privileged access to information. Their expertise, too, is socially institutionalized and linked to a specific context and its functional requirements, even though in a different way from the expertise grounded on the professional role.[10]

The decoupling of the term expert from the professional role does not imply an inflationary extension of the circle of individuals eligible for an expert interview. The frequently used phrase "expert on one's own behalf" is out of place here. Of those who have something to report on account of personal observation and experience, not each and every individual is to be interviewed as an expert. Schmid-Urban and others (1992, p. 85) rank among experts, for example, also pub-owners and kiosk-operators, since these "often are in touch with certain groups." They are informants who, in our view, can definitely contribute important background information, but do not give an expert opinion. Such individuals do not meet the criterion of active participation. They have not acquired their knowledge of a particular problem (for example housing shortage, poverty, health risks) through an activity which is aimed at the problem and, therefore, with a view to analyzing and/or helping to solve the problem in any way. The contacts and observations from which they derive their knowledge are embedded in structures of relevance, which are not focused on a problem but, for example, determined by economic motives. The definition of experts as active participants emphasizes the specific functions such individuals have with regard to problems – whether by virtue of a profes-sional role, or as a volunteer. Special knowledge acquired through carrying out such functions is the subject matter of the expert interview.

It is reasonable to decouple the term expert from holding a formal position in a hierarchy of occupational status positions and to argue, accordingly, that the expert interview shall be used also with interviewees who are active participants. While integrating the active participants into the group of potential experts we are avoiding the risk involved in a narrow definition of the term expert – the risk that "professionalisation of a solution for a problem [is] connected with a momentous narrowing of a problem definition" (Sprondel, 1979, p. 143). Certainly, also an expertise issued by a citizens' group or an NGO is knowledge- and science-based, however, it is a different view, different with regard to the determinative relevances as compared to those of a head of a public authority or a minister of state.[11]

Viewing the status of the expert and the extra-professional social settings of production of expertise from the wider perspective just outlined, and taking into account the reflections on Mode 2-knowledge production (Gibbons and others, 1994), a more differentiated account of relevant aspects of expert knowledge comes into sight. In the following, we shall take a closer look at some aspects we believe to be particularly important for the data analysis of expert interviews.

(a) *Socio-cultural conditions of the production of expert knowledge:* In the transition to a pluralized, heterogeneous mode of knowledge production expert knowledge is sensitized regarding stocks of knowledge generated outside the scientific world and acquired, experienced (and suffered) in extra-professional practice. A co-mingling between expert knowledge of active participants and that of professional-scientific experts takes place, resulting in the formation of hybrids between formerly separated fields of knowledge and symbolic orders; in transgression of boundaries between periphery and centre, everyday experience and systematic knowledge, local and global expertise.[12] Under these circumstances experts become sensitized for the context within which their knowledge has to prove itself as useful (Gibbons and others, 1994; Nowotny and others, 2004), while the active participants' advantage is the possession of local knowledge.

Accordingly, while exploring expert knowledge with the tool of the expert interview, the socio-cultural conditions of the production of knowledge become relevant topics of data collection and analysis. Attention is drawn to the embeddedness of the expert in circumstances and milieus; to the heterogeneity of relevant others; to membership in global communities and local networks; to arenas and circles the expert is involved in and orientation is derived from (Schütze, 2002). While following this lead we are exploring if and to what extent the expert is open to mixing different knowledge bases in the sense of transdisciplinarity and hybridity – to a mingling between the perspectives of experts, laymen, and active participants –; whether she or he has an open awareness context with regard to other knowledge orders and a readiness to overcome an "imperialistic" expert position (Welsch, 1993); altogether we are following up the question of plurality, transdisciplinarity, and reflexivity of the production of expert knowledge and the definitions it provides. The focus of analysis, therefore, is directed towards the modes and mechanisms of producing knowledge, that is to an understanding of the process, by which knowledge is generated, checked, communicated, reflected upon, modified, and finalized. The socio-cultural conditions of knowledge production are reviewed as a core dimension of expert knowledge as much as of expert interviewing. We suggest they should be taken into account at all phases of the research process starting from designing the interview schedule, conducting the interview, and analyzing the data.[13] As to methodology, the analysis of expert knowledge thus yields to a process-oriented interpretive approach.

At this point we are going to revise an earlier standpoint regarding the relevances of the expert. We were then arguing that the expert's relevances were defined *exclusively* by the responsibilities attached to his or her position and function in the field of action under study, that is by these relevances alone (Meuser and Nagel, 1991). With regard to the expert's relevancies we are taking on a different view now. The production of expert knowledge being influenced more and more by a plurality of different spheres – including knowledge acquired beyond and independent of the scientific-professional and economic spheres –, it has to be assured that the responsibilities connected with the expert's position are not the only ones to be focused on but also the relevances derived from other realms of experience, p.e. personal life experience as a private person. This reflects a point at issue in the discussion about the expert interview, the question of whether and in which way the biographical motivation and milieu-specific embeddedness of knowledge (-acquisition) should be a subject matter of the interview. In an earlier article (Meuser and Nagel, 1991) we suggested to ignore the private aspects of expert behaviour. Bogner and Menz (2002b, p. 44), however, are in favour of a "methodical integration of the expert as 'private person'." The authors argue that there would hardly be a chance in distinguishing between an interviewee as expert and as private person. As it were only the analysis of the case would show the extent to which "private" relevances were important for the reconstruction of the expert's knowledge and behaviour.

We find this a convincing statement. In addition, a revision of our earlier position is suggested by more recent research in which we used the method of the expert interview. The private person's relevances, however, are examined to see how they affect those relevances, which are of primary importance for the expert's position and responsibilities.

To give an example, in a study on dual career couples (Behnke and Meuser, 2003, 2005) human resources managers of large companies were interviewed as experts; interviewees who showed a commitment to improve the work- life- balance also reported some concern about their highly qualified daughters who, unlike the sons, had great difficulties in finding employment appropriate to the level of their qualification. This shows how experiences made in the private sphere influence the perception and, possibly, the handling of work-related responsibilities. This kind of impact should definitely be thematized in an expert interview, at the same time the expert interview is not be confused with a biographical interview. Biographical structures and processes being the research objective – like the development of an expert's knowledge base, the dynamics of a career, and changes of identity – a narrative biographical interview should be chosen as a tool of data collection and analysis. On the other hand, in exploring expert knowledge, the focus remains on the institutional framework within which the expert moves and on the individual actor involved, her or his position and responsibilities within a particular context.

(b) *Negotiating expert knowledge: practices of communication and organization:* With the development of new socio-cultural forms of knowledge production further relevances of expert knowledge and for its analysis are surfacing. Since knowledge increasingly emerges by way of negotiation within plural, heterogeneous discourse communities, and networks of experts, the patterns and practices of expert communication, of bargaining over definitions and solutions are gaining importance. They are of interest as a collective practice across institutional, professional, and entrepreneurial boundaries – as well as the practice of organizing such negotiation processes. In order to discover the typical traits of an expert's body of knowledge, attention was directed to discourse and networking practices, and in particular to the patterns of establishing consensus as well as differences between opinions, even more so to practices of working on minimum consensus, to negotiating procedures, criteria of participation, and strategies of inclusion and exclusion.

Determining negotiation and networking as basic characteristics of expert knowledge raises the question whether the analysis must yield to an analysis of epistemic cultures – as is suggested by Knorr-Cetina (2002, p. 12) or alternatively by Schütze (2002), the latter favouring the concept of social worlds and arenas. According to Knorr-Cetina, Knowledge Society as structured by epistemic cultures is adequately comprehended by way of exploring the practices of the different knowledge cultures; and she further remarks that in the context of Knowledge Society the inside worlds of knowledge are becoming ever more crucial. Accordingly, and in contrast to older studies focusing on disciplines and specialized fields, the analysis of epistemic cultures is concerned with the procedural rationality and the epistemic practice within fields of knowledge and thus with the complex life-worlds at the insides of modern institutions. As a result, the subject matter of research has changed from the construction of knowledge towards the "construction of the machineries by which knowledge is being constructed" (Knorr-Cetina, 2002, p. 13).[14] This raises the question of the relation between the expert interview and ethnographic methods. While stating that the expert interview plays an important role as an independent method of empirical social research, it can yet be agreed that it is as much open to an ethnographic research design as are other tools of interpretive-qualitative research, for example participant observation. Regarding our concept of the expert interview, it should be added that a basic ethnographic attitude would prove very useful.

(c) *Expert knowledge as construction:* Recognizing expert knowledge as a collective project of producing knowledge by way of negotiation, cooperation, networking and teamwork, it has to be acknowledge that the production of knowledge is to be defined as an open ended process.

Throughout the actual making of the expertise, the outcome regarding the definition of what is the case and the respective problem solving strategies remains an open question, the productive process itself must be seen as bearing an uncertainty regarding its result. In addition, the practices guiding the production of expertise need to be conceived of as being carried out with a view to options "in spe," so to say, that is options not yet to be apprehended but expected to materialize in future. This practice is to be opposed to a mode of decision-making marked by neglect of ambivalences and uncertainties, the expert relying on her or his authority, freedom of judgement and power to define situations.[15] Yet the new-mode-experts as much as their predecessors in Mode 2 are not likely to be acting in a social vacuum devoid of power structures. Their settings, too, are allocating insider and outsider positions, as can be illustrated with regard to the definition of rules of conduct and criteria of validity. In accordance with Foucault's approach to the knowledge-power-relationship and with the discourse analysis developed from his work, expert discourses are to be understood as orderly practices of production of meaning patterns, particularly busy drawing the line between favourable and unfavourable patterns and legitimizing and delegitimizing potential speakers (Keller, 2005).

It has to be assured that a negotiative model of expertise does not imply that procedures and results are arbitrary. An impressive example is given by the Intergovernmental Panel on Climate Change. The panel's "Summary for Policymakers: Climate Change 2007: The Physical Science Basis" (www.ipcc.ch), gives an insight into the production of knowledge by a worldwide network of experts. The network's tasks are defined as following: to systematically check the validity of studies on climate change showing different results; to contrast divergent profiles; to establish a minimal consensus by ranking indicators of qualitative probability (in the sense of likelihood, not quantitative probability) and modelling them in different scenarios. Reflecting on this example of transnational and transdisciplinary knowledge production, one might say that claims of validity of expertise can be measured by criteria of plurality, plurality of negotiations, of actors, of knowledge bodies being processed.

Knowledge production is an open-ended process, moving towards unknown futures, taking into account unforeseen options and developments. Looking at the reciprocal and collective process of discourse among experts with different outlooks and across boundaries of disciplines, professions, and spheres of knowledge, expert knowledge cannot but be recognized as a social construction, as socially created in a societal practice. Depending on its (social) location and other factors, such practice may take on different forms, bring about different results and hence must be seen as a contingency, as appearing not inevitably. The constructiveness and contingency of expert knowledge and standpoints is further underlined by the limited duration of expert networks alluding to the temporality of knowledge bodies and therefore limited claim of validity.

Bearing these characteristics in mind, expertise in the discourse on post-modernity is reflected as an attitude, a non-imperialistic attitude of acknowledging plurality and contingency, the otherness of other systems and practices of knowledge, while at the same time refusing to give up ones' own claim of validity. The practice of plurality as stated by Welsch (1993, p. 322) is said to be an issue of hard work. Plurality is endangered, on the one hand, through superficiality, that is neglect of conflicts and oppositions between concepts and, on the other hand, through indifference or arbitrariness in the sense of "anything goes." Consequently, when analysing expert interviews, attention is drawn to the expert's awareness of contingencies, to his habitus and practice of controlling plurality and contingencies, particularly, following Welsch, to the practices of acknowledgement and erasure of plurality and contingencies, and to the use of irony.

(d) *Explicitness of expert knowledge:* Expert knowledge – in classical sociology of knowledge constructed as an ideal type and not reconstructed empirically – is defined as a special knowledge which the expert is clearly and distinctly aware of. It is located in "discursive consciousness" – to use the terminology of Giddens (1984).[16] For both Schütz (1964) and Sprondel (1979) this constitutes a crucial difference as compared with everyday knowledge. Yet in view of the more recent discussion of the term expert in the sociology of knowledge and of empirical research on expert behaviour, this standpoint cannot be maintained. Contrary to Schütz' and Sprondel's assumption of the explicitness of expert knowledge, light is shone to the tacit parts of expert knowledge, to relevances escaping the experts' awareness and reflection. Not only everyday knowledge, but also expert knowledge comprises pre-theoretical experimental knowledge (Bogner and Menz, 2002b, see also Bogner and Menz, in this volume, Köhler, 1992; Meuser and Nagel, 1994; Schröer, 1994).[17]

The new forms of knowledge production appearing in a pluralized and globalized world are to be considered as accompanied by highly detailed expression and overstatement of viewpoints; by an increased necessity to discuss options thoroughly; and by elaborating maximum contrasts between approaches (Welsch, 1993, p. 323). Therefore, an increased level of explicitness of expert knowledge might rightly be expected. However, together with the change towards a knowledge-based society and continuous growth in differentiation and reflection of knowledge (Schütze, 2002), an increase in non-explicit knowledge is to be observed. According to Rammert (2003), this is not a zero-sum game; the explicitness of knowledge does not necessarily result in a decrease of implicit stocks of knowledge. Paradoxically, it rather were the case "that in the intensified process of explicating and formalizing growing stocks of knowledge [...] the *relevance of non-explicit knowledge* emerges clearer and clearer" (Rammert, 2003, p. 484; emphasis in original), namely, collectively shared experiences, incorporated knowledge, rules of thumb, organizational routines, informal rules. Adopting Knorr-Cetina's understanding of epistemic cultures, a dynamic concept of knowledge needs to be applied: no longer should knowledge be conceptualized as a fixed product, as an "intellectual or technological product" but considered as a "process within definite contexts of production," directing the analytic attention towards "knowledge as it is practiced" (Knorr-Cetina, 2002, pp. 17–18). Yet the operational knowledge guiding and orienting a person's behaviour is difficult to be accessed consciously, it is hardly to "reeled off" just like that in the interview. However, it is seizable in the empirical data and open to reconstruction from what the interviewee tells.[18] It is to be achieved favourably on the basis of narrations of concrete problems, conflict and problem solutions taken from the expert's experience (see below).

Summing up, what follows from the diagnosis of present-day society regarding the analysis of expert knowledge and starting from the concept of expert interview as an open method which is not guided by a script or a preconceived sequential order but solely by topics to be covered in the course of interviewing: Firstly, the diagnosis of our time leads to adopting a process-oriented analytical view on expert knowledge. Questions to be posed may regard reference groups, important spheres of knowledge; accounting of the plurality and globalization of knowledge. Relevant aspects refer to the embeddedness of expert knowledge in milieus and socio-cultural settings. Secondly, expert knowledge is defined by the communicative practice of insider groups and networks; the procedures of negotiating opinions; and the strategies of inclusion and exclusion. Thirdly, another element is the biographical mixture of the expert status within life-worldly, private as well as public spheres of experience. Fourthly, in view of the complexity, uncertainty, and ambiguity of expert knowledge, it is the expert's habitus, his awareness of contingencies, and his strategies of self-assurance, which finally come into focus as an essential component of her or his knowledge.

1.3 Data collection

According to the procedural nature and the non-explicitness of considerable parts of expert knowledge like tacit or pre-theoretical experiential knowledge, the expert interview is not likely to be conceptualized as a process of extracting knowledge from the interviewee by asking questions in the sense of a questionnaire. Referring to Giddens' distinction between practical and discursive consciousness, the expert knowledge connected with habitual ways of problem management can be located in between the two poles. Neither is it a fully pre-reflexive knowledge at the level of basic rules or ethno-methods as analysed by Cicourel (1972), nor is it comparable to the knowledge of grammatical rules, which certainly most individuals intuitively have command of but are only partly capable of making explicit. Experts will report cases of decision-making and state principles they keep to; these are the data necessary for reconstructing the supra-individual, field-specific patterns of expert knowledge.

Against this background, we consider an open interview based on a topic-guide to be appropriate for data collection. As regards the reconstruction of knowledge, which underlies expert behaviour, questionnaires would at best allow for knowledge at the level of the discursive consciousness containing rationalist reasoning corresponding with officially accepted standards. This type of argument is to be found quite often in expert interviews, but apart from the rare case in which the interviewee does not really cooperate, that is answers with semi-official statements, experts do reveal a lot more about relevances and maxims connected with their positions and functions: when they carry on talking about their activities, extemporize, give examples, or use other forms of exploration. The open interview provides the room for the interviewee to unfold his own outlooks and reflections. As to data collection interviewing should be based on general topics but avoid closed questions and a prefixed guideline.

For the interviewer it is a must to prepare the interview topics thoroughly and build up a knowledge base of the field the experts are moving in. Different from the narrative interview, in the expert interview naivety would involve the risk of presenting oneself to the expert as an incompetent interviewer. Such renunciation would also mean taking a wrong course methodically, as the focus is not on the individual expert's biography but on action strategies and criteria of decision-making connected with a particular position.

The effort invested into the design of the topic guide provides the interviewer with the thematic competence enabling him for productive interviewing. The motto "Ignorance as Method" (Hitzler, 1991) led the wrong way. Most of the time the researcher cannot afford to be too naive and ignorant. When collecting expert interviews with managers, Trinczek (1995, p. 65) found that the readiness of the respondents "to bring up their knowledge and viewpoints" is decisively influenced by the competency with which the interviewer is able to present her or himself. It is important to be informed in advance about rules, principles, statutes within the expert's context, for instance about collective agreements and the fundamentals of labour law when making a study on human resources management. Much the same is due to crucial events being published in the media.[19] An uninformed interviewer might cause doubts as much about her or his competence as her or his involvement. To be short of knowledge of events inside the respective institution is forgivable.

The expert interview and the biographical interview differing clearly with regard to objective and methodical design, narrative passages are not excluded from the expert interview. Narratives about episodes in the field of the expert's professional activity turn out to be key points of reference for the reconstruction of orientations guiding conduct. Methodically, this can be put to good use by eliciting narrations through the mode of interviewing. Narratives provide insight into the tacit aspects of expert knowledge, which she or he is not fully aware of and which, on the contrary, become noticed only gradually in the course of the narration.[20] This may be illustrated by a narrative sequence drawn from an interview with a personnel manager who, by tackling a case of decision-making over candidates for a higher position, seeks to illustrate the criteria underlying the final result.[21]

There was a woman, a mechanical engineer, who had been here for an interview, and she should possibly be considered for a position as supervisor of outside work, and then it was argued that it was likely she wouldn't be able to come out on top against a totally male-dominated outdoor staff, where the going is a bit rough, you know, because no one is treated with kid gloves out there. It's unpleasant work, in all weathers, it partially is dirty work, and also there are just distressing decisions to be made in personell [sic] matters and orders to be given and so on, and then it was said, no, she would probably not be able to do that, you know. And then our employees' representative spoke out in favor of that woman and said, why not give her a chance, if one always raises objections, women can never prove themselves, and then the gentlemen in charge who should possibly employ the lady felt more and more uneasy, and I really have to say, and that now is something I meant earlier regarding one's own view, you can leave it on, I don't mind [this refers to the tape recorder; MM/UN], and when you realize, there are about eight or ten candidates, and one of them was a woman, and she enters the room on very high heels, she is wearing a skirt, she sits down and makes a good impression and tells you that her previous employment was in a construction department, a drawing office, where she designed engine heads and was responsible for production and so on, and now she would have to, or this is what one should imagine, that now in this position she really tackles her tasks, then I, too, have had my doubts, you know, and then I finally said, well, all right, that man X certainly is the better choice. That's about how it goes. So despite all efforts to reject common prejudice, once again it comes to the conclusion, that, alas, she wouldn't be able to do the job, after all.

Through this narrative about a particular case, general criteria of decision-making in recruitment become as clear as it becomes apparent how criteria of decision-making in an organization, in connection with gender-related structures of prejudice, bring about a practice which is typical and not unfamiliar. While narrating his story the interviewee becomes aware that he is being recorded and by and by is tangled up in a narrative the unfolding and outcome of which he could not clearly foresee from the start. In doing so he reveals more about the relevance structures underlying his behaviour than he would actually do – and would be able to do – if he were asked directly. It can be presumed that the knowledge coming to light is located at the border of practical and discursive consciousness.

Apart from narratives, reports about breaches of routine activities are particularly instructive (Walter, 1994, p. 275). Mechanisms of orderly functioning become apparent by looking at how breaches and conflicts are controlled. This corresponds to the logic of breaching experiments in early ethnomethodology (Garfinkel, 1967). It is obvious that the occurrence of such reports cannot be anticipated when designing an interview schedule. Therefore, it is all the more important to carry out the interviews in such a way that (a) does not prevent the expert from addressing unforeseen aspects of topics and (b) utilizes such aspects in subsequent interviews. From our experience it is crucial for a successful outcome of an expert interview to use the schedule in a flexible, non-bureaucratic way – that is as a thematic guideline and not as if it were a questionnaire to be administered. It is the relevance structures of the interviewees, which shall be elicited, not those of the interviewer.

Questions should be focused on the how of decision-making and acting. In this way, general principles and maxims can be grasped, and a reconstruction of the logic underlying a decision is facilitated. Furthermore the wording of questions should aim at the supra-personal level of knowledge and relate to the institutions in question. Unless the interviewee retreats to his formal role, his personal qualifications come up anyway. So it becomes clear what the official institutionalized reality is as well as to what extent the expert acts in a field of conflict between perceived institutional directives and his personal interpretation of rules. Questions about decisions made or processes having taken place eventually allow a reconstruction of the logic and procedure of the decision-making process. Follow-up questions should as far as possible evoke accounts of concrete events or generate narrations.

The dynamics of the situation in expert interviewing, like with other types of interviews and other reactive methods, is decisively determined by the mutual perceptions of the participants. The impact of the interviewer's appearance as determined by factors like age, gender, and social status has already been described in the literature on the (structured) interview. In expert interviewing both the status relation and gender relation play a prominent role.

Regarding the status relation it has been stated above that the outcome of the interview is co-determined by whether the expert sees the interviewer as a competent interlocutor. The ascription of competence to the interviewer is based not only on his behaviour, but also on aspects of his formal status. Interviewers who hold a high academic degree are often granted "credit," so to speak, as regards their competence. On the other hand the experts might be sceptical about young researchers who do not yet hold a higher degree, in particular in cases of a high status of the expert. This seems to play a role in management research. In interviews with executive personnel, Trinczek (2002, p. 219, see also Trinczek, in this volume) has observed expectations of the following kind: "If the university hasn't even bothered to send over a 'real' professor, the researcher should at least have got a PhD."

The gender relation appears to be increasingly important in a society, which is not only hierarchically structured but also showing an unequal distribution of acknowledged expertise to the disadvantage of women. In most fields of research the experts under study are males despite all changes in gender-relations. This is to be understood in connection with the development of professions and particularly applies to the functional elites of society (Littig, 2002). In the historical development of occupations and professions, expertise has become a field predominated by males, "a man's business," so to speak (Wetterer, 1992). Methodical and methodological consequences resulting from the dominating "manliness" of the expert status, is an issue raised only rarely, as Littig (2002, p. 191) rightly remarks.

In situations of expert interviewing the female researchers' professional status is often neglected. Young female researchers who are dealing with a male-dominated field are especially affected by the fact that in the experts' understanding gender status dominates over professional status. If this is the case, the female researcher is considered to be "acceptably incompetent" (Gurney, 1985). Abels and Behrens report how they utilized this constellation in interviews with male experts:

> In many talks with experts we claim to have received important pieces of information just because men find it necessary to explain matters through and through or to come up with facts which we as women in an ascribed lower status are not believed to be capable of getting right. These projections and the concomitant frankness can be further increased through naïve and humble questions appealing to the expert's readiness to enlighten us. (1998, p. 86)

The ascription of features and character traits on the basis of gender may foster expectations on the respondent's side, which can become a burden for the female researcher but can also be strategically instrumentalized with regard to the research objectives.

1.4   Analysis[22]

Different from the analytic approach appropriate for case studies, in the analysis of expert interviews attention is focused on thematic units, that is passages with similar topics which are scattered about the interviews. Sequentiality of statements within a single interview is not of interest. Instead, what gains importance is the institutional-organizational context within which the expert's position is embedded and which provides the actor with guiding principles. Right from the beginning of the analysis, the context is taken into account in order to assess the meaning and significance of the expert's statements – no matter at what point in the course of the interview they appear. The context as commonly shared by the experts largely ensures the comparability of the interviews; in addition, comparability is guaranteed through the use of the topic guide. This guideline reflects the relevant topics against a horizon of other possible topics and serves to focus the interviews.

Transcription: As a general rule interviews are being taped. Transcriptions of thematically relevant passages are a prerequisite for the analysis. A transcription of the whole recording – in contrast to working with biographical interviews – is not standard. The transcription is also less detailed; prosodic and paralinguistic elements are noted only to a certain extent.

Paraphrase: The sequencing of the text according to thematic units is easily done, as it were, in the manner of commonsense reasoning. In order to rule out a narrowing of the thematic comparison of passages from the different interviews – the next but one step in the analysis – and to avoid to "give away reality," the paraphrase should follow the unfolding of the conversation and give account of the interviewee's opinions.

Coding: The next step in condensing the material is to order the paraphrased passages thematically. The interpreter keeps close to the text and adopts the terminology of the interviewee. At best a term or phrase can be used as it is. Whether one or more coding categories are attached to a passage depends on how many topics are addressed. It is allowed and necessary to break up the sequentiality of the text also within passages, since the subject matter of the analysis is not the totality of the individual person's life. The frame of reference at this stage in the analysis still is the single interview; condensations, typifications, abstractions remain within its horizon.

Thematic comparison: From this stage onward the analysis surpasses the single passage in the text. The logic of the procedure corresponds to that of coding, but now thematically comparable passages from different interviews are tied together (cf. Nagel, 1986). Category formation close to the language of data has to be maintained; theoretical abstraction should be refrained from, if possible. Since in the course of the thematic comparison a large amount of data is condensed, it is essential to check and if necessary revise coding decisions. The results of the thematic comparison have continuously to be checked in the light of the other relevant passages in the interviews, to examine whether they are sound, complete and valid.

Sociological conceptualization: It is only now that a distant reviewing of the texts and the terminology of the interviewees takes place. Features shared and features differing from interview to interview are elaborated and categorized by drawing on the theoretical knowledge base. The specific characteristics of the commonly shared knowledge of experts are condensed and categorizations formulated. The process of category formation implies a subsumption of phenomena under a term claiming general validity, on the one hand, and a reconstruction of this term as valid for the reality under scrutinization, on the other hand. The level of abstraction is that of empirical generalization. Statements refer to structures of expert knowledge. While establishing links to the academic discourse, the generalizations remain restricted to the empirical data, even though a terminology is used which cannot be found in the material itself.

Theoretical generalization: The researcher arranges the categories according to their internal relations. When representing the results of research the empirically generalized findings are framed by a theoretically inspired perspective. In this reconstructive process the meaning structures of the field of action under study are connected to form typologies and theories – overcoming loose ends and unconnected findings so far handled pragmatically.

Regarding data analysis all stages of the analytical process should be passed through and shortcuts be avoided. What is more, while the process of interpretation is progressing it often proves necessary to go back to an earlier stage in order to check the adequacy of generalizations as grounded in data. This recursiveness is the typical merit of this approach.

Notes

1. See, for example, Hitzler, Honer and Maeder (1994), Brinkmann, Deeke and Völkel (1995), Schulz (1998), Bogner, Littig and Menz (2002, 2nd edition 2005), Mieg and Näf (2006).
2. As we showed elsewhere, the expert interview is one of the most frequently applied methods of empirical research, both as a method in its own right and in the framework of a triangulation of methods. It is applied particularly in industrial sociology, and organizational, educational, and policy research. Although the expert interview has been used frequently for a long time it was hardly ever reflected methodologically and with a view to the characteristics as compared with those of other methods of interviewing. The result is a certain "confusion and inconsistency" as to the understanding of the expert interview (Mieg and Brunner, 2004, p. 199; for a similar view see also Bogner and Menz, 2002a, p. 20). Correspondingly, on checking through relevant handbooks on methods it turns out that the expert interview is at best mentioned as an exploratory method. Exceptions are Flick (1995), von Alemann (1995), Friebertshäuser and Prengel (1997), Nohlen and Schultze (2002), Kühl and Strodtholtz (2002), Bohnsack, Marotzki and Meuser (2003), Becker and Kortendiek (2004). It is widely agreed to locate the expert interview in the context of qualitative social research methodology. Our article is written in this line of thought which however is not unchallenged but criticized as an unjustified option. (Deeke, 1995).
3. Similar Pfadenhauer (2002, pp. 127–8, our translation), for whom the expert interview is "a method of data collection which is highly ambitious involving great effort." See also Pfadenhauer in this volume.
4. Our comments are based on previous articles on expert interview and expert knowledge (Meuser and Nagel, 1991, 1994, 1997, 2002). In this article our former considerations are discussed in the light of changes in knowledge production and extended with a view to the impact on the analysis of expert knowledge. Doubts about our conceptualization of the expert interview as a method in its own right are expressed by Deeke (1995), Kassner and Wassermann (2002).
5. In previous articles we treated this contextualization of the expert and expert knowledge somewhat briefly; meanwhile the changes in knowledge production have become more visible and require to be dealt with – which we shall do in this article. It will be examined whether and in which way the processes of societal change – discussed as newly emerging knowledge cultures and forms of knowledge production – are challenging a revision of concepts drawn from the sociology of knowledge.
   See Gibbons and others (1994) on the change of forms and cultures of knowledge production in different spheres of society (economy, education, the humanities and the social sciences). For an analysis of knowledge cultures in the sciences and high-technology see Knorr-Cetina (2002), and in general Rammert (2003). For critique cf. the contributions in Bender (2001) and a review of publications on the Knowledge Society (Hettlage, 2004).
6. A confusion of terms can occasionally be observed also in the method's literature (cf., for example, Gläser and Laudel, 2004).
7. Cf. Pfadenhauer (2003, p. 171) who assumes that counter-experts have undergone a marked change in status with their expertise being upgraded, and accordingly are no longer labelled as "counter"-experts.

8. For example, not so long ago judges at the German Federal Constitutional Court consulted the Chaos Computer Club, an association of hackers, with regard to the legal processing of safety provisions for computers used in the registration of votes (Kölner Stadt-Anzeiger, 29 August 2007).

9. Cf. the majority of the contributions in Bender (2001). Above all warnings are also concerning the enthusiasm which seems to drive Gibbons and others in view of Mode 2; cf. also Hettlage (2004).

10. An organization like Greenpeace is a good example illustrating the observation that an increase in institutionalization and recognition usually is coupled with a professionalization and scientification of also the non-professional or counter-expertise (For the institutionalization of social movements in general cf. Rucht, Blattert and Rink, 1997).

11. Pfadenhauer (2003, p. 172) points out that the expertise of counter experts is as much opinionated as those of other experts implying that they are not at all covering the role of disinterested third party. It should be mentioned here that the expert interview like other interviewing methods is used to gather information about a subject matter as seen from various perspectives, and although the expert's knowledge may be of a privileged nature it is nonetheless tied to a position like any other knowledge.

12. In postmodern discourse it is claimed that the dividing line between insiders and outsiders, insider and outsider knowledge becomes blurred; we do not share this approach. In accordance with the perspective of the sociology of knowledge we maintain the distinction between expert and lay knowledge, though not the clear-cut distinction between the professional expert and the layman. As mentioned above, we place a fourth figure besides layman, well-informed citizen and professional, namely the active participant with her or his input of new relevances, fulfilling the function of a critical corrective against the side-effects of the modernization process.

13. Thus the production of expert knowledge develops as an independent subject matter to be studied in future research on different groups of experts.

14. We are not going into the question raised by Knorr-Cetina as to whether this logically implies a departure from traditional definitions of knowledge.

15. In contrast to the model of negotiation discussed here cf. the study of Bogner and Menz (2002a) on the rationality of decision-making in the political system.

16. Giddens (1984) distinguishes a discursive consciousness from a practical consciousness. The first can be outlined by a person when asked to do so since it is explicitly represented in the stock of knowledge; the second can only be reconstructed from the implicit stock of knowledge.

17. Cf. Bogner and Menz (2002b, pp. 43–4) who distinguish between three dimensions of expert knowledge to be hold analytically separate: "technical knowledge," "process knowledge," and "interpretive knowledge." Technical knowledge is expert knowledge in the narrower sense; it is explicit knowledge and can be directly communicated in the interview. Process knowledge is conceived of as "practical experiential knowledge" resulting from frequently and repeatedly performed action patterns and interaction routines. Interpretive knowledge is created not only in functional contexts but is additionally shaped by subjective relevances and viewpoints. The aforementioned embeddedness of expert knowledge in the biographical sphere and in the life-world is bearing effect here.

18. Against the background of a tradition of ethnographic research, Pfadenhauer (2003, p. 160) calls into question that the expert interview and interviewing are generally suitable to gain insight into pre-theoretical experiential knowledge.

She thereby touches upon issues of method and methodology under discussion inside the world of qualitative social research which we would prefer to refrain from in this article.

19. For more detailed comments see Pfadenhauer (2002) who even views the expert interview as "a conversation between expert and quasi-expert."
20. This is caused by the structural dynamics of narrations (cf. Schütze, 1982).
21. The interview was carried out for a study of implementation of equal treatment policy in public administration (Meuser, 1989).
22. A detailed presentation of the analytical steps can be found in Meuser and Nagel (1991, reprinted in Bogner, Littig and Menz, 2002).

Further readings

Miller, R. L. (2005) *Biographical Research Methods, Vol. 4, Disputes and Concerns in Biographical Research* (London: Sage).

Nowotny, H., Scott, P. and Gibbons, M. (2001) *Re-Thinking Science: Knowledge and the Public in an Age of Uncertainty* (Oxford: Polity Press).

Schütz, A. (1964) "The Well-Informed Citizen: An Essay on the Social Distribution of Knowledge" in *Collected Papers*, Vol. 2, pp. 120–34 (The Hague: Nijhoff).

References

Abels, G. and Behrens, M. (1998) "ExpertInnen-Interviews in der Politikwissenschaft. Das Beispiel Biotechnologie" in *Österreichische Zeitschrift für Politikwissenschaft 27*, 79–92.

Alemann, U. von (1995) *Politikwissenschaftliche Methoden. Grundriss für Studium und Forschung* (Opladen: Westdeutscher Verlag).

Bauman, Z. (1991) *Modernity and Ambivalence* (Ithaca, NY: Cornell University Press).

Beck, U. (1992) *Risk Society: Towards a New Modernity* (London: Sage).

Beck, U. (1998) *World Risk Society* (Cambridge: Polity Press).

Beck, U., Giddens, A. and Lash, S. (1994) *Reflexive Modernization. Politics, Tradition and Aesthetics in the Modern Social Order* (Cambridge: Polity Press).

Becker, R. and Kortendiek, B. (2004) *Handbuch Frauen- und Geschlechterforschung* (Wiesbaden: VS-Verlag).

Behnke, C. and Meuser, M. (2003) "Doppelkarrieren in Wirtschaft und Wissenschaft" in *Zeitschrift für Frauenforschung und Geschlechterstudien 21*, 62–74.

Behnke, C. and Meuser, M. (2005) "Vereinbarkeitsmanagement. Zuständigkeiten und Karrierechancen bei Doppelkarrierepaaren" in Solga, H. and Wimbauer, C. (eds) *"Wenn zwei das Gleiche tun..." – Ideal und Realität sozialer (Un-)Gleichheit in Dual Career Couples* (Opladen: Verlag Barbara Budrich), pp. 123–39.

Bender, G. (2001) *Neue Formen der Wissenserzeugung* (Frankfurt am Main and New York: Campus).

Bogner, A., Littig, B. and Menz, W. (2002) *Das Experteninterview. Theorie, Methode, Anwendung* (Opladen: Leske and Budrich).

Bogner, A. and Menz, W. (2002a) "Expertenwissen und Forschungspraxis: die modernisierungstheoretische und methodische Debatte um die Experten" in Bogner, A., Littig, B. and Menz, W. (eds) *Das Experteninterview. Theorie, Methode, Anwendung* (Opladen: Leske and Budrich), pp. 7–29.

Bogner, A. and Menz, W. (2002b) "Das theoriegenerierende Experteninterview. Erkenntnisinteresse, Wissensformen, Interaktion" in Bogner, A., Littig, B. and

Menz, W. (eds) *Das Experteninterview. Theorie, Methode, Anwendung* (Opladen: Leske and Budrich), pp. 33–70.

Bohnsack, R., Marotzki, W. and Meuser, M. (2003) *Hauptbegriffe qualitativer Sozialforschung* (Opladen: Leske and Budrich).

Bonss, W. (1998) "*Uneindeutigkeit, Unsicherheit, Pluralisierung, Postmoderne. Eine Bilanz*" in *Merkur 52*, 968–75.

Brinkmann, C., Deeke, A. and Völkel, B. (1995) "Experteninterviews in der Arbeitsmarktforschung. Diskussionsbeiträge zu methodischen Fragen und praktischen Erfahrungen" in *Beiträge zur Arbeitsmarkt- und Berufsforschung 191* (Nürnberg: IAB).

Cicourel, A. V. (1972) "Basic and Normative Rules in the Negotiation of Status and Role" in Sudnow, D. (ed.) *Studies in Social Interaction* (New York: The Free Press), pp. 229–58.

Deeke, A. (1995) "Experteninterviews – ein methodologisches und forschung-spraktisches Problem. Einleitende Bemerkungen und Fragen zum Workshop" in Brinkmann, C., Deeke, A. and Völkel, B. (eds) *Experteninterviews in der Arbeitsmarktforschung. Diskussionsbeiträge zu methodischen Fragen und praktischen Erfahrungen. Beiträge zur Arbeitsmarkt- und Berufsforschung 191* (Nürnberg: IAB), pp. 7–22.

Flick, U. (1995) *Qualitative Forschung. Theorie, Methoden, Anwendung in Psychologie und Sozialwissenschaften* (Reinbek: Rowohlt).

Friebertshäuser, B. and Prengel, A. (1997) *Handbuch Qualitative Forschungsmethoden in der Erziehungswissenschaft* (Weinheim and München: Juventa).

Garfinkel, H. (1967) *Studies in Ethnomethodology* (Englewood Cliffs: Prentice Hall).

Garz, D. and Kraimer, K. (1991) *Qualitaiv-empirische Sozialforschung* (Opladen: Westdeutscher Verlag).

Gibbons, M., Limoges, C., Nowotny, H., Schwartzmann, S., Scott, P. and Trow, M. (1994) *The New Production of Knowledge: The Dynamics of Science and Research in Contemporary Societies* (London: Sage).

Giddens, A. (1984) *The Constitution of Society: Outline of the Theory of Structuration* (Cambridge: Polity).

Gläser, J. and Laudel, G. (2004) *Experteninterviews und qualitative Inhaltsanalyse* (Wiesbaden: VS-Verlag).

Gorden, R. L. (1975) *Interviewing: Strategy, Techniques, and Tactics* (Homewood: Dorsey Press).

Gurney, J. N. (1985) "Not One of the Guys: The Female Researcher in a Male-Dominated Setting" in *Qualitative Sociology 8*, 42–62.

Habermas, J. (1985) *Die neue Unübersichtlichkeit* (Frankfurt am Main: Suhrkamp).

Hettlage, R. (2004) "Die 'Wissensgesellschaft' im Verzauberungs-Entzauberungs-Zirkel" in *Soziologische Revue 27*, 407–21.

Hitzler, R. (1991) "Dummheit als Methode. Eine dramatologische Textinterpretation" in Garz, D. and Kraimer, K. (eds) *Qualitativ-empirische Sozialforschung* (Opladen: Westdeutscher Verlag), pp. 295–318.

Hitzler, R., Honer, A. and Maeder, C. (1994) *Expertenwissen. Die institutionalisierte Kompetenz zur Konstruktion von Wirklichkeit* (Opladen: Westdeutscher Verlag).

Kassner, K. and Wassermann, P. (2002) "Nicht überall, wo Methode draufsteht, ist Methode drin. Zur Problematik der Fundierung von ExpertInneninterviews" in Bogner, A., Littig, B. and Menz, W. (eds) *Das Experteninterview. Theorie, Methode, Anwendung* (Opladen: Leske and Budrich), pp. 95–111.

Keller, R. (2005) *Wissenssoziologische Diskursanalyse. Grundlegung eines Forschungsprogramms* (Wiesbaden: VS-Verlag).

Knorr-Cetina, K. (2002) *Wissenskulturen. Ein Vergleich naturwissenschaftlicher Wissensformen* (Frankfurt am Main: Suhrkamp) (Original: *Epistemic Cultures. How the Sciences make Knowledge* (1999) Cambridge/London: Harvard University Press).

Köhler, G. (1992) "Methodik und Problematik einer mehrstufigen Expertenbefragung" in Hoffmeyer-Zlotnik, J. H. P. (ed.) *Analyse verbaler Daten. Über den Umgang mit qualitativen Daten* (Opladen: Westdeutscher Verlag), pp. 318–32.

Kühl, S. and Strodtholz, P. (2002) *Methoden der Organisationsforschung. Ein Handbuch* (Reinbek: Rowohlt).

Liebold, R. and Trinczek, R. (2002) "Experteninterview" in Kühl, S. and Strodtholz, P. (eds) *Methoden der Organisationsforschung. Ein Handbuch* (Reinbek: Rowohlt), pp. 33–70.

Littig, B. (2002) "Interviews mit Experten und Expertinnen. Überlegungen aus geschlechtertheoretischer Sicht" in Bogner, A., Littig, B. and Menz, W. (eds) *Das Experteninterview. Theorie, Methode, Anwendung* (Opladen: Leske and Budrich), pp. 173–90.

Meuser, M. (1989) *Gleichstellung auf dem Prüfstand. Frauenförderung in der Verwaltungspraxis* (Pfaffenweiler: Centaurus).

Meuser, M. and Nagel, U. (1991) "ExpertInneninterviews – vielfach erprobt, wenig bedacht. Ein Beitrag zur qualitativen Methodendiskussion" in Garz, D. and Kraimer, K. (eds) *Qualitativ-empirische Sozialforschung* (Opladen: Westdeutscher Verlag), pp. 441–71.

Meuser, M. and Nagel, U. (1994) "ExpertInnenwissen und ExpertInneninterview" in Hitzler, R., Honer, A. and Maeder, C. (eds) *Expertenwissen. Die institutionalisierte Kompetenz zur Konstruktion von Wirklichkeit* (Opladen: Westdeutscher Verlag), pp. 180–92.

Meuser, M. and Nagel, U. (1997) "Das ExpertInneninterview – Wissenssoziologische Grundlagen und methodische Durchführung" in Friebertshäuser, B. and Prengel, A. (eds) *Handbuch Qualitative Forschungsmethoden in der Erziehungswissenschaft* (Weinheim and München: Juventa), pp. 481–91.

Meuser, M. and Nagel, U. (2002) "Vom Nutzen der Expertise. ExpertInneninterviews in der Sozialberichterstattung" in Bogner, A., Littig, B. and Menz, W. (eds) *Das Experteninterview. Theorie, Methode, Anwendung* (Opladen: Leske and Budrich), pp. 257–72.

Mieg, H. A. and Brunner, B. (2004) "Experteninterviews. Reflexionen zur Methodologie und Erhebungstechnik" in *Schweizerische Zeitschrift für Soziologie* 30, 199–222.

Mieg, H. A. and Näf, M. (2006) *Experteninterviews in den Umwelt und Planungswissenschaften* (Lengerich: Papst).

Nagel (Matthes-), U. (1986) "Modelle und Methoden rekonstruktiver Theoriebildung" in Gerhard, E. and others (eds) *Subjektorientiertes Lernen und Arbeiten – Ausdeutung einer Gruppeninteraktion* (Bonn: Deutscher Volkshochschulverband), pp. 29–55.

Nohlen, D. and Schultze, R. O. (2002) *Lexikon der Politikwissenschaft*, Vol. 2 (München: Verlag C. H. Beck).

Nowotny, H. (1997) *Im Spannungsfeld der Wissensproduktion und Wissensvermittlung*, http://www.unicom.unizh.ch/unimagazin/archiv/1-97/wissensproduktion.html, accessed on 11 September 2007.

Nowotny, H., Scott, P. and Gibbons, M. (2004) *Wissenschaft neu denken. Wissen und Öffentlichkeit in einem Zeitalter der Ungewissheit* (Weilerswist: Velbrueck Wissenschaft) (Original: *Re-Thinking Science: Knowledge and the Public in an Age of Uncertainty* (2001) Oxford: Polity Press).

Pfadenhauer, M. (2002) "Auf gleicher Augenhöhe reden. Das Experteninterview – ein Gespräch zwischen Experte und Quasi-Experte" in Bogner, A., Littig, B. and

Menz, W. (eds) *Das Experteninterview. Theorie, Methode, Anwendung* (Opladen: Leske and Budrich), pp. 113–30.

Pfadenhauer, M. (2003) *Professionalität. Eine wissenssoziologische Rekonstruktion institutionalisierter Kompetenzdarstellungskompetenz* (Opladen: Leske and Budrich).

Rammert, W. (2003) "Zwei Paradoxien einer innovationsorientierten Wissenspolitik: Die Verknüpfung heterogenen und die Verwertung impliziten Wissens" in *Soziale Welt 54*, 483–508.

Rucht, D., Blattert, B. and Rink, D. (1997) *Soziale Bewegungen auf dem Weg zur Institutionalisierung. Zum Strukturwandel "alternativer" Gruppen in beiden Teilen Deutschlands* (Frankfurt am Main and New York: Campus).

Schmid-Urban, P. (1992) *Kommunale Sozialberichterstattung* (Frankfurt am Main: Deutscher Verein für öffentliche und private Fürsorge).

Schröer, N. (1994) "Routiniertes Expertenwissen. Zur Rekonstruktion des strukturalen Regelwissens von Vernehmungsbeamten" in Hitzler, R., Honer, A. and Maeder, C. (eds) *Expertenwissen. Die institutionalisierte Kompetenz zur Konstruktion von Wirklichkeit* (Opladen: Westdeutscher Verlag), pp. 214–31.

Schütz, A. (1964) "The Well-Informed Citizen: An Essay on the Social Distribution of Knowledge" in *Collected Papers*, Vol. 2 (The Hague: Nijhoff), pp. 120–34.

Schütze, F. (1982) "Narrative Repräsentation kollektiver Schicksalsbetroffenheit" in Lämmert, E. (ed.) *Erzählforschung* (Stuttgart: Metzler), pp. 568–90.

Schütze, F. (2002) "Das Konzept der sozialen Welt im symbolischen Interaktionismus und die Wissensorganisation in modernen Komplexgesellschaften" in Keim, I. and Schütte, W. (eds) *Soziale Welten und kommunikative Stile* (Tübingen: Narr Verlag), pp. 57–83.

Schulz, W. K. (1998) *Expertenwissen. Soziologische, psychologische und pädagogische Perspektiven* (Opladen: Leske and Budrich).

Sprondel, W. M. (1979) " 'Experte' und 'Laie': Zur Entwicklung von Typenbegriffen in der Wissenssoziologie" in Sprondel, W. M. and Grathoff, R. (eds) *Alfred Schütz und die Idee des Alltags in den Sozialwissenschaften* (Stuttgart: Enke), pp. 140–54.

Trinczek, R. (1995) "Experteninterviews mit Managern: Methodische und methodologische Hintergründe" in Brinkmann, C., Deeke, A. and Völkel, B. *Experteninterviews in der Arbeitsmarktforschung. Diskussionsbeiträge zu methodischen Fragen und praktischen Erfahrungen. Beiträge zur Arbeitsmarkt- und Berufsforschung 191* (Nürnberg: IAB), pp. 59–68.

Trinczek, R. (2002) "Wie befrage ich Manager? Methodische und methodologische Aspekte des Experteninterviews als qualitativer Methode empirischer Sozialforschung" in Bogner, A., Littig, B. and Menz, W. (eds) *Das Experteninterview. Theorie, Methode, Anwendung* (Opladen: Leske and Budrich), pp. 209–22.

Walter, W. (1994) "Strategien der Politikberatung. Die Interpretation der Sachverständigen-Rolle im Lichte von Experteninterviews" in Hitzler, R., Honer, A. and Maeder, C. (eds) *Expertenwissen. Die institutionalisierte Kompetenz zur Konstruktion von Wirklichkeit* (Opladen: Westdeutscher Verlag), pp. 268–84.

Welsch, W. (1993) *Unsere postmoderne Moderne* (Berlin: Akademie Verlag).

Wetterer, A. (1992) *Profession und Geschlecht. Über die Marginalität von Frauen in hochqualifzierten Berufen* (Frankfurt am Main and New York: Campus).

2
The Theory-Generating Expert Interview: Epistemological Interest, Forms of Knowledge, Interaction

Alexander Bogner and Wolfgang Menz

2.1 The methodological ambiguity of the expert interview

2.1.1 Introduction: the debate about expert interviews

Expert interviews are a good example of the way in which the everyday practice of social research and theoretical consideration of this practice do not always run parallel to one another. The use of particular methods sometimes precedes their general theoretical reflection. For many years, the widely held view was that expert interviews were conducted frequently but only rarely thought through (Meuser and Nagel, 1991). Only in recent years has the debate about expert interviews gradually become more concrete (see Bogner and Menz, 2008). However, this has certainly not led to a situation in which the different definitions and methodological conceptions of expert interviews have moved closer together. Even today there are disputes not only about *how* expert interviews can be placed on a secure methodological footing, but also about *whether* this is even possible in principle.

Different positions continue to be opposed to one another. Meuser and Nagel (1991, 1994, 1997), for example, have advocated a form of expert interview that is genuinely situated in the qualitative paradigm. They argue that the long period in which methodological reflection was not well developed can be explained by the lack of recognition accorded to the specific strengths of this kind of interview, and by the persistence of a research tradition in which the expert interview is usually seen as having no more than an exploratory function.

Against this view, it has been argued that there is no codified model of "the" expert interview and that there cannot be any such thing; or that, if such a canonization is developed, it is bound to lose any value it may have because it will attribute exaggerated methodological significance to the experience of specific cases (Deeke, 1995, Kassner and Wasserman, 2005). It is argued that the attempt to turn the expert interview into a particular method overlooks the contextual nature of research. This leads to a relativity in this form of interview which places three kinds of obstacle in the way of any attempted methodological generalization. Firstly, all research relies on a relational concept of the expert, which depends on the topic being investigated (Deeke, 1995, p. 7). Secondly, conversations with experts constitute a particular social situation that is especially susceptible to interferences; this may not invalidate the basic principles of how interviews should be conducted, but it sets narrow limits to the range of prescriptive methodological rules available (Vogel, 1995, p. 82). Thirdly and finally, it is argued that one cannot stipulate that expert interviews should be carried out in a certain way. Interviewers will always have their own particular interest in the subject under investigation, and their own concrete question to which they are seeking an answer; this inevitably leads to flexibility in the use of this instrument of enquiry (see Trinczek, in this volume). Depending on the interviewer's interest and the research question under investigation, there will be differences between conversations with experts in respect of the extent to which they are pre-structured, the openness with which they are conducted, and the ways in which they are processed, evaluated and interpreted. This seems to mean that a proliferation of ways of proceeding is unavoidable in the area of expert interviews. And this gives us very few grounds for optimism that this form of interview could ever take on firm, distinctive contours.

In addition, expert consultations are not restricted to qualitative interviews, and neither can they be considered typical representatives of the qualitative paradigm when they are carried out as semi-structured interviews. The expert interview is, on the one hand, suspected of inadequate methodological rigour and of producing little more than impressionistic results because it lacks standardization and quantification of the data, while appearing on the other hand to be too narrow as a way of bringing the interviewee's relevance structures into the open in a "pure" way because the conversation is actively guided and the interviewer occasionally intervenes to redirect it. The expert interview is thus seen as a methodological hybrid which, notwithstanding numerous indications that inter-paradigm debates are rapidly becoming less relevant to the practice of research (see Kelle and Erzberger, 1999), has clear weaknesses because it belongs to both worlds.

This may all sound rather dramatic. In fact, though, the controversy about the methodology of the expert interview is not, in our view, caused by fundamental methodological difficulties. We suspect that the problem lies elsewhere, and that the debate about the expert interview is being kept alive by a lack of clarity in the systematization of the different epistemological interests and research designs.

In this article, we proceed in the *first section* by identifying three dominant forms of expert interview. This is designed to make clear the specific status of, and claims made on behalf of, the expert interview, aspects which are frequently only dealt with implicitly in the debate about methodology. It becomes apparent that methodological generalizations only make sense in relation to expert interviews that are explicitly situated in the "interpretative paradigm" (Wilson, 1970). In accordance with this methodological situation of the issue, we do not treat the object of investigation as a social fact, and we do not treat knowledge about it as the result of an objective comprehension or passive reception of the facts of the situation. Instead, our research attitude is a perspective from the sociology of knowledge, which understands social reality as a construction created by acts of interpretation (Berger and Luckmann, 1966). Academic research, which analyzes the social order on the basis of meanings and structures of relevance, appears as an active-constructive process (Schütz, 1962). Basic social constructivist assumptions like these (see Knorr-Cetina, 1989, Flick, 2004) are central points of reference for the discussion which follows about the nature and knowledge of experts and about suitable interaction strategies for use in interviews.

In the *second section*, we begin by proposing an analytic differentiation between forms of expert knowledge in the framework of the discussion about different approaches to the concept of the expert. Only an explicit concept of expert knowledge as an act of construction performed by the researcher is capable of paving the way for a fundamental change of perspective with regard to the interpretation and conceptualization of the interaction situation. We then outline a concept of the expert, which takes into account the power and the social effects of expert knowledge. This concept owes much to critiques of the theoretical absolutization of the interactionist production of meanings and rules, such as can be found in the work of Blumer (1969) and others. Our own proposal is based on an assessment that the status of experts is not just produced by subjective-situative processes of interpretation, but has its pre-existence confirmed to an equal degree by these processes. This enables us to incorporate into our analysis systematic asymmetries and inequalities that are not limited to local interaction structures and on which expert status essentially rests.[1]

In the *third section*, we discuss this methodologically oriented reconstruction of the expert with regard to interpretations of the interaction situation and the practical consequences they have in interviews. In concrete terms, we argue that what is known as interaction effects should be treated not as variables that distort the situation, but as elements, which are constitutive of the process of data production. This rejection of an "archaeological" model of data production, which conceptualizes expert knowledge as a buried treasure that must be dug up while being kept free from contamination as far as possible, is combined with the outline of a model of typical interaction situations in the expert interview which treats the production of data as a social process.

2.1.2   A typology of the expert interview

There is considerable variation in the concepts of the expert interview employed in the methodological literature on this subject. Meuser and Nagel's (1991) classification of the expert interview as belonging to the paradigm of interpretative social research, which followed the logic of their research orientation, was seen by some critics as an over-hasty attempt to lay claim to a methodologically "neutral" instrument of inquiry on behalf of one particular paradigm (see Deeke, 1995). It is evident that this criticism rests on a competing concept of the expert interview, but this concept is not made explicit in any systematic way. The following discussion therefore proposes a differentiation of the dominant forms of expert interview employed in the methodological debate, in accordance with their epistemological functions. Following suggestions made by Vogel (1995) and with the help of ideas from the relevant works by Meuser and Nagel, we distinguish between exploratory, systematizing, and theory-generating expert interviews.

(1) The expert interview owes its prominence in empirical social research, as a frequently employed instrument for the collection of data, to its function as an *exploratory* tool. In both quantitatively and qualitatively oriented research projects, expert interviews can serve to establish an initial orientation in a field that is either substantively new or poorly defined, as a way of helping the researcher to develop a clearer idea of the problem or as a preliminary move in the identification of a final interview guide. In this sense, exploratory interviews help to structure the area under investigation and to generate hypotheses. The experts interviewed may themselves belong to the target group of the study as part of the field of action, but in many cases experts are also deliberately used as a complementary source of information about the target group that is the actual subject. In the latter case, the expert's role is that of someone who possesses "contextual knowledge."[2]

Exploratory expert interviews should be conducted as openly as possible, but purely on grounds of demonstrative competence it is advisable to structure in advance at least the central dimensions of the planned conversation with reference to a topic guide. In this respect the exploratory expert interview differs from the narrative or episodic interview, though this does not mean that any spontaneous digressions or unexpected changes of subject on the part of the expert should be nipped in the bud. The focus of the exploratory interview, in terms of its subject matter, is on sounding out the subject under investigation. The objective is not to compare data, acquire as much information as possible, or standardize the data. There is thus a fundamental distinction between the exploratory interview and the other two types.

(2) The *systematizing expert interview* is related to the exploratory variant in that it is oriented towards gaining access to exclusive knowledge possessed by the expert. The focus here is on knowledge of action and experience,

which has been derived from practice, is reflexively accessible, and can be spontaneously communicated. This kind of expert interview is an attempt to obtain systematic and complete information. The expert enlightens the researcher on "objective" matters. This means that the expert is treated here primarily as a guide who possesses certain valid pieces of knowledge and information, as someone with a specific kind of specialized knowledge that is not available to the researcher. With the help of a fairly elaborate topic guide, the researcher gains access to this knowledge.[3] The systematizing expert interview is probably the most widespread form of this interview method found in research practice.

The only comprehensive textbook published so far on the expert interview (Gläser and Laudel, 2004) also belongs to this type. It is true that this type does not restrict the concept of the expert to the person who is in possession of particular, specialized knowledge of exceptional quality. This approach also treats knowledge derived from practical everyday experience as a possible object of expert interviews. The main focus, though, is not on the interpretative character of expert knowledge but rather on its capacity to provide researchers with facts concerning the question they are investigating. Experts are a source of information with regard to the reconstruction of sequences of events and social situations: "Experts are people who have special knowledge about social facts, and expert interviews are a way of gaining access to this knowledge" (ibid., p. 10). From this methodological perspective it is not the experts themselves who are the object of the investigation; their function is rather that of informants who provide information about the real objects being investigated.

Even so, systematizing interviews are not necessarily open and qualitative. Standardized surveys – such as those used in, for example, the Delphi method (see Aichholzer, 2009) – are also possible here. The final point to make in this connection is that in the case of systematizing expert interviews, unlike exploratory interviews, it is important for the data to be comparable in relation to the subject matter.

One significant aspect of the systematizing expert interview is the way it has become an important tool for the collection of data in the framework of multi-method approaches (triangulation), for example in organizational sociology. We suspect that the dominance of this form of pure enquiry about information has contributed to the restricted understanding of conversations with experts which leads to the perception of the systematizing type as *pars pro toto*. It may also be a paradoxical consequence of the popularity of the systematizing expert interview that the connection between empirical practice and methodological reflection is so weak in the case of the expert interview.

(3) We use the term *"theory-generating"* for the type of expert interview that was methodologically established by Meuser and Nagel and has been developed further by these authors. In this case the expert no longer serves

as the catalyst of the research process, or to put it another way as the means by which the researcher can obtain useful information and elucidation of the issue being investigated. The essence of the theory-generating interview is that its goal is the communicative opening up and analytic reconstruction of the subjective dimension of expert knowledge. Here, subjective action orientations and implicit decision making maxims of experts from a particular specialist field are the starting-point of the formulation of theory.[4] The researcher seeks to formulate a theoretically rich conceptualization of (implicit) stores of knowledge, conceptions of the world and routines, which the experts develop in their activities and which are constitutive for the functioning of social systems. In ideal terms, this procedure seeks to generate theory via the interpretative generalization of a typology – by contrast with the representative statistical conclusions that result from standardized procedures. Following considerations put forward by Glaser and Strauss (1967) on databased theory, qualitative theory is drawn up here via theoretical sampling and comparative analysis as a process of inductive theory formulation, at the conclusion of which, ideally, the researcher will have a "formal" theory. It follows that the theory-generating expert interview must be classified as part of the methodological canon oriented to the fundamental principles of interpretative sociology.

This means that we have settled the paradigmatic fate of the theory-generating interview. However, we still have to answer the question of whether this kind of expert interview involves a specific method that can be clearly distinguished from those used in paradigmatically related forms of interview.[5] One could challenge our argument so far by objecting that expert interviews have been inadmissibly defined in terms of the object of the investigation or the person being interviewed, and so cannot be a distinct method (see Kassner and Wassermann, 2005). The following discussion of the concept of the expert is a response to this objection.

2.2   Who counts as an expert? A method-oriented reformulation of the concept of the expert

2.2.1   The concept of the expert in the discussion about methods

Three different ways of looking at the definition of an expert can be found in the debate about the methodological foundations of the expert interview. These approaches rely on different analytic and normative perspectives, and in the discussion that follows we identify them as the voluntaristic, the constructivist, and the sociology of knowledge concepts of the expert. However, because of the convergence between the constructivist and the sociology of knowledge approaches, it comes as no surprise that what we encounter in practice is usually a mixture of different conceptualizations oriented towards specific research interests. We argue that a definition which insists exclusively on the knowledge dimension of expertise leads to weaknesses in relation to method and to contradictions, and in the conclusion to this section we outline a concept of the expert which makes use of ideas from modernization theory concerning changes in the figure of the expert.

(1) The *voluntaristic concept of the expert* starts from the undeniable fact that every human being is in possession of particular information, capacities and so on which equip them to deal with their own everyday life; one can thus speak in a general sense of a specific advantage in terms of knowledge relating to personal arrangements. This would mean that in principle, everyone is an expert – an expert on their own life, or as Mayring (1996, p. 49) has put it in methodological terms, "experts on their own meanings." This concept of the expert is inseparable from an unspecific asymmetry in knowledge, and has been criticized (see Meuser and Nagel, 1997, p. 484) on the grounds that we can also enquire about the everyday knowledge of people who are of interest as whole persons by using the methods of narrative or problem-centred interviews. Considerations related to analytic differentiation also mean that it is hard to see why we should extend the concept of the expert in this way. In addition, if every individual is by definition an expert, it becomes difficult to interpret situations in which expert knowledge clearly has specific social effects. Of course, it does not seem appropriate to treat the difference between laypersons and experts as an absolute difference (this strict demarcation is increasingly being called into question, especially in recent work on the sociology of knowledge and the sociology of science – see Meuser and Nagel, in this volume), but it is no more productive to adopt a voluntaristic approach which sees itself subjectively as emancipatory and critical of authority, but which finally does no more than attempt to flatten out existing hierarchies by means of an effort of conceptual will.

(2) The main characteristic of the *constructivist definition* is its focus on the mechanisms involved in the ascription of the role of expert, and it can be divided into a *method-relational* and a *social-representational* approach. The first approach reflects the fact that every expert is also to some degree the "construct" of a researcher's interest. In conducting an investigation, the researcher assumes that the selected expert is in possession of relevant knowledge about a certain subject (Meuser and Nagel, 1997, Deeke, 1995). This perspective understands "being an expert" as something that functions via the ascription of a role by actors who are interested in information and elucidation, in knowledge of the "objective" facts. The consequence of this approach for the practice of research is that one can also look successfully for experts at lower levels of hierarchy within organizations (see Froschauer and Lueger, in this volume). It is not always the case (and one could even say that it is rarely the case) that leading figures who are the public face of an organization are also the experts a researcher is

looking for. In theoretical terms, the method-relational definition reminds us that expertise is not a personal quality or capacity. However, this overlooks the fact that there is always and unavoidably a "material subtext" underlying the method-related construct, since the researcher is never at liberty to select just anyone as an expert. As a rule, researchers fall back on those who have established their reputation by publishing in the relevant literature, who are active in the corresponding associations and organizations, and who have attained prestigious qualifications and occupy prestigious positions. This provides researchers with a reasonable degree of certainty that these are the experts who "really" possess a store of knowledge of relevance to their research. These social ingredients indicate that the relational approach and the *social-representational approach* are closely related. The latter approach states that an expert is anyone who is made into an expert by societal processes, that is who is seen as an expert in social reality. From this perspective, the expert can be described as a trained and specialized professional (an exponent of Weber's "*Fachmenschentum*," Weber, 1980, p. 576), or as a member of the "functional elite" (Meuser and Nagel, 1994, p. 181). The social-representational approach reflects the complex processes of definition which underpin "being an expert," together with all the preliminary assumptions these require, but its strict focus on the societal parameters of expertise means there is a danger that a concept of the expert with elitist implications will be uncritically accepted.

The method-relational and social-representational approaches are so closely interconnected with one another that any distinction between them is of primarily analytic value. In research practice, who is to count as an expert (and who is sought after as an expert) is always defined via specific research interests and simultaneously through the social representativity of the expert. The limits of the constructivist position become clear when one considers that researchers selecting an expert are always practically guided by the form in which they find the social world, the meanings that have been structured into that world before researchers engage with it.

(3) The *focusing of the expert in terms of the sociology of knowledge* has become very influential in the debate about methods. One reason for this is to be found in the paradigmatic orientation of the scholars who have set out the idea of the theory-generating interview as a special form of the qualitative interview. A second reason is the fact that the debate within sociology about the figure and function of the expert was at a fairly early stage initiated by sociologists of knowledge, and it has been largely dominated by these scholars. This certainly does not mean, however, that any consistent concept of the expert has been employed. What unites those who have been engaged in this debate is the way they conceptualize experts in terms of the specific structure of their knowledge.

Schütz (1964) sees the expert as a scientist who acts on the basis of certain, unambiguous knowledge that can be communicated and reflected on at any time. However, because the characteristics of the layperson, in the figures of the "well-informed citizen" who emancipates himself from a "natural world view" with the help of a reflexive way of thinking, and of the "straightforward man in the street", are not very well defined, the figure of the expert becomes unclear and contradictory. As the well-informed citizen weighs up, in a rational way, the arguments put forward by different experts involved in a dispute, we can observe a new way of dealing with knowledge and science in which the first cracks appear in the notion of the expert as an objective and neutral guardian of the truth. In the following discussion, both the sociology of science-related aspects of this question and its implicit relevance to politics, and the theory of democracy were taken up. Sprondel (1979) tries to characterize expert knowledge as "special knowledge" in order to make Schütz's concept of the expert more specific. This special knowledge is unlike general knowledge in that it includes complex, integrated stores of knowledge and is also related constitutively to the pursuit of a profession. This enables Sprondel to differentiate between the expert and the knowledgeable layperson who may have special knowledge (for example, an amateur DIY enthusiast) but who, because his or her functional context is restricted, is unable to constitute "structurally significant social relations" (Sprondel, 1979, p. 149).

Criticism has been voiced of the narrowing of the concept of the expert so as to restrict it to professional activity, in view of the fact that experts participate in extra-parliamentary social movements on a voluntary basis (Meuser and Nagel, 1997). Critics have also objected to the idea that what distinguishes expert knowledge is its reflexivity and explicitness. Sprondel argues, as does Schütz, that the expert's special knowledge is 'immediately accessible' while everyday knowledge is diffuse. Meuser and Nagel (1994, p. 182f.), on the other hand, point out that the basic orientations of the expert, his or her implicit knowledge, that is to say the unwritten laws and decision-making maxims that operate in his or her specific functional area of expertise, are not directly accessible. In terms of method, this means that one cannot enquire directly about the implicit rules of routine action, the expert's habits and traditions; these things have to be reconstructed. In terms of theory, it means that the definition of an expert which argues via a differentiation of forms of knowledge needs to be expanded, though not fundamentally corrected.

Introducing the idea of a special structure or form of knowledge that is available to the expert is neither theoretically satisfactory nor productive in terms of method. The first problem here is that an expert who is conceptualized as *possessing* a specific (additional) store of knowledge seems to have been detached from the societal conditions of recognition of his or her expert status. Because this recognition depends on social parameters which can themselves change, we would argue that it is not in the first instance actually existing differences in competence that characterize the (sought after) expert, but rather the *social relevance* of his or her knowledge. We shall return to this point later. Secondly, conceiving of expert knowledge as a "homogeneous body of knowledge", albeit one that is only implicitly present, means ignoring statements that can be recognized as those of the "private person."[6] Thirdly and finally, this static model is combined with a sociologically unsatisfactory conceptualization of the interaction situation which sets up an ideal communication process that is "natural" and "free of distortion" and in which this "entity" is supposed to be made transparent. It therefore seems to be appropriate to proceed via an analytic differentiation of expert knowledge in order to solve these problems of method.

2.2.2   Expert knowledge as an "analytic construction"

The idea there is such a thing as "special knowledge" rests on the theoretically problematic premise that the validity and generation of subjective meanings and orientations can be thought of as strictly divided into the categories of lifeworld and system. If, on the other hand, we proceed via a process of analytical differentiation that cuts across the traditional distinction between everyday and expert knowledge, we can identify three central dimensions of expert knowledge, which also converge with the different method-related and theoretical claims made by the expert interview: (1) *"technical knowledge,"* which contains information about operations and events governed by rules, application routines that are specific to a field, bureaucratic competences, and so on. This "technical" knowledge remains most closely related to the area of knowledge where knowledge provides a specific advantage, where expert knowledge can be distinguished from everyday knowledge because it is more systematic and more specific in its content. This can be distinguished from (2) *"process knowledge,"* which relates to the inspection of and acquisition of information about sequences of actions, interaction routines, organizational constellations, and past or current events, and where the expert, because of his or her practical activity, is directly involved or about which she or he at least has more precise knowledge because these things are close to his or her field of action. This process knowledge, unlike technical knowledge, is not really specialized knowledge in the narrow sense (something one can acquire through educational qualifications), but is more a matter of knowledge based on practical experience acquired from one's own context of action. The theory-generating interview seeks to gather (3) *"interpretative knowledge,"* that is to say the expert's subjective orientations, rules, points of view and interpretations, which suggest a picture of expert knowledge as a heterogeneous conglomeration. As we reconstruct this interpretative knowledge we enter, to put it in old-fashioned terms, the sphere of ideas and ideologies, of fragmentary, inconsistent configurations of meaning and patterns of explanation. This analytic differentiation makes it possible to describe more precisely the epistemological interest of the theory-generating expert interview, and it also makes clear that expert knowledge cannot be understood satisfactorily if it is thought of as a "homogeneous body of knowledge."

Expert knowledge only becomes identified as interpretative knowledge as the data are gathered and the principles of evaluation are applied; its interpretative character is not a quality of the stores of knowledge themselves. In this respect it does not exist as an entity prior to interpretation, and in this sense interpretative knowledge is always the result of an act of abstraction and systematization performed by the researcher, an "analytic construction."[7] This means that the differentiation we have proposed between three kinds of expert knowledge is not really based on any characteristics of the knowledge itself, but is primarily a construction of the social scientist doing the interpretation. It is almost impossible to tell, on the basis of something said in an interview, whether this statement should be considered "technical knowledge" and so in no need of further interpretation, or "interpretative knowledge," that is as the expression of a subjective construction of meaning on the part of the interviewee.

In general terms, "interpretative knowledge" does not constitute a specific advantage in terms of knowledge available to the expert. In order for a substantively rich investigation of this "interpretative knowledge" to be possible, it is therefore necessary to integrate the expert methodologically as a "private person." It is only in the phase when the data are evaluated that it becomes clear whether the relevance structures and patterns of orientations used by the expert can be reconstructed exclusively by using his or her explanations given from within the professional context, or whether it is also necessary to incorporate comments made from the personal sphere. It is frequently the case that those very passages in an interview where commonplaces and pithy sayings from everyday life are mobilized, or arguments put forward which rely on metaphors from the "private" sphere, are of particular interest. One can hardly distinguish in practice between the interviewee as "expert" and the interviewee as "private person", and it makes no methodological sense to attempt to do this.

2.2.3 The social relevance of expert knowledge

Before examining in more detail the problems of method that are implied by the sociology of knowledge concept of the expert, we need to raise the question of the criteria used in practice to single out experts who interest the researcher. In order to answer this question, one can start by proceeding "reconstructively," so to speak, and asking why certain people are interviewed as experts in empirical investigations. In investigations where the only goal is the gathering of "useful information" (Deeke, 1995), the criterion of "knowledge" does indeed suffice to determine who is considered an expert (for example, in the case of Gläser and Laudel, 2004). However, this does not apply to investigations where the main concern is the "interpretative knowledge" of the actors interviewed. This is of interest for a social-scientific investigation not because the expert is, for example, able to demonstrate access to this knowledge in an especially systematic or reflexive way or because it provides a particularly accurate reflection of reality, but *because it affects practice to a significant degree*. In theory-generating expert interviews, we consult experts because their action orientations, knowledge and assessments decisively structure, or help to structure, the conditions of action of other actors, thereby showing that expert knowledge has a socially relevant dimension. It is not the exclusive nature of his or her knowledge that makes an expert interesting for the purposes of an interview oriented towards interpretative knowledge, but the fact that this knowledge has the power to produce practical effects. As Beck (1992) has shown in his analysis of the radical transformation in the meanings of knowledge and science in conditions where the concepts of nature and society can hardly be kept apart, what constitutes a post-traditional expert is that she or he is, by virtue of his or her specific knowledge, politically influential. Experts can thus be understood as people who, on the basis of specific knowledge that is derived from practice or experience and which relates to a clearly demarcated range of problems, have created a situation where it is possible for their interpretations to structure the concrete field of action in a way that is meaningful and guides action.[8]

"Expert" remains a relational concept inasmuch as the selection of persons to be interviewed depends on the question at issue and the field being investigated by the researcher. When carrying out empirical investigations, we are not usually dealing with people whose activities are "relevant to the whole of society," who shape complex public discourses in a decisive way and have the potential to exercise a great deal of power and influence in ways that determine structural conditions spanning society as a whole. This kind of expert can be found at the centre of discussions about the "Second Modernity." Case studies, though, usually involve a concrete investigation of a smaller unit – a specific organization, company, educational or medical institution, and so on. This means that the question of who is to count as an expert for purposes of method always has to be answered in relation to the concrete field of operation in which the expert acts, and with reference to the investigative spectrum of the empirical study being carried out.

We are now in a position to offer the following approximate methodological definition of the concept of the expert. An expert has technical, process and interpretative knowledge that refers to a specific field of action, by virtue of the fact that the expert acts in a relevant way (for example, in a particular organizational field or the expert's own professional area). In this respect, expert knowledge consists not only of systematized, reflexively accessible knowledge relating to a specialized subject or field, but also has to a considerable extent the character of practical or action knowledge, which incorporates a range of quite disparate maxims for action, individual rules of decision, collective orientations and patterns of social interpretation. An expert's knowledge, his or her action orientations and so on, also (and this is decisive) point to the fact that she or he may become hegemonic in terms of practice in his or her field of action (for example, in a certain organizational-functional context). In other words, the possibility exists that the expert may be able to get his or her orientations enforced (at least in part). As the expert's knowledge has an effect on practice, it structures the conditions of action of other actors in the expert's field in a relevant way.

This definition emphasizes that the goal of the theory-generating expert interview is the reconstruction and analysis of a specific configuration of knowledge. *This means that in terms of method, it cannot be treated as nothing more than a qualitative interview with a particular social group.* The need for a methodologically adequate concept of the expert is closely connected with the problem of the concrete selection of people to be consulted in the empirical investigation. The broader definition of the expert does not just leave us with the problem of localizing the specific knowledge that is relevant to our investigation. It also means that we need to identify those potentials for power and influence, which mean that the expert's interpretative knowledge may succeed in becoming hegemonic. In the first case it is not always leading figures within an organization that have access to the knowledge that is relevant to the investigation, and real influence is not automatically correlated with a person's formal position. Since we often have little idea in advance either of the distribution of relevant knowledge or of the power structures within the field of investigation, the selection of people to be consulted must inevitably be an iterative process. After we have carried out the first round of interviews, we will have further information that may help us in selecting our next group of interviewees. However, the assignment of expert status often cannot be done on the basis of immanent findings from the expert interviews alone; we need to bring into play further sources of data and methods of investigation (for example further interviews) before we are in a position to answer the question of how far the expert knowledge has practical affects and is efficacious.[9]

We must now see whether the concept of the expert we have proposed can demonstrate its usefulness in the framework of method-related considerations. This is the subject of the next section.

2.3 Interaction structures in the expert interview

2.3.1 From the archaeological to the interaction model of the interview

If one compares the relevant contributions to the debate about methods in expert interviews in respect of what they say about the form of consultation and the style of the interview, one can identify parallel features which appear repeatedly even when there are differences of detail. As a consequence of the conceptualization of expert knowledge as a clearly demarcated, stable and homogeneous body of knowledge, all these contributions orient themselves towards a certain standardized ideal of how to conduct an interview successfully, a kind of "one best way" of consulting interviewees which follows an "archaeological model" of the interview. There is a tacit assumption that attitudes, definitions of situations and action orientations exist which are "true" and "real" and are independent of context. These phenomena, it is implicitly assumed, have their roots in a deep stratum of the human psyche, and the task of the researcher is to use appropriate interview techniques to bring them to the surface in a form that is as pure as possible. The interviewer is an essential instrument, but no more than that, and she or he is also a source of mistakes and disturbances, which obstruct or distort the process of "valid" evocation and reconstruction of the "genuine" values.[10] In accordance with this conception, reflection on the interview as a social situation within the debate about the expert interview essentially revolves around the concept of "interaction effects," the term used to describe whatever endangers the interaction structure being striven for and the distortions of and deviations from the ideal kind of interview that is sought after (see Meuser and Nagel, 1991, p. 449ff., Vogel, 1995, Krafft and Ulrich, 1995). The very concept of an "interaction effect" points to the analytic orientation here towards the model of the "archaeological interview." Interactions bring about effects (without them we would have no interaction, just an indistinct noise without meaning), and this is seen as a pathology of communication, a defect of the ideal, distortion-free interview which should be avoided. But the situative effects in the expert conversation diagnosed as "mistakes" and "distortions" can be used productively (see Abels and Behrens, 2009); not only that, they are constitutive for any process in which data are produced.

In the final analysis, the generally propagated ideal of openness in conversations and neutrality on the part of the interviewer is also, notwithstanding the indisputably good reasons that we have for adhering to this ideal, unable to move beyond the idea that the interviewer can in some way remain "invisible" and, by not influencing what the interviewee says, provoke action orientations, attitudes and so on that are as "pure," context-independent and situation-independent, as possible. All too often scholars forget that anything that is said, both in everyday situations and in the particular situation of the interview, is not just said *about* some subject in a social vacuum, but is also said *for* the concrete interaction partner. Nothing that is said can be detached from its social dimension, and so is always a situative statement made in the framework of a specific interaction situation. And this situation is reflected on by the interviewee, either directly and consciously or at the level of "practical consciousness" (Giddens, 1984); the interviewee reacts to this situation and plays an active role in helping to constitute it.

We therefore need an "interaction model of the interview" as a contrast with the "archaeological model." In the following discussion, we would like to single out one particular dimension of the complex interaction mechanisms at work in the expert interview – though this dimension is, in our opinion, a vital one. If statements are always made in relation to another person who is perceived in a certain way, the structuring of the interaction situation is decisively shaped by the "expected expectations," that is the conceptions the interviewee forms, on the basis of various indications and pre-existing knowledge, and also of the experience of communication as it takes place during the interview itself, of the possible expectations of the interviewer/researcher. We therefore want to analyze the interaction structures in the expert interview by looking at the interviewee's perception of the interviewer and the competences ascribed to the latter. In doing this, we assume that whatever is said by the interviewee is in essential respects guided by what she or he believes or suspects to be the case in relation to the interviewer's competence, professional background, normative orientations and attitudes, and possible influence within the relevant field of investigation. This perspective takes as its object of analysis the so-called "interaction effects," which it treats as (necessary) components of the communication structure under examination. This structure is always constituted with reference to a specific situation; it may be reproduced in the course of interaction within the interview, but it may also change. Certain communication structures may, depending on the epistemological interest and goal of the investigation, be more productive than others, because they stimulate the interviewee to articulate specific forms and stores of knowledge in which the interviewer is interested. Nevertheless, one cannot formulate any general ideal (whatever it might look like in detail) of the "right" way to conduct an interview, one that would have overall validity regardless of the particular case. It follows that we must always bear in mind, in general and also when evaluating the data, that statements made in an interview are also a function of the communication structure.

We now want to move on to provide a brief sketch of some selected interaction situations that are typical of expert interviews and which are shaped by certain perceptions, ascriptions and suspicions about competence in relation to the interviewer. These situations are based on our own research experience,[11] and we would like to pose the following questions: How can one recognize that certain role expectations are operating in an interview (*indications*)? What *preconditions* provide the basis for these expectations? What are the *advantages* and *disadvantages* of this kind of interaction situation? In what kinds of investigation, and in relation to what kinds of substantive question, are such interaction situations productive (*area of application*)? The typology of these interaction situations we have drawn up accords with the three dimensions of: the specialist competences attributed to the interviewer; the suspected convergence or coincidence of the normative background against which the concrete interaction in the interview takes place; and the perceived potential of the interviewer as someone with power to act or to exert influence in the field in which the interviewee is active (see Table 2.1).[12]

2.3.2 The expert's perception of the interviewer: six kinds of ascription

(1) If the interviewer is seen as a co-expert, she or he will be treated as a colleague, a partner with equal status, someone with whom the expert can exchange knowledge and information about the specialist field in question. The interviewee assumes a shared store of knowledge, which she or he and the interviewer can fall back on without needing to restate it in detail. The store of knowledge that is assumed to exist is not restricted to technical and process knowledge, but includes a significant proportion of the (largely implicit) normative and practical premises of the interviewee's own orientations (interpretative knowledge). The expert assumes that the interviewer is familiar with the practical conditions of his or her actions and shares their normative implications; there is therefore no need for the interviewee to justify any of these assumptions in the interview. However, this does not mean that the interviewee assumes complete congruence between his or her knowledge and that of the interviewer. In many cases it is assumed that the interviewer has general competences and knowledge in a generalized and systematized form, whereas the interviewee has an advantage in terms of specific knowledge in the concrete case and in the context of his or her background. This rests on a recognition of the interviewer as a representative of a university department or institute which is concerned with questions and subjects similar to those in which the expert specializes.

The standard situation in interviews is an asymmetrical one in which the interviewer consults the expert. In this case, there is a tendency for this to fade and for a polarized division of roles into interviewer and interviewee to be replaced by a more emphatically horizontal communication structure.[13] The interviewee him or herself asks questions in order to obtain information from the interviewer and to familiarize him or herself with the interviewer's own position and assessment, engages in substantive debates with the interviewer, and so on. Not infrequently, the conversation ceases to be a consultation and takes on the character of a discussion between specialists. The expert responds to the interviewer's questions with questions of his or her own, which in terms of interaction theory have the function of testing the role expectations and ascriptions of competence that the expert has formulated in relation to the interviewer. Acceptance of the interviewer as a co-expert can be seen as a preliminary contribution made by the expert at the beginning of the interview. It is based initially on vague indications and impressions, and these are implicitly checked as the conversation develops. Only in the course of the discussion itself does it become clear whether the interviewee's expectations and ascriptions can be confirmed or if they will have to be abandoned. An interaction structure shaped by granting the interviewer "co-expert" status usually only becomes firmly established during the course of the subsequent conversation. Such a structure therefore requires a large number of preliminary assumptions, and – especially in the initial phase of the conversation – needs to be permanently re-established and confirmed by the interviewer's behaviour and discussion style. As a rule, though, this structure does not rest solely on the concrete communication behaviour of the researcher in the interview, but also requires information and impressions that were available in advance such as knowledge of the professional background and institutional connections of the interviewer, and/or pre-existing personal acquaintance.

In the debate about methods, this kind of interaction structure is seen as problematic if and when there is a danger of a reversal taking place in the interview situation: the interviewee tries to bring this about by insisting on posing his or her own questions in such a way that the researcher does not manage to ask all of his or her own questions in the usually limited time available for the interview.[14] In addition, the interviewee may make a strategic decision to pose repeated questions of his or her own in order to give away as little as possible. The recognition of the interviewer as a co-expert can also be a disadvantage if the interviewee displays a tendency to retreat to discussion of specialized, technical scientific aspects of the subject or to limit his or her comments to specialist academic discourse. If this happens, the interview will concern itself with technical details, formulae and statistics rather than subjective evaluations, normative goals and the expert's own action orientations, and will be of less sociological interest.

In another respect, acceptance of the interviewer as a co-expert can turn out to be a specific advantage. If the researcher demonstrates his or her specialist interest in the subject, makes use of his or her own knowledge and engages in a lively discussion on this basis, the interviewee will be prepared to do the same and to reveal information and knowledge she or he would be unlikely to make available if the interviewer's role were assessed differently and competence attributed differently.[15] What Abels and Behrens (1998, p. 87) rather disparagingly refer to as "trading information," and see as something that endangers the interview, thus acquires a dynamism of its own that can be used productively. What is more, a conversation situation that is more strongly oriented towards discussion rather than consultation is frequently in the interest of the researcher if she or he is able to introduce the provisional findings of his or her investigation as part of the discussion, take note of critical comments on his or her position, and even use the discussion on the quiet as a way of helping to validate that position communicatively.

If the expert interview is seen primarily as something that will produce "useful information" and elucidation of "facts" (as is the case with exploratory and systematizing interviews), the high level of specialist inter-action between co-experts will have a productive effect and the interview will be of value for the detailed analysis of the issue at stake. If, on the other hand, the goal of the investigation is the reconstruction of interpret-ative knowledge (as is the case with theory-generating expert interviews), the "technicist element" becomes problematic, since the implicit normative and practical premises of expert opinion will be presupposed as a shared basis of the conversation between expert and co-expert, and it will be diffi-cult to gain access to them for the purposes of analysis.

(2) Another attribution of competence we encounter frequently in the practice of expert interviews is the idea of *the interviewer as expert from a different knowledge culture*. What characterizes this attribution is that the interviewee assumes that the interviewer possesses significant specialist competence and knowledge (in this respect, it works in a similar way to the expectation that the interviewer will behave as a co-expert), but takes into account the fact that the interviewer comes from a different professional background. The conversation is focused by a shared substantive interest in the core issues, but it is clear that each participant in the conversation is arguing against the background of his or her own stores of knowledge, normative goals and practical obligations to act. The interviewer appears as an expert, but as the representative of a different discipline rather than as a specialist colleague.

If the interviewee orients his or her style of answering questions and dis-cussion to role expectations of this kind, the answers she or he gives will as a rule be formulated in more didactic terms than in circumstances where the interviewer is perceived as a co-expert. Less frequent use will be made of specialist terms from the interviewee's own discipline, and she or he will go to greater lengths to make clear the background to his or her own action orientations. One quite frequently finds that the interviewee behaves rather uncertain, because she or he is not really sure to what extent special-ist knowledge about his or her own discipline can be presupposed. In this kind of interaction structure, the interviewee will typically ask how much explanation the interviewer requires of the specialist context of his or her remarks, whether the concepts being used are familiar, and so on.

As a rule, the expert also attempts to do justice to (what she or he imag-ines to be) the epistemological interest of the researcher and to adapt his or her response to the latter's specialist and disciplinary background. In inter-views of this type the answers frequently contain introductory passages in which the interviewee says something like: "I'm sure you'll find this inter-esting from a social-scientific perspective...", or "As a sociologist you may see this differently, but...". In this way the difference between the participants' perspectives is openly acknowledged, which contrasts with the assumption of shared specialist interest in cases where the interviewer is treated as a co-expert. One frequently finds explicit references in the argument to the fact that the views being expressed by the interviewee can be traced back to his or her own specialist and professional experience, that is the expert states explicitly that she or he is not assuming any shared horizon of meaning as the basis of the conversation. This also indicates an expectation that there will be differences between interviewer and interviewee not only with regard to (assumed) "technical" specialist knowledge, but also in relation to normative premises.

The role expectations and competence ascriptions we have set out here as types are, of course, primarily a matter of assumptions made by the interviewee, but as a rule these assumptions are based on interviewees' actual experience with interviewers and on the (usually vague) knowledge and expectations the former have of the latter. For the practice of interviews it is not always important whether these assumptions are completely accurate. Nevertheless, the "interviewer as representative of a different knowledge culture" is not only a type of role assessment we encounter frequently in practice, it also corresponds as a rule to the actual distribution of competences to a much greater degree than cases where the interviewer is treated as a co-expert. This means that an interaction structure shaped by the model of a conversation between experts belonging to different knowledge cultures requires fewer preconditions. Unlike the "co-expert," the "expert from a different knowledge culture" does not permanently have to demonstrate his or her specialist knowledge, take care to use the correct terminology, and show that she or he is well informed about every detail of the issue under discussion. Initially, presenting a visiting card from a university or a respected institute or showing that one has an academic qualification is usually enough to ensure that the interviewee will form an expectation that she or he is dealing with an expert in sociology. However, in this case, too, he or she must contribute actively to sustaining this expectation as the interview progresses. Here too, signs of ignorance of the expert's specialist field of action, repeated recourse to everyday language, and a general lack of professionalism will cause the interviewee to revise his or her attribution of competence.

In cases where the interaction situation of an interview is shaped by the competence assessment of the "interviewer as expert from a different knowledge culture," a range of different dynamics can develop in the course of the conversation. Ideally, the interviewee reacts in a sensitive, interested way to the researcher's social-scientific epistemological interest and orientates his or her responses towards this interest, though without abandoning his or her specialist context as the expert whose knowledge is relevant to the investigation. Both of the participants in the conversation "accept" the different models of interpretation, the divergent forms of background knowledge, and the different normative implications of the two knowledge cultures. However, there are two quite different ways in which the interview can diverge from this course. The first possibility is that the interviewee may feel him or herself obliged or forced to defend his or her own "culture" (knowledge culture or specialist culture) actively, and to demonstrate the superiority of that culture. The expert insists on the legitimacy of his or her own perspective in the face of the suspected epistemological interest (and possible criticism) of an interviewer who comes from a "different" specialist world. If things go particularly badly, the conversation develops in the direction of an allocation of roles in which the interviewer is seen in advance as a "potential critic."

If things go differently, the interviewee will go out of his or her way to demonstrate willingness to respond to questions posed from a social-scientific perspective, and will consciously put aside his or her own point of view on the grounds that it is probably not very interesting "for a sociologist." This conversation situation can become problematic if it goes beyond a preparedness to recognize the epistemological interest of the researcher, which of course is as a rule productive for the interview, and turns into an exaggerated adaptation to suspected expectations or, as all too frequently happens, if the imagined interest of the social scientist diverges too sharply from his or her real interest. It is also possible for the interviewee's preparedness to accommodate the interviewer to go so far as to take on elements of a "paternalistic" style of communication. In this case, the communication situation will be hard to distinguish from one in which the interviewer appears as a "layperson."

The competence ascription of the "interviewer as expert from a different knowledge culture" proves advantageous by virtue of the fact that as a rule, the expert's specialist patterns of argument and orientations become more apparent here than when the interviewer is treated as a co-expert, since in the latter case it is assumed without question that the interviewer shares them. Theory-generating approaches, or those concerned with the analysis of interpretative knowledge, are therefore well placed to benefit from this structuring of roles in interviews. The disadvantage, however, is that detailed specialist knowledge is rarely made explicit in such interviews. This interaction constellation is therefore less fruitful for expert interviews of the exploratory or systematizing type where the primary purpose is the acquisition of "technical knowledge."

(3) In the literature on methods, the kind of interaction in expert interviews that treats the *interviewer as layperson* is usually considered to be a negative example alerting us to dangers, and the result of a failure to conduct the conversation in the proper way. Trinczek, for example, argues that interviewers who want to conduct successful expert interviews with managers must, as an indispensable precondition, have expert status themselves or, as a minimum requirement, "at least appear reasonably compatible with and 'equal' to" the interviewee in respect of their age and qualifications" (Trinczek, 1995, p. 65). Vogel (1995, p. 80) complains about the "demonstrative good nature" of some interviewees, their attempts to show how well

disposed they are, and the efforts of the interviewee to dictate the content of the conversation to the (seemingly) inexperienced or inferior interviewer, which "has a lasting effect" by making it difficult to "build up a conversational atmosphere of reciprocal productivity." However, instead of reacting to these "paternalistic effects" (ibid.) with a display of resentment at not being perceived or taken seriously as an expert in the desired way, interviewers would be better advised to "turn this discriminatory paternalism to their strategic advantage, as a way of making the collection of data more productive" (Abels and Behrens, 1998, p. 86).[16] Vogel and Trinczek are too eager to try to live up to what they imagine to be the expectations of their interview partners; the idea that only older men with doctorates are able to conduct expert interviews successfully is not very convincing.

If we want to characterize what distinguishes this kind of competence ascription, and if we want to go on to weigh up its specific advantages and disadvantages, we need to reflect on the fact that this distribution of roles is fundamentally ambivalent. This is because the expert can perceive the interviewer as either a *"welcome"* or an *"unwelcome"* layperson. If the interviewer is welcome, the expert acts as someone with the didactic task of transmitting his or her experience, views, and stores of knowledge. The interviewer is offered a painstaking introduction to the specialist foundations of the field under investigation and the factual preconditions of specific action orientations. Because the interviewer is not expected to ask any further constructive questions in the course of this exposition or, to put it another way, because everything the expert says is assumed to be equally relevant, the conversation can easily become a monologue. As this happens, a situatively generated "pressure to narrate" can be constituted which leads to deeper levels of the expert's knowledge. If the lay interviewer is seen as unwelcome, however, any further questions she or he may ask will be seen by the interviewee as unwanted interruptions. As a result of verbal and non-verbal refusal[17] of a dialogic form of conversation, the interviewer is forced to accept the role of a silent, attentive receiver of knowledge. Displaying no interest in the researcher's specific requirements, the expert does not say a great deal and says it quickly. This competence ascription leads to a strictly hierarchical communication situation.[18]

There are a number of strengths and problems which are features of an interaction situation structured in this way and which correspond to the fundamental ambivalence of this distribution of roles. One the one hand, naïve questions stand a good chance of producing the most interesting and productive answers – especially in the framework of a research design that seeks to generate theory. Once the image of the interviewer as a layperson has become stabilized in the course of the interview, and if it is also accepted by the interviewer, this removes a considerable burden from the interviewer because she or he no longer has to demonstrate his or her own expert status or take care to avoid annoying the interviewee. The interviewer has the freedom to do whatever she or he wants, and can ask questions that under other circumstances would have endangered the stabilized schema of expectation. This can make it possible to gain access to information that might not otherwise be revealed, particularly because a naïve interviewer is seen as especially trustworthy (see Abels and Behrens, in this volume). In this situation, experts see hardly any danger that the interviewer will be able to make any strategic use of the information obtained, ask supplementary, excessively critical questions, or put the interviewee in a position where she or he will have to justify his or her position; experts therefore act more freely and informally. If the interviewee thinks she or he needs to explain the most basic elements of his or her ways of thinking and acting, this can be of great interest for analyses of interpretative knowledge because even simple patterns of argument that are not usually made explicit by the expert will be set out in detail. Things are quite different when the interviewer is perceived as a "co-expert," and they do not go as far as this when the interviewee considers him or herself to be dealing with an "expert from a different knowledge culture."

The disadvantages of the competence assumption to the effect that the interviewer is a layperson are obvious: interviewees sometimes bore researchers with interminable monologues about trivia or things they already know, they plod through the contents of textbooks, or they retreat to commonplaces.[19] There is hardly any likelihood that difficult specialist issues can be clarified, it is easier to ignore supplementary questions, and there is a tendency for the interviewee to take over the structuring of the course the interview takes (see Gillham, 2000, p. 82). We have already mentioned, in connection with the perception of the interviewer as an "unwelcome layperson," the danger that the interview will be a short one if the interviewer is not able to demonstrate his or her own competence. In addition, it is very difficult to challenge and correct this kind of competence ascription. And, last but not least, being treated as a layperson is an unpleasant experience for the interviewer, who feels the expert has not understood him/her and has underestimated him/her.

(4) The antithesis of the type just described is the perception of the *interviewer as an authority*. There are two variants of this. In the first variant, the interviewer is seen as a *superior specialist in the field*, who seems to be trying to find out whether the interviewee possesses appropriate knowledge in his or her field of action or is acting "correctly." The interviewer is seen as an expert who has come down from a higher sphere, equipped with the insignia and academic competences of someone who belongs to a university or other institute; this expert descends to the lowlands of practice in order to pass judgment on a colleague with inferior qualifications, or at best to find out how those involved in practical affairs see things. In this first variant, the assumption of superiority relates in the first instance to specialist competences. In the second variant, where the interviewer is seen as an *evaluator*,

it is the power dimension where the interviewer is considered to be superior. In this case the researcher is seen as an envoy dispatched by a higher authority, someone who wants to examine the interviewee's organization and on whose judgment the future of the organization or the interviewee depends. The interviewee's assessment is that the researcher has been sent to carry out tasks such as monitoring the efficiency of a measure, checking on the use of funds that have been allocated, or asking critical questions about the interviewee's qualifications. The interviewee feels placed in a position where she or he must justify him or herself, wants to present him or herself in the best possible light, and seeks to legitimize his or her actions and views in the most perfect way possible in the eyes of the (supposed) authority.[20]

The interaction situation in which the interviewer acquires an authoritative function in this way is characterized by mistrust about the confidential use of the information provided, and by what seems to be exaggeratedly positive self-promotion or, on the other hand, deliberate obsequiousness towards the researcher. This expectation (or fear) of the researcher's role can frequently be observed in the fields of action of experts who are under particular political pressure to legitimize their work, for example in connection with pilot schemes where success does not seem assured, with controversial methods of treatment in social-pedagogical practice, and so on. A perception of the interviewer as evaluator means that one of the most important criteria for a successful interview cannot be met – the assumption that it will have no social repercussions. At least, this criterion is not met in the mind of the interviewee, and that is what counts. There is an absence of trust as a basis for spontaneous and honest answers. Problematic or "critical" facts are not mentioned, and there is no way of getting at them by asking skilfully phrased questions in the interview, because as a rule there seems to be so much at stake from the point of view of the interviewee – future financial support, admitting that one's own concepts may have failed, or simply the honour of one's profession. But although there is hardly any point trying to set up such interaction situations, interviews conducted on these lines are not altogether without value. For example, one can learn a great deal about the interviewees' legitimation and self-justification strategies, the patterns of argument they use in pursuit of their interests, and strategies employed to immunize one's own position against internal and external criticism. The interviewer is no longer in a neutral position, no longer an external observer. She or he becomes a target and object of strategic ways of acting by the actors in the field under investigation.

(5) If the interviewer is seen as a *potential critic*, there is an assumption that she or he is not capable of judging the facts and issues at stake in the interview in an objective way that does justice to the subject. The interviewer is not considered to be a conscientious researcher with a value-neutral epistemological interest, but is seen as the ideologically prejudiced representative of a certain undesirable worldview. The assumption is that she or he cannot

be trusted because she or he wants to use the findings of the interview strategically for political or personal purposes rather than to place them at the disposal of "neutral" science. The interviewee assumes that there is a fundamental divergence between the normative assumptions underlying the investigation and his or her own principles. Even though the "interviewer as expert from a different knowledge culture" may not necessarily share the normative assumptions that prevail in the expert's specialist field either, she or he can still be reasonably sure that the interviewee will treat the "different culture" with interest and respect. In the case of the "interviewer as potential critic," though, the result is rejection of the interviewer, which can even go as far as concealed or open hostility. The expert feels that the interview questions are a form of criticism and believes that the integrity of his or her function or even of his or her person is being questioned. This becomes obvious if the interviewee says things like: "You can think what you like, but we as representatives of the management have to think of the economic health of the company," or: "Let me tell you, if you are not a practitioner with responsibility for dealing with such questions, it's easy to adopt a moralising tone." It is also possible for the first indications of this attitude to emerge in the shape of insistent critical questions about the influence of funding bodies on the investigation, if this amounts to a suggestion that what is going on is not a scientific investigation but something where the findings have already been decided in advance. There is no clearly defined boundary between this kind of response and paternalistic ways of treating the interviewer as a layperson. If the interviewee suspects that the difference between his or her normative frame of reference and that of the interviewer is only caused by the latter's ignorance and incompetence, the interviewee often argues in a manner somewhere between benevolence and condescension (in much the same way as when the interviewer is seen as a layperson), on the basis of the conviction that his or her words will be able to provide some improving knowledge for "the sociologist." If the interviewer is suspected of being a potential critic, sociologists (as representatives of a profession that does not always enjoy a reputation for ideological neutrality) will have a difficult time – especially when investigating politically or ethically controversial fields of action (for a good example of this from research in a normatively sensitive specialist field, see Bogner, 2005a, p. 105ff.).

It hardly needs saying that if this is the interviewee's role expectation of the interviewer, it will almost always be disadvantageous for the interview. This interaction situation is characterized by limited preparedness to answer questions because of a lack of trust, the interviewee's desire to get the interview over with as quickly as possible, and a reluctance to do anything to support the research project (for example by putting the researcher in touch with further potential interviewees). There are some possible benefits, but they are limited to the way in which the interviewee, if she or he feels his or her status as an expert is being challenged, usually spends more time seeking to legitimize his or her own action orientations, views and interpretations, so that the normative premises of the argument which usually remain implicit become more clearly visible.

(6) The role assessment of the interviewer as a potential critic rests on the assumption that there is a divergence between the normative background of the investigation and the corresponding implications of the expert's profession or field of action. The core of the judgment that the interviewer is an *accomplice* lies in the assumption of identity between the normative orientations of the interviewee and those of the interviewer. In this case, the interviewer is seen as a comrade-in-arms in a field of action where power struggles are going on. This turns him/her into someone who is seen as particularly worthy of trust, so that concealed strategies will be explained, and confidential information will be revealed. The atmosphere of complicity is as a rule created via the definition of a shared adversary (see Hermanns, 2004). The interviewee explains quite candidly what is directly normative about his or her ways of acting and patterns of argumentation and what is factual or purely strategic. The interviewer becomes an intimate accessory in these disputes, and the implicit rules according to which they are conducted are disclosed. This happens because the interviewee is convinced that the interviewer is completely honest and discreet. In this respect, this role assessment on the part of the interviewee requires that a large number of preconditions be met. As a rule, interviewer and interviewee need to have been personally acquainted before the interview, so that the interviewee is already informed about the researcher's normative views – for example, as a result of their participation in politically oriented organizations, or via knowledge of the researcher's publications in the field, or even as a result of personal friendship. The fact that the researcher belongs to a university, an institute, or a profession, which often gives the interviewee enough guidance for him/her to be able to identify the interviewer as a "co-expert" or "expert from a different knowledge culture," is not enough on its own as long as it does not say enough about the researcher's normative orientations. The existence of this common ground is expressed symbolically in the interview, for example by informal und personal codes of communication, reference to shared experiences, and so on.[21]

The assessment that the researcher is an "accomplice" is an incalculable advantage for the interview. The interviewer gains access to confidential information, she or he can build on the high level of openness and honesty of the answers, and she or he is given insights into real strategies and action orientations that go well beyond official aims and objectives or legitimation patterns. However, there is also a problematic element: the normative premises must remain largely unstated. Tacit agreement on the common ground uniting interviewer and interviewee means that one cannot question this situation by anything one says in the interview; if one did this, the relationship of trust that has been stabilized over a long period would be unilaterally brought to an end (see Table 2.1).

Table 2.1 Typology of interaction situations and interview strategies

	Dimension of typification	Indications of the communication situation	(Ascribed) preconditions on the interviewer's side
Interviewer as *(1) co-expert* *(2) expert from* *a different* *knowledge culture*	specialist competence (of same type [1], of equal value [2])	symmetrical interaction situation; numerous counterquestions asked by the interviewee	mastery of the specialist vocabulary (esp. 1), specialist knowledge, institutional background, academic titles
(3) Interviewer as *lay-person*	specialist competence (low level)	asymmetrical interaction situation in favour of interviewee: monologues delivered by interviewee, demonstratively good-natured manner; paternalism	status of interviewer is lower than that of interviewee; interviewer is not a specialist in this particular field
(4) Interviewer as *authority*	"evaluator:" power, "superior expert:" (greater) specialist competence	asymmetrical interaction situation in favour of the interviewer; interviewee's legitimation strategy	institutional background: interviewer has status of a specialist authority or a significant position in terms of political power
(5) Interviewer as *accomplice*	normative background (shared)	secret knowledge is revealed, interviewee speaks in a "personal" way (for example by addressing the interviewer informally)	personal acquaintance, background of shared experience (for example membership of political organizations)
(6) Interviewer as *potential critic*	normative background (divergent)	rejection of the interviewer, brief replies, critical counter questions, expert anticipates the interviewer's questions	interviewer is publicly known to be a "critic;" institutional background in organizations the interviewee does not approve of

Interview and question style	Possible advantages	Possible disadvantages	Main area of application
oriented towards dialogue, repeated supplementary questions, rapid exchange of questions and answers, "trading information"	high level of specialist knowledge, high density of facts (1, 2), more explicit setting out of grounds and orientations (2)	interview remains within interviewee's professional frame of reference; "technicist element"	exploratory or systematizing expert interviews; investigations mainly concerned with gathering facts and data
interviewer is primarily a receiver of knowledge, questions generate narrative, committed but naïve supplementary questions	high level of trust on the part of the interviewee, pressure is taken off interviewer	difficult to guide interview in desired direction	theory-generating expert interview; investigations oriented towards interpretative knowledge
authoritarian style of questioning, critical supplementary questions, interviewer interrupts interviewee	increased self-presentation of the interviewee	rule that the interview will have no social repercussions is contravened; "critical" issues are not addressed	not to be recommended as an interview situation; sometimes unavoidable in the case of evaluations
interview is conducted in a "personal" style and everyday language is used; repeated confirmation of common ground; range of different kinds of question possible	high level of trust on the part of the interviewee; access to confidential information	normative premises are not revealed	exploratory, systematizing and theory-generating expert interviews; investigations where the object is technical and process knowledge
critical or tendentious interview questions; no verbal or non-verbal confirmation of the interviewee's status	normative premises are set out at length	danger that the conversation will be broken off	not recommended as an interview situation; this situation can come about in investigations of ethically or politically controversial fields; sometimes productive in investigations oriented towards interpretative knowledge

2.3.3   Farewell to the ideal of neutrality:
on the methodological advantages of the interaction typology

Needless to say, the typology we have sketched of interaction situations in the expert interview is by no means exhaustive. The types it constructs are compressed, extreme cases, which implies that they rarely appear in their pure forms in the practice of interviews. It is possible for combinations of specific competence and power ascriptions to arise in accordance with the three dimensions in which types are constructed (for example through a perception of the interviewer as layperson *and* evaluator), and also for ascriptions related to competence and to normative orientations to be combined (for example the interviewer as co-expert *and* accomplice). Furthermore, the interaction structure of the entire course of a concrete interview can rarely be classified as belonging to one or more particular types. What is more likely to happen is that in the conversation process, expectations and attributions that were initially based on vague suspicions are either stabilized or revised.[22]

We have constructed these types not just as a contribution to descriptive analyses of interaction situations that occur empirically. When we interpret data collected in interviews, we need to reflect that the data cannot be understood as an expression of abstract, general "expert knowledge" but also as a variable produced by the interaction, and that the interviewee's statements are responses to a person seen as having concrete competences and interests – and thus as statements that would have been different had the interviewee had a different conception of the interviewer. Secondly, certain ascriptions of competence, and so on can be deliberately provoked and used strategically as a way of pursuing the researcher's own interest in the investigation. Which role expectations and competence ascriptions are dominant depends on a range of factors – the interviewer's age and sex, specialist knowledge as evidenced by an ability to use specialist terms, linguistic competence, institutional background, academic titles, and so on. The most significant factor, though, is the way in which the researcher presents him or herself and his or her research interest, both in the interview itself and in preparatory contacts with the expert. Of course, it is only the last of these elements that can be influenced by the researcher him or herself.[23] In addition, it is hardly possible for a researcher to outline in advance, on the drawing board, the "ideal" role expectation for a given project (and it will often be the case that the different interaction situations described will be desirable at different stages of the investigation). But it certainly makes sense to "play" with the role expectations and to employ different self-presentation and conversational strategies in different interviews conducted during an investigation, as a way of finding out which of these ways of proceeding is best suited to one's own epistemological interest. This will not always be the "co-expert" self-presentation, which is usually considered the only productive one.

We frequently notice in interviews that interviewees attempt to use vague indications to build up a picture of the interviewer and, on this basis, decide what discussion style and arguments they will use (and often miscalculate). When this happens, the interviewer serves as a screen onto which imagined expectations and counter-expectations are projected. Alternatively, the interviewee may react to an unspecific interview situation by giving a "rhetorical interview" (Meuser and Nagel, 1991, p. 451) containing nothing more than the standard aims and objectives of the expert's field of work, which are already well known to the interviewer. It is therefore a good idea to provide interviewees with some pointers so that they can form an impression of the interviewer. Being explicit about one's own position, that is both about one's epistemological interest and about one's view of the relevant issues, can be far more productive for a successful conversation than playing hide-and-seek. This places a question mark over the ideal of the interviewer whose attitude is somewhere between neutrality and empathy, an ideal, which is held to be applicable to qualitative interviews in general and to expert interviews in particular.[24] Where expert interviews are concerned, we are not usually dealing with people who need to be encouraged to express their own opinions and views and offered support so that they can seize the opportunity to speak freely. In expert interviews, "getting the interviewee to speak" is not normally a problem – and if it is, this is not usually because the expert cannot articulate his or her own position or because she or he is excessively respectful towards the interviewer, who "comes from research." Because of the practical work they do every day, experts are used to adopting controversial positions and defending these positions against critical objections. The complexity of the interaction strategies used to anticipate this specific understanding of the expert's own role and the particular competences of experts, and the extent to which we are able to differentiate these strategies, combine to distinguish the expert interview from other procedures that aim, in a similar way, to reconstruct subjective action orientations and implicit decision-making maxims. And there is an additional objection, which carries even more weight: neutrality in interviews is, in the end, not credible. In expert interviews the interviewee knows very well that the interviewer has already made a detailed study of the subject of the investigation and has formed an opinion of his or her own (see Kaufmann, 1996). Insisting on a claim to be neutral looks more like an attempt to conceal one's own position in a situation where there is no serious possibility of being "genuinely" neutral. Moreover, the interviewer can show his or her own "commitment" in respect of the substantive issues in such a way that the interviewee is encouraged to respond by expounding his or her own stores of knowledge and information.[25]

We have not constructed this typology of interaction constellations as a way of identifying a communication ideal that will be binding for "the" expert interview. The decisive consideration should be that the rules according to which the conversation is conducted must be drawn up in relation to the actual or desired role expectations and ascriptions of competence. What one expects from a "co-expert" is an interview style oriented towards specialized discussion; in order to sustain the role expectation of "accomplice", the repeated confirmation of common ground is needed; the "critic" is permitted to ask waspish counterquestions now and then; the "layperson", unlike the co-expert, need have no qualms about making general appeals to the expert to say something.

2.4   Conclusion: the methodological pluralism of the expert interview

As we argued in the first section of this article, it only makes sense to debate whether or not the expert interview can justifiably be considered a distinctive and autonomous method for the collection of data when we are concerned with the theory-generating expert interview. The methodological specificity of this kind of interview, though, does not lie in "the expert" as an object of research, but rather in the researcher's interest in a specific configuration of knowledge. This configuration is characterized on the cognitive level as a conglomeration of subjective, not necessarily consistent orientations and patterns of explanation ("interpretative knowledge"), and at the social level as determinants of action for others (the efficaciousness of the expert knowledge). This concept of the expert interview (in terms of the sociology of knowledge, as a specific kind of reconstructive interview) signifies a rejection of a concept of the expert that either treats experts as no more than products of the researcher's interest or defines their function solely with the help of a special form of knowledge. In the second section of the article, we therefore proposed a reformulation of the constructivist concept of the expert as used in the sociology of knowledge. The expert should be seen as a person who disposes of, or is believed to dispose of, particular competences, and who consequently has a social status, or exercises a function, which places him/her in a position where she or he may be able to gain general acceptance for his or her action orientations and situation definitions. At the same time, there are grounds for criticism of the widely accepted model of expert knowledge with regard to what it says about the specific epistemological interest that operates in theory-generating expert interviews. From the perspective of a reconstruction of "interpretative knowledge," expert knowledge should be seen as an "analytic construction" rather than, as has been the case up until now, "special knowledge." This redefinition, which removes the close connection between expert status and exclusive stores of knowledge, makes it possible to go beyond conventionally accepted rules for conducting interviews which are theoretically unsatisfactory and methodologically inadequate. Giving up the idea that expert knowledge is a homogeneous entity is connected with criticism of an unsatisfactory conceptualization of the interaction situation which assumes that the expert knowledge the researcher is interested in can be dug up like a buried treasure, in as intact a condition as possible. The third section of the article focused on a critique of this kind of "archaeological model," which is closely related to the dogmatic view that there is a single, correct way of conducting interviews, and went on to present an alternative outline of an "interaction model."

We have argued against this ideal of how to conduct an interview, which is implicitly fixated on the view that there is "one best way" of doing so, in favour of a range of different interview strategies, which are all seen as equally valuable. Which of these strategies is appropriate in different specific circumstances depends on the competence of the interviewer and the interest being pursued in any given investigation. However, the idea that each of these strategies is equally valuable does not mean that anything goes: one cannot use just any interaction strategy to open up the field of analysis in which one is interested. What "equal value" means here is simply that the complexity of expert knowledge can be opened up with the help of a variety of (competing) approaches. Each interaction strategy, though, is connected with a certain type of analytic goal. The (re)construction of interpretative knowledge in expert interviews depends on the interaction strategies, and it never identifies more than one segment of the expert's knowledge.

It is time to abandon the idea that we can move step by step to identify a perfect communication situation in which distortion is reduced to an absolute minimum. In the end, this notion supposes that we can produce data in laboratory-like conditions. We need to appreciate that the interaction effects, which are usually treated as distortions, are constitutive and even productive components of the course of every interview. The specific presuppositions, expectations, and reactions that pre-structure and accompany every conversation should be interpreted as situation-specific and person-specific ascriptions which can be used strategically in anticipation and can be used reflexively when the data are evaluated.

Our alternative outline of an "interaction model" is thus an attempt to rethink the debate about the methodology of the expert interview. There can be no *single*, unified set of methodological rules for qualitative interviews; we can only have different rules for different kinds of qualitative interview. Nor is it possible to draw up a unified canon of methods for use in expert interviews. A methodology of the expert interview must bear in mind that interaction structures in such interviews are bound to diverge, and we should adopt the principle of "pluralist methodology."

Notes

1. See Bourdieu 1998 on the theoretical foundations of an observer position that is not dependent on the cult of the subject or the mysticism of structure.

2. On the distinction in research logic between "contextual knowledge" and "operational knowledge," see Meuser and Nagel, in this volume.

3. We are unable to deal in more detail here with the theoretical and practical aspects of this topic guide. For more on this, see Meuser and Nagel, 1991, p. 448f., 1997, p. 486f., Deeke, 1995, p. 18f., Gläser and Laudel, 2004, p. 59ff., Helfferich, 2005, p. 158ff. For an early warning about the danger of using the topic guide in a schematic, inflexible way, see Hopf, 1978.

4. This includes cases where the analytic purpose of an investigation of the subjective dimension of meaning is the reconstruction of *collective* orientations and patterns of interpretation.

5. Meuser and Nagel (1997) claim that the expert interview can be distinguished from "problem-centred" and "focused interviews" in respect of the way the conversation is conducted and analysed, but they provide no systematic account of these differences. It seems to be relatively easy to distinguish the expert interview from the focused interview (Merton and Kendall, 1946) on the basis of the latter's closeness to quantitative methodology, which follows from its deductive orientation. The epistemological logic of the problem-centred interview (Witzel, 2000), on the other hand, is a combination of induction and deduction, which is comparable to the logic of the expert interview in that both are guided by a topic guide. In the end, though, the difference between the procedures lies in the role of the interviewee in the conversation, which is determined by specific epistemological interests and so is more a matter of practical research requirements than of criteria related to method.

6. Meuser and Nagel (1991, p. 450) treat "private" comments made by the expert as an indication that something is going wrong with the interview discourse, but in more recent work they have revised this position (Meuser and Nagel, 2009).

7. Our argument that expert knowledge should be seen as an "analytic construction" is put forward as a way of sharpening the methodological profile of the *theory-generating* expert interview. No problem arises in applying the concept of "special knowledge" to the *exploratory* or *systematizing* expert interview. Indeed, it would make no sense to conduct these "informative" expert interviews if one did not assume that the expert involved had some kind of specific store of knowledge or advantage in this respect.

8. This aspect emerges occasionally in the debate about method in the shape of the creation of converging concepts, which stress the interpretative role of the expert. Hitzer, Honer and Maeder (1994) speak of "the institutionalized competence of being able to construct reality", and Sprondel (1979) speaks of "the constitution of relevant social relations"; from the perspective we are developing systematically here, these concepts refer to the power of expert knowledge to shape outcomes.

9. The theory-generating expert interview, unlike for example Witzel's problem-centred interview, need not always be combined with a specific investigative design. It is more likely to be the case that the position of the expert interview changes during the course of the investigation. If the reconstruction of experts' orientations is an independent goal of the investigation, expert interviews may be the only empirical material needed (and the selection of people to be interviewed can be made according to formal criteria). If, on the other hand, the expert interviews are used in the framework of case studies where the goal is an analysis of organizational orders, it is self-evident that they can only constitute part of the study. After all, no concrete field of action is structured exclusively by the orientations and knowledge of experts.

10. This model, which distinguishes between a desirable (as defined by traditional quality criteria) but never achievable ideal and the way in which this ideal is never realized because of situative effects, predominates even in cases where the concrete structures of action and communication are examined more closely in the (quantitative) interview, for example in Lueger, 1989. For a critique of the "archaeological model" in relation to standardized surveys based on an conversation analysis, see Houtkoop-Steenstra, 2000. See also Kvale's metaphorical description of conventional conceptualizations of the knowledge sought after in qualitative interviews as "buried metal....[which] is waiting in the subjects' interior to be uncovered, uncontaminated by the miner" (Kvale, 1996, p. 3). However, Kvale does not go on to draw any significant conclusions for the interview strategy or the analysis of the interaction situation.

11. Our own empirical work, which provides the basis for the development of this typology, has been largely in the fields of labour and industrial sociology and research on expertise and science (for example Bogner, 2005a, 2005b, Bogner and Menz, 2005, 2006, Bogner and others, 2008, Menz and others, 2003, Menz, 2009).

12. See Martens and Brüggemann 2006 for a distinction between kinds of expert in the interaction constellations of the interview, which is developed according to the dimensions of the expert's communication style and intentions.

13. The symmetrical relationship should be seen as a special case which characterizes this type of expert interview. Horizontal interaction structures are by no means typical of the expert interview as such, as is misleadingly suggested by Köhler's analysis (1992).

14. Abels and Behrens (2009) and Vogel (1995, p. 80) describe this as an unwanted "feedback effect."

15. Kaufmann, for example, argues that the interviewer's own "commitment" (rather than the neutrality and restraint we are usually told is necessary) is an important criterion for the success of the "understanding interview:" Only to the extent that the interviewer gets involved will the interviewee do the same and be prepared to reveal everything he knows (Kaufmann, 1996). See Trinczek's contribution to this volume.

16. Of course, this does not mean avoiding any analysis of discriminatory paternalism in the interview situation, and it certainly does not mean one should approve of it.

17. Disapproval expressed through shaking of the head or dismissive hand gestures as reactions to the interviewer's objections or supplementary questions are certainly extreme forms of refusal. One frequently finds, though, that the expert expresses his or her "internal emigration," his or her retreat to sacrosanct regulatory knowledge that is not accessible via dialogue, by means of a setting that excludes the interviewer as a partner in the conversation: the expert presents him or herself in profile, speaks while looking out of the office window, and so on.

18. For an empirical illustration of this kind of interaction, see Bogner, 2005a, p. 109ff.

19. Martens and Brüggemann (2006, p. 10) also indicate that there is a danger of experts who think they need to instruct the interviewer using over-simplified examples, so that it frequently becomes unclear whether these are real cases or imaginary ones constructed for pedagogical purposes.

20. Even though this assessment of roles occurs in practice, as a rule, predominantly in cases of evaluation (see Leitner and Wroblewski, 2009, on this point),

individual elements of this type are encountered fairly frequently in practice. For example, we have in our own interviews encountered fears that the interviewer is there as an evaluator on the part of members of factory committees who suspected they were being checked on by the trade union, and on the part of interviewees in state-run hospitals who were afraid of rationalization measures and perceived the interviewer in his function as a representative of an institution close to the government.

21. Constructions of common ground in interviews can, however, have other causes, which have nothing to do with shared normative convictions. They may be caused by such things as a shared regional background or the fact that two people speak the same dialect. The reverse also applies: diverging language conventions can prove to be invisible social barriers in an expert interview.

22. Typical examples of this are interviews where the interaction structure is initially shaped by the role expectation of "the interviewer as critic," after which the interviewee revises this view and starts to see the interviewer as a representative of a different knowledge culture. Another possibility: the interviewee finds that his or her initial expectation that the researcher is a co-expert is not confirmed, and shifts for the rest of the conversation to the model of the interviewer as layperson.

23. Interviewees will not normally be deceived for long by attempts on the part of researchers to feign possession of specialist knowledge simply in order to be perceived as a co-expert. However, this does not mean that this type is necessarily the most difficult one to construct, since a 60-year old professor is equally unlikely to be able to play convincingly the part of a clueless layperson. Needless to say, there are considerations of research ethics that set limits to the role expectations that can be "selected." It would obviously be quite unethical for the researcher to pretend to be a reliable "accomplice" when this would amount to misleading the interviewee.

24. See Scheuch, 1967 and Koolwijk, 1974 for the initial and influential conceptions of interview styles to be used in qualitative investigations in Germany; for more specific treatments relating to the methodology of qualitative social research, see Hoffmann-Riem, 1980 and Lamnek, 1995, p. 21ff. For approaches, which explicitly challenge the postulate of neutrality, see Douglas, 1985, Fontana and Frey, 1998 and Holstein and Gubrium, 1999.

25. Reference is frequently made to the "iceberg effect" (Vogel, 1995, p. 79, Abels and Behrens, 2009), which means that the interviewee seems to be unenthusiastic and uninterested, and is reluctant to give much away. In practice, the reason for this is frequently to be found in ways of conducting the interview that lack commitment and any self-positioning on the part of the interviewer. On the other hand, one should not forget that the expert status of the interviewee also means there are limits beyond which she or he cannot go in the forms of argument used. The expert knows that she or he is a quasi-public representative of his or her profession, field of action, organization, and so on, and is not in a position where she or he can break their rules of discussion and self-presentation. It can sometimes be more difficult for experts than for other interviewees to admit to inconsistencies, give accounts of mistakes that have been made, or express "deviant opinions." In addition, an expert often feels obliged to reaffirm his or her expert status, and tries to avoid saying anything that sounds "banal" or everyday. In this respect even the guarantee of anonymity, which the researcher must of course provide, does not usually help.

Further readings

Flick, Uwe (2006) *An Introduction to Qualitative Research*, 3rd edn (London and others: Sage Publications), esp. pp. 147ff.
Fontana, A. and Frey, J. H. (1998) "Interviewing. The Art of Science" in Denzin, N. K. and Lincoln, Y. S. (eds) *Collecting and Interpreting Qualitative Materials* (Thousand Oaks and others: Sage Publications), pp. 47–78.
Kvale, S. and Brinkmann, S. (2009) *InterViews: Learning the Craft of Qualitative Research Interviewing*, 2nd edn (Thousand Oaks and others: Sage Publications).

References

Abels, G. and Behrens, M. (1998) "ExpertInnen-Interviews in der Politikwissenschaft. Das Beispiel der Biotechnologie" in *Österreichische Zeitschrift für Politikwissenschaft, vol. 27*, pp. 79–92.
Abels, G. and Behrens, M. (2009) "Interviewing Experts in Political Science. A Reflexion on Gender and Policy Effects Based on Secondary Analysis", in this volume.
Aichholzer, G. (2009) "The Delphi Method: Eliciting Expert's Knowledge in Technology Foresight," in this volume.
Beck, U. (1992) *Risk Society: Towards a New Modernity* (London: Sage Publications).
Berger, P. L. and Luckmann, T. (1966) *The Social Construction of Reality: A Treatise in the Sociology of Knowledge* (Garden City, NY: Anchor Books).
Blumer, H. (1969) *Symbolic Interaction: Perspective and Method* (Englewood Cliffs: Prentice Hall).
Bogner, A. (2005a) *Grenzpolitik der Experten. Vom Umgang mit Ungewissheit und Nichtwissen in pränataler Diagnostik und Beratung* (Weilerswist: Velbrück).
Bogner, A. (2005b): "Moralische Expertise? Zur Produktionsweise von Kommissionsethik" in Bogner, A. and Torgersen, H. (eds) *Wozu Experten? Ambivalenzen der Beziehung von Wissenschaft und Politik* (Wiesbaden: VS-Verlag), pp. 172–93.
Bogner, A., Littig, B. and Menz, W. (eds) (2005) *Das Experteninterview. Theorie, Methode, Anwendung*, 2nd edn (Wiesbaden: VS-Verlag).
Bogner, A. and Menz, W. (2005) "Bioethical Controversies and Policy Advice: The Production of Ethical Expertise und its Role in the Substantiation of Political Decision-Making" in Maasen, S. and Weingart, P. (eds) *Democratization of Expertise? Exploring Novel Forms of Scientific Advice in Political Decision-Making. Sociology of the Sciences, Vol. 24* (Dordrecht: Springer), pp. 21–40.
Bogner, A. and Menz, W. (2006) "Wissen und Werte als Verhandlungsform. Ethikexpertise in der Regulation der Stammzellforschung" in Wink, R. (ed.) *Deutsche Stammzellpolitik im Zeitalter der Transnationalisierung* (Baden Baden: Nomos), pp. 141–63.
Bogner, A., Littig, B. and Menz, W. (2009) "Expert Interviews. An Introduction to a New Methodological Debate," in this volume.
Bogner, A., Menz, W. and Schumm, W. (2008) "Ethikexpertise in Wertkonflikten. Zur Produktion und politischen Verwendung von Kommissionsethik in Deutschland und Österreich" in Mayntz, R., Neidhardt, F., Weingart, P. and Wengenroth, U. (eds) *Wissensproduktion und Wissenstransfer. Wissen im Spannungsfeld von Wissenschaft, Politik und Öffentlichkeit* (Bielefeld: Transcript), pp. 243–68.
Bourdieu, P. (1998) *Practical Reason: On the Theory of Action* (Palo Alto: Stanford University Press).

Brinkmann, C., Deeke, A. and Völkel, B. (1995) "Experteninterviews in der Arbeitsmarktforschung. Diskussionsbeiträge zu methodischen Fragen und praktischen Erfahrungen" in *Beiträge zur Arbeitsmarkt- und Berufsforschung 191* (Nürnberg: IAB).

Deeke, A. (1995) "Experteninterviews – ein methodologisches und forschungspraktisches Problem. Einleitende Bemerkungen und Fragen zum Workshop" in Brinkmann, C., Deeke, A. and Völkel, B. (eds) *Experteninterviews in der Arbeitsmarktforschung. Diskussionsbeiträge zu methodischen Fragen und praktischen Erfahrungen. Beiträge zur Arbeitsmarkt- und Berufsforschung 191* (Nürnberg: IAB), pp. 7–22.

Douglas, J. D. (1985) *Creative Interviewing* (Bevely Hills: Sage Publications).

Flick, U. (2004) "Constructivism" in Flick, U., Kardorff, E. von and Steinke, I. (eds) *A Companion to Qualitative Research* (Thousand Oaks, London: Sage Publications), pp. 88–94.

Fontana, A. and Frey, J. H. (1998) Interviewing. "The Art of Science" in Denzin, N. K. and Lincoln, Y. S. (eds) *Collecting and Interpreting Qualitative Materials* (Thousand Oaks and others: Sage Publications), pp. 47–78.

Froschauer, U. and Lueger, M. (2009) "Expert Interviews in Interpretative Organisational Research," in this volume.

Giddens, A. (1984) *The Constitution of Society. Outline of the Theory of Structuration* (Cambridge: Polity).

Giddens, A. (1990) *The Consequences of Modernity* (Cambridge: Polity).

Gillham, B. (2000) *The Research Interview* (London und New York: Continuum).

Glaser, B. G. and Strauss, A. L. (1967) *Discovery of Grounded Theory. Strategies for Qualitative Research* (Mill valley: Sociology Press).

Hägele, H. (1995) "Experteninterviews in der öffentlichen Verwaltung: Ausgewählte praktische Probleme" in Brinkmann, C., Deeke, A. and Völkel, B. (eds) *Experteninterviews in der Arbeitsmarktforschung. Diskussionsbeiträge zu methodischen Fragen und praktischen Erfahrungen. Beiträge zur Arbeitsmarkt- und Berufsforschung 191* (Nürnberg: IAB), pp. 69–72.

Helfferich, C. (2004) *Die Qualität qualitativer Daten* (Wiesbaden: VS-Verlag).

Hermanns, H. (2004) "Interviewing as an Activity" in Flick, U., Kardorff, E. von and Steinke, I. (eds) *A Companion to Qualitative Research* (Thousand Oaks, London: Sage Publications), pp. 209–113.

Hitzler, R., Honer, A. and Maeder, C. (1994) *Expertenwissen. Die institutionalisierte Kompetenz zur Konstruktion von Wirklichkeit* (Opladen: Westdeutscher Verlag).

Hoffmann-Riem, C. (1980) "Die Sozialforschung einer interpretativen Soziologie. Der Datengewinn" in *Kölner Zeitschrift für Soziologie und Sozialpsychologie, Jg. 32*, pp. 339–72.

Holstein, J. A. and Gubrium, J. F. (1999) "Active Interviewing" in Bryman, A. and Burgess, R. G. (eds) *Qualitative Research, vol. II* (London and others: Sage Publications), pp. 105–21.

Hopf, C. (1978) "Die Pseudo-Exploration – Überlegungen zur Technik qualitativer Interviews in der Sozialforschung" in *Zeitschrift für Soziologie 7*, pp. 97–115.

Houtkoop-Steenstra, H. (2000) *Interaction and the Standardized Interview. The Living Questionnaire* (Cambridge: Cambridge University Press).

Kassner, K. and Wassermann, P. (2005) "Nicht überall, wo Methode draufsteht, ist Methode drin. Zur Problematik der Fundierung von ExpertInneninterviews" in Bogner, A., Littig, B. and Menz, W. (eds) *Das Experteninterview. Theorie, Methode, Anwendung* (Opladen: Leske and Budrich), pp. 95–111.

Kaufmann, J. C. (1996) *L'entretien compréhensif* (Paris: Nathan).

Kelle, U. and Erzberger, C. (1999) "Integration Qualitativer und Quantitativer Methoden. Methodologische Modelle und ihre Bedeutung für die Forschungspraxis" in *Kölner Zeitschrift für Soziologie und Sozialpsychologie 51*, pp. 509–31.

Knorr-Cetina, K. (1989) "Spielarten des Konstruktivismus" in *Soziale Welt 40*, pp. 86–96.

Köhler, G. (1992) "Methodik und Problematik einer mehrstufigen Expertenbefragung" in Hoffmeyer-Zlotnik, J. H. P. (ed.) *Analyse verbaler Daten. Über den Umgang mit qualitativen Daten* (Opladen: Westdeutscher Verlag), pp. 318–32.

Koolwijk, J. van (1974) "Die Befragungsmethode" in Koolwijk, J. van. and Wieken-Mayser, M. (eds) *Techniken der empirischen Sozialforschung, 4. Band: Erhebungsmethoden: Die Befragung* (München, Wien: Oldenbourg), pp. 9–23.

Krafft, A. and Ulrich, G. (1995) "Akteure in der Sozialforschung" in Brinkmann, C., Deeke, A. and Völkel, B. (eds) *Experteninterviews in der Arbeitsmarktforschung. Diskussionsbeiträge zu methodischen Fragen und praktischen Erfahrungen. Beiträge zur Arbeitsmarkt- und Berufsforschung 191* (Nürnberg: IAB), pp. 23–33.

Kvale, S. (1996) *InterViews. An Introduction to Qualitative Research Interviewing* (Thousand Oaks and others: Sage Publications).

Lamnek, S. (1995) *Qualitative Sozialforschung, Bd. 1: Methodologie*, 3rd edn (Weinheim: Beltz).

Leitner, A. and Wroblewski, A. (2009) "Between Scientific Standards and Claims of Efficiency. Expert Interviews in Programme Evaluation," in this volume.

Lueger, M. (1989) "Die soziale Situation im Interview" in *Österreichische Zeitschrift für Soziologie 14*, pp. 22–36.

Martens, K. and Brüggemann, M. (2006) *Kein Experte ist wie der andere. Vom Umgang mit Missionaren und Geschichtenerzählern* (TranState Working Papers No. 39, Bremen).

Mayring, P. (1996) *Einführung in die qualitative Sozialforschung*, 3rd edn (Weinheim: Beltz).

Menz, W. (2009) *Die Legitimität des Marktregimes. Leistungs- und Gerechtigkeitsorientierungen in neuen Formen betrieblicher Leistungspolitik* (Wiesbaden: VS-Verlag).

Menz, W., Siegel, T. and Vogel, M. (2003) *Leistungs- und Interessenpolitik aus der Perspektive von Beschäftigten. Abschlussbericht an die Hans-Böckler-Stiftung* (Frankfurt am Main: JWG-Universität).

Merton, R. K. and Kendall, P. L. (1946) "The focused interview" in *American Journal of Sociology, Jg. 51, Heft*, pp. 541–57.

Meuser, M. and Nagel, U. (1991) "ExpertInneninterviews – vielfach erprobt, wenig bedacht. Ein Beitrag zur qualitativen Methodendiskussion" in Garz, D. and Kraimer, K. (eds) *Qualitativ-empirische Sozialforschung. Konzepte, Methoden, Analysen* (Opladen: Westdeutscher Verlag), pp. 441–71.

Meuser, M. and Nagel, U. (1994) "Expertenwissen und Experteninterview" in Hitzler, R., Honer, A. and Maeder, C. (eds) *Expertenwissen. Die institutionalisierte Kompetenz zur Konstruktion von Wirklichkeit* (Opladen: Westdeutscher Verlag), pp. 180–92.

Meuser, M. and Nagel, U. (1997) "Das ExpertInneninterview – Wissenssoziologische Voraussetzungen und methodische Durchführung" in Friebertshäuser, B. and Prengel, A. (eds) *Handbuch Qualitative Forschungsmethoden in der Erziehungswissenschaft* (Weinheim/München: Juventa), pp. 481–91.

Meuser, M. and Nagel, U. (2009) "The Expert Interview and Changes in Knowledge Production," in this volume.

Plath, H. E. (1995) "Zum 'Experteninterview' – ein Diskussionsbeitrag" in Brinkmann, C., Deeke, A. and Völkel, B. (eds) *Experteninterviews in der Arbeitsmarktforschung. Diskussionsbeiträge zu methodischen Fragen und praktischen Erfahrungen. Beiträge zur Arbeitsmarkt- und Berufsforschung 191* (Nürnberg: IAB), pp. 85–9.

Scheuch, E. (1967) "Das Interview in der Sozialforschung" in König, R. (ed.) *Handbuch der Empirischen Sozialforschung, I. Band*, 2nd edn(Stuttgart: Enke), pp. 136–96.

Schmid, J. (1995) "Expertenbefragung und Informationsgespräch in der Parteienforschung: Wie föderalistisch ist die CDU?" in Alemann, U. von (ed.) *Politikwissenschaftliche Methoden. Grundriss für Studium und Forschung* (Opladen: Leske und Budrich), pp. 293–326.

Schütz, A. (1962) "Common-sense and Scientific Interpretation of Human Action" in *Collected Papers, Vol. 1* (The Hague: Nijhoff), pp. 3–47.

Schütz, A. (1964) "The Well-Informed Citizen: An Essay on the Social Distribution of Knowl-edge" in *Collected Papers, Vol. 2* (The Hague: Nijhoff), pp. 120–34.

Sprondel, W. M. (1979) "'Experte' und 'Laie'. Zur Entwicklung von Typenbegriffen in der Wissenssoziologie" in Sprondel, W. M. and Grathoff, R. (eds) *Alfred Schütz und die Idee des Alltags in den Sozialwissenschaften* (Stuttgart: Enke), pp. 140–54.

Trinczek, R. (1995) "Experteninterviews mit Managern: Methodische und methodologische Hintergründe" in Brinkmann, C., Deeke, A. and Völkel, B. (eds) *Experteninterviews in der Arbeitsmarktforschung.* BeitrAB191 (Nürnberg: IAB), pp. 59–67.

Trinczek, R. (2009) "How to Interview Managers? Methodical and Methodological Aspects of Expert Interviews as a Qualitative Method in Empirical Social Research," in this volume.

Voelzkow, H. (1995) "'Iterative Experteninterviews': Forschungspraktische Erfahrungen mit einem Erhebungsinstrument" in Brinkmann, C., Deeke, A. and Völkel, B. (eds) *Experteninterviews in der Arbeitsmarktforschung.* BeitrAB191 (Nürnberg: IAB),, pp. 51–7.

Vogel, B. (1995) "'Wenn der Eisberg zu schmelzen beginnt...' – Einige Reflexionen über den Stellenwert und die Probleme des Experteninterviews in der Praxis der empirischen Sozialforschung" in Brinkmann, C., Deeke, A. and Völkel, B. (eds) *Experteninterviews in der Arbeitsmarktforschung.* BeitrAB191 (Nürnberg: IAB), pp. 73–83.

Weber, M. (1980) *Wirtschaft und Gesellschaft. Grundriss einer verstehenden Sozialwissenschaft*, 5. Auflage (Tübingen: J. C. B. Mohr).

Thomas P. W. (1970) "Normative and Interpretive Paradigms in Sociology" in Douglas, J. D. (ed.) *Understanding everyday life. Toward the reconstruction of sociological knowledge* (Chicago: Aldine), pp. 57–79.

Witzel, A. (2000) "The problem-centered interview" in *Forum Qualitative Sozialforschung/ Forum: Qualitative Social Research [Online Journal], 1(1)*, available at http://www. qualitative-research.net/fqs-texte/1-00/1-00witzel-e.htm.

3
At Eye Level: The Expert Interview – a Talk between Expert and Quasi-expert

Michaela Pfadenhauer

Even though this is generally assumed and persistently conveyed in research methodology: The questioning of persons who are regarded as experts – according to which criteria soever – does not constitute the specific characteristic of the expert interview.[1] Due to its underlying epistemological interest (1) for one thing and due to the special kind of interview technique (2) for another thing, the expert interview is an independent procedure within the canon of what is known as the "qualitative interview" (Hopf, 2000). In recent years, it has often been practised and has also been reflected upon methodically and methodologically. The specific character of the interlocutory form makes it necessary, (at least) for the interview of certain (types of) experts, to embed this procedure in an ethnographic research design (3).

3.1 The epistomological interest of the expert interview

The whole purpose of expert interviews seems to be obvious: They are geared to the reconstruction of specific knowledge stocks, or of particularly exclusive, detailed or comprehensive knowledge about particular knowledge stocks and practices, in short: to the reconstruction of expert knowledge. This must, however, be qualified as regards "habitual," or "implicit" elements of expert knowledge. For as all interviews, expert interviews too lend themselves especially to the reconstruction of explainable knowledge stocks.

One must therefore be sceptical about the suitability of the expert interview as an instrument for the ascertainment and analysis of strategies and relevances "that, in fact, apply in the decision behaviour, but that are not necessarily reflectively available to the experts" (Meuser and Nagel, 1997, p. 485). With this, it shall by no means be disputed that experts too – just as incidentally as a matter of course – apply "implicit knowledge" that is not "clear and precise" (Schütz, 1972a, p. 87), but in fact profoundly diffuse and that can at best be verbalized in a piecemeal fashion by them.[2] Such "routinised expert knowledge" (Schröer, 1994) can, however, hardly be reconstructed by means of an expert interview. As regards the reconstruction of situated skills, of performance routines and of quasi-automatic behaviour patterns, all kinds of interviews typically produce deficient or misleading results (cf. Hitzler 2000, p. 22).[3] However, for the reconstruction of stocks of knowledge that can be thematically distinguished and explained, that is for the reconstruction of knowledge that is memorable as having been learned and is hence as a rule known as knowledge (cf. Honer, 1993, p. 88), interviews prove to be suitable instruments.

3.1.1 The knowledge of experts

The epistemological object of the expert interview proves to be focused on a particular knowledge asset within the social knowledge stock: on specialist knowledge, which in the course of the progressive division of labour is increasing proportionally to general knowledge as regards extent and importance (cf. Schütz and Luckmann, 1979, p. 363). The societal specialist knowledge assets are increasingly being differentiated and often have to be acquired in protracted "secondary" socialization processes, from which that type of knower emerges, which is referred to as "specialist." He disposes of a task-related, relatively well-defined partial knowledge within a specialist knowledge field, which he needs to fulfil his specialist function. As opposed to the specialist, the "expert" is that type of knower who has a good overview of the overall known knowledge in one field, that is an overview of a specialist knowledge field, in other words who "knows what the (respective) specialists know in their fields of knowledge – and how what they know relates to each other" (Hitzler, 1994, p. 25).

The differentiation between special(ist) knowledge on the one hand and expert knowledge as a kind of "overview knowledge" about specialist knowledge fields on the other hand makes it clear that by no means all kinds of special knowledge can be equated with expert knowledge (cf. also Sprondel, 1979). Expert knowledge is not "only" a specific, not generally available problem-solving knowledge. At a more fundamental level, it signifies the knowledge one needs to probe into the causes of problems and the principles of problem-solving strategies. As opposed to specialists, the expert thus has a more comprehensive knowledge that enables him not only to solve problems, but moreover to identify and to account for problem causes as well as for solution principles. In short: The expert "typically knows the knowledge stock that is "characteristic" or "relevant" for a certain field, he has, so to speak, an overview of a specialist knowledge field and can offer fundamental problem solutions or can apply these to individual problems within this area" (Hitzler, 1994, p. 26).

With his knowledge about the principles of the issue respectively the factual logic, the expert – in comparison to other persons concerned with the problem area, that is in comparison to non-experts (including specialists) – has a relatively exclusive knowledge asset that is on principle not available to everyone. His knowledge about the factual logic enables the expert to clarify the logical consistency of the issue at hand. And as Soeffner (1989, p. 222) makes clear using the example of interrogators, "the question, how something should have been [to be] logically consistent is more important [to experts] than what 'actually' happened."

3.1.2 The competence of experts

According to Michael Meuser and Ulrike Nagel (1991, p. 443), experts have "privileged accesses to information." However, not only the information at the exclusive disposal of the expert is of decisive importance for his expertise, but furthermore also the (attributable) responsibility for problem-solving related decisions. This refers to competence in the broader sense: "Competence is obviously somehow connected to responsibility and to skills and to willingness and to the fact that responsibility, skills and willingness coincide" (Marquardt, 1981, p. 24). In the sense that the responsibility for finding problem solutions is incumbent upon the expert as quasi ultimate authority, expert competence transcends (exclusive) abilities and (special) skills.[4]

Thus not only his exclusive knowledge stock – in comparison to other persons dealing with the problem – is characteristic for the expert, but moreover his responsibility (resulting from his knowledge of causes) for the provision of possible problem solutions, that is of expertises. Responsibility also means that irrespective of who else (apart from him) was involved in whichever function or to whichever extent in its development process, the ultimate responsibility for the expertise lies with the expert. This (ultimate) responsibility is quasi the other side of the coin of the relative autonomy of the expert, which follows from the fact that his knowledge is superior to the "knowledge that is recallable or claimable from others, that is [that he has] a (hardly ore even completely uncontrollable) advice and help competence" (Hitzler, 1994, p. 26). For according to the "objective meaning" of responsibility, it is ultimately he, who can be called to account by others for the things that are done or not done (by him or by others) regarding the solution of problems.[5]

Bringing the definition proposal of Meuser and Nagel (1991) to a head, we[6] thus regard those persons as "experts," who have privileged access to information and – moreover – who can be made responsible for the planning and provision of problem solutions. From an elite theoretical perspective, "experts" according to this definition appear less as members of a functional elite (cf. Meuser and Nagel, 1994, p. 181), than as members of what can, following Jaeggi (1960), be referred to as "relative," that is local elites as opposed to global elites and, following Dreitzel (1962), as "performance elites," that is as providers of socially desired or demanded services, who as a result of these services are granted (significant) privileges, options, resources and/or esteem.[7]

The expert interview thus primarily lends itself as a data generating instrument in those cases in which the research focuses on the exclusive knowledge assets of experts in the context of their (ultimate) responsibility for problem solutions. In this broad sense, the epistemological interest of the expert interview is aimed at the reconstruction of (explicit) expert knowledge.

3.2   Interview techniques

As is generally known, a basic requirement of non-standardized social research as opposed to standardized interview techniques consists in forbearing from imposing an external relevance system upon the interviewed actor, letting him develop and formulate his own relevances instead. However, one can by no means assume without further query that the "interviewees can best develop their subjective attributions of meaning and relevance structures in an interview situation characterised by far-reaching non-intervention on the part of the interviewer."[8]

Seeing that "the interviewed persons – just as the conventionally working social scientists – envisage an interview as an onesided question-and-answer relation," Anne Honer (1994, p. 629) makes a case – especially for the first interview phase of the explorative interview developed by her – for a "normalization" or "everydaying" of the relatively extraordinary communication situation of the interview to the effect that it should comply as much as possible with the cultural habits prevailing in the respective contexts of speaking to each other. In principle, the aim of the expert interview is neither to subject the interview partner to an interrogation-like nor to an artificial "non-directive" interview situation, but rather to create a communication situation with which he is familiar, that is to conduct a quasinormal conversation (for further details see Honer, 1993, p. 74).

3.2.1   The interview setting

The question of the ideal interview setting for the undisturbed development of subjective relevance structures is discussed by Trinczek (1995 and in this volume) using the example of interviews with managers. According to him, communication in the companies is seldomly characterized by a narrative basic structure. The structure of everyday communication in the company-managerial context that as a rule features team-like work structures, in fact most closely corresponds to a "discursive-argumentative professional discussion" within the scope of a (more or less) relaxed discussion situation.

In general it can be stated that the communication of experts (of the same provenance) amongst each other is characterized by the following features: thematic focusing, use of professional terminology, deployment of indexical language, in short by the fact that experts (of the same provenance) share a "communicative universe" (Schütz, 1972a, p. 97). This is not least due to the fact that in discussions with his "peers," an expert can assume that he can take the knowledge of basic facts or interrelations for granted and that he need not be afraid of being misunderstood – neither literally nor figuratively – because his counterpart is not familiar with the technical terms and most notably with the relevances of his field of activity that structure his thinking and acting. The individual knowledge stock of the expert is structured by a given system of "imposed relevances" of the specific field of knowledge that is, it is not connected with his spontaneously chosen goals. This relevance system is imposed upon him by the assumed problems of his field of activity; with his decision to become an "expert," he, at the same time, accepts it as the only significant relevance system for his thinking and acting (see Schütz, 1972a, p. 96).

On the other hand, particularly the awareness of diverging relevance systems leads experts in communication with non-experts (observable for example in interviews with journalists) to enrich their speech with metaphors and analogies, to play down or to dramatize or to be inclined to adopt a paternalistic or self-legitimizing conversational behaviour.[9] The respective semantics – for example lingo towards other "experts," "translations" towards "well-informed citizens," simplistic statements towards "laypersons" – reveals which knowledge type the interviewee believes his counterpart to be.[10]

In contrast, discussions among experts (of the same provenance) either serve to augment their privileged knowledge access – in terms of two-way briefing – or the reciprocal explanation of their actions with regard to their competence and responsibility for the development and provision of solutions to problems. What takes place in the process is not instruction[11] or (placating) justification,[12] which one can typically observe towards a non-expert (public), but a description and a discursive explanation of what he is doing and why he is doing what he is doing in the way he is doing it.[13] Thus experts typically debate the significance and practical management of their competence and responsibility for the development, implementation and/or control of solutions to problems amongst each other.[14] In general terms, the basic conditions and implications of expert competence are the typical subject matter of communication among experts.

A *different* information content from that normally meted out to a lay (public) is being exchanged. For: "The expert knows [on the other hand] that only another expert will understand all technical details and implications of a problem in his field, and he will never accept a layperson or an amateur as a competent judge of his attainment" (Schütz, 1972a, p. 88).

Insofar as the epistemological interest of the expert interview is directed at issues that are regarded as relevant or are being debated among experts, the accompanying basic concern of the expert interview is to create an interview setting that approaches the conversation situation among experts as closely as possible. And a fundamental requirement and condition for this is precisely not only the status of the interviewed actor as an expert but also a similar status of the interviewer.[15]

3.2.2   The status of the interviewer

In view of the two core components of expert competence mentioned above, the – appropriately as well as privilegedly informed – interviewer typically at best achieves the status of a quasi-expert, inasmuch as he interacts unfettered by responsibility for the development and provision of problem solutions – and thus with the essential difference of being free from the burden of action.

Consequently, the demeanour of the interviewed expert vis-à-vis the interviewing quasi-expert does not only not correspond to that, which, for instance, expresses itself in a paternalistic "mannerism" or justification pressure towards a lay public, but also not ("really") to the demeanour towards other experts. For the meeting between experts (of the same provenance) it is typically marked by a – though not necessarily concrete, but at least fundamental – competitive pressure. Therefore it is characterized by a (at any rate in principle) inherent reserve regarding the disclosure of "trade secrets." As the epistemological interest of the expert interview is directed precisely towards this "operational knowledge" of experts, the "freedom from the burden of competition" inherent in the exchange between an expert and a quasi-expert represents a particular advantage. Thus Trinczek (1995, p. 63, own translation) observes that the fact that the interview is free from the burden of action and from social consequences "sometimes [allows] the managers a degree of openness and candid self-reflection that they normally do not thus concede themselves in their everyday working environment with its predominantly strategically oriented communication and interaction style."[16]

Trinczek (1995, p. 65, own translation) too emphasises that the thematic competence of the interviewer is a necessary condition for a successful expert interview with managers: "The more one is able to slip in qualified assessments, reasons and counterarguments every now and then in the course of the interview, the more the managers on their part are prepared to disclose their knowledge and their positions – and to reveal their subjective relevance structures and orientation patterns in non-strategic intent."

(At least) amongst the representatives of what is known as "qualitative social research" there is a wide consensus to the effect that an orientation on the situational-subjective agenda setting and relevance structuring of the interview partner is significantly facilitated by means of the "flexible interview-situational" use of a "guideline," which is necessary to "guarantee the openness of the interview course" (Meuser and Nagel, 1991, p. 449; in this spirit also already Dexter, 1970). Opinions differ, however, as regards the extent to which the researcher should actually let himself be guided by his guideline during the interview.[17] As a matter of principle, it must be pointed out that only the detached stance of the interpreter when analysing the whole interview text permits a decision regarding the "importance" or "triviality" of a statement. Of much greater significance in this context, however, is that the conceptual design of this – ideally only "mentally" present – guideline already presupposes an as comprehensive and appropriate as possible knowledge on the part of its "designer" (cf. Honer, 1994 as well as Hitzler, 2000).

3.3   The ethnographic embedding of the expert interview

The here developed conception of the expert interview that essentially follows the pertinent note of Anne Honer (1994, p. 633), is based on the premise that people speak differently to other people – both as regards the "how" and the "what" of communication – depending on whether they regard their conversation partners as competent or incompetent (and thus in a way also as relevant or irrelevant) concerning the debated issue. Contrary to the well-nigh inflationary labelling of all kinds of interviews as "expert interviews," we advocate that only those forms of interviews be referred to as "expert interviews" that are characterized by a discussion on an equal footing.

The special conversational form which characterizes the expert interview – the researcher as quasi-expert under discussion with an expert – makes it seem essential to us on at least two counts to embed the method in an ethnographic research design: for one thing with regard to the identification of experts and, for another things, with regard to the qualification of the interviewer.[18]

3.3.1   The identification of experts

The picture that the relevant literature draws of experts largely corresponds to the figure of the professional, who obtains his skills by complying with formal training requirements and who can also provide formal evidence for his expert status by means of certificates issued by professional organizations: "Today, holding a professionally organised expert role in all cases presupposes the completion of general as well as special training, in which the special knowledge that is considered relevant is obtained. The acquisition of this knowledge is sanctioned in corresponding certificates with societal validity" (Sprondel, 1979, p. 151).

The expert status of the professional can be made plausible using doctors as an example, who were for a long time regarded as the "prototype" of the professional in the sociology of professions: The doctor has privileged access to information and he is (ultimately) responsible for the development and provision of medical problem solutions. The professional claim to competence of the medical fraternity essentially aims at permanently and exclusively binding not only the entitlement to alleviate or cure ailments but also that of medical expertises to that group of persons, which verifiably meet the qualification standards defined by the profession: to the duly qualified medical practioners (for further information see Hitzler and Pfadenhauer, 1999).

Unlike for other types of experts, it is characteristic for the professional that he acquires a canonized special knowledge asset via an institutionally specialized and – as regards extent and duration – formalized training in typically "public" institutions that the acquisition of this professional special knowledge is tested (often in cooperation between state and professional organisations) and that he is issued a certificate that "certifies" his professional competence – not only in terms of qualification but also in terms of authorisation. In particular due to these characteristics, the professional is a typically modern – and thus historically relatively "young" – manifestation of the expert (see Hitzler, 1994, as well as Pfadenhauer, 1997).

Peter L. Berger and Thomas Luckmann (1969, p. 133) specify the "educated person" and the "intellectual" as further types of experts. They characterize the latter as a (counter) expert "whose expertise is not desired by society," because he provides a counter design for the determination of reality. According to Zygmunt Bauman (1987), the role of the intellectual is changing from "legislator" to "interpreter" under postmodern conditions. Under the generic term "Man of Knowledge," Znaniecki (1975) presented a so far largely unheeded typology of socially sanctioned "knowers," which differentiates between users of knowledge, administrators of knowledge and discoverers of (new) knowledge. The following simple contrasting of this modern expert with the premodern expert must suffice for now to make our argument clear that experts are not congruent with professionals.

The first empirical manifestation of the expert is probably the shaman. According to Mircea Eliade (1975), his social function is that of an expert for the extraordinary, "who gains strength and authority to come to terms with specific collective and individual borderline situations by dint of his 'voyages to the otherworld', which only he is capable of" (Hitzler, 1982, p. 55). As he is able to get in touch with spirits, he not only has privileged access to information but is moreover responsible for the provision of problem solutions that essentially consist in "fending off evil or wrong" or in "effecting good or right." His competences and special skills are the result or "outflow" of the ecstatic spirit-edness of his body, which is preceded by a biographical disruption or an identity crisis and which leads to the formation of a new identity (cf. in more detail Hitzler, 1982).

This short excursion into shamanism is by no means aimed at mystifying or putting the expert on a pedestal. The experts of today only seldom have competences they gained by extraordinary means (such as divine inspiration or gifted birth). But unlike the professional, they are by all means endued with competences, whose acquirement demand other, to wit mainly non-formalized, in fact diffuse, not clearly designated gateways. In this connection, the focus "on the (...) expertise crystallised primarily in an occupational role" (Sprondel, 1979, p. 141) construes the concept of expert knowledge too narrowly. The expert is neither – as I wanted to show by means of the example of the shaman – identical with the professional, nor can expert knowledge "per se" be equated with canonised specialised knowledge that is formally conveyed and certified in educational institutions. And least of all does an university degree represent a necessary or even sufficient precondition for the expert status.[19]

In societies like ours too, the expert status is in no way necessarily linked to schooling and training in – typically "public" – educational institutions. In dynamic growth sectors, currently for instance in the IT and multimedia sectors, the "provenance" or the proof of relevant skills by means of state-approved certificates issued by professional organizations play a secondary role. In particular the acquisition of hard and software related knowledge and skills is supplied to a large extent autodidactically or in a net-based exchange amongst each other. The same goes for event management practice (cf. Pfadenhauer, 2000/2007). Here the emphasis is persistently placed on "learning by doing" and "training on the job." A further ongoing trend in this field is that of lateral entry, that is the entry from a course of studies in another subject or even without a diploma or degree. Formal certificates of competence are only assigned a higher priority as selection criteria – in particular for executive positions or expert functions – in the course of consolidation processes and decreasing manpower requirements.

Generally one has to take into account that the question who is an expert – here or elsewhere – depends on the approach, on the "framing" – in the sense of Goffman (1977) – determined by the research interest or the research object (cf. Meuser and Nagel, 1991). And if one assumes that for each grouping, also within a society, other forms of knowledge and most notably other hierarchies of knowledge types are relevant or can be relevant (cf. Hitzler, 1999), already the possibility of being able to identify the expert as such presupposes a relatively detailed ethnographic[20] inventarization of the research field in many spheres of activity and culture, inasmuch as the ethnographic epistemological interest is generally directed at the reconstruction of the culturally typical (subjective and objective) stock of knowledge.[21]

For a start, this requires that the researcher suspend his pre-conceptions and ex ante certainties concerning the research field he is about to examine and instead enquires into how the actors themselves see their world (and what they see) (see for example Pfadenhauer, 2001b). As regards the question of expert knowledge, he has to screen the specific cultural knowledge to the effect which "constituents" are in principle known by everyone, that is belong to the specific general education and which socially relevant stocks of knowledge, that is the (exclusive) knowledge regarded as essential for solving the impending problems, stand out against the general knowledge. As to the identification of experts, he has to find out which (types of) persons have a privileged access to information concerning these matters and are being made responsible for the provision of solutions to problems.

3.3.2 The qualification of the interviewer

Apart from the sometimes quite problematic identification of experts, the acquisition of a high degree of thematic competence on the part of the interviewer before he conducts the interview is constitutive for an expert interview. This implies that the interviewer must do his utmost to acquire as much as possible of the – relatively exclusive – special knowledge that the expert has normally acquired in the course of a long (secondary) socialization process.

To the extent that the knowledge corpus, which the experts must typically command in their fields, is relatively well – defined, viz. is put down in study and examination regulations, in task and job descriptions and so on the social researcher has numerous ways and means of acquiring this knowledge. First and foremost, he will be inclined to obtain and to study different types of "canonical documents" that impart the relevant special and specialized knowledge, thus, for instance, textbooks, course books, scientific journals and documentations as well as work reports, minutes of meetings and discussions, professional codes of conduct and much more.[22] Furthermore, there is the possibility of participating in (further) education and training measures in public and private institutions in which the professional expert himself acquires and extends his knowledge.

It is, however, obvious that this only concerns theoretical knowledge, insofar as the prevalent work descriptions too (textbook explanations, instruction sheets and so on) are always "theoretical" or at best impart "how-to-do-recipes." What they precisely mean only becomes discernible in "practice," in the practical implementation: "It is only in the course of practical work that the actor acquires the competence to carry out work processes 'correctly', to cope with imponderabilities and unpredicatable events and to come to 'sensible' decisions situational" (Eberle, 1997, p. 267, own translation).[23] The researcher too typically only acquires a basic or background knowledge in this manner and thus at best that measure of insight that enables him to competently assess expert competence – and thence to conduct expert interviews in the sense advocated here.

The interviewers are, however, faced with particularly grave problems in those action or research fields, in which the expert knowledge precisely does not assume the shape of formalised and certified stocks of special knowledge. While one can acquire the canonized, formally designated stocks of knowledge of professionals – albeit partly only with great effort – via well-known knowledge transfer paths that are more or less accessible to "everyone," the acquisition of non-certified, rather diffuse stocks of special knowledge of "other" experts is invariably only successful if the researcher follows those "tracks" through (initially) "alien" worlds that show him how these actors acquire their skills, which make them into experts of certain socio-cultural contexts.[24]

In principle, the basic non-standardized techniques of data generation – which, as is generally known, consist of following the proceedings, of procuring documents and of speaking to the people – lend themselves to this purpose. All ethnographic variants have in common that the researchers go into the field more or less intensively and at the same time act in the field in such a way that they change it as little as possible. The importance ethnographers assign to "existential involvement" (Honer, 1993, p. 40), that is practical participation, last but not least results from a fundamental scepticism towards the quality of data that have been generated by others, as these are on principle data on how others situational present facts and circumstances (a fact sometimes overlooked not only in the case of accounts "congealed" in written texts) – and not data on the facts themselves.

For the qualification of the researcher as (quasi-) expert this entails that he has to be present and participate as far as possible in all activities that the experts identified by him undertake as experts. That is to say, the ideal basis for the acquisition of a comprehensive as possible pertinent prior knowledge – which is constitutive for conducting expert interviews – is the "acquisition of a virtual membership in the events that are being researched, and thus the advantage of an existential interior view" (Honer, 2000, p. 198, own translation). Therewith the researcher gains a practical familiarity with the research field that expresses itself as (at least potential) action competence and sufficiently qualifies the interviewer to conduct a conversation "on equal footing."

3.4   Conclusion

The form of interview we suggest be referred to as expert interview represents a data generating instrument that is ridden with prerequisites and is thus very time-consuming. Therefore its use proves to be expedient only in view of definite research interests. It is quite certainly not suited, as assumed by Renate Mayntz and others (1972, p. 103), as a substitute for "procedures of direct data collection" that are "more time-consuming, costly or failing due to practical-technical problems." That is to say, the expert interview in the sense referred to above, is far less suited as an instrument for the swift generation of data, compensating as it were the time-consuming travail of participation, than as a kind of surplus procedure, whose competent use already more or less imperatively requires a high degree of field skills and of field acceptance.

Notes

1. Cf. (representatively for many) Deeke (1995, p. 7), according to whom "the term 'expert interview' already denotes that its distinctive feature does not consist of a specific form of interview but in the fact that 'experts' are interviewed." According to Deeke, an expert interview is therefore not a special procedure and does not involve a particular method.
2. Routine knowledge is a structural element of each subjective stock of knowledge and can – following the phenomenologically oriented sociology of knowledge (cf. Schütz and Luckmann, 1979, p. 139) – be analytically subdivided into skills, useful knowledge and knowledge of recipes.
3. Bergmann (1985, p. 307) in particular emphasizes the problem of using the interview as an investigation instrument, as it "produces reconstructively transformed data that is only analysable to a certain extent"; on this fundamental insight see also already Oevermann, 1983 as well as Reichertz, 1988. An impressive portrayal of the problems of prompting do-it-yourselfers to explain their routine knowledge is provided by Honer, 1993. Like Honer Soeffner (1989, p. 211) too emphasizes the usefullness of ethnographic procedures for the reconstruction of implicit routine knowledge (just as Schröer 1994, using the police interrogarion of juvenile suspects as an example).
4. From a stage management perspective, a fundamental question arises concerning the recognizability of facts: Then the expert does not appear as "someone who has special competencies, but as someone who is skilled in making it plausible to society that he has special competencies" (Hitzler, 1994, p. 27, own translation, cf. also Pfadenhauer, 1998 for this perspective on professionals).
5. Schütz (1972b, p. 256) distinguishes the subjective aspect of responsibility (in terms of "being responsible towards") from the "objective meaning" (in the sense of being "responsible for"): "If I only feel subjectively responsible for that what I did or failed to do, without being held responsible by others, the consequence of my wrongdoing will not be reproach, criticism, censure or another form of punishment that someone imposes on me, but regret, pangs of conscience or remorse."
6. As I make no claim to originality for many aspects of the view advanced in this text, but see myself as moving within the discussion context of ethnographically-oriented sociologists, I make use of we-form in various passages.
7. Experts no more than elites can simply be derived from the functional needs of the social and policial system, but can rather be determined on the basis of their personal performance. Whether or even that these perfomances are functional for the existence of a "system" of whichever nature, is another matter (for further details cf. Pfadenhauer, 2001a).
8. Cf. Trinczek (1995, p. 60), who harshly criticizes the "fetishising of" as weak as possible interviewer intervention in the interpretative paradigm.
9. Unlike Vogel (1995, p. 80), who first and foremost puts the "paternalism effects," as he calls them, down to age and status differences, we primarily regard the (real or supposed) competence gap as the factor "triggering" these effects. For more information on the manifold communication styles of experts cf. also Martens, Brüggemann, 2006.

10. For a sociology of knowledge perspective on the differentiation of these three types regarding their individual knowledge assets see Schütz, 1972a.
11. A characteristic feature of the communicative genre "instruction" is statements designated as explicit knowledge (cf. Keppler and Luckmann, 1991).
12. In the tradition of discourse analytical ethnomethodology, justifications (as well as excuses) can be conceived as accounts, that is as linguistic devices employed "whenever an action is subjected to evaluative inquiry" (Scott and Lyman, 1976, p. 74).
13. I would like to point out again that the expert – even with the best of intentions – can and will only disclose knowledge of which he is consciously aware.
14. Strictly speaking, this is also a form of accounting, which is here (in terms of "theoretical" explanations) to all intents and purposes understood to include scientific causal explanations or explanations with a similar epistemological claim. In this context, it is noteworthy that parts of the respective essay of Scott and Lyman (1976) were originally published under the title "responsibilities" in the German translation by Heinz Steinert.
15. Cf. on another setting of priorities Maindok (1996), who in fact explicitly speaks of "experts for conducting interviews," but who in doing so in particular addresses the strategic-communicative meta(competence) of a "professional" interviewer in discussions with laypersons.
16. "The appeal of this consequence – free interview situation also manifests itself in the fact that the interviewees sometimes considerably exceed the time limit, even if every quarter of an hour had been bargained over during the arrangement of the meeting; frequently the researchers rather than the managers end the interview on their own accord" (Trinczek, 1995, p. 63, own translation).
17. For a favourable opinion on a departure from the guideline in support of what is known as "catharsis effects" cf. Kern, Kern and Schumann, 1988, Vogel, 1995; critical as regards the "lapse" into personal and private matters Meuser and Nagel, 1991.
18. As already indicated above, it seems essential to us to integrate expert interviews into an ethnographic research design also with respect to an "overall ascertainment" of the knowledge of experts, that is with respect to the reconstruction of the implicit elements of expert knowledge too, as well as – without expatiating on this at large – as condition for a context-related analysis of all the collected data. On the different methods or techniques of data evaluation subsumed under the label of "social scientific hermeneutics" within the scope of ethnographic research work see Honer, 1993, pp. 89–110 as well as the contributions in Hitzler and Honer, 1997, on the "rules of procedure" they have in common cf. Hitzler, 2000, pp. 25–28.
19. On this note cf. also Meuser and Nagel (1994, p.180) and their criticism of the expert concept of Hartmann and Hartmann, 1982.
20. For a basic description cf. Hitzler, 2007, for an overview of different types of ethnography see Hitzler, 2000 and for a contrastive comparison of conventional and focused ethnography Knoblauch, 2001 and Knoblauch, 2003.
21. In the process of research, as many and as varied as possible data – with respect to the research interest – are collected and analysed. In doing so, the ethnographic "ideal" is the combination of as varied as possible methods while following specific theoretical guidelines of data collection (cf., once more, Honer, 1993).
22. The (partly highly specialized) educational series on television and radio as well as the well-nigh unfathomable possibilities of the internet sometimes provide

effective opportunities for a first introduction into the knowledge acquirement and accumulation of professionals.

23. The interest of the ethnomethodologically-oriented "studies of work" is therefore directed at the concrete work execution in occupational practice. And the programme of "workplace studies" that is interested in work execution in complex technical surroundings, has already firmly integrated the ethnographic approach (for an overview see Eberle, 2007).

24. To stick to the chosen and by no means only "archaic" example: The typically subjective stock of knowledge of the shaman at best reveals itself to the researcher if he tries to acquaint himself intensely with the world of the shamans. There seems to us to be the only possibility for researchers to acquire the as comprehensive as possible appropriate prior knowledge that is constitutive for expert interviews. The interviewer must, as it were, seek to become a (quasi-) shaman himself, to be able to speak with shamans on an "equal footing. Therefore the intense existential involvement of the ethnographer is crucial in this case."

Further readings

Gillham, B. (2005) "Elite Interviewing" in Gillham, B. (ed.) *Research Interviewing: The Range of Techniques* (London: Continuum).

Holstein, J. A. and Gubrium, J. F. (1997) "Active Interviewing" in Silverman, D. (ed.) *Qualitative Research: Theory, Method and Practice* (London: Sage), pp. 113–29.

Knoblauch, H. (2005) "Focused Ethnography" in *Forum Qualitative Sozialforschung 6 (3),* http://www.qualitative-research.net/fqs-texte/3-05/05-3-44-e.htm.

References

Bauman, Z. (1987) *Legislators and Interpreters. On Modernity, Postmodernity and Intellectual* (Cambridge: Polity Press).

Berger, P. L. and Luckmann, T. (1969) *Die gesellschaftliche Konstruktion von Wirklichkeit* (Frankfurt am Main: Fischer).

Bergmann, J. (1985) "Flüchtigkeit und methodische Fixierung sozialer Wirklichkeit" in Bonß, W. and Hartmann, H. (eds) *Entzauberte Wissenschaft, Special volume 3 of the Soziale Welt* (Göttingen: Schwartz), pp. 299–320.

Deeke, A. (1995) "Experteninterviews – ein methodologisches und forschungspraktisches Problem" in Brinkmann, C., Deeke, A. and Völkel, B. (eds) *Experteninterviews in der Arbeitsmarktforschung*, BeitrAB191 (Nürnberg: IAB), pp. 7–22.

Dexter, L. A. (1970) *Elite and specialized interviewing* (Evanston: Northwestern University Press).

Dreitzel, H. P. (1962) *Elitebegriff und Sozialstruktur* (Stuttgart: Enke).

Eberle, T. S. (1997) "Ethnomethodologische Konversationsanalyse" in Hitzler, R. and Honer, A. (eds) *Sozialwissenschaftliche Hermeneutik* (Opladen: Leske and Budrich), pp. 245–79.

Eberle, T. S. (2007) "Ethnomethodologie und Konversationsanalyse" in Schützeichel, R. (ed.) *Handbuch Wissenssoziologie und Wissensforschung* (Konstanz: UVK), pp. 139 –60.

Eliade, M. (1975) *Schamanismus und archaische Ekstasetechnik* (Frankfurt am Main: Suhrkamp).

Fontana, A. and Frey, J. H. (2000) "The Interview: from structured questions to negotiated text" in Denzin, N. K. and Lincoln, Y. S. (eds) *Handbook of qualitative research*, 2nd edn (Thousand Oaks, CA: Sage), pp. 645–72.

Gillham, B. (2005) "Elite Interviewing" in Gillham, B. (ed.) *Research Interviewing: The Range of Techniques* (London: Continuum).

Goffman, E. (1977) *Rahmenanalyse* (Frankfurt am Main: Suhrkamp).

Gorden, R. L. (1975) *Interviewing: Strategy, Techniques and Tactics* (Homewood, III: Dorsey).

Gubrium, J. F. and Holstein, J. A. (2002) *Handbook of Interview Research: Context and Method* (Thousand Oaks, CA: Sage Publications).

Hartmann, H. and Hartmann, M. (1982) "Vom Elend der Experten: Zwischen Akademisierung und Deprofessionalisierung" in *Kölner Zeitschrift für Soziologie und Sozialpsychologie 34*, 193–223.

Hitzler, R. (1982) "Der 'begeisterte' Körper. Zur persönlichen Identität von Schamanen" in Gehlen, R. and Wolf, B. (eds) *Unter dem Pflaster liegt der Stand*, Vol. 11 (Berlin: Kramer), pp. 53–73.

Hitzler, R. (1994) "Wissen und Wesen des Experten. Ein Annäherungsversuch – zur Einleitung" in Hitzler, R., Honer, A. and Maeder, C. (eds) *Expertenwissen. Die institutionalisierte Kompetenz zur Konstruktion von Wirklichkeit* (Opladen: Westdeutscher Verlag), pp. 13–30.

Hitzler, R. (1999) "Welten erkunden. Soziologie als (eine Art) Ethnologie der eigenen Gesellschaft" in *Soziale Welt 50*, 473–83.

Hitzler, R. (2000) "Die Erkundung des Feldes und die Deutung der Daten. Annäherungen an die (lebensweltliche) Ethnographie" in Lindner, W. (ed.) *Ethnographische Methoden in der Jugendarbeit* (Opladen: Leske and Budrich), pp. 17–31.

Hitzler, R. (2007) "Ethnographie" in Buber, R. and Holzmüller, H. (eds) *Qualitative Marktforschung. Konzepte – Methoden – Analysen* (Wiesbaden: Gabler), pp. 207–18.

Hitzler, R. and Honer, A. (1997) *Sozialwissenschaftliche Hermeneutik* (Opladen: Leske and Budrich).

Hitzler, R. and Pfadenhauer, M. (1999) "Reflexive Mediziner? Die Definition professioneller Kompetenz als standespolitisches Problem am Übergang zu einer 'anderen' Moderne" in Maeder, C., Burton-Jeangros, C. and Haour-Knipe, C. (eds) *Gesundheit, Medizin und Gesellschaft. Beiträge zur Soziologie der Gesundheit* (Zürich: Seismo), pp. 94–111.

Hitzler, R. and Pfadenhauer, M. (2000) "Die Lage ist hoffnungslos, aber nicht ernst! (Erwerbs-) Probleme junger Leute heute und die anderen Welten von Jugendlichen" in Hettlage, R. and Vogt, L. (eds) *Identitäten im Umbruch* (Opladen: Westdeutscher Verlag), pp. 361–80.

Holstein, J. A. and Gubrium, J. F. (1997) "Active Interviewing" in Silverman, D. (ed.) *Qualitative Research: Theory, Method and Practice* (London: Sage), pp. 113–29.

Honer, A. (1993) *Lebensweltliche Ethnographie* (Wiesbaden: DUV).

Honer, A. (1994) "Das explorative Interview. Zur Rekonstruktion der Relevanzen von Expertinnen und anderen Leuten" in *Schweizerische Zeitung für Soziologie 20*, 623–40.

Honer, A. (2000) "Lebensweltanalyse in der Ethnographie" in Flick, U., Kardoff, E. von and Steinke, I. (eds) *Qualitative Forschung* (Reinbek: Rowohlt), pp. 194–204.

Hopf, C. (2000) "Qualitative Interviews – ein Überblick" in Flick, U., Kardoff, E. von and Steinke, I. (eds) *Qualitative Forschung* (Reinbek: Rowohlt), pp. 349–60.

Hunt, H. W., Crane, W. W. and Wahlke, J. C. (1964/65) "Interviewing Political Elites in Cross-Cultural Comparative Research" in *American Journal of Sociology 70*, 59–68.

Jaeggi, U. (1960) *Die gesellschaftliche Elite* (Bern: Haupt).

Keppler, A. and Luckmann, T. (1991) "'Teaching': Conversational Transmission of Knowledge" in Markova, I. and Foppa, K. (eds) *Asymmetries in Dialogue* (Hempstead: Harvester Wheatsheaf), pp. 143–65.

Kern, B., Kern, H. and Schumann, M. (1988) "Industriesoziologie als Katharsis" in *Soziale Welt 39*, 86–96.

Knoblauch, H. (2001) "Fokussierte Ethnographie" in *Sozialer Sinn 1*, 123–41.

Knoblauch, H. (2003) *Qualitative Religionsforschung: Religionsethnographie in der eigenen Gesellschaft* (München/Zürich: Vandenhoeck and Ruprecht).

Maindok, H. (1996) *Professionelle Interviewführung in der Sozialforschung* (Pfaffenweiler: Centaurus).

Marquardt, O. (1981) "Inkompetenzkompensationskompetenz? Über Kompetenz und Inkompetenz der Philosophie" in Marquardt, O. *Abschied vom Prinzipiellen. Philosophische – Studien* (Stuttgart: Reclam), pp. 23–38.

Martens, K. and Brüggemann, M. (2006) *Kein Experte ist wie der andere. Vom Umgang mit Missionaren und Geschichtenerzählern* (Bremen: Arbeitspapier 39 des SFB 597 "Staatlichkeit im Wandel" an der Universität Bremen).

Mayntz, R., Holm, K. and Hübner, P. (1972) *Einführung in die Methoden der empirischen Soziologie* (Opladen: Westdeutscher Verlag).

Meuser, M. and Nagel, U. (1991) "ExpertInneninterviews – vielfach erprobt, wenig bedacht. Ein Beitrag zur qualitativen Methodendiskussion" in Garz, D. and Kraimer, K. (eds) *Qualitativ-empirische Sozialforschung. Konzepte, Methoden, Analysen* (Opladen: Westdeutscher Verlag), pp. 441–71.

Meuser, M. and Nagel, U. (1994) "Expertenwissen und Experteninterview" in Hitzler, R., Honer, A. and Maeder, C. (eds) *Expertenwissen. Die institutionalisierte Kompetenz zur Konstruktion von Wirklichkeit* (Opladen: Westdeutscher Verlag), pp. 180–92.

Meuser, M. and Nagel, U. (1997) "Das ExpertInneninterview – Wissenssoziologische Voraussetzungen und methodische Durchführung" in Friebertshäuser, B. and Prengel, A. (eds) *Handbuch Qualitative Forschungsmethoden in der Erziehungswissenschaft* (Weinheim/München: Juventa), pp. 481–91.

Oevermann, U. (1983) "Zur Sache. Die Bedeutung von Adornos methodologischem Selbstverständnis für die Begründung einer materialen soziologischen Strukturanalyse" in Friedeburg, L. von and Habermas, J. (eds) *Adorno-Konferenz 1983* (Frankfurt am Main: Suhrkamp), pp. 234–89.

Pfadenhauer, M. (1997) "Die (Re-)Konstruktion professionellen Handelns. Überlegungen zur Annäherung an den Forschungsgegenstand" in M. Pfadenhauer (ed.) *Explorationen zum Begriff des professionellen Handelns. Dokumentation des 1. Workshops des Arbeitskreises "Professionelles Handeln" am 28.02. und 1.03.1997 in München* (München: Eigendruck), pp. 3–6.

Pfadenhauer, M. (1998) "Problem zur Lösung. Inszenierung von Professionalität" in Willems, H. and Jurga, M. (eds) *Inszenierungsgesellschaft* (Opladen: Westdeutscher Verlag), pp. 209–304.

Pfadenhauer, M. (2000) "Spielerisches Unternehmertum. Zur Professionalität von Event-Produzenten in der Techno-Szene" in Gebhardt, W., Hitzler, R. and Pfadenhauer, M. (eds) *Events. Zur Soziologie des Außergewöhnlichen* (Opladen: Leske and Budrich), pp. 95–114.

Pfadenhauer, M. (2001a) "Macht – Funktion – Leistung. Elitentheoretische Überlegungen zur Profession" in Mieg, H. and Pfadenhauer, M. (eds) *Professionelle Leistung – Positionen zur Professionssoziologie* (Reihe "Wissen und Studium" im Universitätsverlag Konstanz: UVK), pp. 81–7.

Pfadenhauer, M. (2001b) "Was andere Augen sehen. Perspektiven der Rezeption des Techno-Videoclips 'Sonic Empire'" in Hitzler, R. and Pfadenhauer, M. (eds) *Techno-Soziologie. Erkundungen einer Jugendkultur* (Opladen: Leske and Budrich), pp. 235–52.

Pfadenhauer, M. (2007) "Das Experteninterview. Ein Gespräch auf gleicher Augenhöhe" in Buber, R. and Holzmüller, H. (eds) *Qualitative Marktforschung. Konzepte – Methoden – Analysen* (Wiesbaden: Gabler), pp. 449–61.

Reichertz, J. (1988) "Verstehende Soziologie ohne Subjekt?" in *Kölner Zeitschrift für Soziologie und Sozialpsychologie 40*, 207–22.

Schröer, N. (1994) "Routinisiertes Expertenwissen. Zur Rekonstruktion des strukturalen Regelwissens von Vernehmungsbeamten" in Hitzler, R., Honer, A. and Maeder, C. (eds) *Expertenwissen. Die institutionalisierte Kompetenz zur Konstruktion von Wirklichkeit* (Opladen: Westdeutscher Verlag), pp. 214–31.

Schütz, A. (1972a) "Der gut informierte Bürger" in Schütz, A. *Gesammelte Aufsätze*, Vol. 2 (Den Haag: Nijhoff), pp. 85–101.

Schütz, A. (1972b) "Einige Äquivationen im Begriff der Verantwortlichkeit" in Schütz, A. *Gesammelte Aufsätze*, Vol. 2 (Den Haag: Nijhoff), pp. 256–58.

Schütz, A. and Luckmann, T. (1979) *Strukturen der Lebenswelt*, Vol. 1 (Frankfurt am Main: Suhrkamp).

Scott, M. B. and Lyman, S. M. (1976) "Praktische Erklärungen" in Anwärter, M., Kirsch, E. and Schröter, M. (eds) *Seminar: Kommunikation, Interaktion, Identität* (Frankfurt am Main: Suhrkamp), pp. 73–114.

Soeffner, H. G. (1989) *Auslegung des Alltags – Der Alltag der Auslegung. Zur wissenssoziologischen Konzeption einer sozialwissenschaftlichen Hermeneutik* (Frankfurt am Main: Suhrkamp).

Sprondel, W. M. (1979) " 'Experte' und 'Laie'. Zur Entwicklung von Typenbegriffen in der Wissenssoziologie" in Sprondel, W. M. and Grathoff, R. (eds) *Alfred Schütz und die Idee des Alltags in den Sozialwissenschaften* (Stuttgart: Enke), pp. 140–54.

Strauss, A. (1987) *Qualitative Analysis for Social Scientists* (Cambridge: University Press).

Trinczek, R. (1995) "Experteninterviews mit Managern: Methodische und methodologische Hintergründe" in Brinkmann, C., Deeke, A. and Völkel, B. (eds) *Experteninterviews in der Arbeitsmarktforschung*. BeitrAB191 (Nürnberg: IAB), pp. 59–67.

Vogel, B. (1995) " 'Wenn der Eisberg zu schmelzen beginnt...' – Einige Reflexionen über den Stellenwert und die Probleme des Experteninterviews in der Praxis der empirischen Sozialforschung" in Brinkmann, C., Deeke, A. and Völkel, B. (eds) *Experteninterviews in der Arbeitsmarktforschung*. BeitrAB191 (Nürnberg: IAB), pp. 73–83.

Znaniecki, F. (1975) *The Social Role of the Man of Knowledge* (New York: Octagon).

4
Interviewing the Elite – Interviewing Experts: Is There a Difference?[1]

Beate Littig

4.1 Introduction

A comparison of the Anglo-American methodological debate in the social sciences with its counterpart in the German-speaking world reveals that scientists in the latter have now regarded expert interviews as a distinct interview form for some years (Flick and others, 2003, Bogner and others, 2005, Gläser and Laudel, 2004, Mieg and Näf, 2006). With few exceptions, for example (Brandl and Klinger, 2006), the notion of the elite interview is rarely, if ever, encountered in German-speaking countries. Yet the reverse is the case in the Anglo-American and (given the dominance of English as the language of scientific publication) international social sciences debate see, for example (Gubrium and Holstein, 2002 or Denzin and Lincoln, 2000), where the concept of the expert interview appears largely unknown. However, closer study reveals that in many respects the content of publications on these two interview forms does not really differ fundamentally. In fact, quite the opposite applies: central themes in both methodological traditions include the problems of gaining access to the elite or to experts (particularly at a high level) as well as the specifics of interaction and the actual interview process itself. Although not identical, even the respective target group definitions (experts and the elite) for such interviews overlap. The focus of interest in both generally lies on the professional (functional) elite and on professional experts. Indeed, it would seem that the differences between interviews with the elite and interviews with experts lie primarily in differing social and political sciences research traditions and interests. The following article discusses the commonalities and differences in these two methodological approaches, thereby bringing together current insights on comparable techniques and contributing to establishing a more detailed specification of the methodology of expert interviews. It concludes with a sociology of knowledge based appeal that the (professional) functional elite – given their positions of power – be considered as a specific group of experts. From a methodological perspective and as a result of their specific interpretive knowledge ("know why") and procedural knowledge ("know-how"), experts (and thus also the elite) are of relevance to social and political sciences research. Consequently, interviews with the elite aimed at generating explicit, tacit, professional or occupational knowledge should be seen as expert interviews.

4.2 Experts and the elite as interview partners

The terms "elite interview" or "expert interview" raise the assumption that the methodological rationale behind them (as unique interview forms) is linked to specific characteristics in their respective target groups. So what actually makes a person a member of the elite or an expert? Similarly, what makes these particular groups so interesting from a social or political sciences perspective?

One aspect, which quickly becomes apparent in literature on interviewing the elite is that authors generally presume the notion of the elite to be clear and see no need to explain it further. For the most part, reflections begin and end with a more or less vague working definition of what constitutes the elite. Consequently, the elite are often defined by their comparatively high social status and the associated privileges they enjoy: "However the whole notion of an elite, implies a group of individuals, who hold, or have held, a privileged position in society and, as such, as far as a political scientist is concerned, are likely to have had more influence on political outcomes than general members of the public." (Richards, 1996, p. 199).

As Dexter notes in his now classic book on interviewing the elite,[2] this group's members are "the influential, the prominent, and the well informed" (Dexter 2006/1969, p. 19), a definition that, in essence, has remained constant in methodological literature to this day.[3] Indeed, any search for a clear definition is usually in vain see, for example (Moyser and Wagstaffe, 1987, Seldon, 1996, Odendahl and Shaw, 2002, Lilleker, 2003).

One exception is the 2002 article by Welch and others reflecting on the methodology behind in-depth interviews with the corporate elite in which the authors define the elite in relation to their field of research (international business research) as: "an informant (usually male) who occupies a senior or middle management position; has functional responsibility in an area which enjoys high status in accordance with corporate values; has considerable industry experience and frequently also long tenure with the company; possesses a broad network of personal relationships; and has considerable international exposure" (Welch and others, 2002, p. 613).

This definition comes close to the definition of experts proposed by Meuser and Nagel in their groundbreaking 1991 article:[4] "The target group for expert interviews is wide. Examples in literature include top-level managers from politics, business, the judiciary, associations and the sciences, along with teachers, social workers or staff representatives. Most are members of the functional elite, although categorizing some of them in this way, for example staff representatives or social workers might be misleading." (Meuser and Nagel, 2005, p. 73, transl. from German B.L.)

Meuser and Nagel also relate expert status to the field of research. Selected individuals are defined as experts, a status accorded to them by the researchers. Social scientific interest in experts is targeted at their specific contextual knowledge of a given research field or their internal knowledge of the structures, procedures and events in a given organization. In other words, experts serve as informants and possess knowledge otherwise not accessible to researchers. They are often also people in positions of power, that is managers with greater decision-making responsibility. However, they do not necessarily have to be the people who make the high-level decisions at the top of an organization. Ultimately, anyone who is responsible for and has privileged access to the knowledge of specific groups of people or decision-making processes can be seen as an expert. Bogner and Menz (in this volume, Chapter 2) formulate this as follows: *"An expert has technical, process and interpretative knowledge that refers to a specific field of action, by virtue of the fact that the expert acts in a relevant way (for example, in a particular organisational field or the expert's own professional area). In this respect, expert knowledge consists not only of systematised, reflexively accessible knowledge relating to a specialised subject or field, but also has to a considerable extent the character of practical or action knowledge, which incorporates a range of quite disparate maxims for action, individual rules of decision, collective orientations, and patterns of social interpretation. An expert's knowledge, his/her action orientations etc., also (and this is decisive) point to the fact that s/he may become hegemonic in terms of practice in his/her field of action (for example, in a certain organisational-functional context). In other words, the possibility exists that the expert may be able to get his/her orientations enforced (at least in part). As the expert's knowledge has an effect on practice, it structures the conditions of action of other actors in the expert's field in a relevant way."* (italic in the original)

The explication and reconstruction of these different forms of knowledge and their practical consequences form the focus of expert interviews and their subsequent analysis (cf. the articles in Bogner and others, 2005). In contrast, "the experts" own biographical experiences and personal opinions take very much a back seat.

The scientific objective is rarely formulated in quite such an explicit manner in literature in interviewing the elite. However, even at the end of the 1960s, Dexter already drew attention to the fact that the purpose of interviewing the elite was not simply to gather objective facts and knowledge. Indeed, he presented an initial concept for a "transactional theory of the interview" based on an interaction approach to the interview situation: "What this means is, of course, that whether investigators wish it or not, interviewing is a social relationship and the interviewer is part of the relationship. The interviewee's *inarticulate* and *unexamined* conception of the audience guides and determines what he says." (Dexter, 2006/1969, p. 115 italics in original, B.L).

Furthermore, interviews with the elite in Dexter's tradition are not seen as a precise research tool. The sampling is not representative, the statements made by interviewees can be distorted by gaps in their memories, different interviewees can give different information on the same topic, and so on, for example (Richards, 1996, p. 200f).

In comparison, the German-language debate on interviews with experts is strongly influenced by the sociology of knowledge and takes a more differentiated approach to the status of the data obtained (Bogner and others, 2005, Hitzler and others, 1994). However, it is also clear here that there is no one such thing as *the* expert interview. Indeed, there is considerable plurality regarding the underlying notion of what constitutes an expert and the fields of research in the use of this instrument.[5]

According to Bogner and Menz (2005, p. 36ff, see also Bogner and Menz, in this volume), there are three different types of expert interviews:

- exploratory expert interviews (used in a relatively unknown field of research),
- systemizing expert interviews (used to reconstruct "objective" knowledge in a specific field), and
- theory generating expert interviews (targeted not only at the expert's explicit specialist knowledge, but also at his or her tacit specific interpretive knowledge (know-why) and procedural knowledge (know-how) obtained through (professional) practice).

Based on this differentiation, the understanding of interviewing the elite in Anglo-American methodological literature can be classified as exploratory or systemizing in nature. Members of the elite serve as sources of information on specific areas of knowledge that would otherwise be inaccessible. Correspondingly, and depending on the field of research, the comparative analysis of different interviews seeks to provide an objective reconstruction of the facts, problems, decision-making processes, networks and other aspects described by the individual interviewees for example (Welch and others, 2002, p. 613). Richards describes a similar situation in the political sciences: "One of the most important functions of an elite interview is to try to assist the political scientist in understanding the theoretical position/s of the interviewee; his or her perceptions, belief and ideologies. Such information can rarely be gleaned from examining books, documents or records. By their very nature, elite interviews provide a subjective account of an event or issue" (Richards, 1996, pp. 99–200).

Even if the effects of interaction cannot be ignored, they should nonetheless be kept to a minimum to enable maximum proximity to scientific insight into a positivistically accepted, objective reality (cf. Dexter,

2006/1969, p. 115ff.). This is the prevailing goal of the use of expert interviews – using experts as informants – at least in applied social and policy research in the German-speaking world, as well as in political sciences and many other branches of sociology (Gläser and Laudel, 2004, Mieg and Näf, 2006).

Consequently, the dividing line does not run between expert interviews and elite interviews and their different target data sources. Instead, it runs far more within such interviews through their different cognitive interests and the epistemological view of the status of the data they provide. What divides them is their view of science and social reality, namely a positivist versus a social constructivist, that is always interpretive hermeneutic, view:

> However...the hermeneutic argumentation is in essence anti-Cartesian. ... It is based on historical-sociological constructions of reality (realities). It sees individuals interacting with each other and their a priori intersubjectivity *in* not *in contrast to* the interpreted world. It is directed not only at the observing, describing, understanding and explaining of social phenomena, but with that as one also the social aspects of the typal, historically changing perception and articulation patterns and purposes of observing, describing, understanding and explaining... (Soeffner 1989, p. 56f; italics in original; transl. from German B.L.)

Whereas exploratory and systemizing expert interviews are grounded in a more positivist attitude and, consequently, an objectivist cognitive ideal of both the generation and the analysis of the data, the so-called theory generating expert interview proposed by Bogner and Menz in line with Meuser and Nagel (both in Bogner and others, 2005) emanates from the assumption of a social-constructivist production of reality. Ergo, research is also viewed as an active process of creating meaning and relevance. In addition to obtaining information on a particular area of research, theory generating expert interviews also follow sociology of knowledge based goals. In the process, the generation, emergence, functioning, practice, content and effect of explicit and tacit expert knowledge alike become the object of the research. The expert knowledge is understood here as an analytical construct realized depending on the interview strategy in an interactive interview situation. In this respect, the expert knowledge is not simply neatly packaged up waiting to be collected, it is an externalization of different levels of knowledge that is only formed in the course of the interview. According to this social-constructivist oriented view, an (expert) interview is not a "neutral" interview situation from which interaction effects (through gender, age, status, and so on) should be excluded wherever possible.[6] Such influences are not only unavoidable, they are also – just like expectations, emotions, sympathy, antipathy, and so on – a constituent part of an (expert) interview (Helfferich, 2004).[7] As with all other interview forms, the interviewees (and the interviewers) in expert interviews should orient their behaviour (and what they say) on those issues that are of specific relevance to the actual situation in question.

4.3 Specifics of access and interviewing

Literature on both forms of interview, that is interviews with the elite and interviews with experts often focuses on the issues of sampling, the specific access problems faced and the challenges of conducting the interviews for example (Dexter, 2006/1969, Moyser and Wagstaffe, 1987, Vogel, 1995, Odendahl and Shaw, 2002, Welch and others, 2002, Lilleker, 2003 and the articles in Bogner and others, 2005).[8]

4.3.1 Sampling

The first issue usually discussed is sampling. This does not adhere to quantitative conceptions of representativity, since there is no clearly defined pool of experts and members of the elite from which a sample might be chosen in line with specific guidelines. Indeed, the attributed expert or elite status is more often set by the actual field of research and research goals. As Meuser and Nagel (2005, p. 73) note, researchers to a certain extent attribute expert status that is limited to a specific area of research. If the research focuses on corporate human resources issues (for example hiring or redundancy practices), human resources managers and directors, managing directors, and also even representatives of specific lobbying groups (such as associations for the disabled) take on expert status. If it focuses on the drafting of a particular law and the related negotiation and decision-making processes, the civil servants, party functionaries, assessors and – where applicable – representatives of affected citizens' action groups, and so on are the experts to interview. Welch (and others, 2002, p. 613) also describe the attribution of elite status to certain individuals in a similar manner, namely in relation to the research question (in their case international business). Their interest focused primarily on the long-term professional experiences of 90 interviewees in middle management positions in international companies. Notable in their description is the explicit attribution of elite status to representatives of middle not top management, a group typically viewed as a reservoir of the elite. They base this extension of the notion of the elite on their topic of research: their interest lay in operational matters, and they expected to encounter more knowledge of such activities at middle management level than at the top. The actual interviewees were identified and recruited in this case via company profiles (now available on the internet), telephone directories, media reports, prior studies and so-called snowball sampling (that is recommendations from other interviewees). To ensure no important people were omitted from the sample, extensive experience in the particular field was a prerequisite where participation in certain (for example legislative) processes was concerned. Recommendations from interviewees can prove useful in assessing the importance of particular individuals.[9] Theoretical sampling (Strauss and Corbin, 1996, Glaser and Strauss, 1998) is an established selection procedure in cases involving issues linked to specific positions (for example middle management in large companies).

4.3.2   Access problems

As one way of distinguishing themselves, members of the elite seek to distance themselves from the non-elite by setting up access barriers to their private and working lives (Hertz and Imber, 1995, p. viii). The following rule seemingly applies: the higher the social class, the more difficult access becomes.[10] This also applies to the high-level experts described in the previous section. These access barriers can be personified in the form of secretaries, personal assistants and, in the case of the economic and political top elite, entire PR departments. The researcher has to quasi overcome this first hurdle by convincing these guardians of the meaningfulness and necessity of an interview with their respective superiors. Lack of time is another possible access barrier. High-level individuals are frequently obliged to keep to a tight schedule and thus give strict order of precedence to important and unimportant appointments and activities (Brandl and Klinger, 2006, p. 47). Scientific research does not always feature highly on this list of priorities, and since requests for interviews with the experts who are in demand can quickly mount up, they have to be even more selective when choosing those they actually want to accept (Imbusch, 2003, p. 11f).

In addition to distancing themselves, members of the elite also cultivate network contacts to others of their ilk. Although such networks are still characterized by a strong tendency towards social closure and homogenization, access barriers to elite networks have, in the meantime, become more penetrable (Hornbostel, 2004, p. 12, Hartmann, 2007). If the researcher succeeds in gaining initial access, elite networks can prove a rich source of information for scientific research.

A number of strategic suggestions on how to overcome these access problems can be found in literature on both expert interviews and elite interviews alike. Such suggestions are often founded on exploiting the possible motives of potential interviewees for participation in such interviews. Brandl and Klinger (2006), for example, refer to instrumental interests on the part of the target group – such as the hope of gaining useful or utilizable information in the course of the interview. Advantage can be taken of such a motive by offering quick access to the research results in return for participation. A further instrumental motive is the possible public relations value to be gained from cooperating with a well-known research institute. Other interviewees may be interested in participating for reasons independent of the actual research project. Psychosocial motives – such as a lack of competent people to talk to or loneliness – can come into play as well. Similarly, altruism can also be a motivation for agreeing to participate in such interviews, for example a desire to support young researchers in their scientific endeavours or generally make a contribution to scientific advance.

To enhance their own status, making targeted references to the excellent reputation of their research institute, the sponsoring body or their supervising tutors is particularly recommended for students or lower-level scientists. Also recommended is the use of personal contacts or references to commonalities with the high-level interviewee (for example having studied at the same university, originating from the same city, and so on).

4.3.3   Interviewing

The goal of both expert and elite interviews alike is to generate knowledge for scientific purposes. In other words, the interviewees should provide information on a specific topic related to the research. The interviews themselves are open-ended and do not follow a standardized format, thus providing the interviewees with ample space to express their views. Dexter mapped out his definition of an elite interview in 1969 as follows:

> It is an interview with any interviewee – and stress should be placed on the word "any" – who in terms of the current purposes of the interviewer is given special, nonstandardized treatment. By special, nonstandard treatment I mean:
> 1. stressing the interviewee's definition of the situation,
> 2. encouraging the interviewee to structure an account of the situation,
> 3. letting the interviewee introduce to a considerable extent (an extent which will of course vary from project to project and interviewer to interviewer) his notion of what he regards as relevant, instead of relying upon the investigator's notions of relevance. (Dexter, 2006/1969, p. 18)

Interviewers usually work with a set of flexible guidelines, which also contain a list of the relevant issues. As a rule, experts and members of the elite are accustomed to talking about their field of expertise and explaining to others what they know – frequently for strategic purposes. Managers are also often loath to be told what to do and tend more towards testing others. To handle such situations, interviewers need certain skills and abilities. Firstly, they must be extremely flexible, allowing interviewees to lead the conversation, yet not losing sight of the information they are actually interested in. At the same time, they must show themselves to be competent partners. Pfadenhauer (2005, see also Pfadenhauer, this volume) aptly describes this as "talking at eye level." In other words, interviewers may even be required to present themselves in preliminary meetings as quasi-experts and competent partners who are familiar with the expert's area of expertise. To pursue an interaction model based on quasi-expertise, interviewers must prepare extensively for such meetings to ensure they are familiar with the subject matter, speak the "right language" and have the necessary insider knowledge of the field. To a certain extent, this counteracts any differences in status between the interviewer and the interviewee that might lessen the latter's interest in the interview.

Bogner and Menz (2005, p. 60ff., see also Bogner and Menz, in this volume) do however; note that interviewees can perceive their interviewers in different ways and that differences in status are not necessarily disadvantageous in an interview setting. Interviewees can categorize interviewers into the following types:

- Co-experts or experts from another knowledge culture
- Lay people
- People in positions of authority
- Accomplices
- Potential critics.

As far as the interview is concerned, each of these types has its own advantages and disadvantages, which can be strengthened or reduced using appropriate strategic interventions.[11] Although not described as such in the methodological literature on the subject, the same applies to interviews with members of the professional elite, who (as will be discussed in more detail below) can also be viewed as high-level experts.

4.4   Summary and conclusions

Given the above, what conclusions can be drawn on the commonalities and differences in expert interviews and interviews with the elite?

On a practical, methodological level, the same problems are discussed in both sets of literature. No systematic differences can be determined as far as access to the field and actual interaction in the interview are concerned. Similarly, there are no fundamental differences between the target groups for expert interviews or interviews with the elite. In fact, the notion of the expert and the notion of the elite overlap in two key criteria: the knowledge and the power at their disposal. Yet, at the same time, both criteria also play a decisive role in distinguishing experts from the elite (see below for further details).

Bogner and Menz (1995, p. 40f., see also Bogner and Menz, in this volume) differentiate and discuss a voluntarist, constructivist, sociology of knowledge based concept of the expert (cf. also Hitzler, 1994). Following the line of argumentation in Bogner and Menz (2005, see also Bogner and Menz, in this volume), simply possessing specific knowledge does not alone suffice to determine who constitutes an expert. From a sociology of knowledge perspective, professional or occupational experts have such special or specialized knowledge. Sprondel (1979) refers to people with specialized professional or occupational knowledge as experts. He differentiates between such experts and lay specialists, who also possess specialized knowledge, but not related to their work or occupation for example (DIY hobbyists or amateur sports people). For the purposes of linguistic differentiation, individuals with occupational expertise should be referred to as specialists (Hitzler, 1994, p. 21f.). Aside from their specific knowledge, what sets experts apart is the possibility that their knowledge – at least in principle – will also have a practical effect and, thus, significantly influences the freedom of others to act. At the same time, this concept of the expert distinguishes itself from the voluntarist definition, whereby each individual is the expert in his or her own life (cf. Gläser and Laudel, 2004). However, expanding the notion of the expert in this way blurs existing differences in knowledge and evens out differences in social status. Furthermore, such a broader concept of the expert also raises methodological questions. If, as a consequence, every interview were then considered an expert interview, what is the difference between expert interviews and narrative, biographical, focused, topic-oriented or other forms of interview?

These considerations lead to the following conclusions as far as differentiating between expert and elite interviews is concerned: if the expertise (that is specific interpretive knowledge ("know-why") and procedural knowledge ("know-how") in a particular occupational or professional field) is central to the area of research, then the interview can be regarded as an expert interview (Bogner and Menz, 2005, p. 46, see also Bogner and Menz, in this volume). People should only be referred to as experts if they also have a certain degree of power. This vague formulation not only permits a restriction of the notion of the expert to top-level economic, political and governmental (that is the elite) decision-makers (Meuser and Nagel, 2005), it also, at the same time, permits a differentiation between experts and specialists or (specialized) lay people.

Further distinguishing between the elite and experts requires a differentiation of the concept of power: experts can have both formative and/or interpretive power (Bogner, 2005, p. 201f.). According to Bogner's (*ibid.*) line of argumentation, having formative power means having the authority to establish socially binding definitions of problems and predetermine solutions. This can apply both to individual decisions concerning the immediate professional or occupational environment (for example in the case of medical directives or work procedures) as well as to broader matters of social control (for example the ordering of compulsory mass screenings or, more generally, the passing of legal acts). In contrast, interpretive power describes the opportunity open to the expert to provide and establish significant terms and concepts for interpreting phenomena, for legitimizing decisions and, thus, ultimately for the social confrontation with certain phenomena (Bogner, 2005, p. 201f). By way of example, Bogner (ibid.) refers to prenatal diagnostics, where medical expertise is of legitimate relevance in diagnosing possible disabilities. In addition (for example in genetic consultation), such expertise serves as the central guideline and, thus, plays a decisive role in any decisions taken. Ultimately, it is argued, this differentiation between the different ways of exercising power is relevant for distinguishing between experts and the elite. Hence, the elite have more formative power, because they occupy the positions in which the higher decisions legitimized by this form of power are taken. However, they do not necessarily have significant interpretive power because the experts – with their notions, concepts and relevance – have established themselves the opportunity of conferring or starting to confer meaning to decision and negotiation processes (Bogner, 2005, p. 201f.). So-called knowledge workers exert a far higher degree of interpretive power, although they may not necessarily have far-reaching formative power (Willke, 1998).

Figure 4.1 illustrates the differences between specialized lay people, specialists, experts and the elite with regard to knowledge and power.

A summary of the ideas presented in this article leads to the conclusion that the answer to the question posed in the title is yes: there are indeed differences between interviews with the elite and interviews with experts, but also commonalities.

Interviews with the elite can but do not necessarily also have to be expert interviews. Experts, who are defined by their occupational or professional

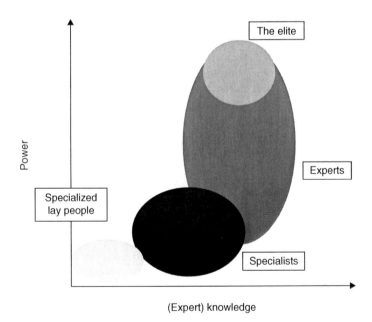

Figure 4.1   Differentiating between experts and the elite

knowledge and their decision-making competences, can but do not have to be members of an elite group. This depends on the extent of their power to act (in the sense of formative power). The ultimate decision on whether an interview is an expert interview or not depends on the field of research and interest. When it comes to researching professional or occupational explicit or tacit interpretive knowledge (know-why), procedural knowledge (know-how) and process knowledge, experts (even elitist experts) are the obvious interview candidates. When the focus lies on issues relating to elite research, questions regarding membership, the (re)production, career paths, social power, lifestyles and thought patterns, and so on of the elite (cf. Wasner, 2004), preference will be given (along with other data) to focused, biographical, subject-matter oriented interviews with representatives of the elite (Mey and others, 2004). In many cases, research into the elite is confronted with similar methodological problems to those encountered in the interviewing of experts. If the actual experts in question are also members of the elite, the access problems will be considerable.[12]

The interview also requires careful preparation on the part of the interviewer: a set of guidelines must be drawn up and extensive knowledge obtained on the actual area of expertise to indicate the interviewer's competence to the interviewee. The latter is presumably of particular importance in the case of experts with a high degree of interpretive power.

Acknowledgements

I would like to thank all the participants in my "Interviewing Experts" course at the ECPR (European Consortium for Political Research) methodology summer school organized in cooperation with the University of Ljubljana in 2006 and 2007 for the inspiring debates on the commonalities and differences between expert interviews and interviews with the elite.

Notes

1. A German Version of this article has also been published in the Open Access Journal Forum Qualitative Research as Littig, B. (2008). Interviews mit Eliten – Interviews mit ExpertInnen: Gibt es Unterschiede? [37 Absätze]. Forum Qualitative Sozialforschung/Forum: Qualitative Social Research, 9(3), Art. 16, http://nbn-resolving.de/urn:nbn:de:0114-fqs0803161.
2. The new edition of Dexter's 1969 book "Elite and Specialized Interviewing" was published in 2006 by the European Consortium for Political Research (ECPR) in the ECPR Classics series. The political scientist's essay-like book significantly influenced the English-language methodological debate on interviewing the elite and, despite the complexity that has since entered this debate, many of his arguments are still valid to this day. In this respect, the book can rightfully be described as a classic (cf. Littig, 2008).

3. One popular definition refers to the elite as a "group in society considered to be superior because of the power, talent, privileges and so on of its members" (Hornby, Cowie and Gimson, 1983, p. 280). However, sociological studies of the elite, link this group not only to social, economic and political influence but also to position (Hartmann, 2007, p. 18, Wasner, 2004). The linking of elite status to a specific office or position (and not an individual) provides continuity to the power held by top politicians, managers or high-level economic officials. Contrary to popular belief, this excludes people like artists, scientists, sportsmen and women, pop stars, actors or other celebrities from the elite. In contrast to Hartmann, Bude maintains that the notion of the elite needs to be taken further if it is to encompass a required performance condition, noting that the Chairman of the Board of Daimler Chrysler is just as much a member of the German elite as the Chairman of the Federal Government Finance Committee. The same applies to the publisher of the Feuilleton in the Frankfurter Allgemeine Zeitung and the Head of Entertainment at the SAT1 television station or Günter Grass and Franz Beckenbauer (Bude, 2004, p. 300f).

4. The 1991 article entitled "Expert interviews – often tested, less considered" (in German: "ExpertInneninterviews – vielfach erprobt, wenig bedacht" – translation from German B.L.) is reprinted in Bogner and others (2005). But it would take about ten years for Meuser and Nagel's conclusions to gain momentum (cf. the anthology on expert interviews by Bogner and others, 2005/2002 or Gläser and Laudel, 2004).

5. The articles in the anthology by Hitzler, Honer and Maeder (1994) offer a detailed discussion of what constitutes an expert and what differentiates experts from specialists and lay people from a sociology of knowledge perspective (cf. also Bogner and Menz 2005, p. 40f.). In addition, Mieg and Brunner (2004) discuss various cognitive psychological conceptions of the expert.

6. For more on the meaning of gender in expert interviews see Littig, 2005 and Abels and Behrens, 2005.

7. They can even be used as a resource in conducting the interview (cf. various articles in Bogner and others, 2005). See also the following section.

8. In the case of interviews with the elite, this often takes the form of essay-like experience reports from research practice with hints on how to address these difficulties (for example, Dexter, 2006/1969, also Lilleker, 2003 or Richards, 1996).

9. The fact that high-level experts and members of the elite frequently occupy exposed positions often complicates the issue of anonymity in such interviews. Nonetheless, anonymity and confidentiality in the treatment of interview material should be assured, except with the express permission to the contrary of the interviewees. Indeed, Dexter (2006/1969, Chapter 2) first cautioned against the unauthorized use of interview material for teaching purposes over 30 years ago.

10. Almost the reverse can be applied to the non-elite: the lower the social status, the easier the entry to the field, even if establishing trust is not always easy where the non-elite are concerned either. This is perhaps one of the reasons why the living conditions of the poor have been studied from a social sciences perspective to such a greater extent than those of the rich.

11. Abels and Behrens (2005, see also Abels and Behrens in this volume) came to comparable conclusions for gender differentiating interaction effects.

12. One aspect that should, in any case, be weighed up with regard to the research question is whether the anticipated results justify the actual effort involved in obtaining an interview. In some cases, an interview with representatives of the lower hierarchical levels may prove more fruitful.

Further readings

Dexter, L. A. (2006/1969) *Elite and specialized interviewing, with a new introduction by Ware, A. and Sánchez-Jankowski, M.* (University of Essex, Colchester: ECPR Press – ECPR classics, 1st edn (1969) Evanston: Northwestern University Press).
Welch, C., Marschan-Piekkari, R., Penttinen, H. and Tahvanainen, M. (2002) "Corporate elites as informants in qualitative international business research" in *International Business Research Review 11*, 611–28.
Weiss, R. S. (1995) *Learning from Strangers. The Art and Method of Qualitative Interview Studies* (New York: The Free Press).

References

Abels, G. and Behrens, M. (2005) "ExpertInnen-Interviews in der Politikwissenschaft. Geschlechtertheoretische und politikfeldanalytische Reflexion einer Methode" in Bogner, A., Littig, B. and Menz, W. (eds) *Das Experteninterview – Theorie, Methode, Anwendung*, 2nd edn (Wiesbaden: Verlag für Sozialwissenschaften), pp. 173–90.
Bogner, A. (2005) *Grenzpolitik der Experten. Vom Umgang mit Ungewißheit und Nichtwissen in pränataler Diagnostik und Beratung* (Weilerswist: Velbrück Wissenschaft).
Bogner, A. and Menz, W. (2005) "Das theoriegenerierende Experteninterview. Erkenntnisinteresse, Wissensformen, Interaktion" in Bogner, A., Littig, B. and Menz, W. (eds) *Das Experteninterview – Theorie, Methode, Anwendung*, 2nd edn (Wiesbaden: Verlag für Sozialwissenschaften), pp. 33–70.
Bogner, A., Littig, B. and Menz, W. (eds) (2005) *Das Experteninterview – Theorie, Methode, Anwendung*, 2nd edn/1st edn (2002) (Wiesbaden: Verlag für Sozialwissenschaften).
Brandl, J. and Klinger, S. (2006) "Probleme des Feldzugangs zu Eliten" in *Österreichische Zeitschrift für Soziologie 31(1)*, 44–65.
Bude, H. (2004) "Elitewechsel. Deutsche Führungsgruppen zwischen 'Bonner' und 'Berliner Republik'" in Hitzler, R., Hornbostel, S. and Mohr, C. (eds) *Elitenmacht* (Wiesbaden: Verlag für Sozialwissenschaften), pp. 295–313.
Denzin, N. and Lincoln, Y. S. K. (eds) (2000) *Handbook of Qualitative Research*, 2nd edn (Thousand Oaks: Sage Publications).
Dexter, L. A. (2006/1969) *Elite and specialized interviewing, with a new introduction by Ware, A. and Sánchez-Jankowski, M.* (University of Essex, Colchester: ECPR Press – ECPR classics, 1st edn (1969) Evanston: Northwestern University Press).
Flick, U., Kardorff, E. v. and Steinke, I. (eds) (2003) *Qualitative Sozialforschung. Ein Handbuch*, 2nd edn (Reinbek bei Hamburg: Rowolth).
Glaser, B. G. and Strauss, A. M. (1998) *Grounded Theory. Strategien qualitativer Forschung*, (Göttingen: H. Huber).
Gläser, J. and Laudel, G. (2004) *Experteninterviews und qualitative Inhaltsanalyse* (Wiesbaden: Verlag für Sozialwissenschaften).
Goffman, E. (1969) *Wir alle spielen Theater* (München: Piper).
Gubrium, J. and Holstein, J. (eds) (2002) *Handbook of Interview Research: Context and Methodology* (Thousand Oaks, CA: Sage Publications).
Hartmann, M. (2007) *Eliten und Macht in Europa. Ein internationaler Vergleich* (Frankfurt am Main: Campus).
Helfferich, C. (2004) *Die Qualität qualitativer Daten. Manual für die Durchführung qualitativer Interviews* (Wiesbaden: Verlag für Sozialwissenschaften).
Hertz, R. and Imber, J. B. (eds) (1995) *Studying Elites Using Qualitative Methods* (Thousand Oaks, CA: Sage Publications).

Hitzler, R. (2004) "Wissen und Wesen des Experten. Ein Annäherungsversuch – Zur Einleitung" in Hitzler, R., Hornbostel, S. and Mohr, C. (eds) *Elitenmacht* (Wiesbaden: Verlag für Sozialwissenschaften), pp. 13–30.

Hitzler, R., Hornbostel, S. and Mohr, C. (eds) (2004) *Elitenmacht* (Wiesbaden: Verlag für Sozialwissenschaften).

Hitzler, R., Honer, A. and Maeder, C. (eds) (1994) *Expertenwissen. Die institutionalisierte Kompetenz zur Konstruktion von Wirklichkeit* (Opladen: Leske und Budrich).

Hornbostel, S. (2004) "Denn viele sind berufen, aber wenige sind auserwählt" in Hitzler, R., Hornbostel, S. and Mohr, C. (eds) *Elitenmacht* (Wiesbaden: Verlag für Sozialwissenschaften), pp. 9–21.

Hornby, A. S., Cowie, A.P. and Gimson, A.C. (eds) (1983) *Oxford Advanced Learner's Dictionary* (Oxford: Oxford University Press).

Imbusch, P. (2003) "Konjunkturen, Probleme und Desiderata sozialwissenschaftlicher Eliteforschung" in Hradil, S. and Imbusch, P. (eds) *Oberschichten – Eliten – Herrschende Klassen* (Opladen: Leske und Budrich), pp. 11–34.

Lilleker, D. G. (2003) "Interviewing the political elite: Navigating a potential minefield" in *Politics 2003*, 23(3), pp. 207–14.

Littig, B. (2005) "Interviews mit Experten und Expertinnen. Überlegungen aus geschlechtertheoretischer Sicht" in Bogner, A., Littig, B. and Menz, W. (eds) *Das Experteninterview – Theorie, Methode, Anwendung*, 2nd edn (Wiesbaden: Verlag für Sozialwissenschaften), pp. 191–206.

Littig, B. (2008) Rezension zu: Lewis A. Dexter (2006) "Elite and specialized interviewing" in *With a new introduction by A. Ware and M. Sánchez-Jankowski* [16 articles] (Forum Qualitative Sozialforschung/Forum: Qualitative Social Research), 9(1), Art. 5., http://www.qualitative-research.net/fqs-texte/1-08/08-1-5-d.htm.

Meuser, M. and Nagel, U. (1991) "ExpertInneninterviews – vielfach erprobt, wenig bedacht. Ein Beitrag zur qualitativen Methodendiskussion" in Garz, D. and Kraimer, K. (eds) *Qualitative empirische Sozialforschung: Konzepte, Methoden, Analysen* (Opladen: Westdeutscher Verlag), pp. 441–71.

Meuser, M. and Nagel, U. (2005) "ExpertInneninterviews – vielfach erprobt, wenig bedacht" in Bogner, A., Littig, B. and Menz, W. (eds) *Das Experteninterview – Theorie, Methode, Anwendung*, 2nd edn (Wiesbaden: Verlag für Sozialwissenschaften), pp. 71–93.

Mey, G., Puebla, C. C. A. and Faux, R. (eds) (2004) "Interviews" in *Forum Qualitative Sozialforschung* 5(3), Special Issue, http://www.qualitative-research.net/fqs/fqs-d/inhalt3-04-d.htm, date accessed in June 2008.

Mieg, H. A. and Brunner, B. (2004) "Experteninterviews. Reflexionen zur Methodologie und Erhebungstechnik" in *Schweizerische Zeitschrift für Soziologie 30*, 1999–2022.

Mieg, H. A. and Näf, M. (2006) *Experteninterviews in den Umwelt- und Planungswissenschaften. Eine Einführung und Anleitug* (Lengerich: Papst).

Moyser, G. and Wagstaffe, M. (eds) (1987) *Research Methods for Elite Studies* (London: Allen and Unwin).

Odendahl, T. and Shaw, A. M. (2002) "Interviewing elites" in Gubrium, J. and Holstein, J. (eds) *Handbook of Interview Research: Context and Methodology* (Thousand Oaks, CA: Sage Publications), pp. 299–316.

Richards, D. (1996) "Elite interviewing: Approaches and pitfalls" *Politics 16(3)*, 199–204.

Pfadenhauer, M. (2005) "Das Experteninterview – ein Gespräch zwischen Experte und Quasi-Experte" in Bogner, A., Littig, B. and Menz, W. (eds) *Das Experteninterview – Theorie, Methode, Anwendung*, 2nd edn (Wiesbaden: Verlag für Sozialwissenschaften), pp. 113–30.

Seldon, A. (1996) "Elite Interviews" in Brivati, B. and others (eds) *The Contemporary History Handbook* (Manchester: Manchester University Press), pp. 353–65.

Soeffner, H-G. (1989) "Anmerkungen zu gemeinsamen Standards standardisierter und nicht-standardisierter Verfahren in der Sozialforschung" in Soeffner, H-G. *Auslegung des Alltags – Der Alltag der Auslegung. Zur wissenssoziologischen Konzeption einer sozialwissenschaftlichen Hermeneutik* (Frankfurt am Main: Suhrkamp), pp. 51–65.

Sprondel, W. M. (1979) " 'Experte' und 'Laie': Zur Entwicklung von Typenbegriffen in der Wissenssoziologie" in Sprondel, W. and Grathoff, R. (eds) *Alfred Schütz und die Idee des Alltags in den Sozialwissenschaften* (Stuttgart: Enke), pp. 140–54.

Strauss, A. and Corbin, L. and J. (1996) *Grounded Theory: Grundlagen qualitativer Sozialforschung* (Weinheim: Beltz/PVU).

Vogel, B. (1995) " 'Wenn der Eisberg zu schmelzen beginnt...' – Einige Reflexionen über den Stellenwert und die Probleme des Experteninterviews in der Praxis der empirischen Sozialforschung" in Brinkmann, C., Deeke, A. and Völkel, B. (eds) *Experteninterviews in der Arbeitsmarktforschung. Diskussionsbeiträge zu methodischen Fragen und praktischen Erfahrungen* (Nürnberg: Landesarbeitsamt Nordbayern, Geschäftsstelle für Veröffentlichungen), pp. 73–83.

Wasner, B. (2004) *Eliten in Europa. Einführung in Theorien, Konzepte und Befunde* (Wiesbaden: Verlag für Sozialwissenschaften).

Welch, C., Marschan-Piekkari, R., Penttinen, H. and Tahvanainen, M. (2002) "Corporate elites as informants in qualitative international business research" in *International Business Research Review 11*, 611–28.

Willke, H. (1998) "Organisierte Wissensarbeit" in *Zeitschrift für Soziologie 27(3)*, 161–77.

Part II

Methodological Practice: Generating Data

5
On Interviewing "Good" and "Bad" Experts

Jochen Gläser and Grit Laudel

5.1 The "quality" of interviewees matters

The success of interview-based investigations considerably depends on the "quality" of the interviewees, that is on the extent to which they meet our expectations in the interview situation. We expect interviewees to understand which information we need, to provide this information in extensive, complete and detailed responses, and to adjust their communication to our steering of the conversation. We also hope to meet respondents which reflect on their own social situation and who are able to provide information about their perceptions, social relations and motives.[1]

These aspects of "quality" are particularly important in interviews that are intended to "mine" a respondent's special knowledge about a social situation or a social process. We consider all interviews that have this function to be "expert interviews." Thus, we define "experts" as people who possess special knowledge of a social phenomenon which the interviewer is interested in, and expert interviews as a specific method for collecting data about this social phenomenon. This conceptualization of the "expert interview" is based on the *expert role of the interviewee in the interview.* Thus understood, expert interviews are a distinct method that is applied in investigations of a specific type, namely investigations that reconstruct social situations or processes and use interviewees as a source of information (Gläser and Laudel, 2009, pp. 11–14). This understanding of "expert interviews" has been introduced to the German methodological discussion by Hopf (1993). In the Anglo-American literature, the distinction between the roles of interviewees as sources of information respectively objects of study is reflected by the concepts of "informants" and "respondents" (for an early reference to this distinction see Zelditch, 1962).

Another approach to "expert interviews" is their conceptualization as interviews with people who have an *expert role in the investigated social setting.* In that perspective, which dominates the wider literature as well as the contributions to this volume, experts are people who are set apart from other actors in the social setting under investigation by their specific knowledge and skills. Such superior knowledge is usually produced by designated processes of learning and training (for example vocational training). Members of professions such as physicians, lawyers, or architects are the best-known examples of "trained" experts. However, expert roles in social settings are not limited to the professions.

This understanding of experts ties the concept "expert interview" to a specific kind of respondents or informants but does not limit the forms or functions of interviews with them. It also focuses the methodological interest on the particularities of an interview that result from the expert status of the interviewee in the investigated field. Thus understood, the expert interview is not a specific method of data collection but includes all forms of qualitative interviews that are conducted with experts. In our opinion, this is the reason why there is no specific methodological discussion of the expert interview as a method of data collection, as has been noted by Bogner and Menz (Bogner and Menz, 2005, pp. 11–16).

Since the roles of "interviewees as experts" and "experts as interviewees" are constructed in different social situations (the interview respectively the investigated social settings), the two definitions of expert interviews are not disjunct (Figure 5.1). In many social science investigations only one of the roles is relevant. The left (white) area in Figure 5.1 represents investigations in which interviews are aimed at the reconstruction of social processes and situations but are conducted with people who don't have an expert role in the field. For example, interviews about health care could be conducted not only with physicians but also with patients. The latter don't have an acknowledged expert role in health care but possess special knowledge about the way health organizations handle patients and thus would be interviewed as experts for this aspect of the investigation. The right (black) area stands for interviews with people who have an expert role in the investigated social field but who are not interviewed as sources of information about social processes in which they participate. An example of this would be a study of biographical self-representations of physicians, where the reflection of social processes by physicians rather than the processes themselves are the subject matter of the investigation. In the middle (grey area) we find the area of overlap between the two definitions. The overlap refers to interviews with "experts in the field" who serve as sources of information about a part of the social reality.

For this specific group of interviews an additional aspect of the "quality" of interviewees becomes important. If we use "experts in the field" as sources of information, our interviews depend not only on their performance in their role as interviewees but also on their "quality" in their expert role in the field. We must ask ourselves whether we receive the same information about medical treatments from good and bad physicians, the same information about baking from good and bad bakers, and the same information about competitive sports from world champions and average athletes.

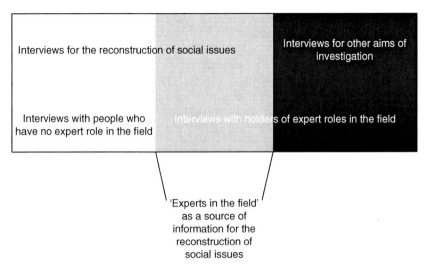

Figure 5.1 Area of overlap of the two definitions of expert interviews
Source: Gläser and Laudel, this volume.

This problem has not yet explicitly been dealt with in the literature even though it might be implicit to discussions about interview responses. We address it in this chapter by using examples from our own empirical investigations, in which we must compare and synthesize statements of researchers. In doing so, we face the above-described quality problem: Do "good" researchers describe their situations in other ways than "bad" ones? What does it mean that certain issues are described in the same way by good and by bad researchers? How can we find out how "good" our informants are in their researcher roles?

5.2 "Good" and "bad" researchers as information sources of science studies

There can be little doubt that researchers are "experts in the field." It also is no secret that the abilities of researchers differ and that the quality differences between very good ("excellent") and medium or even bad researchers are huge. Nevertheless, science studies hardly ever took the abilities of the investigated researchers into account. The abilities of researchers who act as informants in qualitative investigations have not been a topic of methodological reflection at all. This may be due to the fact that outsiders are hardly able to judge the abilities of a researcher. Indeed, there are only very few researchers who are regarded as outstanding and are well-known outside science, such as Nobel price winners and – to a lesser extent – members of the learned academies. Below this threshold of visibility the quality of researchers remains hidden in the implicit judgements of their scientific communities.

Two kinds of empirical science studies can be distinguished according to their handling of the quality problem. Most studies ignore the problem of quality differences between respondents. The first interview-based investigations are classical examples of this neglect (for example Hagstrom, 1965, Crane, 1972). The subsequent ethnographic studies also ignored the "quality" of the observed researchers and possible influences of this aspect on the outcomes of observations (Knorr-Cetina, 1984, Lynch, 1985, Latour and Woolgar, 1986 [1979]). This is surprising because we cannot a priori assume that the observed processes of the social construction of knowledge is performed the same way by "good" and "bad" researchers. The laboratory studies are implicitly based on this very assumption because they do not include the quality as intervening factor – in spite of the obvious importance of researchers' abilities to the observed scientists. The quality discourse among the observed scientists was reported (Latour and Woolgar, 1986 [1979], pp. 163–65) but the quality problem neither influenced the empirical strategy of laboratory studies nor their interpretation. Since the constructivist tradition – which constitutes the mainstream of the sociology of science since the 1980s – still disregards the quality of the makers of scientific knowledge, we still don't know for sure whether good researchers construct knowledge differently from bad ones.

A second group of studies chose research performance as its topic and made the performance levels (productivity, creativity) of researchers the dependent variable of their investigations. The aim of these studies was to identify influences on the productivity and the quality of scientific work. While investigating the influence of organizational research conditions on the productivity of scientists, Pelz and Andrews included the quality – measured by the number of publications – as a dependent variable (Pelz und Andrews, 1966). These kinds of studies were taken up later in the context of investigating scientific excellence and scientific creativity (Jackson and Rushton, 1987, Zuckerman and Cole, 1994). In her study of Nobel Prize winners, Zuckerman did not encounter the problem of quality differences because the study was limited to a homogeneous group of a visible elite (Zuckerman, 1977). Thus, she did not address quality differences in her methodological reflections but instead wrote about the specifics of interviews with members of the elite (Zuckerman, 1972).

With the development of the *Science Citation Index* it became possible to use a more sophisticated measure of quality, namely the frequency with which publications are cited by other scientists. This measure was first introduced by Cole and Cole who started to treat quality not only as a dependent but also as an independent or intervening variable (Cole and Cole, 1967, Cole, 1970, Cole and Cole, 1972). Their use of citations created a new research tradition within bibliometrics for which the measurement of the quality of researchers, organizations and national science systems is an important topic. Shortly thereafter, research policy became interested and began to generate an ever-increasing demand for performance measurements. Today these measurements also utilise other than bibliometric indicators, particularly the amount of external research funding. All these indicator measures are somewhat problematic, only work in some research fields, and are of questionable validity at the level that is of interest here, namely that of the individual researcher (Laudel, 2005, Gläser and Laudel, 2007a).

This short overview demonstrates that science studies have either ignored the varying performance levels of researchers or turned them into the subject matter of their investigations. The methodological question about different responses from "good" and "bad" researchers and the consequences of such differences for studies that are based on interviews with researchers has not yet been asked.

5.3 The dependence of data on the performance levels of researchers

5.3.1 Different phenomena, different perceptions

In our own research we are interested in the influence of institutional and institutionally produced conditions of research on the content of knowledge production. We use qualitative interviews with researchers and research managers as the main method of data collection. We ask researchers about their research projects (the problems they are working on, the methods and objects they use, their collaborations, and so on) and about the specific resource requirements of these projects. Another set of questions focuses on the conditions of research, particularly the available time for research, access to resources and possible influence of the organizational environment on the content of research. From the responses to these questions we reconstruct the changes in the content of research that result from the adaptation of topics, objects, methods and collaborations to the conditions of work.

We had to learn that in our investigations talking to "good" or "bad" researchers makes a difference. The "quality" of the interviewees influences our investigations at two levels. Firstly, the situations of "good" and "bad" researchers may differ, for example with regard to the availability of external funding, the workload, or the status of the interviewees in their organization. In this case, the researchers experience *different phenomena*. Secondly, it is possible that "good" and "bad" researchers provide *different descriptions of the experienced phenomena* because their perceptions or communication behaviour differ. If we combine these two variations we can construct four variants of communication in the interview (Table 5.1).

Table 5.1　Quality-dependent communication situations in interviews with researchers

| | | Descriptions of the phenomena | |
		Same	Different
Phenomena	Same	(False) implicit premise of science studies	Appears as contradiction in the responses. Main problem: identifying the "real" situation
	Different	Not visible in the responses. Main problem: Recognising that a difference exists	Most common situation. Main problem: Recognizing how the data are influenced by quality differences

The left upper cell of the table describes the implicit premise of science studies, namely that all responses are equal in both dimensions. Of course, nobody has ever said that this is actually the case. However, disregarding the quality problem in interview-based and ethnographic studies means that data collection and analysis is in fact based on this presumption.

The common situation in science studies is the direct opposite of this presumption. It is situated in the right lower cell of the table, indicating that the "good" and the "bad" researchers experience different things and provide descriptions of their experiences that are influenced by their "quality." For example, a historian explained during the interview that he can freely choose his topics because the publishers take everything that he writes. In contrast, another historian described that his book project has been rejected by several publishers, and therefore he will now change the topic of his research. The publishers neither requested reviews about the book project from peers nor did they tell him the reasons for the rejections. He assumed that the topic was regarded as not profitable. In the course of the ethnographic observation both historians were interviewed. We found a clear quality difference between the two historians, which let us assume that the insufficient quality of the book project was the reason for the repeated rejections and that the reference to the topic as reason was merely a rationalization of the respondent. However, the ethnographic observation also showed that publishers indeed reject books for thematic reasons. Given that the two historians worked in two entirely different areas, a mix of different experiences and quality differences occurred that was difficult to untangle.

In the "standard case," the complexity of an analysis is dramatically increased because two dimensions must be added in the interpretation of interview statements. We avoid this case in our following demonstration of the problem because its discussion would require a large amount of background knowledge that cannot be provided in a book chapter. Instead, we use the two "pure" cases that only vary in one of the two dimensions. In our experience the pure cases are rare – it does not often happen that "good" and "bad" researchers give identical descriptions of different phenomena or different descriptions of the same phenomena. However, in our current investigation we conducted enough interviews to obtain these kinds of responses. We use them in order to demonstrate how difficult the standard situation is. It is the right lower cell of the table that describes the real challenge because in most situations we are confronted by different descriptions that are likely to point to different phenomena. It is up to us to determine how the performance levels of interviewees influences their descriptions.

5.3.2 Identical descriptions of different phenomena

Our interviews contained several questions that targeted adaptations of the research content to the resource and institutional conditions of research.[2] We intentionally phrased these questions in an indirect and open way in order to avoid an orientating influence on the interviewee. One of the questions was: "Are there research topics that you would like to work on but can't?" The answers to this question varied considerably. The most frequent answer was yes, there are indeed research problems that would be nice to work on but there is not sufficient time. Other interviewees mentioned their resource base as limiting factor. A third group did not feel any restrictions. Among those were two historians who worked at the same university. One of them is a professor who has published numerous books that are read and cited beyond Australia. He regularly acquires external research funding and is a member of the Australian Academy of the Humanities. The other historian obtained his doctoral degree six years ago, but has neither published his PhD thesis nor any other substantial research result. He has never acquired external research funding and was unable to describe research projects of his own even after being repeatedly asked in different phases of the interview. Who is who?

Interviewer: And are there research topics that you are interested in but can't work on?

Historian 1: No. I've been very lucky.

Historian 2: ... that I'm interested in but I can't work on? No. No, I think there is still ample freedom to pursue that curiosity driven approach. If I was to be seized with a particular idea, the resources are here, all the resources are available [...], because I think with historical research, the demands, the cost issues, are relatively modest. It's really my own time, photocopies, inter-library loans and travel. Put all those together and that's really all you need for historical research. So, for that reason, I think most projects that I would be interested in pursuing, are always going to have fairly modest resource implications, and that's definitely no real reason why I couldn't pursue them.

Both interviewees perceive a situation, which does not limit their research financially, institutionally or in any other way. In both cases the aspiration levels concerning the conditions of research correspond to the actual conditions of research. However, the satisfaction of both interviewees is situated at significantly different levels. One of the interviewees has sufficient time and resources for the projects he wants to conduct (not the least because he can use the external funding to reduce his teaching load), while the other one doesn't conduct projects and therefore also perceived a correspondence between his interests and his conditions of work. The difference between a situation with sufficient external funding and a situation in which even the recurrent funding is only intermittent and based on internal grant proposals is not visible in the two assessments of the respective situations.

Researchers from other disciplines also gave near-identical answers that resulted from different aspiration levels. One of the two mathematicians and one of the two geologists rarely publish, are hardly cited, don't acquire external grants and don't have a clear research programme, while the other two publish a lot, are cited above average, continuously get grants and pursue long-term research programmes.

> *Interviewer*: Now, are there any research topics that you are interested in but can't work on?
>
> *Mathematician 1*: Not really, not really at all. I mean I'd like to have, I'm hindered in the financial maths to some extent by not having someone to talk to. Well, there is one other person here that does work in it but he works on it from a different angle so, in some respects I would like to do more in financial maths, but on the other hand I'd like to do more in symmetries because that's what I really like to do. But, no, I don't think that there's an area that I can think of that I really want to do.
>
> *Mathematician 2*: I don't think so. No, I feel at the moment I have quite a few research topics and I'm not looking for – I'm not actively looking for more. I mean, often research projects just arise naturally. You just get into them because you're looking at some problem that leads into something else. So I don't sort of look to start a project from scratch. It always comes from another source. No, I just follow what happens.
>
> *Geologist 1*: I guess, at the moment it's sufficient to keep me going at this stage. I think I've got sufficient projects to keep me occupied at this stage. So I'm not really thinking about other opportunities.
>
> *Geologist 2*: No, not really, I mean everything I am interested in…I can maintain this balance between the applied and pure aspects enough to keep me going now.

We found yet another example of identical descriptions of different phenomena in the self-evaluations of research performance that was sometimes given by the interviewees. The questions about the performance expectations of universities and evaluations of research performance inspired two political scientists at the same university to reflect on how they meet the expectations of their university. One of the two publishes irregularly (with interruptions of up to four years). His only journal publications are book reviews. The other publishes regularly, writes articles in refereed journals, and is internationally visible.

> *Interviewer*: So, my last question about the evaluations would be: What are the consequences of these evaluations for you?
>
> *Political Scientist 1*: In terms of, obviously, promotion. It's whether you get promoted or not. In terms of professional development – *I mean, I am not highly productive but I produce on a reasonably regular basis*. I've never been in a situation where someone said, you haven't produced anything and you're going to. I can always say I'm in the middle of a book now and it's going to come out next year or the year after. So I've never been in a position where anyone's questioned me so I don't know on what basis they would.
>
> *Interviewer*: Are there also specific special expectations in terms of the quality of your research from the University or School?
>
> *Political Scientist 2*: Well, no there is always some talk I guess again, [...] As far as I know there is nothing on that type of functions. And it is clearly that for most people in all universities never mind in [our university], where it's the number of publications that seems to matter more than quality. And I don't see any staff pressure counteracting that. *I don't publish very much*. Even though I keep count of my rate, which is now slowing down because of too much teaching. I don't think I feel affected by any pressures either way. I am aware of the pressures, but only a small number of us can do it.

The two passages in italics highlight the problem: without additional data about the publication activities of respondents we would consider both interviewees as not being particularly productive and as equally productive. We would even consider the first (*"I produce on a resonably regular basis"*) as the more productive and the second as less productive. But it is exactly the other way around. Now let us imagine the many descriptions of this kind that we cannot check independently of the interview...

5.3.3 Different descriptions of identical phenomena

We encountered the other of our pure cases in description of evaluations, that is of situations in which the university assessed the quality of its academics and based decisions on these assessments. Among these evaluations, those that were conducted in the contexts of internal research funding and promotions had the strongest influence on the situation of researchers. The evaluations for promotions are based on a university-wide standard procedure that is only slightly modified in order to accommodate differences between disciplines. The following example includes two historians from the same university who faced the same procedure and evaluation criteria when it came to promotions. From the quotations it is clear which interviewee is "good" and which is "bad." It is far less clear that they both describe the same procedure.

Interviewee: And is this the only occasion when your research is evaluated? When you apply for internal grants?

Historian 1: No it's evaluated if I was to submit an application for study leave, which I have done, and to submit an application for promotion. And I prepared an application under the previous Dean back in 2000 and the then Dean made it quite clear even before I submitted the application that she wasn't going to support it because the first thing she said to me, I had a meeting with her, was my research profile is not very good.

Interviewer: And since then you didn't try again to ...?

Historian 1: I revised my application and again got as far as having a meeting with the Dean last year but it was indicated that I would be ... And my Head of School has indicated to me that I can be sure of being successful in my application for promotion, this is only to Lecturer C, once I submit the book manuscript. So in other words he's telling me that I will only be successful in promotion from a Lecturer B to a Lecturer C if I publish the book, which to my mind is ... We have people in the faculty and elsewhere who've been promoted to Associate Professor and we've had people who've been appointed as Professor who don't even have a book and yet I've been told as a condition of my application for promotion being successful that I have to have submitted a book manuscript which seems to me unfair.

Interviewer: And, how does the university evaluate your research?

Historian 2: Okay. Well, promotions would be the major mechanism. [...] Yes, so on the individual level it's promotion and career development interviews.

Interviewer: What are the consequences of these evaluations for you?

Historian 2: Well, in my case, because I'm quite productive, it's usually good in the sense of getting promoted. But at present there haven't been negative consequences. But if, say, within the Faculty, people are not being very productive, then they're given mentoring, and I've done that as well. You engage with people and you advise them on what they could do to get together a great application or what kinds of publication strategies they need to have.

Both descriptions refer to the same promotion procedure. Academics write an application in which they describe their achievements in teaching, research, and academic administration. They discuss this application with their supervisors (first with the head of school and thereafter with the dean of their faculty), who advise them on the content of the application and on their chances of success. When the application is moving up the hierarchy, each supervisor adds their comments. The final decision is made by a university committee. If the supervisors believe the application would be unsuccessful they advise academics to withdraw it. Such a withdrawal is in the interest of both the applicant and their supervisor. Academics whose application is rejected must wait several years before they can apply again, while postponing an application that has little chance of success enables another application with better chances in the following year. A weak application that goes ahead also creates a dilemma for the supervisors. If they support it, they lose their credibility at the higher levels of the hierarchy. If they don't support it they lose their credibility with the applicant.

The application procedure is strictly regulated. The rules are made publicly available and are strictly followed. Both interviewees we quoted above wrote their applications and had consultations in which they received advice. However, their perceptions of the process are quite different. One interviewee mentions his promotions only casually and gives the impression that they were not problematic. For him, the stronger and more present experience is that of his involvement as a mentor, a role, which has been introduced to support weak applicants. The other interviewee applied with achievements that were considered as insufficient by two deans and the head of school. The supervisors advised against an application. The applicant regarded this as an unfair interpretation of performance criteria, a rather unlikely interpretation given the strict rules and the consistent judgment by the two deans and the head of school. However, it is interesting to note that something that is interpreted by the "bad" applicant as an unfair intervention that prevented the promotion is of no personal concern to the "good" applicant, who hardly even mentions it. The different performance levels of the two interviewees have a massive impact on their perceptions and descriptions of what is essentially the same phenomenon, namely the promotion procedure. This would not be a problem if only their perceptions would matter for the investigation. However, we also need to know the promotion procedure. While in this particular case the "true" procedure could be established by triangulation from many different sources, it is again easy to imagine situations where this would be impossible, and quality-dependent descriptions were the only information about a phenomenon.

5.3.4   Implications for the investigation

In our comments on the quotations from interviews we have already hinted at their different informational yield for our project. Now we would like to systematize these consequences of the quality problem. The differences in the performance levels of our respondents shaped their communication about two aspects of their work that were central to our investigation. The first aspect is a respondent's *content of work*. When we ask for an explanation of the respondent's research problem, reasons for the selection of specific research objects and methods, or other information about the content of research, "bad" researchers provide information that is different from that provided by "good" researchers. This information about the content of work is crucial for our investigation because the content of work shapes the resource demand. "Good" researchers formulate more challenging research problems, and their assessment of strategic aspects of their research such as the solvability of problems or the applicability of methods to their problems differs from assessments of the same aspects by "bad" researchers. These strategic choices and assessments produce the specific resource requirements of the respondent's research, which constituted one of the central variables of our investigation. This is why the results of our study partly depend on what the biochemists tell us about *their* biochemistry, geologists about *their* geology and political scientists about *their* political science.[3]

In addition to the specific information about the respondents' own research the interview also yields general information about the characteristic epistemic practices of their research field. Some characteristics of fields (for example the typical duration of research processes, specific uncertainties or heterogeneity of the used knowledge claims) are important intervening variables in our investigation because they explain the varying implications of uniform resource allocation mechanisms in different research fields. This is why we must extract such field-specific factors from the statements of all respondents belonging to the same field. A description of field-specific practices must be synthesized from statements by researchers of varying performance levels.

This "learning from the field," that is the use of experts as a source of information about characteristics of the content of work, occurs in many science studies projects and probably in many other studies that are based on expert interviews. It is always a means to an end because the knowledge about work processes of experts is needed to answer sociological questions. This is why a second aspect of our respondents' work – the *conditions of work* under which the research was conducted – was more important to us than the content of research, and why most of our examples refer to these conditions. The performance levels of respondents strongly affected the data about conditions of work. Our examples illustrated that

- the statement "my research is not constrained by limitations to my access to resources" may reflect two completely different situations, namely one of a researcher whose aspiration level is so low that it can be met by any resource base, or one of a researcher who is so "good" that they receive all the resources they ask for; and that

- the perception of organizational routines largely depends on the performance levels of respondents, that is that largely identical routines may be differently perceived by "good" and "bad" researchers.

For these reasons we could not simply extract general, university-specific or faculty-specific conditions or routines but also had to include the performance levels of interviewees in our interpretation. We could not avoid this problem by relying on documents describing the formal bureaucratic routines because the actual use of these routines in everyday university life (which mediates the influence of institutions on the content of research) inevitably deviates from the formal prescriptions in documents.

If we tentatively generalize our experiences we find that quality differences between experts interfere with two essential tasks of expert interviews:

(1) If we need to learn something about the content of an interviewee's work, interviews with "good" experts provide information about this work that is different from that provided by "bad" experts.
(2) If we need to learn something about the interviewee's conditions of work we obtain quality-affected information for two reasons. Firstly "good" experts have higher aspiration levels and higher standards against which conditions of work are assessed. Secondly, interventions by the environment are dealt with in different ways by respondents depending on their performance levels, and are thus different for "good" and "bad" experts.

Investigations that rely on at least one of these kinds of information have to face the quality problem.

5.4   Quality differences as a methodological problem of expert interviews and their analysis

5.4.1   How do we assess experts?

Whenever the performance levels of the expert affects their responses, we must know these performancel levels and take them into account when interpreting statements. However, a quality assessment of experts seems to be an impossible task. After all, we interview experts for the very reason of accessing their special knowledge, that is knowledge we don't possess. How could we possibly assess how much of this knowledge they have and how well they are able to use it? Apparently there are only few exceptions to this dilemma. Competitive athletes, for example, are subject to a public performance assessment that is comprehensible outside their group because they compete against each other.

On first glance our own task – to assess the quality of researchers – puts us in a quite comfortable position, too. The demands of science policy and management have pushed the development of evaluation methods, which by now have widely diffused throughout public science systems. Unfortunately, this does not make our task much easier. Science studies agree that ultimately only researchers' peers are able to judge the quality of their work, and that even this peer review may get it wrong. "Objective" indicators that can be applied by outside observers because they abstract from the content of research only offer partial insights into the quality of research, and evaluate past rather than current performance. Therefore, they can only be used as additional information in a peer review. Moreover, we have already pointed out that quantitative indicators cannot be regarded as reliable at the individual level that we are interested in.

The limited opportunities of performance measurement are highlighted when we ask which aspect of quality we actually intend to measure. Is it the current *performance* of the investigated researchers or their *ability* to perform? In our investigation we came across two groups of interviewees for which this difference affected assessments. The careers of some scientists were not yet long enough to enable conclusions about extraordinary research abilities although there were some indications of that. The opposite case occurred, too. Researchers who had made outstanding contributions in the past had ceased to do so at the time of the interview because they didn't receive external funding anymore, had moved away from the mainstream of their field, or were close to retirement and didn't want to start new projects. In both cases it is likely that the scientific abilities of the interviewee exceed the level suggested by the current performance. For our purposes, a categorization according to abilities is more important than one according to the current research performance. However, the opportunities to assess abilities are even more limited when current performance is likely to offer a distorted picture.

Given the numerous problems of performance measurement in science, which we have dicscussed in our own publications, we had to be extremely careful in our categorization of researchers. We used as many indicators as possible, supplemented them with "independent" information from the interviews, and compared the researchers of one discipline to each other.

Prior to the interview we downloaded information about research interests and projects, indicators of peer esteem such as prizes for research or memberships of learned academies, publications, citations and external grant acquisition from internet pages, the Web of Science, and other publication databases. All these indicators are discipline-specific (for example, citation analyses are extremely problematic in the social sciences and the humanities) and can only be interpreted by taking the context into account.

In fields with a high degree of collaboration it is not always easy to ascribe achievements to a specific researcher. Researchers may profit from being a member of a strong group and participate in publications and grant acquisitions without making outstanding contributions themselves. We addressed this problem by checking indicators for all co-authors of highly cited publications and of co-applicants for grants.

This information was used for preparing the interviews. The preparation already included a preliminary assessment of performance levels and the selection of an appropriate strategy for handling the quality problem in the interview. We could not rule out that research was a sensitive topic for those interviewees whose performance levels were considerably lower than those of their colleagues. This is why we applied a specific strategy when interviewing academics with apparently sparse research records. We didn't start with questions about research, which would have presumed that the interviewee conducts research as everybody else, but with questions about teaching. In this initial conversation, we established the extent to which the interviewee actually conducts research, and steered the interview towards research activities depending on that information.

Our interviews contributed to the assessment of quality because our question about the research biography, conditions of research and future research plans touched a trait of a researcher that is closely linked to quality. We obtained clear indications concerning the *aspiration level* of the interviewed researchers, that is their standards concerning their own work, their collaborators, other colleagues, and their conditions of research. Thus, the descriptions of the research and conditions of work provided in the interview are important indicators of quality themselves. Another indicator we could use is the *consistency of the research topics*. Do interviewees pursue a consistent research programme, or are they merely responding to external stimuli such as demands by collaborator or supervisors? Does the interviewee independently conduct research at all?

After the interview we refined the information about our indicators and collected additional information from the internet and publication databases. Using the indicators and information from the interviews, we compared the researchers of each discipline with each other and constructed three groups: a high-level group (16 researchers across all disciplines), a medium-level group (79) and a group of academics who hardly conduct any research (23). In order to highlight the borderline cases whose classification was most difficult, we specifically identified those academics in the medium-level group who were close to either the top or the inactive groups. We conducted the categorization together (and largely achieved agreement). The advantage of this collaborative categorization exercise is the necessity to verbalize impressions from the interview (which only one of us had prepared and conducted). These impressions could thus be discussed in the light of the other information that was gathered independently of the interview.

5.4.2   How do we include the "quality" of our experts into the data analysis?

After we got an idea which of our interviewees are "good," "average" or "inactive" researchers, we coded this categorization in the file names of the interview transcripts, which means that this information appears in the source tag of each interview statement that was used in the analysis.

Always knowing how "good" a source/expert is helps but doesn't solve the problem. Being well aware of the problem that the interpretation of the data can never be fully described, we will nevertheless try to demonstrate how we used the information about quality in our analysis. We already mentioned the two possible ways of using the quality information in our short overview of the treatment of research quality by science studies. Firstly, knowledge about the quality of the source must be used for the interpretation of the data. Secondly, in our investigation we also need to know whether the adaptive behaviour of "good" researchers differs from that of "bad" ones. Thus, we must also include the performance level of a researcher as a subject of the investigation.

The way in which we take into account the performance levels of respondents in the interpretation of the data can only partly be made explicit. We are sure that we read interviews and interpret data "differently" because we have an opinion about the performance levels of the sources. This is also a danger for the interpretation if a prejudice against a group occurs. We counteracted these influences by conducting the first step of the qualitative content analysis – the extraction of raw data – prior to determining and coding performance levels. In the subsequent analysis, we used a "check list" and determined whether

- information is shaped by the 'aspiration level' of the interviewee (in our case: for example if above or below average expectations concerning research performance and conditions of work may have influenced a statement);
- a specific content of work that is due to specific performance levels might have shaped the information (in our case: for example if above or below average research performance manifests itself for example in the number of parallel projects a researcher works on or in the continuity of the respondent's publication record),
- differences between performance levels are accompanied by different self-images and valuations (in our case: for example whether different research performance is accompanied by varying assessments of tasks in teaching); and
- whether an interviewee's performance level affects reported causalities (in our case: for example whether unfavourable research conditions are used in a specific way to explain lower research performance).

These questions are particularly important when we find contradictions in the data or when information that is central to the investigation only stems from few sources. An identification of possible influences of performance levels does of course not mean that we discard the data as "unreliable." We are just in a better position to decide the role we assign a certain piece of information in the construction of our explanation. The extent to which critical aspects of our typologies, generalizations and explanations could be influenced by performance levels of the sources becomes visible.

Information about performance levels of respondents was not only used for the interpretation of data but also in a second, more direct way. In our investigation, the quality of the researchers is also an intervening variable. If researchers adapt the content of their research to institutional conditions then we must find out whether the adaptive behaviour of "good" researchers is different from that of "bad" ones. We achieve this by constructing categories of performance levels and separately investigating the adaptative behaviour for each category. An example of that strategy is Grit Laudel's comparative study of conditions for external fund acquisition and their impact on the content of research (Laudel, 2006a, 2006b). Studies of hindering conditions of research frequently face the objection that the complaints of researchers are just the "rationalizations of the loosers," that is that "bad" researchers use unfavourable research conditions as an excuse for performing badly rather than admitting their insufficient abilities. The comparative study of external fund acquisition of experimental physicists in Germany and Australia took this argument into account by distinguishing two performance levels ("top" and "other") and two categories of the scientists' resource bases ("rich" and "other"). A cross-comparison of the four groups showed that all four fields were populated (Table 5.2). There are the expected concentrations in the lower right cells, which indicate that external fund acquisition indeed is related to the performance level of a researcher. The existence of "top other" and "other rich" scientists shows, however, that quality is neither necessary nor sufficient for a good external fund acquisition. This already puts the "rationalization argument" on doubt. Additionally, an analysis of adaptation strategies

Table 5.2 Differentiation of experimental physicists in Australia and Germany according to their research performance and acquisition of external funds

| | Amount of external funding | | | |
| | Germany | | Australia | |
	"Rich"	"Other"	"Rich"	"Other"
"Top" scientists	8	7	3	4
"Other" scientists	7	23	4	10

Soure: Based on Laudel, 2006b, p. 382.

showed their occurence across all performance levels as a reaction to insufficient resource bases. Thus, the "rationalization argument" could be refuted.

The second example is taken from our current investigation that provided the material for this article. During a preliminary analysis of the interviews we discovered that the adaptative behaviour of "good" and "bad" researchers to the conditions of research funding differed. There is a small group of "top" researchers who

- work on a comparatively broad range of research topics and thus *could* adapt to political demands by selecting politically desired (which means in Australia application-oriented) topics but
- *don't have to* surrender to this pressure because they receive the external funding for their favourite projects even if these projects do not correspond to the political orientations of the research landscape (their high performance being the substitute for "thematic correctness").

In the case of these researchers two things come together: a high thematic flexibility and a low pressure to adapt. At the other end of the spectrum are researchers who experience a high adaptation pressure because their current research projects are not successful. However, these researchers are not able to change their research in the required way because their low performance levels also mean that they cannot apply their accumulated knowledge to a new topic.

This observation made us formulate a hypothesis about the relationship between performance levels and adaptative behaviour (Figure 5.2).

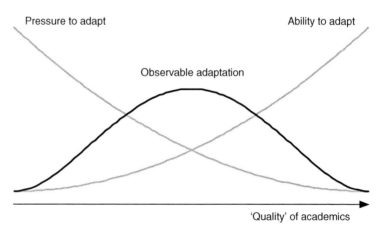

Figure 5.2 Relationship between performance levels and the adaptation of the research content

Source: Gläser and Laudel 2007b.

Adaptations to institutionalized expectations concerning the content of research occur neither at the top level (because these academics perceive little pressure), nor at the weakest performance level (because these academics are not able to make the necessary changes of direction even under strong pressure). The institutionalized pressure to adapt has its main impact at the medium level of academics who are "not good enough" to protect themselves from pressure through "excellence" but good enough to respond to this pressure with changes to the content of their research.

5.5 Concluding remarks

To what extent can our considerations about the role of the quality of experts be generalized? We believe that the problem of "quality-dependent" data in expert interviews affects many investigations because the defining property of an expert – specific knowledge and abilities – varies between experts. We therefore regard it as necessary to consider possible influences of quality differences between experts at the beginning of an investigation. If data may be affected, appropriate strategies for the selection of experts, the conduct of interviews and the data analysis must be developed.

Depending on the aim of a study, the performance levels of experts can also play a role beyond the "area of overlap" identified in the introduction. We might for example be interested to know whether biographical self-represenations of "good" physicians are different from those of "bad" ones. In this case, the quality is explicitly part of the subject matter of the investigation and must be dealt with. Quality differences occur as a "hidden" methodological problem only in studies where "experts in the field" are sources of information about social situations and processes they observed.

Although the techniques of collecting information vary with the research problems and the experts involved, the steps we outlined can presumably be generalized. The main point is to decide early whether the quality of experts could be a problem and whether the strategy of interviewing must be adapted. This includes the decision about using the interviews for collecting data on indicators of quality such as the respondent's aspiration level concerning their own work and conditions of work. With regard to the data analysis a decision must be made whether the quality of experts could have influenced the information they provided. If this is the case, the strategy of data analysis must be adapted accordingly. Our questions about the aspiration levels, work load, self-image, assessments, and rationalizations seem to be applicable beyond interviews with researchers.

Researchers are an interesting "show-and-tell piece" because quality differences between them are a generally recognized and in part publicly negotiated fact, and because quality-relevant information is publicly available. In other investigations that are based on expert interviews it may be far more difficult or even impossible to get "objective" information (that is information that is independent from the interviewer's judgement) about the "quality" of experts. As is the case with all methodological problems in social research, the first necessary step is to emphasize the problem and to accept its relevance for the investigation. It was our aim to initiate this step.

Notes

1. See for those aspects of the interview situation for example Dean and Whyte (1958), Becker and Geer (1970), Bernard and others (1984), Richards (1996), Bernard (2002, pp. 187–91), as well as Gläser and Laudel (2009, pp. 178–82).
2. A description of our project and the empirical methods can be found in Gläser and Laudel (2007b).
3. Unfortunately, it is nearly impossible to find out how information on the content of research is influenced by the performance levels of the interviewees because each research process is unique. Differently from bakers, physicians or managers whose work is repetitive to a large extent, researchers aim at producing new knowledge, which makes each research process unique. Consequently, there is no solid base for a comparison of research processes. Even in the case of collaborative research processes whose participants could all be interviewed, the comparison is hindered by the unique disciplinary perspective of each collaborator. PhD students are the only exception to this "problem of uniqueness" because their supervisor is able to assess the research process as well as the researcher.

Further readings

Bernard, H. R., Killworth, P., Kronenfeld, D. and Sailer, L. (1984) "The Problem of Informant Accuracy: The Validity of Retrospective Data" in *Annual Review of Anthropology 13*, 495–517.

Dean, J. P. and Foote Whyte, W. (1958) "How Do You Know If the Informant is Telling the Truth" in *Human Organization 17*, 34–9.

Laudel, G. (2006) "The 'quality myth': Promoting and hindering conditions for acquiring research funds" in *Higher Education 52*, 375–403.

References

Becker, H. S. and Geer, B. (1970) "Participant Observation and Interviewing: A Comparison" in Filstead, W. J. (ed.) *Qualitative Methodology: Firsthand Involvement with the Social World* (Chicago: Markham Publishing), pp. 133–42.

Bernard, H. R. (2002) *Research Methods in Anthropology: Qualitative and Quantitative Approaches* (Walnut Creek: Altamira Press).

Bernard, H. R., Killworth, P., Kronenfeld, D. and Sailer, L. (1984) "The Problem of Informant Accuracy: The Validity of Retrospective Data" in *Annual Review of Anthropology*, Vol. 13, 495–517.

Bogner, A. and Menz, W. (2005) "Expertenwissen und Forschungspraxis: Die modernisierungstheoretische und die methodische Debatte um die Experten. Zur Einführung in ein unübersichtliches Problemfeld" in Bogner, A., Littig, B. and Menz, W. (eds) *Das Experteninterview – Theorie, Methode, Anwendung*, 2nd edn (Wiesbaden: Verlag für Sozialwissenschaften), pp. 7–30.

Cole, J. R. and Cole, S. (1972) *The Ortega Hypothesis*, Science 178, pp. 368–75.

Cole, J. R. and Cole, S. (1967) "Scientific Output and Recognition, a Study in the Operation of the Reward System in Science" in *American Sociological Review 32*, 377–90.

Cole, S. (1970) "Professional Standing and the Reception of Scientific Discoveries" in *American Journal of Sociology 76*, 286–306.

D. Crane (1972) *Invisible Colleges: Diffusion of Knowledge in Scientific Communities* (Chicago: University of Chicago Press).

Dean, J. P. and Whyte, W. F. (1958) "How Do You Know If the Informant is Telling the Truth" in *Human Organization 17*, 34–9.

Gläser, J. and Laudel, G. (2009) *Experteninterviews und qualitative Inhaltsanalyse als Instrumente rekonstruierender Untersuchungen*, 3rd edn (Wiesbaden: Verlag für Sozialwissenschaften).

Gläser, J. and Laudel, G. (2007a) "The social construction of bibliometric methods" in Barker, K., Gläser, J. and Whitley, R. (eds.) *The Changing Governance of the Sciences: The Advent of Research Evaluation Systems* (Dordrecht: Springer), pp. 101–23.

Gläser, J. and Laudel, G. (2007b) "Evaluation without Evaluators: The impact of funding formulae on Australian University Research" in Gläser, J. and Whitley, R. (eds.) *The Changing Governance of the Sciences: The Advent of Research Evaluation Systems (*Dordrecht: Springer), pp. 127–51.

Hagstrom, W. O. (1965) *The Scientific Community* (Carbondale, IL: Southern Illinois University Press).

Hopf, C. (1993 [1979]) "Soziologie und qualitative Sozialforschung" in Hopf, C and Weingarten, E. (eds.) *Qualitative Sozialforschung* (Stuttgart: Klett-Kotta).

Jackson, D. N. and Rushton, J. P. (eds.) (1987) *Scientific Excellence. Origins and Assessment.* (Newbury Park: SAGE).

Knorr-Cetina, K. (1984) Die Fabrikation von Erkenntnis. Zur Anthropologie der Naturwissenschaft (Frankfurt am Main: Suhrkamp).

Latour, B. and Woolgar, S. (1986 [1979]) *Laboratory Life: The Construction of Scientific Facts* (Princeton: University Press).

Laudel, G. (2005) "Is external funding a valid indicator for research performance?" in *Research Evaluation 14*, 27–34.

Laudel, G. (2006a) "The art of getting funded: How Scientists adapt to their funding conditions" in *Science and Public Policy 33*, 489–504.

Laudel, G. (2006b) "The 'quality myth': Promoting and hindering conditions for acquiring research funds" in *Higher Education 52*, 375–403.

Lynch, M. (1985) *Art and Artifact in Laboratory Science: A Study of Shop Work and Shop Talk in a Research Laboratory* (London: Routledge and Kegan Paul).

Pelz, D. C. and Andrews, F. M. (1966) *Scientists in organizations. Productive Climates for Research and Development* (New York: Wiley).

Richards, D. (1996) "Doing Politics: Elite Interviewing: Approaches and Pitfalls" in *Politics 16*, 199–204.

Zelditch Jr., M. (1961) "Some Methodological Problems of Field Studies" in *American Journal of Sociology 67*, 566–76.

Zuckerman, H. and Cole, J. R. (1994) "Research Strategies in Science: A Preliminary Inquiry" in *Creativity Research Journal 7*, 391–405.

Zuckerman, H. (1977) *Scientific Elite: Nobel Laureates in the United States* (New York: Free Press).

Zuckerman, H. (1972) "Interviewing an Ultra-Elite" in *Public Opinion Quarterly 36*, 159–75.

6
Interviewing Experts in Political Science: A Reflection on Gender and Policy Effects Based on Secondary Analysis

Gabriele Abels and Maria Behrens

6.1 Introduction

Unquestionably, German political science draws from a plurality of methods. In comparison to Anglo-Saxon political science, it is for the most part coined less by the "precedence-position of quantitative methodologies and methods hailing from the natural sciences" (Dackweiler, 2004, p. 53; our translation) – simultaneously, it is also characterized by a lack of methodological reflexion. In his 1991 appraisal of qualitative processes Patzelt points out that the practice of empirical political research was once grasped by the "popularity wave known as qualitative analysis" (Patzelt, 1991, p. 53; our translation) and considered herein a faulty approach. Thus, collective statements "ostensible inclinations in regard to categorizing reflection about research methods as irrelevant or to attribute these to Sociology" (ibid.) should be voiced. Interestingly, gender studies in (German) political science are no exemption. Looking at introductory-, text- and handbooks one has to realize how rarely chapters on methods may be found (Dackweiler, 2004, Ebbecke-Nohlen/Nohlen, 1994).

Since the mid-1990s reflection on methods has indubitably increased and been documented (for examples see von Alemann 1995, Kriz and others 1994, Behrens 2003, Behnke and others 2006a, Behnke and others 2006b, Behrens and Henning 2008). It is notably anchored in professional associations' publications, too.[1] In any case, a debate on basic methods and on the development of sufficient processes that would be fully compatible with the discipline's intricacies is yet to occur.

The debate should, however, not focus on creating or promoting a standard set of disciplinary methods, as it genuinely distinguishes itself from the neighbouring social science disciplines. Simultaneously, German political science lacks certain methodical approaches and processes for data collection and analysis – particularly "de-personalized" approaches to research subjects – preferably strategies and processes requiring methodological and methodical reflection. The expert-interview falls into this category, as its purpose is to explore political action (Meuser and Nagel 1991) as well as to query and evaluate the mundane side of politics and its every day practices (Patzelt, 1994, p. 398). Expert-interviews are vitally important to policy research, in this case especially in implementation studies (Voelzkow, 1995, p. 55) and evaluative analysis.

6.2 What is an expert-interview?

In the methodological classic published in 1970, Dexter (2006) cites an "elite specialized in interviewing," even if his understanding of elite includes a variation of groups. Meuser and Nagel define expert-interviews as a specific type of qualitative interview, differing from other questioning practices in the fashion conversations are conducted, as well as in the evaluation of statements, but also concerning cognitive interests ("Erkenntnisinteresse") and respondent groups ("Befragtengruppen") (Meuser and Nagel, 1997, p. 482, cf. Helfferich, 2004).

This partially connects to Dexter's stipulation; he mentions the following characteristics: (1) the respondent defines the interview's context, (2) he or she structures the framework of relevance/meaning and (3) he or she decides within the interview's course what is and is not meaningful and relevant. However, these criteria may apply for narrative and biographical interviews, too.

The term "informational conversations" ("Informationsgespräche") is used by von Alemann and Forndran (1990, p. 169). More precisely, it defines the scientists' cognitive interests in the process: "gaining"[2] information, leaving the addressee unnamed. The term "expert-interviews," however, puts the respondent into attention's focus and accentuates that the interviewer faces people who are endowed with a specific form of professional wisdom, which differs from the knowledge of a layperson. With this information at hand, the term "expert-interviews" seems more precise than any other alternative definitions or words known to us.

Who is considered to be of expert status is always a social and methodical construction (Deeke, 1995, p. 9). In particular this question can only be answered in relation to the subject researched and cognitive interests (Meuser and Nagel, 1997). Overall experts are "agents bearing specific functions within an organisational or institutional context," who "(re)present solutions to problems and decision-making-processes" (Meuser and Nagel, 2005, p. 74, our translation). Experts do not – as in the investigation by Meuser and Nagel – belong to an organization's management elite,[3] but very often hail from the mid- and lower ranks of organization's. Commonly, they are highly educated individuals, who are very conscious of their status and accustomed to present themselves favourably, to handle inquisitive situations and to elaborate on complex contexts.

While in elite-interviews the respondent's personal inclinations might be of interest (cf. van Schendelen 1984, Aberbach and others 1975, Semmel 1975), this fact does not apply to expert-interviews. The expert is not interviewed as an individual; the interview context "is an organizational or institutional, which is not identical to the individuals acting therein; instead these individuals are merely a "factor" within this framework" (Meuser and Nagel, 2005, pp. 72f., our translation).

In an expert-interview in political science, respondents are present three-fold: as individuals, as representatives and as strategists: an individual interviewed also corresponds to an institution or organization, which he or she represents, and finally he or she is present as a collective, strategic actor (for example a political party, an association, a department) operating in the political sphere. From these findings we derive specific problems for the conversational situation, requiring a systematic reflection on methodological criteria such as validity, reliability and generalization, as the information shared with a researcher could reflect the private opinion of the interviewee, depict the official position of the organization or even be spiked with an instrumental purpose, by deliberately giving out information to coin public discourse, without revealing the actor's strategic interests. At this point the scientist is in danger of being instrumentalized by a collective actor for their official organizational politics (Behrens, 2003, p. 229).

An interview is a "relational space" (Tietel, 2000; our translation); according to Heinzel (1997, p. 100; our translation) "it is fundamental to each dialogical interview-situation that expectations of relations are effectual and patterns of interaction are staged." Hence, the expert is also always present as an individual in the conversation. Moreover: when a respondent's subject-status is negated, this is perceived as a narcissistic offence. This could hurt the temporary relationship of trust required in the fragile situation that is the interview and hence put the interview's success in jeopardy.[4] Dexter already stated that the interview itself is an effectual factor "making the elite feel more special and making them more willing to share information they would not give out under different circumstances"; because the expert's identity is obligatorily bound in his or her belief in their status as expert (Ware and Sánchez-Jankowski, 2006, p. 5). This thinking is therefore part of a collective identity and demands confirmation within the interview's context.

Similarly, the researcher is not a neuter, but all interview participants are also always present not only as subjects, and not only as representatives of their respective organization or "science." Interests, trust, power, control and hierarchy also influence this specific form of social interaction. This implies furthermore – from a gender studies perspective – that the participants in the interview situation will always act as gendered subjects. This in turn calls attention to the question concerning the interviewer's behaviour in the research situation.

In the interpretative paradigm, communication and interaction are considered a main constituent of the research process. The key principle is that "the scientist usually only receives access to relevant and structured data when he [sic!] enters a communicative relation with the researched subject, and consequently instates the conversational rule system of the subject researched" (Hoffmann-Riem, 1980, p. 346f.; our translation). Accordingly, it is recommended to the interviewer to maintain a gesture of interested aloofness, even within the framework of an open and semi-structured expert-interview. The interviewer is to be an "empathic" and "stimulating-passive" individual who merely encourages the respondent to speak, so that the interview protocol may be read and interpreted as a monologue (cf. Lamnek, 1989, pp. 67, 69, 179). Along these lines the interview situation should "strive to adhere to the communicative rules of and be similar to mundane action" (Lamnek, 1988, p. 24; our translation). For expert interviews in political science we can assume that the more professional respondent represents a collective, strategic actor, subjective and mundane codifications become less important.

The problems consequently resulting for political scientific research practice are obvious. On the one hand, the interview's context requires openness, exploration and flexibility. On the other hand, the respondent may retort with counter-questions, strategic comments, or ask the interviewer's take on a specific problem. The scientist must then react. Concerning her or his interest to gain information, an attitude including negation to the respondents' reactions will most likely be unfavourable to the researcher. Schmid (1995, p. 285) recommends – while making political statements for example – to show a "benevolent interest"; however, a "detective's flair" – the use of suggestive questions as inescapable while dealing with critical topics. Moreover "comments, gestures and actions" by the interviewer should be controlled (ibid., p. 311; our translation).

It is clear that the scientist must act as neutral as possible, but does or cannot always act neutral in an interview, while he or she must attempt "luring" information out of the respondent. Many socially constructed and situational factors are out of the researcher's reach; these are communicated verbally and nonverbally and could at best be partially controlled for, and partially applied deliberately in one's favour. Key factors are the following: gender, age, professional status/title, experience and background, idiosyncrasies/attitudes and organizational affiliation. They operate in the specific interview situation not independently, but in sync with each other, effectively enforcing or lessening each other. This makes it simply impossible to single out individual effects and to weigh their precise influence (cf. Bryant and Hoon, 2006). We do not consider these factors as "distortions" and "disturbances," which could and should be minimized. On the contrary: we claim that these factors are always inescapably present in research as a social interaction. For us, the gender factor is a structural social category with a prominent role in the interview situation. Alluding to the "doing-gender" approach it should be noted, "that gender differences in the interview are created by interaction and are present throughout the interview" (Littig 2005).

Considering this, let it be pointed out that the respective literature widely ignores the gender issue. Meuser and Nagel (2005, p. 79; our translation) briefly state that with "certainty...gender differences between the participants of an interview [impact] the situation's definition." Warren (1988, p. 44) remarks it is almost a truism in interview science that women receive more feedback than men most of the time, because they are perceived as less threatening and have higher communicative skills. Van Schendelen (1984, p. 307) mentions that access to parliamentarians in different structures was easier for women, and therefore gender was part of recruitment characteristics when casting an interview team – but without drawing any further conclusions for data collection and data analysis. Padfield and Procter (1996) in contrast plead that gender effects should be minimized to the best of one's capability. These general statements on gender effects are then to be limited so that – taking aside the danger of reification of gender stereotypes – the subject researched and also other changes in social gender relations are to be respected (for example, the slow rise of women into leading positions, paving the way into what are traditionally considered male domains), especially then when the gender hierarchy shifts.

For gender studies, as remarked above, it is certainly not a new insight that gender "accompanies" the whole research context (cf. the discussion in Sarantakos 2004). First methodological reflections on gender-specific effects already exist regarding narrative interviews (McKee and O'Brian, 1983, Padfield and Procter, 1996, Williams and Heikes, 1993, Littig 2005). However, in most of these cases the researched topic is deeply gendered (abortion, single fathers, nursing); therefore, gender relations, the topic and biographical interview technique have most likely influenced the interview's setting. Gurney (1985) in contrast, reflects her research experience in a male domain as greatly coined by problems of access to the field due to sexist behaviour. Until now these types of reflections are more of a "side product"; there is a remarkable lack "of fundamental (meta-)studies on gender category's meaning for an expert-interview" (Littig 2005, p. 203, our translation).

6.3   Effects in conversational interaction and their methodological tracing

In the following sections we will draw on our experience with semi-structured expert-interviews that we collected while being involved in two empiric research projects in the field of biotechnology policy in the mid-1990s.[5] For the interview setting it was relevant for a gigantic difference between the scientist and the respondent to exist. Next to gender, these differences concerned age and qualification, as well as the formal occupational position. Furthermore, the interviews were also influenced by the fact that biotechnology policy is a greatly controversial political and technical topic in society.[6]

A central result of our methodical reflection on the basis of conversational analytic category-building was the identification of specific interaction-effects or patterns within the interview situation, which were in particular embossed by gender, which we take as a fundamental social category. Based on Vogel's suggestions (1995) we identified a general paternalism, catharsis, iceberg and reactionary feedback effect, and added to these the profile-effect. The results, especially those contained in our gender-theorem-interpretation, are traced by means of a secondary analysis.

Secondary analysis of qualitative data, defined as a process during which primary data is made available to another research group, is a technique barely used in political science until today (see in detail Dale and others, 1988, Corti 2000, Corti and Thompson, 2004, van den Berg, 2005). The purpose is to verify validity and reliability of data. For qualitative expert-interviews, interview protocols (that is usually a transcription of a conversation) and memos are archived. Interview memos are recordings made by the original research-team, including personal impressions, as well as information on the non-verbal interview situation (for example where a talk took place, seating plan, gestures made by the respondent).

In a *synchronic* secondary analysis, primary data is exchanged between teams, in order to re-examine and compare interpretations with one's own results. Supported by primary data from previous projects *diachronic* secondary analysis allows reconstructing the subjective characteristics (class or ethnic background, age, gender) of the interview participants and their relevance for the interpretation of data. Based on interview memos taken throughout a research project on the development of young people between 1962 and 1964, Goodwin and O'Connor (2006, p. 390) observed: "Alongside the lens of class, there was also some evidence that gender and gender-based prejudices influenced the interview process [...] For example, the interview memos reveal some evidence that male researchers made assumptions that the girls would give up paid employment for marriage and motherhood at the first opportunity. Likewise, assumptions were also made about the need for male respondents to secure higher paid jobs in order that they could " 'provide' " for their future families."

We consider secondary analysis a very adequate technique for the further development of qualitative methods. We have carried out a diachronic analysis of the memos recorded during and/or after each of our interview. These memos reveal our own subjective impressions; to some extent they resemble a research diary common in ethno-methodological studies. They can consequently be analysed as materials themselves, in order to disclose the researcher's feelings within the interview situation and their projections on the studied objects. Alternatively, systematic supervision accompanying the research process is possible. In both dissertation projects neither data analysis within a team nor independent supervision (due to financial reasons) was an option. This is a quite common situation in social sciences. It is simply assumed that the scientist him- or herself has an adequate professional distance and enough reflexive competences. This assumption can be tested by secondary analysis.

6.4   Interaction-effects in expert-interviews

Interaction-effects in expert interviews are assessed differently throughout the literature. Often they are categorized as failure in the interview's run of communication, and as something the scientist cannot change as the framework of the interview does not permit it (cf. Meuser and Nagel 2005). The informational content of such conversations is believed to be small. Such a development of the conversation can however, like the following examples depict, include very positive elements. We also assume that gender is a constitutive factor in the interview. Gender specific behaviour and resulting interaction-effects or typical patterns were not only "disturbing" or "distorting," but could be used *positively* for gaining information.[7]

In what follows we will allude to four effect-types described by Vogel (1995): paternalism-, catharsis-, iceberg- und feedback-effect, and describe these from a gender perspective. To these we will add the profile-effect. However, individual conversations can only seldom be attributed to one type of effect, as expert-interviews are dynamic social interactions.

Similarly, the effectual type might dominate throughout most of the interview, but each interview phase may change the basic pattern of a conversation due to the participants' adaption or reaction. For example, the iceberg- effect may be succeeded by a catharsis-effect (cf. ibid., p. 81). Furthermore, the scientists' own learning process during the course of the research project and also within interviews is relevant. In a first step we will present the primary analysis results, and then re-examine them by secondary analysis (see Table 6.1).

Table 6.1   Typical effects in conversational interaction

Effect	Basic feature
Paternalism effect	Manifest goodwill by the interviewee towards interviewer
Catharsis effect	Interviewee uses interview as compensation for professional dissatisfaction
Iceberg effect	Interviewee's disinterest and inert willingness to give out information
Feedback effect	Interviewee tries to reverse the question-answer-context
Profile-effect	Interviewee seeks to 'show off' in front of the interviewer

Source: Our compilation.

6.4.1 Paternalism-effect

The paternalism-effect is typically "a manifest goodwill by the interviewee towards the interviewer's research subject" (Vogel, 1995, p. 80; our translation). We often encountered this effect with men, who approached us women in quite a fatherly way as we moved within a male-dominated domain. Here gender, age, professional status and knowledge-hierarchy mingled: the paternalism we as "young" women faced was fed by an informational imbalance inherent in any expert-interview. Behnke and Meuser (1999, p. 78; our translation) state that "young female scientists moving within a male-dominated field, [...] are affected in particular, because in perception of those studied, the scientists gender-status dominates over their professional position. The female scientist is perceived as acceptably incompetent."

A second gender-specific bias was also apparent because we were women interested in male spheres: biotechnology and the politics behind it. We could choose between two reactions to these assumptions about our little knowledge on these political and scientific technical materials: For one, we were partially pressured to present our capability in the matter, meaning our own expert-status which we had acquired throughout time. Being taken despite this seriously offended the female scientist. Then, we often could choose to use the discriminatory paternalism in a productive way. In many conversations with experts, we received especially important information, because our male respondents felt a dire need to explain things to us thoroughly. Or they felt a need to state facts more explicitly, because they assumed that we were unable to correctly analyse these answers.[8] These gendered projections onto us and the therefore existing openness on the research topic, were (optionally) enforced by our questions, which suggested to the expert that we must be naïve and simple-minded, appealing to his willingness to enlighten us.

The *secondary analysis* confirms this paternalism-effect. One of the interview memos reads "X staged himself as a fatherly authority." It is interesting to point to the learn-effect chronicled throughout the timeframe during which interviews were held. Whereas during the first interview, we were inclined to contradict and prove wrong our interview-partners in their thinking that we were uninformed, in consecutive interviews we often accepted the frequent "father-daughter-relation" in order to use it for our own purpose – gaining information – as we realized it was easier to receive access to information in this manner. At this point, the factors gender and age mingled. A handwritten interview memo from an early conversation reads: "what a macho." Aside from linking the gender and age factors, the memo expresses anger to being treated like a dumb girl. Another interview memo reads: "X was more insulting than anything, arrogant as a scientist, [...] when he said that it is difficult to explain certain things to people, who [meaning me] never had done their own research and who had not written proposals for funding." The later diaries document no more entries like the one above or similar showing just how difficult it is to weigh the gender-factor and its interaction with other social factors, like age and qualification.

6.4.2   Catharsis-effect

The catharsis-effect stands for respondents using the interview as compensation in order to give free rein to their professional dissatisfaction (Vogel, 1995, p. 81). The female scientist may be faced with a problem, namely that the interviewee strays off-topic and the "informational harvest" will be little. An interview memo reads: "Y enjoyed speaking about ethics and the German's cultural problems with genomic science." At the same time, there is a chance of receiving detailed statements. We as women, thus our interpretation, were attributed with a lower status, and therefore perceived as less threatening than a male interviewer. Therefore, we encountered the catharsis-effect quite often – but not only in the variation depicted above.

The catharsis-effect might be understood as a broadening of Vogel's definition of the respondent's role change from expert to private individual (for a comparison see Meuser and Nagel, 2005 and in this volume, McKee and O'Brien, 1983). Respondents reported on family-events, the state their garden was in or discussed the capabilities of a new vehicle. In these situations the female scientist can either end the interview and risk not receiving required information or be patient and redirect the interviewee back to the topic of interest.

Female scientists may tend to opt for the latter. A role change by the respondent to the private individual perhaps occurs because women are attributed to the private sphere. For the female scientist it is hard to return the conversation to the research topic, as he might perceive this as disinterest in his person, endangering the fragile situation of trust. A possible consequence is that the respondent might chose to stonewall during the interview's continuation (iceberg-effect).

The *secondary analysis* confirms that the return from private person to expert is particularly difficult. It seems that women are attributed to the private sphere, and simultaneously her professionalism is ignored. When returning to being an expert, we often find that the respondent becomes "bored" while giving out information. While during the first interviews we evaluated private stories positively as an indicator of an existing "relationship of trust," later interviews indicate an increasing lack of patience with straying off-topic in form of a catharsis-effect, which led to tensions during some of the conversations. We suppose that male researchers are not confronted with this specific variation of the catharsis-effect in which the respondent switches between roles of expert to private individual.

6.4.3   Iceberg-effect

The iceberg-effect describes disinterest and inert willingness to give out information (Vogel, 1995, p. 79) caused by a variety of reasons. Perhaps the respondent is not a "real" expert on the topic studied, or he or she is not (or no longer) knowledgeable in the subject area. It could also be due to a widely-distributed scepticism among interviewed natural scientists and company representatives towards hypotheses from political science on bio-technology. An interview memo reads: "he is a full-blooded scientist and has had nothing to do with political decision-making processes," overall the conversation was "difficult and tiring, and it was hard getting him to talk." Meuser and Nagel (2005) recommend cutting such conversations off. In principle, we agree. One should not abort a conversation too early though. Another reason for the effect may be that the respondent wants to quiz the interviewer about her knowledge on the subject, about the (political) stance she takes on the topic, if she is trustworthy, and so on. In case of "liking" the blockade is abandoned and very gainful conversations might evolve. To a certain degree this effect is normal at the beginning of every interview, as a situation of trust should be built up first. This is depicted in the memo from an interview with a company representative: "X was very distrustful at first, what did I want to know anyway, and how would I then use the information, X didn't want the conversation to be recorded, but eventually agreed to do so."

We met the iceberg-effect, in its most rigid form, seldom and broke it in a relatively short period of time. We assume male interviewers might be confronted more forcefully by this effect, due to "quarrels" about status competence perhaps playing a part in the interview. Tietel describes this very vividly for a conversation conducted by a male/female research team. The female interviewer was later completely "butted out" of the conversation and "was excluded from the men's rivalry" (Tietel, 2000, p. 8).

We attribute the fact that our interviews showed very little of this type of the iceberg-effect, on the premise that we as women were received with far less distrust, and that expectations of us were lower. When encountering a lack of knowledge on the subject studied by the respondent, these did not retrieve to a blockade.[9] On the contrary, respondents usually attempted to conceal their lack of knowledge by providing different information or making general statements in order to save face (for a comparison see the profile-effect).

The *secondary analysis* shows that we took on classic female role behaviour – whether consciously or not – in order to break the iceberg effect. An interview memo states the iceberg was melted with "admiring statements regarding his importance for the development of genetic engineering in Germany." This illustrates that "doing gender" allows for the use of interview tactics to which male scientists cannot resort to in the same manner. It also shows that not only the respondents' behaviour should be analysed, but also that of female scientists. It is possible we might have ourselves in some cases provoked a change from iceberg effect to profile-effect.

6.4.4   Feedback-effect

Feedback-effect describes those conversational situations, in which respondents try to reverse the question-answer-context (Vogel, 1995, p. 80). The respondent tries to make the female scientist a co-expert. He or she wants to ask the female scientist how his or her actions are perceived from a societal environment, or would be perceived in case of acting. The feedback-effect may put the female scientist into an awkward situation, when blocking off questions she might seem impolite and when tolerating the contextual change she might not receive information or in fact give suggestions on what socially-accepted or desired answers might be.

In both cases the interview might fail. This effect is in part dependent on the subject; in terms of a conflict-laden topic such as biotechnology it might lead to potentially critical statements being challenged and because social scientists are in general perceived as critical. On the other hand, the feedback-effect is tied to the specifics of a respondent group. As Dexter already remarked (cf. Ware and Sánchez-Jankowski, 2006, p. 10) scientists often try to act as "gatekeepers to information."

We encountered the feedback-effect only seldom and only after several interviews had already taken place. Throughout the project's course, the female scientist becomes an expert herself. Due to her targeted questions, the respondent soon understands the female scientist to be knowledgeable, enticing counter-questions. Particularly in interviews with company representatives, the respondent attempted to receive information from the interviewer on their competitor's positions and strategies or from environmental or consumer-political associations. Aside from obtaining such information, the reversal of the question-answer-direction is beneficial for the company representative as he or she must not reveal much information him- or herself. The second project experienced the same: one tried receiving information on other respondent's positions, asking the interviewer's personal opinion on topics, asking who had been interviewed as well, or even asking for an explanation for other actor's actions. Occasionally, an interesting discussion can evolve; sometimes "trading information" can help. However, it also implies a problem: answers might be distorted. We ascribe the few encounters of this effect-type to the fact that women in political fields are *prima facie* mostly not understood as experts, and that we weren't pressured much during conversations to identify ourselves as capable interview-partners (or competitors).

The *secondary analysis* depicts that the feedback-effect primarily, but not exclusively, was found with experts from enterprises and enterprise associations. Differences resulting from varying scientific cultures could be held accountable, too. Aside from gender, organization-specific factors might deliver an explanation for the seldom arising of the feedback-effect. Furthermore, it is obvious that in "professionals" from a company, the organization's interest and strategic information were employed more often than personal inclination. Here, the gender-factor seemingly slides into the background.

6.4.5 Profile-effect

We encountered the profile-effect quite often. The respondent seeks to prove his (or her) high level of knowledge and is very willing to give out information overall. One interview memo states briefly: "scientific careerist" who "wants to breathe fresh wind into the worn out structures of the old men."

We presume that the profile-effect pops up more often in interviews between men and women, and that it could therefore be a gender-specific effect.[10] The female scientist might react provokingly, as in "but surely you don't have any more detailed knowledge on this, do you?" and thus obtain information. Or affirm admiration concerning the respondent's capabilities in order to "retrieve" more information. In some interviews respondents went as far in strengthening their profile, and succeeded in patting themselves on the back for committing prosecutable actions.

The conversational situation is one of classic gender-specific role distribution. The man is capable and worldly-wise, the woman admires him. To a certain degree, the female scientist can be a part of these gender roles. But there is a great danger of the male respondent dominating the interview as a private individual.

Aside from this, we encountered a case in which the respondents did not want to strengthen their profile through showing how knowledgeable they were on the studied subject, but chose "side show scenery": one respondent scheduled a phone appointment with a TV-reporter while one of the authors was present and listened in. Apparently he sought to demonstrate how highly demanded his opinion was. Or, one interviewer worked at his PC briefly during several times in interview his indispensability and thus signalled his generosity in agreeing to partake in an interview. The female interviewer should probably just react with obvious disinterest and signal the admiration he hoped for shall not arrive. Or the conversation might end with a guided tour through the lab, whilst proudly showing the new DNA sequencer, which the female scientist knows only to appreciate in part, because it reminds her of the "one-armed bandit from the amusement park."

The *secondary analysis* shows that interviews with female respondents are not free of such effects either: "X told a lot about her many public discussions with rivals and irrational fears of genetic engineering." The analysis shows too, that we felt superior in the conversational situation most of the time once the profile-effect surfaced. We could decide when to applaud the respondent, agree with him or her or "punish" them with disinterest. An interview memo, for example, recorded "childish behaviour," because the respondent wanted to impress with supposedly "manifold important contacts to the elite in politics and the economy." The memo documents the interviewer feeling superior.

Another interview memo points out that the respondent was encouraged to make his or her mark several times during the interview. The informational gain from such conversations is questionable, one must distinguish between "real" information and exaggerations or even intentionally false information. A mixed-sex project-team can contribute to avoiding such gender-specific interaction-traps, the disadvantage being that the positive effects may not be used in one's favour then.

6.5   Conclusion

The depicted experiences do not permit any generalizations, but allow merely the formulation of hypotheses that should be systemically examined in future research. The perspective on the relevance of interaction-effects could be sharpened: Aside from age, professional status, background experience and cultural factors, gender is a significant factor. Reports concerning gender-specific interaction-effects clarify that expert interviews are not partner-like discursive talks between equals. Despite differing research areas, questioning-styles and experts, we discovered common ground in our individual conversation contexts. On the one hand, these similarities refer to the behaviour of the (mostly male) respondents towards us (as women), but also allude to the findings of the secondary analysis, particularly how we were "doing gender" in the interview situation and reacted to the behaviour by our counterpart. Simultaneously the result of our secondary analysis showed that in part of the talks with female respondents we experienced and felt – as several interview memos state – a "sisterhood" or "understanding each other in a 'womanly fashion'" on the "men's clique" in science and academia. This is also a gender construction.

Gender-specific biases, whether positive or discriminating, coin the relationship of interaction. They can be used to her benefit by the female scientist. Defence mechanisms (iceberg-effect) are encountered seldom; other effects such as the paternalism or profile-effect can be derived to informational gain. Often damaging to the interview was the often encountered catharsis-effect, when the respondent switched to the private person.

A diachronic secondary analysis clarifies just how difficult it is to weigh each of the different social factors that are intertwined and interact in relation to the complex cause-and-effect-relationship. This points to a considerable need to continue the development of research methods. In open and semi-structured expert-interviews there is also the general problem that political scientists are interested in revealing real-life procedures, while respondents might seek to cover facts behind a veil and aim at creating political myths, because "organisations, too, work in self-interest toward a most positive and consistent depiction of their operations" (Hucke and Wollmann, 1980, p. 224; our translation). One must assume that "political desirability" impinges on all methods of data collecting in every controversial field of politics.

From a methodologist point of view we call for a triangulation of techniques. Detecting traps in methodology does not mean to disapprove the instrument of research as a whole. Expert interviews are indubitably of definite interest, especially with a field that is yet to be explored. Standardized methods are often inadequate for seeking expert-knowledge (for example the Delphi survey, cf. Aichholzer in this volume), because the required reduction of reality is contrary to the expert's experience.

According to Meuser and Nagel (1991, p. 133f.) the cognitive gain from expert-interviews are more in line with a sociology of knowledge approach. Hence, they lie on a level of interpretation-patterns, orientation-patterns and patterns of normality; regarding political operations they aim at "structures of relevance and knowledge patterns in the political system." Also, political activities are "things with an own quality" (Hucke and Wollmann, 1980, p. 220; or translation). Grasping of every day political operational practice can only be reconstructed in detail on the basis of these interviews. Therefore "iterative expert-interviews" are especially common in policy studies, in particular for a qualitative analysis of networks (Voelzkow, 1995, p. 55). Documents, such as, for example, legislative bills, press releases, statements or protocols however are – depending on their type – usually only "landmarks," albeit of relevance; but the empiric complexity of political actions are only in part mirrored in them.

Experts are problematic informants (Dean and Whyte, 2006) leading to pitfalls attached to this research technique. When confronting these issues, we suggest the following possibilities: it is ubiquitous to combine expert-interviews with other methods of data-collection, holding many interviews with experts corresponding to different organizational and institutional contexts in order to validate the data by means of a thematic comparison. The validity and reliability would greatly benefit from being carried out by a team, or at least if they were evaluated by one. Furthermore supervision should render the possibility of reflecting on each individual "relational interview-space" and to analyse its meaning for data collection and evaluation.

Concerning gender effects we see significant need for methodological research in order to improve research techniques: they can be reconstructed in an *ex post* secondary analysis using transcripts and interview memos. In the interest of an increase in methodological self-reflection secondary analyses should be carried out by scientists who are not part of the project-team. However, here we encounter the dilemma of handling confidential information (for a comparison cf. van den Berg, 2005). Also a comparison between experiences from male colleagues, but also including expert-interviews with female respondents, might be insightful. Nevertheless, much fails as political operative spheres are still dominated by male actors, and herewith gender-specific aspects already exist during the sampling-phase.

Mixed-sex research groups in particular grant the opportunity for a systematic comparison. Unfortunately these proposals fail – due to the economic reasons – but also due to a "receptive block" (Dackweiler, 2004, p. 51; our translation) in political science towards gender-theoretic approaches, such as a consequent opening towards methodological questions. In the interest of a methodological "duty of care," this resistance should be overcome.

Notes

1. In the year 2003 an ad-hoc group "empirical methods in political science" of the German Political Science Association (DVPW) was founded, which has the status of a permanent research group since 2006. Furthermore the thematic sections and working groups regularly debate on methods.
2. In our understanding the English terms "data-making" or "data-creation procedures" allude precisely to methods primarily producing data.
3. The term refers to individuals, which "[are] part of the operative field, whose problems are sought to be solved." In this sense our interviewees would belong to the functional elite. The term elite and the processes to identify the members are however subject to controversy; cf. Meuser and Nagel, 1994, pp. 181–4.
4. Inverting a formulation by Becker-Schmidt (1985, p. 95) formulated for the feminist debate it may be questioned for expert-interviews if the object status of the expert is missed because their subjectivity is denied.
5. For lack of space we only mention the most important information on the projects, for a more detailed description see Abels and Behrens, 2002. One project reconstructed political processes on the EC-Human Genome Programme (Abels, 2000). For this purpose many actors from project development from science and research administrations were interviewed. The other project (Behrens and others, 1996) compares the implementation of research programmes in the field of biotechnology in The Netherlands and The Federal Republic of Germany and analysed the process of societal context-formation of genetic procedures for food stuff production (Behrens and others, 1997 and 2001). Aside from political experts, company representatives were interviewed. The majority of conversations was recorded, in single cases this was not possible or the respondents did not agree to being recorded. In total 127 interviews were conducted. Most of the 107 male respondents were between 50 and 60 years old, 22 of female respondents between 35 and 45 years of age. Almost all respondents had an academic background, many had acquired a PhD, some even habilitated. Most had studied the natural sciences, many were lawyers or economists. Most of the time actors corresponded to the lower and mid-levels of the hierarchy, and were included in the preparing of decisions and their implementation (for example as subject specialists) and therefore had detailed knowledge, and were only in very rare cases part of the leading elite. The authors/interviewers are political scientists and were in their early and mid-thirties, striving for their PhDs, when conducting the interviews.
6. On problems of interview in a conflict-laden context see Kacen and Chaitin, 2006.
7. By consciously using gender-specific biases to attain information, one risks strengthening existing gender stereotypes. However, it is fairly common to make use of biases held by the experts towards the scientists, not only concerning gender-specific questions, but also concerning, for example, political attitudes that

are expressed with help of certain clothes (Schmid, 1995). Whether or not the end justifies the means is a question of research ethics.

8. There are also forms of cultural and ethical paternalism, as an interview-note proves: "XY was (as is typical for Brits!) very sceptical of EU-Programmes."
9. We only ended a conversation earlier than intended in two cases.
10. Furthermore we assume that also in conversations between men a profile-effect takes place in relation to conflicts over status and competencies. This one is also gender-specific, due to this being a display of masculinity. The staging of gender can also be found in the paternalism-effect in the figure of the fatherly type.

Further readings

Bryant, L. and Hoon, E. (2006) "How can the intersections between gender, class, and sexuality be translated to an empirical agenda?" in *International Journal of Qualitative Methods 5(1)*, http://www.ualberta.ca/~iiqm/backissues/5_1/pdf/bryant. pdf, accessed 14 May 2007.
Corti, L. and Thompson, P. (2004) "Secondary analysis of archive data" in Seale, C., Gobo, G., Gubrium, J. F. and Silverman, D. (eds) *Qualitative Research Practice* (London: Sage), 327–43.
Sarantakos, S. (2004) *Social Research*, 3rd edn. (Houndsmill: Palgrave).

References

Abels, G. (2000) *Strategische Forschung in den Biowissenschaften. Der Politikprozess zum europäischen Humangenomprogramm* (Berlin: Edition Sigma).
Aberbach, J. D., Chesney, J. D. and Rockmann, B. A. (1975) "Exploring elite political attitudes: some methodological lessons" in *Political Methodology 2(1)*, 1–27.
Alemann, U. von (ed.) (1995) *Politikwissenschaftliche Methoden. Grundriss für Studium und Forschung* (Opladen: Westdeutscher Verlag).
Alemann, U. von and Forndran, E. (1990) *Methodik der Politikwissenschaft*, 4th edn (Stuttgart, Berlin, Köln: Kohlhammer).
Becker-Schmidt, R. (1985) "Probleme einer feministischen Theorie und Empirie in den Sozialwissenschaften" in *Feministische Studien 4(2)*, 93–104.
Behnke, C. and Meuser, M. (1999) *Geschlechterforschung und qualitative Methoden* (Opladen: Leske & Budrich).
Behnke, J., Baur, N. and Behnke, N. (2006a) *Empirische Methoden der Politikwissenschaft* (Paderborn, München, Wien, Zürich: Schöningh).
Behnke, J., Gschwend, T., Schindler, D. and Schnapp, K. -U. (eds) (2006b) *Methoden der Politikwissenschaft. Neuere qualitative und quantitative Analyseverfahren* (Baden-Baden: Nomos).
Behrens, M. (2001) *Staaten im Innovationskonflikt. Vergleichende Analyse staatlicher Handlungsspielräume im gentechnischen Innovationsprozess Deutschlands und den Niederlanden* (Frankfurt am Main: Peter Lang).
Behrens, M. (2003) "Quantitative und qualitative Methoden in der Politikfeldanalyse" in Schubert, K. and Bandelow, N. C. (eds) *Lehrbuch der Politikfeldanalyse* (München, Wien: Oldenbourg), pp. 205–38.
Behrens, M., Meyer-Stumborg, S. and Simonis, G. (1996) *Gentechnik und die Nahrungsmittelindustrie* (Opladen: Verlag für Sozialwissenschaften).
Behrens, M., Meyer-Stumborg, S. and Simonis, G. (1997) *GenFood: Einführung und Verbreitung, Konflikte und Gestaltungsmöglichkeiten* (Berlin: edition sigma).

Behrens, M. and Hennig, E. (2009) "Qualitative Methoden der Internationalen Politik" in Wilhelm, A. and Masala, C. (eds) *Handbuch der Internationalen Politik* (Wiesbaden: VS Verlag) (forthcoming).

Berg, H. v. d. (2005) "Reanalyzing Qualitative Interviews from Different Angles: The Risk of Decontextualization and Other Problems of Sharing Qualitative Data" in *Forum Qualitative Sozialforschung/Forum: Qualitative Social Research 6(1)*, art. 30, http://www.qualitative-research.net/fqs-texte/1-05/05-1-30-e.htm, date accessed 16 May 2007.

Brosi, W. H., Hembach, K. and Peters, G. (1981) *Expertengespräche. Vorgehensweise und Fallstricke. Arbeitspapier des Forschungsprojekts Berufliche Bildung und regionale Entwicklung* (Trier: Universität).

Bryant, L. and Hoon, E. (2006) "How can the intersections between gender, class, and sexuality be translated to an empirical agenda?" in *International Journal of Qualitative Methods 5(1)*, http://www.ualberta.ca/~iiqm/backissues/5_1/pdf/bryant.pdf, date accessed 14 may 2007.

Corti, L. (2000) "Progress and Problems of Preserving and Providing Access to Qualitative Data for Social Research – The International Picture of an Emerging Culture" in *Forum Qualitative Sozialforschung / Forum: Qualitative Social Research 1(3)*, http://qualitativeresearch.net/fqs/fqs-eng.htm, date accessed 14 May 2007.

Corti, L. and Thompson, P. (2004) "Secondary analysis of archive data" in Seale, C., Gobo, G., Gubrium, J. F. and Silverman, D. (eds) *Qualitative Research Practice* (London: Sage), pp. 327–43.

Dackweiler, R.-M. (2004) "Wissenschaftskritik – Methodologie – Methoden" in Rosenberger, S. K. and Sauer, B. (eds) *Politikwissenschaft und Geschlecht* (Wien: UTB-WUV), pp. 45–63.

Dale, A., Arber, S. and Proctor, M. (1988) *Doing Secondary Analysis* (London: Unwyn Hyman).

Dean, J. P. and Foote Whyte, W. (2006) "How do you know if the informant is telling the truth?" in Dexter, L. A. *Elite and Specialized Interviewing* (Colchester: ECPR Press), pp. 100–7.

Deeke, A. (1995) "Experteninterviews – ein methodologisches und forschungspraktisches Problem" in Brinkmann, C., Deeke, A. and Völkel, B. (eds) *Experteninterviews in der Arbeitsmarktforschung. Diskussionsbeiträge zu methodischen Fragen und praktischen Erfahrungen. Beiträge zur Arbeitsmarkt- und Berufsforschung Nr. 191* (Nürnberg: Bundesanstalt für Arbeit), pp. 7–22.

Dexter, L. A. (1970/2006) *Elite and Specialized Interviewing* (Colchester: ECPR Press).

Ebbecke-Nohlen, A. and Nohlen, D. (1994) "Feministische Ansätze" in Nohlen, D. (ed.) *Lexikon der Politik*, vol. 2: Politikwissenschaftliche Methoden (München: Beck), pp. 130–37.

Goodwin, J. and O'Connor, H. (2006) "Contextualising the Research Process: Using Interviewer Notes in the Secondary Analysis of Qualitative Data" in *The Qualitative Report 11(2)*, 374–92.

Gurney, J. N. (1985) "Not one of the guys: The female researcher in a male-dominated setting" in *Qualitative Sociology 8(1)*, 42–62.

Heinzel, F. (1997) "Biographische Methode und wiederholte Gesprächsinteraktion. Ein Verfahren zur Erforschung weiblicher Politisierungsprozesse" in *femina politica: Zeitschrift für feministische Politik-Wissenschaft 6(1)*, 96–104.

Helfferich, C. (2004) *Die Qualität qualitativer Daten. Manual für die Durchführung qualitativer Interviews* (Wiesbaden: Verlag für Sozialwissenschaften).

Hoffmann-Riem, C. (1980) "Der Datengewinn" in *Kölner Zeitschrift für Soziologie und Sozialpsychologie 32*, 339–72.

Hucke, J. and Wollmann, H. (1980) "Methodenprobleme der Implementationsforschung" in Mayntz, R. (ed.) *Implementation politischer Programme: empirische Forschungsberichte* (Königstein/Ts.: Anton Hain), pp. 216–35.

Kacen, L. and Chaitin, J. (2006) "'The Times They are a Changing': Undertaking Qualitative Research in Ambiguous, Conflictual, and Changing Contexts" in *The Qualitative Report 11(2)*, 209–28.

Kriz, J., Nohlen, D. and Schultze, R. -O. (eds) (1994) *Lexikon der Politik*, vol. 2: Politikwissenschaftliche Methoden (München: Beck).

Lamnek, S. (1988/1989) *Qualitative Sozialforschung*, vols 1 and 2 (München: Psychologie Verlags Union).

Littig, B. (2005) "Interviews mit Experten und Expertinnen. Überlegungen aus geschlechtertheoretischer Sicht" in Bogner, A., Littig, B. and Menz, W. (eds) *Das Experteninterview – Theorie, Methode, Anwendung*, 2nd edn (Wiesbaden: Verlag für Sozialwissenschaften), pp. 191–206.

McKee, L. and O'Brien, M. (1983) "Interviewing men: taking gender seriously" in Gamarnikow, E., Morgan, D. H. H., Purvis, J. and Taylerson, D. (eds) *The Public and the Private* (London: Heinemann), pp. 147–61.

Meuser, M. and Nagel, U. (1991) "Experteninterviews als Instrument zur Erforschung politischen Handelns" in Bering, H., Hitzler, R. and Neckel, S. (eds) *Politisches Handeln/Experteninterviews. Dok. Nr. 1 des AK Soziologie politischen Handeln* (Bamberg: University press), pp. 133–40.

Meuser, M. and Nagel, U. (1994) "Expertenwissen und Experteninterview" in Hitzler, R., Honer, A. and Maeder, C. (eds) *Expertenwissen. Die institutionalisierte Kompetenz zur Konstruktion von Wirklichkeit* (Opladen: Westdeutscher Verlag), pp. 180–92.

Meuser, M. and Nagel, U. (1997) "Das ExpertInneninterview – Wissenssoziologische Voraussetzungen und methodische Durchführung" in Friebertshäuser, B. and Prengel, A. (eds) *Handbuch Qualitative Forschungsmethoden in der Erziehungswissenschaft* (Weinheim: Juventa Verlag), pp. 481–91.

Meuser, M. and Nagel, U. (2005) "ExpertInneninterviews – vielfach erprobt, wenig bedacht. Ein Beitrag zur qualitativen Methodendiskussion" in Bogner, A., Littig, B. and Menz, W. (eds) *Das Experteninterview – Theorie, Methode, Anwendung*, 2nd edn (Wiesbaden: Verlag für Sozialwissenschaften), pp. 71–93.

Padfield, M. and Procter, J. (1996) "The effect of interviewer's gender on the interviewing process: a comparative enquiry" in *Sociology 30(2)*, 355–66.

Patzelt, W. (1991) "Politikwissenschaft" in Flick, U., Kardorff, E. von, Keupp, H., Rosenstiel, L. von and Wolff, S. (eds) *Handbuch Qualitative Sozialforschung* (München: Psychologie Verlags Union), pp. 53–5.

Patzelt, W. (1994) "Qualitative Politikforschung" in Kriz, J., Nohlen, D. and Schultze, R.-O. (eds) *Lexikon der Politik*, vol. 2: Politikwissenschaftliche Methoden (München: Beck), pp. 395–98.

Schendelen, M. P. C. M. van (1984) "Interviewing members of parliament" in *Political Methodology, 10(3)*, 301–21.

Schmid, J. (1995) "Expertenbefragung und Informationsgespräch in der Parteienforschung: Wie föderalistisch ist die CDU?" in Alemann, U. von (ed.) *Politikwissenschaftliche Methoden. Grundriss für Studium und Forschung* (Opladen: Westdeutscher Verlag), pp. 293–26.

Semmel, A. K. (1975) "Deriving perceptual data from foreign policy elites: a methodological narrative" in *Political Methodology 2(1)*, 29–49.

Tietel, E. (2000) "Das Interview als Beziehungsraum" in *Forum Qualitative Sozialforschung/Forum: Qualitative Social Research* [Online Journal], *1(2)*, http://qualitative-research.net/fqs/fqs-d/2-00inhalt.htm, accessed 13 May 2007.

Voelzkow, H. (1995) " 'Iterative Experteninterviews': Forschungspraktische Erfahrungen mit einem Erhebungsinstrument" in Brinkmann, C., Deeke, A. and Völkel, B. (eds) *Experteninterviews in der Arbeitsmarktforschung. Diskussionsbeiträge zu methodischen Fragen und praktischen Erfahrungen. Beiträge zur Arbeitsmarkt- und Berufsforschung Nr. 191* (Nürnberg: Bundesanstalt für Arbeit), pp. 51–57.

Vogel, B. (1995) " 'Wenn der Eisberg zu schmelzen beginnt ...' – Einige Reflexionen über den Stellenwert und die Probleme des Experteninterviews in der Praxis der empirischen Sozialforschung" in Brinkmann, C., Deeke, A. and Völkel, B. (eds) *Experteninterviews in der Arbeitsmarktforschung. Diskussionsbeiträge zu methodischen Fragen und praktischen Erfahrungen. Beiträge zur Arbeitsmarkt- und Berufsforschung Nr. 191* (Nürnberg: Bundesanstalt für Arbeit), pp. 73–83.

Ware, A. and Sánchez-Jankowski, M. (2006) "New Introduction" in Dexter, L. A. *Elite and Specialized Interviewing* (Colchester: ECPR Press), pp. 1–11.

Warren, C. A. B. (1988) *Gender Issues in Field Research* (London: Sage).

Williams, C. L. and Heikes, E. J. (1993) "The importance of researcher's gender in the in-depth interview" in *Gender and Society 7(2)*, 280–91.

7
Expert Interviews on the Telephone: A Difficult Undertaking

Gabriela B. Christmann

7.1 Introduction: reason and methodical context of the study

The topic of this contribution is the method chosen for a sub-project, which was carried out in the context of a more extended study on "Demographic Change at Universities," Saxony being the focal point.[1] For the sub-project qualitative expert interviews were used, part of them being conducted on the telephone. For the time being, qualitative telephone (expert) interviews have seldomly been discussed in literature. By this contribution the few indications offered by literature and our own methodical experiences will be reflected on.

As already indicated, the sub-project was integrated into an extended project – consisting of five sub-projects and multi-methodically planned – in the field of university research (see Figure 7.1). The starting point of the entire project was the question of which effect demographic change will have on the university system and the academic labour market particularly in Saxony. Based on existing statistics, the first sub-project was about presenting predictions on the future numbers of university beginners in Saxony and on estimating the offer of academic graduates until 2035. The second one predicted the need in numbers of academically educated workforce on the Saxonian labour market until 2020. To give reason to predictions and estimations, a quantitative survey among experts by way of the Delphi method was carried out in the course of the third sub-project. By way of given items, experts from Saxony and the other federal states were asked to give their estimations on expected trends on the labour market, in the field of universities, and in educational policy. Accordingly, experts came from the fields of "business," "educational/university system," and "politics." As it had to be assumed that steps by decision-makers at universities and in the field of the politics of the federal state may considerably influence the demand for studies, more deep-reaching studies by way of qualitative expert interviews with decision-makers[2] were carried out by a fourth and a fifth sub-project.

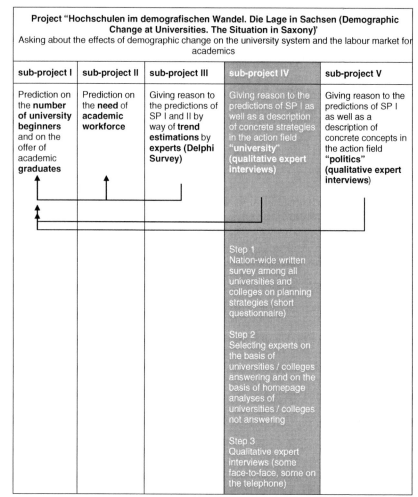

Figure 7.1   The research design in the context of the extended project
Source: Developed by the author.

With them, the questions of which concrete strategies are developed at universities to be fit for competition in the future (sub-project IV) and which steps are planned by political actors to organize the university system (sub-project V) were in the fore. Ideas from other federal states were supposed to be included into both sub-projects, due to which decision-makers from the entire Federal Republic were taken into consideration. Thus, the overall project pursued an application-related goal: foundations for university-planning and educational-political acting were supposed to be provided.

For this contribution the method of the sub-project is in the fore, which dealt with strategies in the action-field of universities (see the specially marked column in Figure 7.1).

The sub-project was meant to analyse if and – if yes – how (in times of demographic change) universities make their institutions attractive for future students. "Best practice" examples of demography-according university planning should be identified and described. On the one hand results served for giving reason to assumptions by the prediction model of sub-project I particularly for Saxony, and on the other hand for providing information on further strategies of nationwide university planning.

By a first step, a written survey among universities by way of a short questionnaire was carried out. The questionnaire addressed university leaderships.[3] It asked about essential topics of university planning by way of standardized and open questions. Questions were derived from expert literature on university research and from the public discourse on university development in Germany. A total of 268 institutions of academic education received this questionnaire. After a "reminding action" it was possible to achieve a total return of 41 per cent.

Based on this, at first information on basic strategies of universities was gained. It served for selecting universities by a second step which seemed to be promising for the then following – now: qualitative – round of expert interviews. As by the short questionnaire universities were also asked to name contact partners for a possible qualitative expert interview, it was not difficult anymore to win over concrete interview partners. However, we did not always follow the suggestions (see Chapter 2). Selecting those universities, which were supposed to be included into the sample of the qualitative expert survey was not only based on those universities as having participated in the written survey. It was additionally based on homepage analyses (of offers of studies, models) of those universities, which had not answered in the context of the written survey. On the whole, such universities were chosen which according to our analysis looked particularly active and innovative in respect of strategy development. In retrospect it turned out that a great part of universities chosen this way also belonged to the group of those universities as being chosen for support in the context of the initiative of excellency of the Federal Government and the federal states. By a third step, a total of 22 qualitative expert interviews were carried out.[4] As already indicated, these expert interviews were meant to achieve deeper insight into how institutions of academic education prepare for the future. The experts were asked which strategies of university planning their respective university had actually developed and was expected to develop and which experiences they had made with previous steps.[5]

There were 14 face-to-face and eight telephone interviews. The decision for expert interviews on the telephone was motivated by research-economic reasons – in respect of the project's chronological and financial resources.

Our assumption was that if telephone interviews were an appropriate way at all in the context of qualitative analyses, this would most probably be the case with a project like ours, as the interview partners were academically educated experts holding positions with university leadership/administration, who – as we could assume – showed the following core competences: a high ability to think in the abstract, strong orientation at topical criteria, high level of competence in respect of giving explanations, experience with presenting themselves to the outside world[6] by way of interviews, even on the telephone, most of all towards journalists but also towards fellow scientists. Furthermore, our research interest was not directed at the reconstruction of life world or implicit knowledge, that is a kind of knowledge being "difficult to ask about," but rather at finding out about estimations, experiences, suggestions and intended ways of action within a field of practical acting and thus at explicit, reflected knowledge, a good deal of which is characterized by inner-university negotiation processes and to a certain extent by public discourses on the development of universities. Given this target group and these questions, we assumed that telephone interviews were suitable for extending those data as being collected by way of face-to-face interviews and that we would not be confronted with more serious methodical problems.

As intended, we were able to topically extend our study by way of telephone interviews. Also experts interviewed on the telephone provided us with much valuable information about their actual strategies of university planning; it was even possible to find out about new aspects in this way. However, interviews happened in a less unproblematic way than expected by us. This will be described in the following (see Chapter 4). Before this however, there will be reflecting on which kind of interview was carried out or which kind of interaction situation was typical for collecting data (see Chapter 2). Furthermore, there will be a critical look at the literature on methods of telephone (expert) interviews (see Chapter 3).

7.2   Explorative-systematizing expert interview at eye level

It has already been mentioned that experts were (not only but most of them) recruited by way of written questionnaires. There we had asked for naming contact partners for possible oral expert interviews. This request was met by almost all universities answering. Usually, universities named their vice presidents as contact partners, colleges always named their presidents. Sometimes both universities and colleges recommended the president's personal assistant, the head of the department of planning and development, the head of the department of academic matters, or one of their study advisers. If study advisers had been named as contact partners, in most cases we did not follow the recommendation, as we were rather interested in people being included in university planning at a higher level. In this context we assumed that experts are found not only at the level of immediate decision-making (members of university leaderships) but also at the level of preparing decisions (assistants and heads of departments).[7]

Always the first contact was made by e-mail, that is both for face-to-face interviews and for telephone interviews (on this see also Gläser and Laudel, 2006, pp. 153–61; Mieg and Näf, 2006, p. 26). Potential interview partners were shortly informed about the research project. Most of all they were asked if they were ready to give an interview and if they agreed with an audio-recording. Also, at the same time they were sent the interview guideline, after first experiences had shown that experts (that is particularly interview partners intended for telephone interviews) connected their agreement to being informed about actual questions in advance and in more detail (see Chapter 4). After their agreement the dates for the interviews were fixed on the telephone, sometimes via secretaries.

Bogner and Menz (2005b, see also Bogner and Menz, in this volume) for their typology distinguish between the explorative, the systematizing, and the theory-generating interview (see also Vogel, 1995, p. 74). On the one hand, our project might be counted among the category of the systematizing interview because it was about finding out about "action knowledge and experience-based knowledge gained by practical work and being reflexively available and spontaneously communicatable." On the other hand, however, it was not that a strict "topical comparability of data in the fore," due to which this attribution is not completely adequate. It would also be inappropriate to call our expert interviews purely explorative, even more as according to Bogner and Menz (2005b, see also Bogner and Menz, in this volume) the latter only serve "for preliminary orientation in a topically new or confusing field." However, one maxim of explorative interviews was definitely a guideline for us: the interviews were supposed to be as open as possible, and were supposed to find out about the universities' action or, to have it more exactly: planning emphasis. Thus in respect of method, interviews practiced by us are of a mixed type, here we like to call them explorative-systematizing expert interviews.

The basis of the interview was an interview guideline. This guideline consisted of four main questions which were very openly designed, were aimed at inner-university strategies, and which were asked all interview partners. They were followed by additional questions, which addressed a total of 11 subjects and for the purpose of improved clarity were divided into three blocks. For – as shown by the analysis of our short questionnaires – not every university has worked out concepts on every topical field, not for every interview was it necessary to "work off" all additional questions. As already mentioned, the study did not aim at all interviews to be comparable but at finding out about "best practice" examples from certain fields. As the interview guideline was previously given to the interview partners by e-mail, they were told at the same time that they would not have to deal with every aspect of the additional questions but only with those being relevant for their university/college or with those they considered relevant. This way it was guaranteed that on the one hand the experts perceived our range of interests. On the other hand, however, they could lay their emphasis on those fields in which they were able to talk about concepts and experiences. As Vogel (1995, p. 76) has it, this was important not at least for atmospheric reasons, for the interviewees were supposed to feel they were being taken seriously as a competent partner (status!). Thus, the experts were provided with enough leeway for those aspects as being important for them. Within a certain frame, in respect of answering the questionnaire they were able to structure their use of time according to their own preferences. However, indeed further questions by the interviewers had a certain effect. Both for face-to-face and for telephone interviews this strategy proved to be practical.

Different from what Bogner and Menz (2005b, see also Bogner and Menz, in this volume) state to be typical for the type of the systematizing interview, the interviewer was in a position to have expert knowledge of the topical fields she was asking about. She was familiar with cross-university discourses and relevant research literature influencing universities' internal debates. However, she was not herself included into the experts' respective contexts of university planning and decision-making, but she was provided with basic knowledge. Thus, she approached the experts not as a "laywoman" but to a certain degree as a "co-expert."[8] This is not to say that the expert interviews took on the nature of debates among experts (see Bogner and Menz, 2005b, see also Bogner and Menz, in this volume). Rather, the expert's knowledge advantage in his or her particular field and context was taken seriously. But in any case it was possible to conduct the interviews "at eye level" (Pfadenhauer, 2005, see also Pfadenhauer, in this volume).

The strategy for additional questions was based on the "question technique between pre-knowledge and naivety" as suggested by Walter (1994, p. 274). Walter pointed out to the fact that it is favourable if interviewers include a certain degree of pre-knowledge into the interview. Apart from the fact that this will increase the interviewer's reputation, it challenges the expert to deal with the topic more intensively and in more detail. At the same time it will also be advantageous if naïve questions are asked. This will provoke answers "which do not in any case fit to the interviewer's expectations, and it will bring up aspects which rather express the interviewee's point of view" (Walter, 1994, p. 274; on this see also Gläser and Laudel, 2006, p. 129f).

7.3   Entering methodically "unknown territory": the qualitative-oriented expert interview on the telephone

In several respects, extended literature research on qualitative telephone interviews in the Anglo-American and German-speaking countries produce a disappointing result: the number of *methodical-systematic* contributions is extremely small, furthermore there are only essays with a low number of pages (five to eight pages), and in respect of content one misses fundamental reflections on the suitability of this kind of interview for the field of qualitative social research.

However, this is not meant to say that qualitative telephone (expert) interviews are not conducted. According to statements by Opdenakker (2006, Abstract), this kind of interview has become common: "Face-to-face interviews have long been the dominant interview technique in the field of qualitative research. In the last two decades, telephone interviewing became more and more common."

However, this statement may be supposed to be true most of all for Anglo-American countries. There, qualitative interviews are used rather frequently and also very pragmatically (see for example studies by Brody, Geronemus and Farris, 2003, Galster, 2006, Mitchell and Zmud, 1993). These works are very much topic-related and provide only little information about the actual methodical way of proceeding. Discussing methods is completely missing. In German-speaking countries qualitative telephone interviews are comparatively less common. However, a number of entries on current research projects in the "Informationssystem Sozialwissenschaften" (FORIS) indicate that the use of qualitative telephone interviews is increasing. Some entries make obvious that qualitative telephone interviews with decision-makers and people having special knowledge – that is experts – are intended for the respective projects. Nevertheless, interviews in the context of these projects are not called *expert interviews*. Thus it becomes obvious that qualitative-oriented expert interviews on the telephone are definitely used but that this methodical practice is not reflected on.

The few contributions, which are explicitly meant as *methodical* contributions to *qualitative telephone interviews* (see Burke and Miller, 2001, Busse, 2000) do not offer anything else than practical-technical instructions on how to proceed. There are no (explicit) considerations on the question of which kind of target group or question this method is suitable, or not.

However, it is remarkable that Busse (2003, p. 28, own translation) at the beginning of his contribution calls the telephone interview an "expert interview on the telephone." But this is done only in passing. Thus, implicitly he restricts the application field of the qualitative telephone interview to expert interviews, without explaining in more detail or giving reasons. Instead, Busse speaks of the advantage of the telephone interview: "The guideline-based telephone interview, that is the expert interview on the telephone by help of a question catalogue, is a very efficient and economic kind of qualitative data survey, as neither travelling is necessary nor are there any expenses if an interview shall be conducted" (Busse, 2003, p. 28, own translation).

In the following paragraphs the author will explain in detail how a guideline must be constructed, how contact is made with potential interview partners, and how a telephone interview is practically done. Other than it is mostly the case with contributions on qualitative face-to-face interviews, he recommends a strongly structured guideline which "is similar to a standardized questionnaire, the only difference being the fact that it includes more so called "open questions" than the latter" (Busse, 2003, p. 30, own translation).

By the way, here a phenomenon becomes obvious which Bogner and Menz (2005b, this volume) state also for face-to-face interviews with experts: even if interviews are conducted as partly structured interviews, they must not be considered "genuine representatives of the qualitative paradigm."

According to Busse (2003), the guideline should be organized for an interview of about 45 minutes. For making contact he recommends a three-step-procedure: By way of a letter – purposefully addressing the potential interview partner – the expert shall at first be informed about the goals and the subject of the project. This letter should also announce a first telephone call. This call should be some days later and inform the expert about what to expect in respect of time expenditure and content, to then talking about his readiness for an interview. By a third step, the actual telephone interview is conducted.

In the context of conducting the actual interview Busse (2003) also emphasizes the advantages, which in his opinion are connected to the guideline being formulated and structured as best as possible. The latter is said to be the best means to prevent problems of understanding which may occur particularly with *telephone* interviews, as "during the interview" one "is restricted to the verbal part of communication" (Busse, 2003, p. 31, own translation). It is outspokenly important, Busse (2003, p. 31, own translation) says, "to formulate questions as clearly and precisely as possible." Finally the author discusses the necessity of further asking in case of uncertainties, of the audio recording, and of the interview record, in the context of which it stays unclear if by this "record" he means a complete word-for-word transcript.

On the whole, a certain sensitiveness for the special nature of the telephone interview in comparison to the face-to-face interview becomes obvious in Busse (2003). As early as at the beginning of his contribution he states, "However, one disadvantage of this method is in the fact that in contrast to the common interview procedure, when one sits face to face with one's interview partner, quite an important part of human communication (gestures, facial expressions) is lost: one is restricted to the interview partner's voice as a source of information, and he or she only hears the interviewer's voice" (Busse, 2003, p. 28, own translation).

As we have already seen, however, the author suggests the interview to be strongly structured as a possible solution for potential interaction problems.

This way advantages are given away which are promised by (more) openly structured interviews, something, which Busse (2003) does not discuss, however.

In Burke's and Miller's (2001) contribution discussions in respect of the technically mediated kind of interaction of the telephone interview are completely missing. Explicitly, the authors understand their explanations to be "practical recommendations," most of all they address novices in the field of qualitative interviews (Burke and Miller, 2001, p. 3). Against this background they deal in very much detail with subjects such as the pre-test, recording technology, making contact, and scheduling.

Burke and Miller (2001, p. 4) structure the interview process by three phases: the phases before, during, and after the interview. In the context of the preparatory phase the authors recommend to make preliminarily contact with the interview partner by a letter, which already informs about actual questions. This way it becomes implicitly obvious that in the context of telephone interviews as described by them they must have certain kinds of questions and a certain type of interview partners in mind: "We found it useful to communicate our interview questions ahead of time to participants, along with a general introductory letter about our study. This would be especially relevant if you are researching a topic that is abstract, such as intuitive decision-making. Participants need time to reflect and think about their responses, and we found that this padding of time ultimately yielded more thick, rich descriptive data from participants" (Burke and Miller, 2001, p. 7).

Practically, the authors derived their methodical recommendations from interviews with managers, which were focused on the latter's decision-making behaviour. Thus, the research interest was in the professional way of acting of people who may be considered experts. This means that Burke's and Miller's methodical contribution – just as also Busse's – actually deal with *expert interviews* on the telephone, without the authors explicitly saying so.

As already indicated, in the context of the "pre-interview phase" Burke and Miller (2001, p. 5) deal in detail most of all with questions of making contact as well as with technological possibilities of audio recordings. During the phase of conducting the interview the interviewer's way of talking is in the fore. Methodical recommendations are similar to relevant instructions for qualitative interviews. It is explained in detail how interview partners can be motivated to go on with talking by help of signals from the recipient. It is then surprising in this context that Burke and Miller suggest a strongly structured interview guideline, which apart from open questions also provides closed ones. The answers to open questions are said to have the function of providing an explanation horizon for the answering behaviour with closed questions: "Ensure you have a mix of open-ended and close-ended questions. It is helpful to have some questions where people respond, for example, in a specific Likert scale fashion (that is, close-ended response options), so that you have some easy-to-score data. The open-ended questions will then provide you with the rich filler to elaborate upon such responses" (Burke and Miller, 2001, p. 21).

Recommending a semi-standardized way of proceeding is similar to Busse, the latter – as already explained – offering this as a solution for difficult interaction situations during a *telephone interview*, whereas Burke and Miller do not give any reason for their way of proceeding.[9]

In respect of the duration of the telephone interview, the authors talk about their experience that during the pre-test many interview partners considered a duration of 15 to 20 minutes too long. Thus, in the context of the actual field phase individual durations of interviews were agreed on with the respective interview partners. According to the interviewees' time budget and the study's maximum need of information, the interview guideline was individually composed.

Ideas for the "post-interview phase" are comparatively short. They are restricted to mentioning mainly content-analytical or categorizing ways of proceeding.

Both in Busse's and in Burke's and Miller's contributions it is conspicuous that there is no systematic comparison of telephone and face-to-face interviews. This is done by Opdenakker (2006) who compares qualitative face-to-face interviews and technology-mediated ones, while for the latter category he takes telephone, MSN messenger, and e-mail interviews into consideration. The comparison is done very fundamentally in respect of the chronological and spatial (a-) synchronicity of interaction situations (see Opdenakker, 2006, p. 4). According to this, the telephone interview has in common with the MSN messenger and also with the face-to-face interview that the interaction happens in a *chronologically synchronous* way, in contrast to the chronologically asynchronous e-mail interview. On the other hand, *in respect of space* the telephone interview is characterized by an *asynchronous* interaction situation which by the way is also true for the MSN messenger and the e-mail interview, in contrast to the spatially synchronous face-to-face interview. Opdenakker particularly discusses the advantage connected to spatial synchronicity in respect of method: spatially co-present interaction partners are able to perceive social signals ("social cues") in the form of non-verbal elements. The author assumes that the importance of non-verbal elements of interviews varies according to the kind of questions and the target group of a study: "Due to this synchronous communication, as no other interview method FtF [face-to-face; G.C.] interviews can take its advantage of social cues. Social cues, such as voice, intonation, body language and so on of the interviewee can give the interviewer a lot of extra information that can be added to the verbal answer of the interviewee on a question. Of course the value of social cues also depends on what the interviewer wants to know from the interviewee. If the interviewee is seen as a subject, and as an irreplaceable person, from whom the interviewer wants to know the attitude towards for example the labour union, then social cues are very important. When the interviewer interviews an expert about things or persons that have nothing to do with the expert as a subject, then social cues become less important" (Opdenakker, 2006, p. 7).

It is remarkable that here Opdenakker also refers to expert interviews, in the context of which he estimates that for the target group of experts the importance of "social cues" is less than with others. This would mean that sheer "voice-to-voice" communication during qualitative telephone interviews (Ball, 1968, p. 61) may at best be considered unproblematic if it is an expert interview.

However, possibly Opdenakker underestimates that "social cues" alone are of great importance for smoothly maintaining the atmosphere of the interview.[10] Conversation-analytical studies on telephone calls in private and institutional contexts, which for the time being have focused on opening and terminating a conversation (on this see the "classics": Schegloff and Sacks, 1973, Schegloff, 1977), showed that telephone interaction – due to lacking visual perception – means much more coordination efforts for the interaction partners even if it is only about identifying each other at the beginning or about finishing the conversation.[11] In the latter case the conversation partners must carefully prepare each other for the receiver being replaced. Finishing the conversation too abruptly is not a good option, as according to cultural conventions on maintaining social contacts it would result in considerable irritation (see also Höflich, 1989, p. 205f). The assumption suggests itself that even during the phase *between* starting and finishing the conversation the lack of non-verbal signals may result in increased coordination efforts and may also result in the organization of the conversation being disturbed, even more as this phase is much less ritualized than those of starting and finishing.

This assumption is contrasted by results of psychological laboratory experiments showing that compared to direct conversation situations telephone-mediated conversations do not prove to be more considerably affected in respect of organizing a conversation (see for example Butterworth, Hine and Brady, 1977, Cook and Lalljee, 1972). However, it must at once be added that for these laboratory examinations interaction situations from daily life and work contexts were simulated. In these contexts it is mostly no problem if there happens the – wide-spread – short-time overlapping of speech and negotiations on the right to speak. This is much more problematic in situations of scientific interviews, particularly in contexts of qualitative research where a different level of conversational skill is demanded than in everyday life. The interviewer tries to act according to the methodical imperative of the "minimum-invasive" way of proceeding. He or she is asked not to interrupt his or her opposite. Most of all he or she should avoid disturbing the interview partner's thoughts during pauses for thought. Thus, to be able to correctly judge an interaction situation the interviewer depends highly on non-verbal signals (on this see also Chapter 4 as well as Jordan, Marcus and Reeder, 1980, p. 217). Thus the following is valid: "the entire stock of non-linguistic signs of gestures, facial expressions, posture is not an unnecessary concomitant of speaking which might be blended out (...) but is constitutive for producing unambiguity for an act of speaking" (Bülow, 1990, p. 307, own translation).

Now it is remarkable that in methods-related literature on *standardized* interviews the possibilities and limitations of telephone interviews are discussed much more critically than in literature on qualitative interviews.[12] One is highly aware of the fact that the significance of non-verbal elements may not be underestimated (on others see most of all Friedrichs, 1990).

It is considered to be proven that telephone interviews are only suitable for interviews with simple question patterns and guidelines for answers (see Anders, 1990, Friedrichs, 1990, Hillmann, 2007, p. 890, Hippler and Schwarz, 1990, Schnell, Hill and Esser, 1999, p. 345). Against this background Noelle-Neumann and Petersen (2000, p. 184) state the fear that after all the wide-spread telephone surveys will result in methodical "impoverishment." The debate is contradictious in respect of the question of in how far the standardized telephone interview implies lower or higher quota of refusals. Hillmann (2007, p. 890) assumes that telephone interviews are regarded to be more anonymous and less personally embarrassing, from which he derives a lower quota of refusals. Noelle-Neumann and Petersen (2000, p. 193), however, point to the telephone interview being regarded "as less interesting and a bigger disturbance and more stress" in comparison to face-to-face interviews. This way they explain the then evidently higher quota of refusals of telephone interviews. The assumption that telephone interviews should be rather short (see for example Hillmann, 2007, p. 890) is also debated. Frey, Kunz and Lüschen (1990, p. 22) point out to the fact that longer telephone interviews may definitely be successful (on this see also Schnell, Hill and Esser, 1999, p. 351, Cockerham, Kunz and Lüschen, 1990, p. 405, own translation): "Also, in case of a short interview the interviewee will rather have the impression that in case of only a few questions the project cannot be respectable. Experience shows that in case of appropriate preparation, previous information, and a good and interesting course of the interview which is closely connected to the topic of the project telephone interviews of 30 minutes or even more are possible."

Interesting is the result that interviewees perceive (standardized) interviews as "less interesting" and short interviews as "not respectable." It is an open question in how far these results can be transferred to qualitative-oriented expert interviews on the telephone. At least it cannot be completely ruled out that these observations might also – and particularly – be true for experts, even more as this target group (as we may assume) is provided with a particularly high level of reflexivity.

7.4   Problems previous to and during expert interviews on the telephone

Bogner and Menz (2005a) state that usually it is easier to win experts over for an interview than people from an "unfiltered public" because they are professionally interested in their own field and they are basically more open towards research. Indeed, in the course of our study we were able to find that it is easy to win experts over if it is a face-to-face interview, but not if it is a telephone interview. Whereas experts meant for an interview at the place were quick to agree and as fast with offering a date for an interview, potential telephone interview partners were considerably reluctant with agreeing. This happened independently of which type of academic education institution these experts belonged or which function they had. A total of 12 telephone interviews was intended. However, due to delays – beyond the time limit – it was only possible to realize eight.

This is surprising in so far as the face-to-face interview was announced to be 60 minutes long and the telephone interview to be 20 or 30 minutes long. We assumed that experts, permanently suffering from time pressure, would be much more ready for interviews if these required comparably little time. But this was a misjudgement. Interestingly, also Burke and Miller (2001, p. 11) talk about the experience that fixing dates for telephone interviews was a lengthy thing; however in their case things were somewhat less problematic, as dates were fixed on the telephone: "We found participants more responsive to setting up interview appointments via the phone, compared to email. But this process can also become a scheduling quagmire that takes as much time as conducting the interviews themselves."

We conclude that with experts a shorter interview does not automatically work as a factor motivating for agreeing to an interview and fixing a date. In respect of its motivating effect, the attention paid to an expert by the interviewer's more or less time-consuming journey (across all of Germany) and a one-hour interview must not be underestimated. In this respect, the request for a rather short telephone interview is a different signal.

However, also it may be supposed that to play an important role the short period of 20 to 30 minutes for answering important questions of university planning is only a minor incentive for the expert, as it offers only little leeway for explaining or it forces him or her to give a compressed explanation. Thus, a rather short interview is not necessarily a relief. Possibly, in such a situation experts feel the need to previously prepare themselves (more intensively).

This consideration is supported by the observation that most telephone interview partners were only ready to agree after they had seen the interview guideline, something which due to lack of time was not always immediately possible. Further problems resulted from some telephone interview partners using the telephone call's basic flexibility with regard to scheduling. Compared to the face-to-face interview, there is no need for the interviewer to make a journey, appropriately it may be fixed or changed at short notice. One expert right at the beginning suggested a spontaneous date at very short notice – depending on an unforeseen gap in his schedule. Two interview partners changed a fixed date at short notice when the interviewer called them at the agreed time. Thus, telephone dates are less binding than face-to-face dates, as the telephone contact may be made again without effort at any other time. The flexibility expected from the interviewer in this context may be supposed to be a challenge for every research team.

But not only fixing dates for interviews was challenging. Also actually conducting the telephone interviews turned out to be a difficult matter. Mitchell (1984, p. 249) rightly points to the fact that due to lacking nonverbal elements interaction partners must organize the interaction process exclusively by way of language and voice, due to which conversations on the telephone require much more attention in respect of what is happening linguistically than immediately personal interaction: "The voice must express all that there is to say. It must cover both the content of the message and the necessary nonverbal instructions on how to interpret that content. Thus, talking by telephone demands a good deal more attention to vocal nuance than face to face communication does."

This statement is particularly valid for scientifically motivated telephone interviews (see also Chapter 3). In the following, by the example of selected transcript segments from three different telephone interviews we like to show interaction problems happening several times or being typical. Although the first phenomenon was not as often and frequently found in the data material as the second one, it could at least be observed in four cases, due to which it deserves attention.

Transcript segment 1[13]

01	IP1	Also es war ja die Frage danach so wie sich so ((nennt die
02		Hochschule)) positioniert,
03	I	Mhm,
04	IP1	ähm (--) gibt's denk ich schon: zu einem gewissen Antei:l, äh::
05		den Punkt, dass man sagt ähm 'hh äh (.) wir sind da nicht
06		vergleichbar,
07	I	Mhm,
08	IP1	un:d was man nicht gut vergleichbar- vergleichen kann, das ist
09		auch schwierig miteinander in Wettbewerb zu bringen.
10	I	Mhm,
11	IP1	Das hat ja auch (.) soweit erstmal eine gewisse Logik.
12	I	Ja.
13		(--)
14	IP1	Ähm:: (2,25) ja. 'hh Ähm: (---) ansonsten, (--) hat die ähm (.)

```
15          ((nennt Hochschule)) sich auch beteiligt an den Eliterun⌐den
16    I                                                        ⌊Mhm,
17    IP1   äh zu bewerben, also in der ersten Runde und jetzt auch in
18          der nächsten Runde, ⌐'hh und hat (--) 'hh sich insofern: also
19    I                         ⌊Mhm,
20    IP1   erstmal von der Forschungsschiene her (--) sehr stark (-) damit
21          beschäftigt, wo sind 'hh unsere Kernfelder, gleich ob das dann
22          Forschungsschwerpunkt oder Forschungscluster heißen soll,
23    I     Mhm,
24    IP1   eines von beiden äh:: gibt's da, hat das also für sich (--)
25          definiert, (1,5) un::d- (3.0) *was war noch die Frage*?
26    I     Ähm
27    IP1   'hh ach ja (.) um- um:: sich auch in diese Richtung dann zu
28          bewe⌐gen.
29    I        ⌊Mhm, mhm,
30    IP1   Ähm (--) ich denke dass- (2,25) 'hh ähm:: (2,0) ansonsten war
31          die- ((nennt Hochschule)) die letzten zwei Jahre und sicherlich
32          auch das nächste halbe oder ganze Jahr (.) 'hh sehr stark damit
33          beschäftigt, diese Modularisierung der Studiengänge
34          voran⌐zutreiben.
35    I           ⌊Mhm,
```

Translation:

(Due to language differences the transcripts only reflect the original (German) transcript to provide the reader with an idea of what the interviews were like.)

IP1	*Well, the question was how ((names university)) positions itself, after all,*
I	*uhm,*
IP1	*well, (--) I think this exists to a certain degree, ehm there is the point when you say 'hh well (.) we can't be compared to this,*
I	*uhm,*
IP1	*and what you can't really compare is also difficult to see competing*
I	*uhm,*
IP1	*after all, this is (.) also logical to a certain degree.*
I	*yes.*
	(--)
IP1	*Ehm, (2.25) yes. 'hh Ehm (---), also (--) ((names university)) has taken part in the elite rounds*
I	*uhm,*
IP1	*ehm, to apply, that is during the first round and now also in the second round, 'hh and (--)' hh in so far has under the research aspect (--) been dealing very much (-) with, where are*

	'hh our essential fields, no matter if you call it research focus or research cluster,
I	uhm,
IP1	it is one of these, ehm there is- has defined that for (--) himself, (1.5) and- (3.0) what was the question again?
I	Ehm
IP1	'hh Oh yes (.) to- to move towards this direction then.
I	uhm, uhm,
IP1	well (--) I think that – (2.25) 'hh ehm (2.0) otherwise during the last two years and surely also the next half or the whole year ((names university)) 'hh was very much occupied with driving on this modularization of courses.
I	uhm,

With segment 1, a number of linguistic irregularities (re-formulations, break-ings off) and longer breaks are conspicuous (lines 04–08, 14–17, 24–8, 30). Indeed, linguistic irregularities are not at all unusual with oral language, particularly if it is a daily life conversational situation. They even appear with very formal conversational contexts; however usually this happens to a very low degree. Accordingly, in our case the experts we interviewed (including the above quoted one) were in the overwhelming majority of interviews able to realize a rather "written" style. Compared to the remaining data material, the above quoted segment is thus conspicuous. In line 25 it is additionally the case that according to his statement the interview partner has forgotten the question (for a short time). On the whole it becomes obvious that the expert is not concentrating.

As already mentioned, the situation was similar also with three more telephone interviews. This raises the question if the interview partners were distracted by a third person, such as the secretary entering the room, and/or by a short-time activity (signing a document, looking for some information among the documents held ready for the interview). In the literature on methods of qualitative interviews one is aware of the fact that external disturbances may have effects on the content of the interview. Due to this there is trying to avoid situations prone to disturbances as far as possible. However, during a telephone interview it is not possible to make sure that the expert will exclusively pay attention to the interview (see also Engel and Behr 2008). In this respect, interviewers have no control over the interview situation.

But even more serious is the fact that often external disturbances cannot be identified as such, except the interview partner does so. This means that conspicuous linguistic irritations in the context of telephone interviews cannot be conclusively interpreted. It is not possible to judge if irritations are caused by external factors (as explained above), are due to topical reasons, or are caused by a "sheer" concentration deficit.

In our research context one reason for linguistic irritations might be that on the one hand the interview partners want to be cooperative and want to provide their opposite with useful information but that on the other hand, due to reasons of competition, they must at the same time very much consider which information to give without talking about a "trade secret." With some interviews there are explicit indications that for reasons of competition one does not want to further explain a subject.

If, on the other hand, linguistic frictions are "only" due to a temporary concentration deficit, there is the question of how far this is due to lack of support by the interviewer by way of *non-verbal* attention signals. Not without reason, literature on methods of qualitative face-to-face interviews emphasize that gestures addressing the interview partner, eye contact, and nodding – apart from linguistic reception signals – are of essential importance for the course of the interview.

Furthermore non-verbal aspects, particularly in the form of eye contact, are significant also for the interviewer, and that is when it must be ascertained if the interview partner has finished his answer, that is if should be a change of speakers and the next question may be asked. Segments 2 and 3 show which insecurities develop if these non-verbal elements are lacking:

Transcript segment 2

```
01   IP2   Was ich sehr kritisch- oder was ich m::h gewisserweise
02         beklage, ist äh das Akkreditierungsgeschäft,
03   I     Ja,
04   IP2   'hh
05         (--)
06   IP2   das ist natürlich ähm: (1,25) sehr auf⌈wändig, und 'hhh (.)
07   I                                         ⌊Mhm,
08   IP2   äh: ich sag mal trotzdem nicht immer ähm (1.0) streng rational,
09   I     Mhm, (.) mhm,
10         (1,25)
11   I     Ja. (--) 'hh Ja; neben Bachelor und Masterstudiengängen (...)
```

Translation:

IP2	*What I complain about very critically or ehm to a certain degree is the 'hh accreditation business,*
I	*yes,*
IP2	*'hh*
	(--)
IP2	*of course, this needs ehm (1.25) very much effort, and 'hhh (.)*
I	*uhm,*
IP2	*well, I'd say nevertheless it is not always ehm (1.0) strictly rational,*

I   *uhm, (.) uhm,*
             (1.25)
I   *yes. (--)'hh well, apart from BA and MA courses (...)*

The interview partner of segment 2 answers the question about which experiences were made at his university with the introduction of BA and MA courses. He was asked to formulate advantages and disadvantages of these new kinds of courses and, if necessary, to discuss necessities of change. Accordingly, in the previous sequences he mentioned various aspects, which he considers positive or negative. For example, he mentions the accreditation procedure, which is connected to the new courses. After the completion of line 02, mentioning the "accreditation business" will probably be completed by giving a reason, for one may expect an explanation why the expert judges "critically" on the procedure. In line 03, during a break by the expert the interviewer at first reacts by a reception signal. After taking breath and another short break (l. 04/05) the expert starts giving reason for his judgement (l. 06). At the end of the statement in line 08 on the one hand a thought has been completed, but on the other hand, given the weakly rising contour of intonation, one might think that reason-giving will be continued. The interviewer must make sure if the expert makes a break to further structure his speech or if he considers his contribution to be finished and is waiting for the next question. According to experience, in face-to-face situations eye contact is helpful with solving such cases of doubt. During a telephone interview this is not possible. Carefully, the interviewer reacts by a second "Mhm," the first signal being divided from the second one by a micro pause (l. 09). Then there is a break (l. 10): obviously still the interviewer is not sure about which kind of situation she is confronted with; in any case she does not dare interfering (possibly too early). But there is no change: no reaction by the interview partner becomes obvious. Reluctantly, the interviewer at first says "yes," followed by a short break, then, finally, she starts her next question (l. 11).

A similar situation is shown by segment 3 with another interview partner.

Transcript segment 3

```
01   IP3   Äh: das andere ist, dass wir äh: temporär Schwankungen hatten,
02         ⌈es gab also (--) Einbrüche als wir auf Bachelor Master
03   I     ⌊Mhm,
04   IP3   umgestellt haben,
05   I     Mhm,
06   IP3   äh:: die waren aber temporär, und haben sich jetzt ins
07         Gegenteil umgekehrt, ⌈also 'hh äh (--) äh: ja das- äh das sind
08   I                          ⌊Mhm,
09   IP3   eben auch statistische Pro⌈zesse; (--) n⌈re,
10   I                               ⌊Ja, ja,   ⌊mhm,
```

11	IP3	'h⌐h
12	I	└Mhm,
13	IP3	Gut.
14	I	Gut.
15		(1,0)
16	I	Sie wollten noch zur Internationalisier⌐ung etwas sagen?
17	IP3	└Ja. Inter- also
18	I	'hh
19	IP3	Internationali⌐sierung, (...)
20	I	└Mhm,

Translation:

IP3	*Ehm the other aspect is that we ehm had temporary fluctuations, that is there were sharp falls when we changed to Bachelor Master,*
I	*uhm,*
IP3	*ehm but those were temporary, and have now reversed, that is*
I	*uhm,*
IP3	*'hh ehm (--) ehm well, these- ehm these are also statistical processes; (--) you see,*
I	*yes, yes, uhm,*
IP3	*'hh*
I	*uhm,*
IP3	*well.*
I	*All right.*
	(1.0)
I	*You were also going to say something about internationalization?*
IP3	*Yes. Inter- Internationalization, (...)*
I	*uhm*

Also here it is about experiences with BA and MA courses. The interview partner talks about sharp declines in numbers of applicants after the change to the new courses, but he emphasizes that these had only been temporary and that meanwhile the process had reversed. In line 09, discussing this aspect is completed both in respect of thought and intonation. However, it stays an open question if the expert intends to further explain this aspect or if he intends to give several other aspects. The interview partner audibly taking breath in line 11 may be interpreted as indicating his speech to be continued. In line 12 the interviewer by the reception signal "Mhm" indicates her readiness to listen further. However, the expert by taking breath has not made himself ready for further explanations but for saying the word "well" which due to its strongly declining intonation is of a concluding nature (l. 13). This indicates an end of speech. Against this background the interviewer takes up the word "well" by saying "all right" (l. 14), this way ratifying the end of speech by the expert. By way of a following break, however, she leaves her opposite on the telephone the option of beginning to speak again (l. 15). Then she changes to another topic (l. 16). She reminds the expert of something which he has marked as a topic which must be dealt with in his previous statements and thus formulates a conversation-immanent request to narrate.

The comparative analysis of the change of situations of speech with face-to-face interviews produced the result that coping with this was much faster and easier.

On the whole, the interviewer subjectively perceived telephone interviews much more exhausting than immediate interview situations at the place, although the former were shorter than face-to-face interviews. Even if with face-to-face interviews the degree of attention is unquestionably higher, it is still even higher with telephone interviews, as lacking non-verbal signals must be compensated by much more work of interpreting what has been said, and that is in respect of structuring speech both topically and formally. Rightly so, Gläser and Laudel (2006, p. 169) emphasize that by intervening with the "apparent emptiness" of a pause for thought one will miss "important information." Thus, almost all the time the interviewer was in a situation of insecurity. On the one hand she was aware of the danger of interpreting a break not as an inner-speech break but as an indication of ending speech and that against this background she might interfere too early with the interview partner's thought. On the other hand she felt to be under the pressure of not allowing too long breaks. Not at all – if there was a speech vacancy – she wanted the interview partner to have the impression of lacking attention and to make him feel uncertain. It is also that periods of silence on the telephone, as shown by Hess-Lüttich (1990, p. 286, own translation), are risky for another reason: "Being silent together on the telephone is much more difficult to go on with than with direct conversation because both sides interpret it as a danger or even an interruption of the contact ("Hallo," "Are you still there?") (...) Thus, activities of securing the contact are more typical for the type of telephone conversation than for example activities of securing understanding."

However, Hess-Lüttich (1990) looks at daily-life telephone calls. But this thought is also – and particularly – of significance for telephone interviews, as for methodical reasons any uncertainty of interview partners must be avoided. This may also explain why with telephone interviews much more often the interviewer produced reception signals in the form of "yes" and "uhm" than was the case with direct interviews. On the one hand this was the only way to indicate attention, on the other hand these signals served also for communicating to the opposite that the telephone-technical contact was still intact. Also, vice versa strategies by the experts of reducing breaks became obvious, as conspicuously more often than their colleagues during face-to-face interviews they produced fillers by way of lengthening and other lengthening of syllables.

7.5 Conclusion

In respect of method, qualitative telephone interviews are a very demanding and thus difficult undertaking. This is not to say that due to this they are generally useless. It may depend on the kind of questions of a study whether telephone interviews are useful. In the context of the here presented "explorative-systematizing" study (see Chapter 2), which was first of all on finding out about examples of "best practice" in the field of university planning, we were able to gain outspokenly useful information by help of telephone interviews. However, the more strongly expert interviews are directed at generating theory, the more problematic the telephone method may be supposed to be. Due to the lack of non-verbal elements, the interaction process may be disturbed much more than with face-to-face interviews. Furthermore, potential external disturbances (such as the entering of third parties) are usually not recognized. This means that interviewers are not able to know if the interview partner's attention is exclusively directed at the interview. Thus, telephone interviews generate a kind of data material, which for the following interpretation process may leave many questions open. This may considerably obstruct theory generation.

There would have to be a much more systematic analysis of the question whether telephone interviews should be rather short – that is not longer than 20 to 30 minutes – or whether they may be much longer. Statements by methods-related literature are contradictious. Also our own empirical experiences do not allow for any clear statement: on the one hand there were indications that short telephone interviews, due to fewer possibilities of presentation and stronger necessities to compress, must be considered rather unattractive and not being relieving per se. This would suggest longer telephone interviews. On the other hand, probably not only for the interviewer telephone interview situations are particularly "attention-intensive" and thus exhausting. This might increase in the case of longer interviews. Thus, this might provoke unwanted interview mistakes and loss of concentration with interview partners.

What concerns the interaction problem of change of speakers during telephone interviews, this may be reduced by an interview strategy. In the context of the above presented analysis it could be shown that during potentially speech-vacant breaks the interviewer (due to her fear of blocking the interview partner by her next question) at first reacted carefully by reception signals and breaks, this way successfully leaving the interview partner enough freedom for answering the questions. This unconscious behaviour by the interviewer might be developed to become an interview strategy which would be: breaks by interview partners must be *systematically* accompanied by recipient signals and short breaks, and this way one must wait for further reactions until the situation is clear.

Notes

1. The client was the Saxonian State Ministry of Arts and Sciences, the conducting institution was the "Zentrum demographischer Wandel (Centre of Demographic Change)" of the Technical University of Dresden, heads of the project were Karl Lenz and Winfried Killisch.
2. Following Meuser and Nagel, by an expert we understand most of all somebody who "influences decisions and problem-solving beyond the routines of decision-making" (see also Bogner and Menz 2005a, Pfadenhauer 2005, see also Pfadenhauer, in this volume, and Köhler, 1992, p. 319f.). Meuser and Nagel consider expert interviews to be particularly interesting as "they inform about those action concepts and knowledge stocks as controlling, driving, and retarding processes of social change and the modernization of society." (Meuser and Nagel, 2005b) See also the most extended volume for the time being on "Expertise and Expert Performance" by Ericsson and others (2006), and see the volume "Eliten am Telefon" (Elites on the Telephone) by Martens and Ritter (2008).
3. Every state and Church university and college including art and music colleges as well as all vocational academies in the Federal Republic of Germany were written to.
4. Twelve interviews were conducted at universities, nine at colleges, and one at a vocational academy. Ten experts were from the so called "old" federal states, 12 from the "new ones." Thirteen federal states were represented, some of them several times, particularly Saxony, as the emphasis of the overall project was there.
5. Experts were concretely asked about their experiences for the time being with BA and MA courses and how they were judging on them in respect of their future attractivity. It was also asked which particular kinds of courses are and will be important for the respective university and for what reasons, and which target groups institutions of academic education try to win over as university beginners. Not least there was the question of which developments universities and colleges expect for the Federal Republic's university system: if they assume the university system to be de-differentiated (in respect of the three traditional "columns" of university, college, vocational academy), how they judge on future competitive behaviour among universities, and if in respect of relationships between universities they rather count on competition or on co-operation.
6. Also Bogner and Menz (2005a) are of this opinion when writing that "often" the expert "is used to acting in a publicity-effective way and close to the public."
7. On choosing experts see also Deeke (1995, p. 17) and Meuser and Nagel (2005a).
8. The status of co-expert was supported in so far as the interviewer, being a "Privatdozent" (having successfully completed a habilitation thesis but has not been offered a chair yet), was close to the expert at least in respect of the academic degree.
9. The semi-standardized method not even connected by the authors to their original target group – that of managers – who, as made clear by Trinczek (2005, see also Trinczek, in this volume), in the context of expert interviews do not expect leeway for extended narrations but a clearly structured guideline and a rapid game of questions and answers. Giving such a reason would have been plausible in so far as the communication process during an expert interview should possibly be "adjusted to the interviewee's cultural context" (Gläser and Laudel 2006, p. 110).

10. According to Reid (1977, p. 397), "social cues" have the following functions for a conversation: "1. Mutual attention and responsiveness (to provide evidence that the other person is attending). 2. Channel control (to indicate the way participants should take turns in speaking and listening). 3. Interpersonal attitudes (to indicate attitudes and intentions). 4. Illustrations (to accompany and illustrate what is being said – for example by gesture). 5. Feedback (to indicate whether the other person understands, believes, or disbelieves, is surprised, agrees or disagrees, is pleased or annoyed)."

11. See also the numerous linguistic works on telephone and language in situations of daily life conversations, such as by Bülow (1990), Hahn (1990), Hess-Lüttich (1990), Wiegmann (1990).

12. On this see Noelle-Neumann and Petersen (2000, p. 183) who write: The seemingly unstoppable increase of telephone surveys since the end of the 1970s is accompanied by the continuously rising number of books and articles in expert magazines where the advantages and disadvantages of telephone interviews are compared to those of oral-personal "face to face" interviews. See for example the works by Anders (1990), Brückner and others (1982), Buschmann (2001), Cockerham and others (1990), Friedrichs (1990), Frey and others (1990), Henkel (2001), Mc Cormick and others 1993, Noack (2003), Noelle-Neumann and Petersen (2000), Schenk (1990), Schnell and others (1999), Waleczek (2003). However, in the latest volume about telephone interviewing "elites" (edited by Martens and Ritter 2008) most of the articles only deal with the techniques of interviewing experts in the context of telephone surveys. It seems as if critical aspects fade into the background.

13. Transcript conventions: **IP** = interview partner, **I** = interviewer; [= beginning of an overlapping in case of speaking at the same time; (.) = short stop; (-) (--) (---) = breaks shorter than 1 sec., each (-) representing about 0.25 sec.; **(1.5)** = breaks being 1 sec. long or longer; ***yes*** = speaking in a low voice; 'hh = audible breathing in; punctuation marks, and **?** symbolize a weakly or strongly rising contour of intonation; punctuation marks ; and . symbolize a weakly or strongly falling contour of intonation; **yes:::** = lenghtening; the number of colons somewhat symbolizes the lengthening, each : symbolizing about 0.25 sec.; **mayb-** = unfinished statement; (( )) = remarks by the one making the transcript; (...) = omission in the transcript.

Further readings

Burke, L. A. and Miller, M. K. (2001) "Phone Interviewing as a Means of Data Collection: Lessons Learned and Practical Recommendations" in *Forum Qualitative Sozialforschung / Forum: Qualitative Social Research 2*, available at: http://qualitative-research.net/fqs/fqs-eng.htm, date accessed 11 June 2006.

Ericsson, K. A., Charness, N., Feltovich, P. J. and Hoffman, R. R. (eds) (2006) *The Cambridge Handbook of Expertise and Expert Performance* (Cambridge: Cambridge University Press).

McCormick, M. C., Workman-Daniels, K., Brooks-Gunn, J. and Peckham, G. J. (1993) "When You're Only a Phone Call Away. A Comparison of the Information in Telephone and Face-to-Face Interviews" in *Journal of Developmental and Behavioral Pediatrics 14*, 250–55.

References

Anders, M. (1990) "Praxis der Telefonberatung" in Forschungsgruppe Telefonkommunikation (ed.), pp. 426–36.

Ball, D. W. (1968) "Toward a Sociology of Telephones and Telephoners" in Truzzi, M. (ed.) *Sociology and Everyday Life* (Englewood Cliffs, NJ: Prentice-Hall), pp. 59–75.

Bogner, A. and Menz, W. (2005a) "Expertenwissen und Forschungspraxis: Die modernisierungstheoretische und die methodische Debatte um die Experten. Zur Einführung in ein unübersichtliches Problemfeld" in Bogner, A., Littig, B. and Menz, W. (eds) *Das Experteninterview – Theorie, Methode, Anwendung*, 2nd edn (Wiesbaden: Verlag für Sozialwissenschaften), pp. 7–30.

Bogner, A. and Menz, W. (2005b) "Das theoriegenerierende Experteninterview. Erkenntnisinteresse, Wissensformen, Interaktion" in Bogner, A., Littig, B. and Menz, W. (eds) *Das Experteninterview – Theorie, Methode, Anwendung*, 2nd edn (Wiesbaden: Verlag für Sozialwissenschaften), pp. 33–70.

Brinkmann, C., Deeke, A. and Völkel, B. (eds) (1995) *Experteninterviews in der Arbeitsmarktforschung. Diskussionsbeiträge zu methodischen Fragen und praktischen Erfahrungen* (Beiträge zur Arbeitsmarkt- und Berufsforschung: BeitrAB 191) (Nürnberg: Institut für Arbeitsmarkt- und Berufsforschung der Bundesanstalt für Arbeit).

Brody, H., Geronemus, J., Roy, G. and Farris, P. K. (2003) "Beauty Versus Medicine: The Nonphysician Practice of Dermatologic Surgery" in *Dermatologic Surgery 29*, 319–24.

Brückner, E., Hormuth, St. W. and Sagawe, H. (1982) "Telefoninterviews – Ein alternatives Erhebungsverfahren? Ergebnisse einer Pilotstudie" in *ZUMA Nachrichten 11*, 9–36.

Bülow, E. (1990) "Sprechakt und Textsorte in der Telefonkommunikation" in Forschungsgruppe Telefonkommunikation (ed.), pp. 300–12.

Burke, L. A. and Miller, M. K. (2001) "Phone Interviewing as a Means of Data Collection: Lessons Learned and Practical Recommendations" in *Forum Qualitative Sozialforschung / Forum: Qualitative Social Research 2*, available at: http://qualitative-research.net/fqs/fqs-eng.htm, date accessed 11 June 2006.

Buschmann, N. (2001) *Auswirkungen von Befragungsmodi. Andere Antworten bei Telefoninterviews als bei Face-to-face-Umfragen und Fragebogenerhebungen* (München: Grin-Verlag).

Busse, G. (2003) "Leitfadengestützte, qualitative Telefoninterviews" in Katenkamp, O., Kopp, R. and Schröder, A. (eds) *Praxishandbuch Empirische Sozialforschung* (Münster u.a.: LIT), pp. 27–33.

Butterworth, B., Hine, R. R. and Bradyleen, K. D. (1977) "Speech and Interaction in Sound-Only Communication Channels" in *Semiotica 20*, 81–99.

Cockerham, W. C., Kunz, G. and Lüschen, G. (1990) "Sozialforschung per Telefon: BRD und USA im Vergleich" in Forschungsgruppe Telefonkommunikation (ed.), pp. 400–12.

Cook, M. and Lalljee, M. G. (1972) "Verbal Substitutes for Visual Signals in Interaction" in *Semiotica 6*, 212–21.

Deeke, A. (1995) "Experteninterviews – ein methodologisches und forschungspraktisches Problem" in Brinkmann, C., Deeke, A. and Völkel, B. (eds) *Experteninterviews in der Arbeitsmarktforschung. Diskussionsbeiträge zu methodischen Fragen und praktischen Erfahrungen. Beiträge zur Arbeitsmarkt- und Berufsforschung Nr. 191* (Nürnberg: Bundesanstalt für Arbeit), pp. 7–22.

Engel, T. (2008) "Das eine tun, ohne das Andere zu lassen – Experteninterviews mit Managern am Telefon. Nutzen, Anforderungen, Praxis" in Martens, B. and Ritter, T. (eds) *Eliten am Telefon: neue Formen von Experteninterviews in der Praxis* (Baden-Baden: Nomos), pp. 75–94.

Ericsson, K. A., Charness, N., Feltovich, P. J. and Hoffman, R. R. (eds) (2006) *The Cambridge Handbook of Expertise and Expert Performance* (Cambridge: Cambridge University Press).

Forschungsgruppe Telefonkommunikation (ed.) *Telefon und Gesellschaft. Band 2: Internationaler Vergleich – Sprache und Telefon – Telefonseelsorge und Beratungsdienste – Telefoninterviews* (Berlin: Spiess).

Frey, J. H., Kunz, G. and Lüschen, G. (1990) *Telefonumfragen in der Sozialforschung. Methoden, Techniken, Befragungspraxis* (Opladen: Westdeutscher Verlag).

Friedrichs, J. (1990) "Gesprächsführung im telefonischen Interview" in Forschungsgruppe Telefonkommunikation (ed.), pp. 413–25.

Galster, G. C. (2006) "What's the Hood Got to Do With It? Parental Perceptions about How Neighborhood Mechanisms Affect Their Children" in *Journal of Urban Affairs 28*, 201–26.

Gläser, J. and Laudel, G. (2006) *Experteninterviews und qualitative Inhaltsanalyse als Instrumente rekonstruierender Untersuchungen* (Wiesbaden: VS).

Hahn, W. von (1990) "Telefon und Sprache. Einleitende Zusammenfassung" in Forschungsgruppe Telefonkommunikation (ed.), pp. 275–80.

Henkel, J. (2001) *Das Telefoninterview* (München: Grin-Verlag).

Hess-Lüttich, E. W. B. (1990) "Das Telefonat als Mediengesprächstyp" in Forschungsgruppe Telefonkommunikation (ed.), pp. 281–99.

Hillmann, K. -H. (2007) *Wörterbuch der Soziologie* (Stuttgart: Kröner), p. 890.

Hitzler, R., Honer, A. and Maeder, C. (eds) *Expertenwissen. Die institutionalisierte Kompetenz zur Konstruktion von Wirklichkeit* (Opladen: Westdeutscher Verlag).

Höflich, J. R. (1989) "Telefon und interpersonale Kommunikation – Vermittelte Kommunikation aus einer regelorientierten Perspektive" in Forschungsgruppe Telefonkommunikation (ed.), pp. 197–220.

Jordan, L. A., Marcus, A. C. and Reeder, L. G. (1980) "Response Styles in Telephone and Household Interviewing: A Field Experiment" in *Public Opinion Quarterly 44*, 210–22.

Köhler, G. (1992) "Methodik und Problematik einer mehrstufigen Expertenbefragung" in Hoffmeyer-Zlotnik, J. H. P. (ed.) *Analyse verbaler Daten. Über den Umgang mit qualitativen Daten* (Opladen: Westdeutscher Verlag), pp. 318–32.

Martens, B. and Ritter, T. (eds) (2008) *Eliten am Telefon. Neue Formen von Experteninterviews in der Praxis* (Baden-Baden: Nomos).

Mayring, P. (2000) *Qualitative Inhaltsanalyse. Grundlagen und Techniken* (Weinheim: Deutscher Studienverlag).

McCormick, M. C., Workman-Daniels, K., Brooks-Gunn, J. and Peckham, G. J. (1993) "When You're Only a Phone Call Away. A Comparison of the Information in Telephone and Face-to-Face Interviews" in *Journal of Developmental and Behavioral Pediatrics 14*, 250–55.

Meuser, M. and Nagel, U. (1994) "Expertenwissen und Experteninterview" in Hitzler, R., Honer, A. and Maeder, C. (eds) *Expertenwissen. Die institutionalisierte Kompetenz zur Konstruktion von Wirklichkeit* (Opladen: Westdeutscher Verlag), pp. 180–92.

Meuser, M. and Nagel, U. (2005a) "ExpertInneninterviews – vielfach erprobt, wenig bedacht. Ein Beitrag zur qualitativen Methodendiskussion" in Bogner, A., Littig, B. and Menz, W. (eds) *Das Experteninterview – Theorie, Methode, Anwendung*, 2nd edn (Wiesbaden: Verlag für Sozialwissenschaften), pp. 71–93.

Meuser, M. and Nagel, U. (2005b) "Vom Nutzen der Expertise. ExpertInneninterviews in der Sozialberichterstattung" in Bogner, A., Littig, B. and Menz, W. (eds) *Das Experteninterview – Theorie, Methode, Anwendung,* 2nd edn (Wiesbaden: Verlag für Sozialwissenschaften), pp. 7–30.

Mieg, H. A. and Näf, M. (2006) *Experteninterviews in den Umwelt- und Planungswissenschaften. Eine Einführung und Anleitung* (Lengerich and others: Pabst).

Mitchell, G. (1984) "Some Aspects of Telephone Socialization" in Thomas, S. (ed.) *Studies in Communication* (Norwood NJ: Ablex), pp. 249–52.

Mitchell, V. L. and Zmud, R. W. (1999) "The Effects of Coupling IT and Work Process Strategies in Redesign Projects" in *Organization Science 10,* 424–38.

Noack, G. (2003) *Online-Befragung und Telefoninterview* (München: Grin-Verlag).

Noelle-Neumann, E. and Petersen, T. (2000) "Das halbe Instrument, die halbe Reaktion. Zum Vergleich von Telefon- und Face-to-face Umfragen" in Hüfken, V. (ed.) *Methoden in Telefonumfragen* (Wiesbaden: Westdeutscher Verlag), pp. 183–200.

Opdenakker, R. (2006) "Advantages and Disadvantages of Four Interview Techniques in Qualitative Research" in *Forum Qualitative Sozialforschung / Forum: Qualitative Social Research 7,* available at: http://qualitative-research.net/fqs-texte/4-06-4-11-e htm, date accessed 14 March 2007.

Pfadenhauer, M. (2005) "Auf gleicher Augenhöhe reden. Das Experteninterview – ein Gespräch zwischen Experte und Quasi-Experte" in Bogner, A., Littig, B. and Menz, W. (eds) *Das Experteninterview – Theorie, Methode, Anwendung,* 2nd edn (Wiesbaden: Verlag für Sozialwissenschaften), pp. 113–30.

Reid, A. A. L. (1977) "Comparing Telephone with Face-to-Face Contact" in Sola Pool, I. de (ed.), pp. 386–414.

Schegloff, E. A. (1977) "Identification and Recognition in Interactional Openings" in Sola Pool, I. de (ed.), pp. 415–50.

Schegloff, E. A. and Sacks, H. (1973) "Opening up Closings" in *Semiotica 8,* 289–327.

Schenk, M. (1990) "Das Telefon als Instrument der Sozialforschung" in Forschungsgruppe Telefonkommunikation (ed.), pp. 379–85.

Schnell, R., Hill, P. B. and Esser, E. (1999) *Methoden der empirischen Sozialforschung* (München/Wien: Oldenbourg).

Sola Pool, I. de (ed.) *The Social Impact of the Telephone* (Cambridge u.a.: The MIT Press).

Trinczek, R. (2005) "Wie befrage ich Manager? Methodische und methodologische Aspekte des Experteninterviews als qualitative Methoden empirischer Sozialforschung" in Bogner, A., Littig, B. and Menz, W. (eds) *Das Experteninterview – Theorie, Methode, Anwendung,* 2nd edn (Wiesbaden: Verlag für Sozialwissenschaften), pp. 209–22.

Vogel, B. (1995) " 'Wenn der Eisberg zu schmelzen beginnt ...' – Einige Reflexionen über den Stellenwert und die Probleme des Experteninterviews in der Praxis der empirischen Sozialforschung" in Brinkmann, C., Deeke, A. and Völkel, B. (eds) *Experteninterviews in der Arbeitsmarktforschung. Diskussionsbeiträge zu methodischen Fragen und praktischen Erfahrungen. Beiträge zur Arbeitsmarkt- und Berufsforschung Nr. 191* (Nürnberg: Bundesanstalt für Arbeit).

Waleczek, T. (2003) *Das Telefoninterview in der empirischen Sozialforschung* (München: Grin-Verlag).

Walter, W. (1994) "Strategien der Politikberatung. Die Interpretation der Sachverständigen-Rolle im Lichte von Experteninterviews" in Hitzler, R., Honer, A.

and Maeder, C. (eds) *Expertenwissen. Die institutionalisierte Kompetenz zur Konstruktion von Wirklichkeit* (Opladen: Westdeutscher Verlag), pp. 268–84.

Wiegmann, H. (1990) "Zur Rhetorik telefonischer Kommunikation" in Forschungsgruppe Telefonkommunikation (ed.), pp. 313–18.

Williams, M. L. (1993) "Measuring Business Starts, Success and Survival. Some Database Considerations" in *Journal of Business Venturing 8*, 295–300.

8
Expert versus Researcher: Ethical Considerations in the Process of Bargaining a Study

Vaida Obelenė

8.1   Introduction

This chapter explores the dilemmas faced when interviewing experts by reflecting my own experiences in relation to the ideals of ethical research. In general, ethical issues encountered when doing a study are multiple; they arrive prior to, during and after a study (for example Mauthner and others, 2002, Homan, 1991, Kimmel, 1988, Kvale, 1996, Ali and Kelly, 2004). Ethical dilemmas are also acknowledged by researchers who work on powerful and knowledgeable research subjects (for example Odendahl and Shaw, 2001, Hertz and Imber, 1995, Moyser and Wagstaffe, 1987, Dexter, 1970). Against this background, it is the purpose of this chapter to reflect the extent to which the propositions of the democratic research literature – that is research that argues in favour of assigning equal rights to research subjects by turning them into co-researchers and, accordingly, engaging them at all levels of a study process – are relevant to an expert researcher. Furthermore, I seek to reflect the dilemma of the researcher who has a commitment to protect the study from harm and simultaneously owes a duty to protect the research subject from harm.

The argument is structured in the following way. As a first step I elaborate the understanding of the expert as a research subject, and review propositions derived from the literature on democratic and ethical research. As a second step, I discuss whether the democratic practices are at all appropriate for an expert researcher that simultaneously has to protect the research subject and the study from harm. The expert researcher has to manage relationships with powerful research subjects, and simultaneously he or she has to find a position of control in order to secure the purpose of scholarly investigation. On the basis of my own experiences of bargaining with experts I conclude that these practices do not necessarily mean more ethics in research, and that the participatory ideals and practices, however noble they are, may not be transferable to and even inappropriate for research based on expert interviewing. The question remains whether the researcher is able to accomplish such a twofold task of protecting the study and the expert, and how? The third part addresses this issue by discussing how the powerful experts are themselves vulnerable to impacts a study may have. Two issues can be distinguished. On the one hand, there is the question of how researchers may exploit information on strengths and weaknesses of an expert to their advantage when assuming a strong bargaining position and when motivating experts to engage with a study in a role assigned to them by the researcher. On the other hand, there is the question of how the researcher, who is committed to minimizing harm to a subject in a study context, may use such information on strengths and weaknesses of an expert in following the ideals of ethical research.

8.2   The expert, democratic and ethical research

The question is, in which way the interests of researcher and the expert should be balanced in the context of a study? Just as researchers have a duty of protecting their subjects from harm, so researchers have the duty of protecting themselves from harm; the tension which may turn to be resolvable only as "either one or the other" choice. Needless to say, a study potentially is linked to a variety of harms. Harm reduction targets to minimize negative consequences of participation in a study for a research subject. But most importantly it is the idea of benefit that facilitates their decision to take part in a study. It thus becomes important to acknowledge that the problem of harm is not resolved by minimizing the negative influence of the study: harm also occurs if the subjects do not benefit from the study in the way they anticipated. On the other hand, ethical stance is about securing the interests of scholarly investigation. Therefore, as another tension point in this discussion I want to consider the interests of the researcher that represent academic freedom to study phenomena and report findings. To sum up: the researcher owes a duty to ensure the purpose of the scholarly investigation and a simultaneous duty to protect the research subject from harm.

To do a study, among other things, means to embark on a process of negotiating and constructing the researcher's own position and the position to be assumed by the research subject at all levels of a study. The literature about managing relations with respondents suggests many professional tricks to avoid causing harm to the respondent and to achieve rapport and disclosure in an interview situation. Furthermore, there is advice on the need to foster and maintain the relationship with subjects or, in this case, co-researchers in a study beyond the interview situation. For example, the respondents ought to have the right to access their data and be given a chance to fix the transcripts; they should be provided a chance to look into reports prior to their dissemination and once more invited to give their "informed consent" to proceed. Respondents should even be offered opportunity to withdraw from a study at any point. In the meantime, the practices of doing research such as those conceived by the term "communicative validity" (Kvale, 1996) invite the researcher to engage in a process of validating the interpretation with the interviewees. All in all, the democratic research literature may suggest that such democratic practices facilitate research tactically, methodologically and are a requirement for ethical research (Hammersley, 1995, pp. 48–9). In the meantime, the literature specialized in knowledgeable and powerful respondents indicates that expert researchers may find themselves in a situation to pursue such good practices due to the nature of their subject. For example, the interviewees may claim their rights in a study as far as censoring the writings. Altogether, the survey of this literature and its arguments may be overwhelming and disempowering rather than instructive for arranging the practical aspects of research. For instance, by following the emphasis on the power of the subject and the necessity of permanent negotiation one may lose sight of defending the original research purpose.

It is true, however, that the literature warns the researcher on particularities of studying the powerful and knowledgeable. For example, feminist researchers, altogether proponents of democratic research practices, to refer to the hierarchical order in research arrangements acknowledged the difference between "studying up" and "studying down" (Harding, 1987, p. 8). There are situations, specifically they may occur when "studying up," that "imply important qualification to the feminist commitment to non-hierarchical research techniques" (Hammersley, 1995, p. 56). Hammersley furthermore argues that these situations may require from researchers to "exploit whatever resources they have to exert control over the relationship, on the grounds that in present circumstances the only choice is between being *dominant or being dominated*" (1995, p. 56). In a similar way, Luff by reflecting her own experience of "studying up" suggests that research practices developed in "studying down" *"may be not transferable, indeed may be counter-productive"* (1999, p. 692) when "studying up."

This chapter, for the most part, reiterates those themes and concerns expressed by researchers with regard to studying powerful people. Yet it is important to remind oneself of the particularity of the experts as research subjects, including their potentially dominating stand in the interaction with the researcher. Experts are knowledgeable and with power capacity (Bogner, 2005, see also the contributions of Bogner, Menz and Littig, in this volume). The expert researcher will encounter highly literate and knowledgeable people capable of offering their interpretation of reality, who, however, are also capable of exerting influence on a study. The question is, should the researcher and the expert be assigned equal power and at all levels of the research process? What happens when the conflict of interests ensues? It is common to regard a study in the perspective of power dynamics: such images of a study as a battlefield may become highly relevant for a study based on expert interviews. For example, as much as knowledge is perspectival and value implicated, there may be no means to resolve the interpretative conflicts. In this context, the question to ask is, how the choices the researcher makes in managing the relationships with the expert serve to cause such conflicts? While ethical stance, as described above, means a process of balancing study decisions in such a way that the harm to the subject and the researcher is minimized, which is a difficult but nevertheless worthwhile ideal to achieve, based on my own experiences in the following section I seek to demonstrate that the democratic research practices may be counterproductive and do not immediately mean that the research is more ethical.

This chapter is based on a reflection of my experience of interviewing people who were communist functionaries 15–19 years ago. In the meantime, they moved ahead to establish themselves in relation to new forms of knowledge and power. It is true, that the reasons to propose such a study as an instance of expert interviewing are not immediately obvious. While many people I studied may be described as those who may "influence the freedom of others to act" (Littig, in this volume), these capabilities ensue not immediately from the know-how I studied. This, however, merely draws attention to the constructed nature of the expert's position: the expert researchers would grant the experts' status in relation to the present day roles in society to the same people I was studying. The underlying purpose of the study was to contribute to the understanding of the communist recruitment system but also to explore the construction of the devalued condition of a communist functionary. In other words, the study was concerned with a sensitive and devalued topic; accepting the expert's status in such a study meant that individuals admit belonging to a blameworthy group in society. This implicated that the study had to overcome their reluctance to recognize themselves as experts. Besides, it had to expect that the experts would claim the control position in a study in order to protect themselves from harm in a context of such a topic.

8.3   The process of bargaining in practice

While the literature may propose the democratic research practices as a means to avoid ethical dilemmas, and possibly may even argue that the ethical research consists of such practices, it is important to note that such practices may not only facilitate but also thwart the research efforts, including the researcher's duty to pursue research in an ethical way. In this section on the basis of my own experiences of bargaining with experts I seek to reflect the democratic research practices as problematic choices for research based on expert interviewing, particularly by anticipating their potentially dominating stand in the interaction with the researcher. However, it is important to understand that whatever arrangement with the research subject the researcher achieves – the exclusion or invitation of the expert to become co-researcher – the tensions and dilemmas will follow from either approach. Finally, "bargaining," in the way I mean, does not imply abandoning the researcher's position, on the contrary, the simple point I wanted to make here is about the researcher in a strong bargaining position. This emphasis on bargaining, however, communicates my experience that a study of experts will be a form of bargained research and the interests of both parties will have to be considered.

Initially, when entering the field, I did not problematise this power relationship between me as researcher and the respondents in terms of their impact on my further work (for example, when writing on data). While I acknowledged the risks of giving in to the interests of the respondents, I was predisposed to secure the most urgent objectives. In particular, there was uncertainty whether, given the sensitivity of the topic and the small population that constituted the field, I will be able to secure my objectives in terms of data collection. For example, I had a list of 60 experts in Lithuania drawn from the archive sources going back as far as 16–19 years. Locating these people after so many years did not mean yet that they would be available for interviewing. For instance, the most radical case of accessing (although not exceptional) is represented by interview negotiation extending across three months with 19 answered phone calls. Furthermore, I identified about one third of those 60 experts as "irreplaceable" in relation to two criteria: on the one hand, it was a unique know-how this particular individual could offer; on the other hand, there were experts I had to access in order to generate credible grounds for the study. Besides, I was learning about inaccessible people (for example, death, illness, imprisonment, emigration). The pressure caused by my commitment to meet the study objectives was enormous. At these moments of negotiating I thought least about how I will have to write on the data I was accessing "at any cost" and by accepting everything that experts were offering.

For example, the "irreplaceable" expert informed me that he cannot accept taking part in a study as long as there is a communist perspective: either the topic is wrong or *"I think I am a wrong subject for you."* During our 40-minute negotiation process he recurrently tried to make me understand: *"This was just a job for me nothing more. I worked there like in many other places during my life."* He, however, not merely disagreed to support the main interest of the study but engaged with contemplation what could be a topic of his interest. When he accepted the interview, it was clear that he did not change his understanding on being a wrong subject. Besides, the topics to be addressed during the interview were reworked to consider his interests. Furthermore, it was obvious that my choices in analysis, interpreting and writing will have to develop a way to represent his opinion. This example shows how the expert was capable of influencing the study by exploiting my vulnerability ensuing from pressure to get access to data.

It is in light of this uncertainty that I embarked on the process of negotiating the study with the experts and making promises to them with regard to which benefits the study will generate and how I would minimize harms the study may cause. The practices of democratic research at that moment, among other things, appeared to be offering a valuable bargaining chip. I thought that such arrangements, for example, would generate sense of control and predictability on the part of the experts (for example, this seemed important given their social prominence and the fact that communist functionary is a devalued condition), and in this way eventually would motivate the experts to accept the invitation to take part in the study. However, during the first interviews I acknowledged the possibly thwarting implications of the democratic research practices. Partially in order to facilitate the interview interaction, partially in order to assess the validity of my interpretation, during the interview I was returning the question by interpreting the interviewee's preceding response in terms of the study's research questions. My efforts to interpret their words by "reading through or beyond the data" (Mason, 2002, p. 149) happened to be evaluated by *"I might have been not clear enough"* or *"That's not what I said"* phrases. Already at this point the most accurate interpretations were responded by using *"Yes, but"* construction. In other words, the likelihood of "interpretative conflict" (Yow, 2005, p. 142) was immediately obvious.

It was, for example, entirely obvious that I would not be able to engage with each research subject into a *"discussion, emerging as each of us granted the other interpretative space and stretched to understand the other's perspective"* (Borland, 1998, p. 331). Moreover, such conflicts are not easy to be resolved by appealing to academic standards of analysis, and interpretation as developed by the researcher is always at risk of being discounted as value implicated. Most importantly, what happens when the subject is not interested to understand the researcher's perspective? I certainly was experiencing how some of the interviewees were assuming the roles of "teachers" to explain that the questions I was asking were "wrong" which implied that my perspective and thus ability to understand the phenomena I was studying was also "limited." For example, when I sought information about hierarchical structure in response it was explained to me that I was observing an entirely irrelevant factor. Instead I was advised to focus on functional structure. This certainly was a valuable insight but I was not given information on hierarchical structure because the interviewee did not accept it was important (without even considering explaining why it was not important). Furthermore, there were instances when interviewees refused to accept my perspectives, even when corroborated with factual data. For example, I asked one of them whether he could explain why a rather significant proportion of people who were recruited by the system were those who simultaneously had an alternative option of engaging with academic career. *"There were* not many like that among us,"* he refused to accept the unanticipated perspective that

I was offering. My second attempt to elaborate on data I had did not change his stance. Yet now the most interesting part was to begin: "I can't get what are you getting at by asking this question," he eventually requested I delivered an explanation. The innovative perspective dislodged the expert from the position of control: he was not able to predict the consequences his reply may entail, but most importantly, he realized that he was not certain what the study's purpose was. These examples on how those people who experience themselves as knowledgeable respond, invite projecting the response the researcher could expect in case they are invited to "validate" propositions and conclusions of a study. Most importantly, what could be the consequences of a conflict over the interpretation given that the expert is not only capable of offering her or his interpretation of reality but may be capable of obstructing an alternative account proposed by the researcher?

One has to realize that when accessing "irreplaceable" and dominating experts, the researcher may experience pressures to comply with requests from experts, which may harm the interests of a study. Above all, it is important to understand that various potentially counterproductive arrangements are even necessary in order to protect research subjects from harm. It is true that the practices of engaging experts at all levels of a study may be the only way to go about the study (for example Raab, 1987). However, bargaining behaviour researchers have argued that bargainers might be offering more than necessary to motivate the other party to accept the contract (for example Corfman and Lehmann, 1993) and this is certainly a valuable insight for an expert researcher who faces a challenge of defending the interests of study and not only those of an expert. For example, I rather quickly during the fieldwork assumed a stance that experts are not to be engaged at all levels in a study process. By defending this stance I interviewed 36 experts in Lithuania and only four declined but even not for the reasons of lacking control. I received five offers "to help" but only if I wanted. However, partially because of my choices to accept the topics from the "irreplaceable" experts by making their concerns a part of the study; partially because of interesting exploratory opportunities offered by the unanticipated topics that were emerging from data which I collected; and partially because of what my commitment to protect the anonymity of experts and confidentiality of their data requested (the challenge which I did not anticipate to the full when distributing promises), I ended up doing a rather different study from what I designed initially. Certainly, my advantage was that I could allow this flexibility in research decisions.

However, eliminating the subject from the participation at all levels of research merely means that one problematic issue is replaced with another: the beliefs on the necessity of engaging subjects in harm and benefit management's have their good reasons. For the researcher, inferring the subject's perceptions of harm is not easy, if possible at all. Making sure that subjects are not harmed will require a high sensitivity; such an awareness will also result from the researcher's empathic ability to see things from another's perspective (Stewart, 1955, p. 132). But the risk exists that such perceptions are merely "a kind of subjective colonialism" (Nealon, 1998, p. 32). Furthermore, even if the expert leaves the study at the researcher's own discretion, it is still likely that the writings of the researcher will have to go through scrutiny of the subjects as audience and any mismanagement of data may bear immediate implications on the prominent research subjects. While there are plenty of possibilities to consider the experts as vulnerable, studying the experts entails a range of mechanisms, which invite the researcher to consider the impact of the researcher's work, including how the researcher could be harmed. The expert researcher has to have a perception of not only entering but also leaving and once again returning to the field. In light of these considerations, the expert may be defined as the subject the researcher can never completely disengage from, the expert is highly vulnerable to the impact of a study and the expert has the capacity to protect oneself from harm or, alternatively, is capable to push for benefit in a study context. Given that in my work I chose not to engage the experts as co-researchers, I had to tackle a difficult task given such a demanding research subject: first, the researcher has to motivate the prospective subjects to take part in a study, and then the researcher has to find a way to motivate them to leave the rest at the researcher's own discretion. Therefore, in the next section I turn to explore how I engaged with expert's motivation management. Simultaneously I aim to illuminate on the issues of expert's strength and vulnerability assessment.

8.4   Managing relationships with a motivated subject

What is the researcher's role in producing the motivated research subject? Dodge and Geis (2004) present an example of a study which failed to recruit a single participant on account of having provided unmotivating information. It is true that the reasons why an expert is motivated to take part in a study may be different and, for example, not once I experienced that factors such as their sense of duty to serve as a research subject on the topic were motivating the experts. In particular, this section aims to consider the researcher's responsibility in producing motivation of an expert to request a position of control in a study. I want to look into two types of motivation by offering them as something specifically an expert researcher should be cautious about. On the one hand, there is motivation, which is directed by the idea that participation in a study will provide benefits to an expert. When reflecting on this type of motivation I particularly want to emphasize the importance of understanding the researcher's own role in producing a perception of shared agenda in a study context. I also want to emphasize the ethical interviewing as a choice that eventually may result in irresolvable tensions when also pursuing the ideal of ethical writing. On the other hand, there is motivation, which is directed by fear that participation in a study will cause harm to the subject. Learning strengths and vulnerabilities of research subjects remains an important task if the researcher wants to do a study in a way that complies to criteria of being ethical. Such information also enables the researcher to predict resulting motivations on the part of the research subject and helps to understand strengths and weaknesses of the researcher's position in negotiating and implementing the study.

8.4.1   The benefit motivation

This type of motivation may be enhanced by offering incentives which lead experts to believe that their participation in a study will contribute to generating a range of beneficial outcomes as seen by them. I felt it was crucial to understand the expectations of experts with regard to the study but also more generally what type of study would be most relevant to answer their urgent concerns. This knowledge gave me a broader understanding of the expertise I chose to observe and allowed me to accommodate the study I wanted to do with reference to the urgent issues in the domain of a given expertise. Now I was able to speak about the study in their language of motives by clarifying to which extent the study will be able to fulfil such expectations. While it was certainly not applied or expert purpose driven research that I intended, the ability to "translate" the objectives of the study in terms of experts' vocabulary was a particularly valuable tactic when talking to experts with pragmatic interests and concerns.

From my experience in this process of negotiation it was vital to begin with the package of propositions with regard to the impact of the study that would appear attractive but also intriguing and somewhat amusing for experts. For example, when negotiating with former functionaries in order to emphasize a public moment of their experience and to imply their duty to take part in a study, I was sharing with them my belief that they have a duty to history writing due to their unique position in the past. This argument was something that was just too much for some of them to make any sense (considering that the communist past is devalued). One of them bitterly commented: *"You have to start writing history 10 years after everybody is dead,"* and almost without a pause he added: *"Shall we start?"* Indeed he might doubt the high ambition of the study, which pursues the controversial and highly devalued purpose in society and he warned me about the possible implications if such data – when used "too early" – may have on his life. But, among other things, his choice to accept the role of the research subject may mean that when his condition for history writing is met there is a chance that also his views will be considered.

Experts themselves facilitate the impression of shared agenda. I was asked perpetually by them when negotiating the interview: *"What is there in it for me?"* or *"Why should I care?"* If I failed to provide satisfying answers, the experts would themselves suggest what type of study interested them.

Furthermore, experts might try to show they are not only knowledgeable subjects but that they also are able to cope with issues as complex as research questions. Dexter (1970) shares his experience of elite as people who like to "teach." However, the decision to open a space for an expert to reflect the study implicates that the expert develops his or her own ideas about how the study should be done. It is true that evading a response to such questions or failing to satisfy the expert's desire to "teach" is not the best strategy for a researcher who has to recruit an irreplaceable expert or achieve consent to use data. However, once the researcher answers the question such as *"what is there in it for me?"* convincingly enough she or he might have recruited somebody who thinks of himself as not merely a research subject but a partner.

This brief excursus into what motivates experts to take part in a study gives an understanding that the researcher should be cautious that there are established topics and concerns in the field to such an extent that working on the topics as desired by the researcher might be difficult, if possible at all. Among other things, success depends on creating a sense of interest and support to the study on the part of the research subjects. While researchers experience difficulties in gaining the experts' cooperation in research efforts, they will have to think about the ways to motivate the reluctant to contribute, disinterested or highly busy experts to take part in a study. And, of course, the opposite of this is also true: the expert researcher may encounter highly motivated individuals who have a particular interest or strong feelings about the topic and want to participate actively in a study. Moreover, they may have their own ideas about the benefit the study will generate. But here await decisions to engage or not engage in study bargaining, as discussed in preceding sections.

In my work I discerned the interview interaction as a particularly problematic source in building the notion of shared agenda. The interview negotiation is explicitly marked with the purpose of shaping a shared agenda, but in the interview interaction this explicitness typically will be lost. The issue to contemplate for an expert researcher is that the fieldwork ethics (for example Ryen, 2004) might turn to be another choice that will put a further spoke in the researcher's wheel. Literature typically emphasizes the importance of maintaining a balance between different roles: researchers find themselves experiencing tension between professional obligation to seek the best information possible and interpersonal obligation to respect the subject's privacy and well-being. Advice on ethical fieldwork typically considers the issue of informed consent and focuses on building the rapport and on the "tricks" of maintaining it throughout the interview. The subject will not be judged even if the researcher disagrees with the subject's views; instead the researcher seeks to understand and displays an understanding. Clearly it may only mean that these encouragement techniques are interpreted by the subject in terms of agreement and shared views. It was not once during my fieldwork that while experts accepted reluctantly to engage with the study, it was throughout this investment in the interview inter-action that they developed their ideas of the agenda the study pursued and came to care about the outcome it produced: by contemplating the subject matter they understood the purpose and usefulness of the study (but in their own way).

8.4.2   The harm motivation

Certainly there are actions the researcher can take to limit and regulate the experts' exposure to vulnerability in a study. On the one hand, under-standing the expected harm perceptions on the part of the experts invites the researcher to engage with management of motivation such as the steps targeted at reducing the collection of potentially harmful data, particularly those which are not even necessary for a study. On the other hand, collect-ing data on sensitivities, competence and social embeddedness of experts in my work proved to be a valuable source of information when projecting which of my choices when analysing, interpreting and writing may cause harm to experts. In the following I seek to discuss these issues in relation to three images of an expert, namely the sensitive subject, the competent sub-ject and the socially embedded subject.

8.4.2.1   *The sensitive expert*

The way the researcher delivers an image of a trustworthy individual and a credible professional capable of preventing the harm is but only one aspect the researcher ought to be cautious about. An equally important task during my fieldwork was reducing the collection of sensitive material in the context of the sensitive topic, including the task of not asking unnecessary and pro-vocative questions. Some of these tasks I was tackling certainly may be con-sidered as an instance of self-censoring but my unwillingness to endanger the interviewees won out. My decisions reduced the problems of collecting such data but it is also true that these sensitive and often provocative topics were entering the study in other ways. For example, I refrained from addressing the topics of property stealth, one of the crimes that the stigma theory tends to assign to the people I was studying in Lithuania, by instead establishing that I am interested in production and transfer of know-how. However, the inter-viewees were addressing the sensitive issues, for example, by accounting how others were stealing and by expressing their regrets that I was not interested in the issues which, according to them, were the topics of the utmost import-ance. While I explicitly omitted the possibility that the study will tackle such topics, my perception was that this information invited the experts to think that they could openly talk about such urgent for them topics without even occasionally bothering to enter "off-the-record" passage.

Nevertheless during the interviews there were always sensitive issues to address and they tended to vary unpredictably among the people I was interviewing. To my relief, it often happened that when after a lengthy hesitation I accumulated courage and asked, the experts appeared to be highly eager to explore an "interesting" perspective. When reflecting on what misleadingly appeared to be the sensitive issues to me, I realized that often such perceptions resulted from my own mismanagement of the study: I experienced the issues as potentially sensitive when I felt that the interviewee would think that the topic is not a part of an agreement about the interview. I realized that the issues were sensitive only when the interviewees asked to stop the recording or when they were moving closer to me, as if they wanted to tell a secret.

Yet it is true that the experts grow increasingly comfortable during the interview; they become engaged and committed to the study. At these moments they are ready to go to great lengths to make sure the researcher will be equipped to do the study. Moreover, the experts do not only breach the limits of their own privacy, they also breach the privacy of others and disclose the secrets of organizations. Accounts of expert researchers are full with descriptions of such "miracles" when their respondents "open up" and this is how I experienced the process. In that context, it was important for me to understand how the length of the interview was producing the exposure of experts to vulnerability. My perception of an interview dynamics was that after a very desirable development such as "opening up" the moment of "breaking down" follows. I achieved understanding that two hours of interaction almost certainly meant that a productive time of an interview was exhausted and the experts by now were wandering into issues which increased their exposure to harm and, among other things, requested that I give away the researcher's role.

I collected plenty "off-the-record" or "not for press" episodes during the interview. However, there was also plenty of apparently sensitive information without such markers involved. It is obvious that when at first the researcher struggles to recruit respondents amid the risk they may decline the sensitive topic, now the researcher faces decisions how to go about the sensitive data collected, possibly by wrongly assessing which issues are sensitive. The guidelines the experts give may be vague. What should, for example, the phrase "I trust you" pronounced recurrently throughout the interview entail for what to do with data? To understand the possible impact of my decisions of working with data, I sought to explore whether the specific topics appeared to be sensitive in the context of other interviews. In my work such consideration proved to be a valuable tool, albeit still limited, in developing sensitivity to vulnerabilities of the experts and an additional source of judgement when taking decisions.

8.4.2.2   *The competence of the expert*

The reason to assign the research subjects with the status of an expert alone draws the attention to the fact that they are knowledgeable and invites the researcher to assume their competence. I, for example, anticipated from the beginning that being of the age which means that I was too young to experience the past events might generate an impression of my incompetence. I anticipated a certain patronizing and, accordingly, exhaustive explanations. However, the experts accounted by mentioning names of people without explaining who they were, they used the slang words without explaining them, they were interrupting my questions by implying that they understand what I want to know, and they spoke about past events without contextualizing them as if I was taking part in them. The experts assumed my competence to understand such highly specific references and they assumed they understand my purpose. But as much as such a format was difficult to follow, it seems, it also demonstrates disregard of the experts to the competence of the researcher. This illuminates the problem the researcher has to face: the experts set interaction and produce data under the false assumptions of the researcher's competence.

I found it was crucial to shape the understanding of different senses of competence that characterize the researcher and the expert: it allowed to ease domination relationships by shaping perception of difference and specialization but simultaneously provided a chance of informing the experts about the different perspectives into the topics. For example, it was important to think about how I could articulate the questions I wanted to ask in a way that would make the experts perceive them as innovative perspectives into the topic. When the expert would say, *"I never though about this in such a way,"* I felt that I was recognized as competent.

Creating a sense of difference in competence of the interacting parties may help to offset experts' desire to teach or overpower, but, of course, the opposite response might be the case. Still such strategies on revealing different competence may helpfully invite experts to express a more profound interest in the study's purposes and, if (like in the example I present below) such perception of incompetence results too late, there is still a chance for them to inform the researcher on the status of the data they delivered under the false assumptions. For example, one expert devoted seven hours of his time to the study (this certainly was one of the exceptionally long interviews which extended from "less than one hour"). Only after five hours had elapsed he, an engineer by education, realised that there was not a single "yes" or "no" question asked. He then tried to figure out how I was going to produce tables with percentages and graphs from the passages that he delivered in the course of our interaction. *"I only hope you do not set me up,"* he then whispered for a goodbye when I was finally leaving. Ideally the principle of informed consent rules out the possibility of covert research and deception. However, regardless of my earnest attempts to inform the experts about the study, I had the sensation of covert research all throughout the fieldwork, similarly like that described by Luff (1999). Not once did I come across experts who felt competent and rushed impatiently through introductory stages by delivering their consent without informing themselves about the study. In fact I got so used to that pattern that I felt highly disturbed when the nineteenth interviewee spent about 30 minutes "examining" the study and carefully taking notes.

All in all, the researcher cannot expect that experts, however knowledgeable they are, will be able to assess the meaning and implication of their account in relation to the interpretative perspectives of the study. When experts assume that they understand hazards and benefits pertaining to their participation in a study, it merely means that they take their point of view for the researcher's point of view. People are competent in their own ways: "there can be no universal criteria of ascertaining competence" (Sin, 2005, p. 280). The examples of the experts, who assume their competence in a study context as discussed above, may mean that they deliver data by controlling for entirely different risks than the study represents. The responsibility that awaits the researcher to protect the experts from harm may turn out to be a challenging task, particularly that there just does not seem to be another way to interpret their data than by ascribing the meanings they assign. Beyond the strategies to encourage the experts to acknowledge different senses of competence, I proposed earlier that my solution to this problem was to find a way to motivate the experts to leave the study at the researcher's own discretion.

8.4.2.3   *The social embeddedness of the expert*

Regardless of how researchers conceive experts in terms of their know-how, the experts are implicated into social hierarchies and associations. Experts are few, they may be interconnected, and they take part in unique events. This signals that securing the anonymity of the expert is a likely problem an expert researcher will face. Furthermore, their close interconnection means that some may harm others by disclosing information others would consider private or secret. For example, by choosing to work on people who worked in one and the same high office, I entered a network of friends and foes; some of these people have not been in contact for as many as 20 years. Talking about their own experience, which is also the experience of others requires a high sensitivity and a skill from the expert of how to go about the topics if others should not be harmed by what a given expert says. And while some failed this task trespassing upon the privacy of others or breaching the secrets of organizations unintentionally, there also were those who took their chance to take revenge on their foes or punish those whom they considered offenders. Furthermore, the questions they asked about others were incredibly direct (even such as, for example, "is he still a heavy drinker?," "is he still a womaniser?" or other references to the "dark," immoral, or sometimes embarrassingly private side of other experts interviewed). These experts' stories, gossips and questions about others, however, in my work became an interesting perspective in developing awareness about sensitive topics. For example, there was one expert who spoke about how a human being is responsible for protecting the devalued accomplishment from destruction. I was interpreting this passage, which he delivered in an abstract and somewhat metaphorical way, as a valuable insight into the knowledge transfer from one system into another. It was with the help of "gossipers," however, that I was able to realize that the criteria in terms of which the expert described the "obligation" correspond to the business project which not once publicly was considered in terms of theft. This certainly influenced me to become cautious in choosing how to exploit such a passage in the text. Furthermore, the expert's skill in delivering the sensitive message by abstracting it to the level where it loses sensitivity inspired some of the choices I made when writing about sensitive topics.

Expertise implicates as a range of beliefs and stereotypes; it may entail a devalued and stigmatized condition. A considerable proportion of the 69 people I interviewed in two societies may be described in terms of being prominent people and some of them, for example, established their post-communist lives without "highlighting" their former communist involvement. The participation in a study may immediately bear implications on the socially embedded life of an expert. Moreover, I certainly experienced myself to be much less a "disinterested observer" than I wanted to be. While the interaction with research subjects starts from the ideas about what type of being I am going to encounter, this is yet another reason why it is helpful to foster somewhat different images of experts: the images would help the researcher to be assertive enough to enter into a negotiation with an expert and seek the data for the purpose of own scholarly investigation; but simultaneously the image of an expert would help the researcher to be cautious and attentive to vulnerabilities of the research subjects.

8.5   Conclusion

In this chapter and drawing on my experiences of studying powerful research subjects, I suggest discussing democratic research practices as a set of possibly counter-productive research tips for expert researchers. While the proponents of democratic research may argue that such practices are also immediately ethical, it is, in my view, important to question this proposition. For example, the discussion of the possibility of interpretative conflicts between researcher and experts as subjects of research suggests that there is a risk that the study may reach an ethical impasse. Instead, the expert researcher needs to anticipate and carefully negotiate the tensions which may follow from the decision to adopt recommendations in the literature on turning the research subjects into co-researchers. The reflection of the status of powerful research subjects has long been an issue in research. Yet it is important to remind oneself of the particularity of the experts as research subjects, including their potentially dominating stand in the interaction with the researcher.

Whatever arrangement the researcher achieves – the exclusion or invitation of the expert to become co-researcher – the question remains what kind of action the researcher could take in order to anticipate the tensions and dilemmas that will follow from either approach. It should be obvious from my discussion that the solution I adopted in my own work is conventional and follows the first strategy: beyond the interview situation the research subject is not invited to participate in the process, while the researcher assumes responsibility with regard to the representation of the interests of the research subjects. While this is certainly not the only solution I conclude on the basis of my experiences and the specific framework of my study, that such a model can sufficiently secure the purpose of the investigation and simultaneously fulfil the duty to represent the interests of the research subjects. Such arrangement, however, implicates that the researcher alone is responsible for decisions with regard to harm and benefit management in a study context. This is an uneasy task given that the expert, among other characteristics, is a research subject difficult to disengage from and is vulnerable to the impact of a study.

In any case, a study of experts will always be a form of bargained research: it will be an outcome of negotiations between the researcher and the expert; the interests of both parties have to be considered. In order not to be corrupted by the experts' interests the researcher needs to stick to the research agenda and to remain assertive enough in defending his or her desired role as well as the topics of the study that need to be supported by the experts. Finally, while underlining the commitment to the ideal of ethical research, the chapter invites caution with regard to motivating the experts to take part in the research. The expert as a respondent is vulnerable to the impact of a study or may be seduced by its apparent benefits. Here I discussed how the expectation and anticipation, on the part of the respondent, of harm and benefit resulting from the study is actually facilitated by the researcher's own techniques of engaging the respondent, techniques that provoke the wish of the respondent to assume control and, eventually, the status of a co-researcher.

Acknowledgements

I wish to thank Alexander Bogner and Herwig Reiter for their comments.

Further readings

Dexter, L. A. (1970) *Elite and specialized interviewing* (Evanston: Northwestern University Press).

Raab, C. (1987) "Oral history as an instrument of research into Scottish educational policy making" in Moyser, G. and Wagstaffe, M. (eds) *Research methods for elite studies* (London: Allen and Unwin), pp. 109–25.

Luff, D. (1999) "Dialogue across the divides: 'Moments of rapport' and power in research with anti-feminist women" in *Sociology 33*, pp. 687–703.

References

Ali, S. and Kelly, M. (2004) "Ethics and social research" in Seale, C. (ed.) *Researching Society and Culture* (London: Sage), pp. 115–28.

Bogner, A. (2005) *Grenzpolitik der Experten. Vom Umgang mit Ungewißheit und Nichtwissen in pränataler Diagnostik und Beratung* (Weilerswist: Velbrück Wissenschaft).

Borland, K. (1998) "'That's not what I said': Interpretative conflict in oral narrative research" in Perks, R. and Thomson, A. (eds) *The Oral History Reader* (London: Routledge), pp. 320–31.

Corfman, K. P. and Lehmann, D. R. (1993) "The Importance of Others' Welfare in Evaluating Bargaining Outcomes" in *The Journal of Consumer Research 20*, pp. 124–37.

Dexter, L. A. (1970) *Elite and specialized interviewing* (Evanston: Northwestern University Press).

Dodge, M. and Geis, G. (2004) "Fieldwork with the elite: interviewing white-collar criminals" in Hobbs, D. and Wright, R. (eds) *The Sage handbook of fieldwork* (London, Thousand Oaks, New Delhi: Sage Publications), pp. 79–92.

Hammersley, M. (1995) *The Politics of Social Research* (London, Thousand Oaks, New Delhi: Sage Publications).

Harding, S. (1987) *Feminism and Methodology* (Bloomington, Milton Keynes: Indiana University Press, Open University Press).

Hertz, R. and Imber, J. B. (eds) (1995) *Studying elites using qualitative methods* (Thousand Oaks, CA: Sage Publications).

Homan, R. (1991) *The Ethics of Social Research* (London: Longman).

Kimmel, A. J. (1988) *Ethics and Values in Applied Social Research* (Newbury Park: Sage Publications).

Kvale, S. (1996) *Interviews: An Introduction to Qualitative Research Interviewing* (Thousand Oaks, CA: Sage Publications).

Luff, D. (1999) "Dialogue across the divides: 'Moments of rapport' and power in research with anti-feminist women" in *Sociology 33*, pp. 687–703.

Mason, J. (2002) *Qualitative Researching* (London, Thousand Oaks, CA: Sage Publications).

Mauthner, M., Birch, M., Jessop, J. and Miller, T. (eds) (2002) *Ethics in Qualitative Research* (London, Thousand Oaks, CA, New Delhi: Sage Publications).

Moyser, G. and Wagstaffe, M. (eds) (1987) *Research methods for elite studies* (London, Boston: Allen and Unwin).

Nealon, J. T. (1998) *Alterity politics: ethics and performative subjectivity* (Durham, NC, London: Duke University Press).

Odendahl, T. and Shaw, A. M. (2001) "Interviewing elites" in Gubrium, J. F. and Holstein, J. A. (eds) *Handbook of Interview Research: context and method* (Thousand Oaks, London, New Delhi: Sage Publications), pp. 299–316.

Raab, C. (1987) "Oral history as an instrument of research into Scottish educational policy making" in Moyser, G. and Wagstaffe, M. (eds) *Research methods for elite studies* (London: Allen and Unwin), pp. 109–25.

Ryen, A. (2004) "Ethical issues" in Seale, C. (ed.) *Qualitative Research Practice* (London, Thousand Oaks, CA: Sage Publications), pp. 230–47.

Sin, C. H. (2005) "Seeking informed consent: reflections on research practice" in *Sociology 39*, pp. 277–94.

Stewart, D. A. (1955) "Empathy, common ground of ethics and of personality theory" in *Psychoanalytic review 42*, pp. 131–41.

Yow, V. R. (2005) *Recording Oral History: A Guide for the Humanities and Social Sciences* (Walnut Creek, CA, Oxford: AltaMira Press).

Part III

Fields of Application: Applications of Expert Interviews in Different Fields of Research

9

How to Interview Managers? Methodical and Methodological Aspects of Expert Interviews as a Qualitative Method in Empirical Social Research*

Rainer Trinczek

9.1 Introduction

In discussions on methodology, purists frequently raise objections to the expert interview[1] on grounds of it being a "dirty" method. Expert interviews, they claim, operate in a "no-man's-land" somewhere between the qualitative and quantitative paradigm[2] devoid of much profound methodological reflection. Flexibly applied in empirical research, relying more or less on an interview schedule depending on the research interests and the specific research question involved, conducted in a more or less open fashion, the data prepared, analysed, and interpreted in some obscure fashion according to homemade recipes, expert interviews, in the eyes of methodology gurus from the ranks of qualitative as well as quantitative methodology, fail to meet the standards of either one of the paradigms. The social researchers M. Meuser and U. Nagel have experienced this with the qualitative research community: "Whenever the word "guided interview" falls, relentless scepticism from hard-line advocates of "soft" methods is guaranteed. Resort to concepts such as semi-structured or focused interview does little to remedy this – quite to the contrary" (Meuser and Nagel, 1989, p. 8, translated from German).

Such discontent with guided expert interviews is also reflected in the relevant literature on methodology, which rarely deals with this method in any detail. Whereas, in the German context, the "narrative interview" and "objective hermeneutics," which tend to be viewed as particularly refined, carefully considered, and highly sophisticated methods of collecting and analysing data respectively, have attracted overwhelming interest, the guided interview has been relegated to the sidelines, even though it is actually much more frequently used in empirical social research.[3]

This article is an attempt in defence of the expert interview as a useful and suitable instrument for data collection. It will be discussed with reference to the qualitative paradigm, since guided expert interviews are typically, and rightfully so, associated with qualitative methodology. Drawing on interviews with managers, the problem of the ideal interview setting for subjective structures of relevance to freely emerge will be discussed, which – as we all know – is a key issue in qualitative methodology.[4]

9.2   Methodological basics

With recourse to symbolic-interactionist and phenomenological approaches, standardized methods of interviewing have been criticized on grounds of systematically shutting the door on opportunities to get at what interviewees "really" think, since such approaches to interviewing fail to adequately consider the specific interview situation as well as the constitutive features of everyday life and everyday communication along with the subjective attribution of meaning that takes place therein. The interview situation, thus the reasoning, is of course no exemption in terms of the significance of ascribing meaning: in light of their everyday knowledge and structures of relevance, interviewees attribute certain meanings to the questions asked and respond based on those subjective interpretations. Accordingly, Cicourel, in his classical text on "Method and Measurement in Sociology" (1970), stresses: "If it is correct to assume that persons in everyday life order their environment, assign meanings or relevances to objects, base their social actions on common-sense rationalitites, then one cannot engage in field research or use any other method of research in the social sciences without taking the principle of subjective interpretation into consideration. (...) To ignore this point is to render both the questions (or conversations) and the answers received as problematic and/or meaningless." (Cicourel, 1970, p. 61) And: "Standardized questions with fixed-choice answers provides a solution to the problem of meaning by simply avoiding it" (Cicourel, 1970, p. 108).

The high degree of sensitivity to context is rightfully regarded as a crucial advantage of qualitative interviews over standardized survey methods; this sensitivity pertains to the context of interviewees' everyday lives and the respective structures of relevance orienting their actions as well as to the context of the interview situation. With this in mind, it has been argued that social scientific research must systematically "adapt to the rules of everyday communication that exist prior to the research process" (Schütze and others, 1981, p. 434, own translation) as an indispensable methodological prerequisite for successful interviewing. The terms "openness" and "communication" refer to two basic norms guiding the process of data collection (Hoffmann-Riem, 1980) that, at the methodical level, are conceived to enable an interpretive sociology to effectively make good on its methodological promises.

However, in the further course of the debate on methodology, a peculiarly one-sided specification of these "prior rules of everyday communication" has taken hold. The fundamental openness of qualitative interviewing for the specific area of research in question, with the key advantage of allowing the researcher to flexibly adapt to the large diversity of differently structured social contexts, has been increasingly displaced by a set of best practice instructions defining "good" qualitative interviewing practice.

With reference to the supposedly largely narrative structure of everyday communication, which research is required to adjust to, it has become a widely unquestioned commonplace that the best possible interview setting for encouraging interviewees to disclose their subjective attributions of meaning and structures of relevance is one in which the interviewer largely refrains from intervening in the interview. The interviewer is called upon to exercise pronounced restraint – such the logically perfectly consistent reverse conclusion – as a means of respecting the "prior rules of everyday communication in the field."[5]

This line of reasoning, indeed, plays a significant role in nourishing the scepticism with which hard-line advocates of qualitative methods view the guided expert interview. In their perception, this method involves too much interviewer intervention and structuring so that interviewees are not given the opportunity to freely develop their own structures of relevance.

In society, however, there exist realms of social reality where everyday communication for the most part follows completely different rules. A company, for instance, represents such a world. Now, if we take the methodological foundations of qualitative research seriously with an eye to companies as areas of research, we must attempt to find ways of interviewing that accord with the prevailing modes of everyday communication in this segment of social reality.

In the following, I will make such an attempt drawing on two management studies. One of the studies focuses on the company level and examines collective orientation patterns of managers regarding the issue of codetermination (Trinczek, 1993). The other study is concerned with the interface of company life and the private life of executives. It looks into how executives (re-)arrange their lives to cope with changed demands in their professional and private lives (cf. Ellguth and others, 1998, Behnke and Liebold, 2000, Liebold, 2000). Both studies involve research objects that can be considered suitable cases for the purpose of the argument proposed here, since in both instances they are sufficiently "soft" to qualify as appropriate cases for qualitative research, even in the eyes of the qualitative paradigm's most devout disciples.[6]

A comparison of the methods applied in both studies is interesting mainly for the purpose of illustrating that due to the fact that managers on a daily basis are engaged in worlds that are very differently structured in terms of the prevailing modes of communication (company – private life), it follows from the tenets of qualitative methodology that, depending on the research question, very different techniques of data collection may be adequate to the task.

9.3   The initial phase of the interview

Any interview with managers in a company environment at the outset faces managers' implicit and explicit expectations of such a conversation, irrespective of the specific research topic involved. These expectations are for the most part shaped by the existing rules of everyday communication in the company. Accordingly, concerning the, for the success of an interview, crucial opening sequence, managers expect the research team to confront them with questions, which they are supposed to respond to. Once the greeting ritual is completed, the "host" typically opens the conversation with words like the following, which express the anticipation of clearly defined roles in the interview setting: "Okay, fire away. What do you want to know? Feel free to ask."

Such initial expectations obviously largely arise from the interviewee's everyday work experience. Being asked questions by superiors or asking the right questions oneself are an integral part of managerial work. Managers project expectations rooted in such experience onto the interview situation. In the interview, the researchers are the ones to ask questions and they are the ones to answer, just as they expect their subordinates to do or their superiors expect them to do: briefly and precisely, to the point and without wandering from the subject. Of course, few managers actually live up to this ideal. When conducting interviews, we regularly come across interviewees who, by constantly straying from the subject, make it difficult for the researcher to successfully accomplish the interview. Nevertheless, the expectations are still in effect; sometimes the interviewee even becomes aware of deviating from this ideal and brings up the subject in the course of the interview. One manager, for instance, before the interview, admitted to having a tendency of getting too caught up in details and asked us to interrupt him whenever he dwelt on a topic too long.

The guided interview, especially in the version employing a more closed interview schedule, defines an interview situation that corresponds perfectly with managers' prevailing expectations in the opening sequence of an interview and therefore, undoubtedly, is the best choice for the opening stage. Switching to other methods of interviewing first requires a cautious process of overcoming managers' predominant question-and-answer orientation. This can take considerable time and demands a high degree of social competence. Opening an interview with an executive by asking him or her to engage in a lengthy narration runs the risk of dooming the whole interview to failure – the reason being that such an interview situation is almost diametrically opposed to the everyday communication structures at the workplace. In the eyes of managers, "time" – especially their own time – is a scarce and valuable resource. In their perception, constantly lacking and being pressured for time marks everyday action in the company setting. Requesting managers right at the beginning of a conversation to take the time for lengthy elaborations is likely to appear provocative in light of this perception of their own work situation. This would create a considerable gap between the interview situation and the rules of everyday communication as they exist in the field and are reflected in managerial expectations that the research team give the conversation a clear structure.

9.4 Developing the interview

Interview situations are not static; typically, they develop a life of their own such that the initial expectations the parties to the interview bring to the interview may change as the interview progresses. For instance, once the interview situation is successfully established and initial insecurities are overcome, it is a quite common experience in interviews with management that the atmosphere of the conversation quickly becomes noticeably more relaxed. Gradually, the interviewees begin to realize the difference between the interview situation and the question-answer situation that is a regular part of their daily work experience. As opposed to the social situation in the company context, the interview puts nobody under scrutiny and no one has to justify shortcomings or failure; in consequence, the initially noticeable strategic handling of information can be relaxed.

This change in the managerial perception of the social situation "interview" becomes apparent in the interviewees readjusting their initial expectations of the distribution of roles in the interview setting. Once the interview enters this stage, the initial, typified expectations of a question-answer-type conversation no longer prevail; as a result, the nature of the interview can change without running the risk of failure. This is precisely the situation when an "openness" in conducting qualitative interviews, which not only allows to flexibly adapt the style of interviewing to the situation but virtually demands to do so, proves its worth.

This is the time when systematic shifts to "other" forms of interviewing can take place with potentially promising results. However, the researcher in this situation is still not fully free to make use of the whole range of interviewing techniques. Rather, there remain limits to what is feasible that clearly have to do with the subject matter that one seeks to approach through the interview. In the following, drawing on the above-mentioned cases of "orientation patterns of managers concerning codetermination" and "life arrangements," I will show that the appropriate choice of interview technique in the "second stage" of interviews with management depends on the nature of the object of research.

The crucial difference between these cases with regard to the form of interviewing is that, in the one case, the object of research solely involves a manager's company life; hence, when topics of this kind are addressed in the interview, the typical rules governing everyday communication in this setting determine the manager's expectations of the interview – and the interviewer is well-advised not to disregard them in the way the interview is conducted. The second case ("life arrangements"), on the other hand, refers to private life outside of the company, where other modes of everyday communication prevail. In this case, it is indeed possible to overcome managers' initial expectations and to shift to more narrative forms of interviewing. The interviewee in the interview situation mentally "leaves" or (in the best case) even "forgets" the company setting with its typically non-narrative modes of communication – even if the interview is conducted in the interviewee's own office on company premises.

9.5   Interviewing managers about business issues

If the topic of the interview primarily relates to the company context, the interview will typically not take on a narrative form even in the second stage when the conversation becomes more relaxed. Attempts at stimulating at least brief narrations in the course of an interview are rarely successful with managers. This is lesser due to managers' desire to not waste valuable time "chattering" – as they would call it. Rather, it has to do with the fact that to the extent that managers' expectations of the interview shift from the familiar initial question-answer focus – which happens frequently although not always – they mostly tend to switch to another structure of everyday communication that is rooted in managerial experience in the company context: the expert discussion, the basic communicative structure of which managers are mainly familiar with from the open discussions in project teams and other team-type working arrangements.

In the course of interviews on company matters, we can thus observe a shift between differently structured forms of conversation, which are both within the range of common company practice. "Good" qualitative interviewing practice requires the interviewer to "go along with" this shift from one form of communication common to a company setting to another.

The new interview situation represents a relaxed discussion setting, in which, although the topics are still structured by a "competent" research team, the interviewees voice their views on issues without any reservations, allow them to be questioned, and critically reflect on them. Since the interview situation is free from the demands of action and socially inconsequential, it occasionally nourishes a degree of candor and open self-reflection on the managers' part, which they, in this form, would normally not allow themselves to engage in in the company context with its mostly strategic communication and interaction style.[7]

The fact that the interviewees at times willingly go considerably over the time limit initially set for the interview, even though seeking just an additional 15 minutes may have required a fair amount of haggling at the point of arranging the interview, shows how attractive this inconsequential conversation situation is to them. It is not uncommon for the researchers to finally take the initiative to end the conversation and not the managers.

Kern and others (1988) speak of a virtually "cathartic effect" in management interviews and have essentially traced this back to the one-dimensional "separation" of the strategic and communicative sides of action in company life. "If even a social contact in an interview situation is experienced as an opportunity for compensation, this must be a consequence of having to suppress discursive communication in everyday life. The reason for this may well be that being confined to what is subjectively perceived to be "purely strategic" action acts to gag the strategist himself" (Kern and others, 1988, p. 93, own translation from German, emphasis in the original).

Under such conditions in a company, "the relationship offered by 'understanding people from the outside'," according to the authors, provides "short-term relief" (Kern and others, 1988, p. 94, own translation from German); the interview situation affords an opportunity to dissolve the "communication blockage." Kern and others have apparently experienced that the managers they interviewed were often inclined to seize the opportunity of the interview as a stage for self-dramatization with cathartic effects, while relegating the sociologists to the role of an audience or the straight man providing the feeds for further elaborations. They report that attempts to question managerial views and to point out problems regularly failed: "At points where their views are in threat of being called into question in discourse, repression of other legitimate worldviews is repeated." (Kern and others, 1988, p. 94, own translation from German) In the view of Kern and associates, such pathogenic forms of communication can occasionally interfere with the task of "successfully" conducting an interview.

As indicated above, I have mainly had other experiences. In my observation, managers appear to seek less a patient audience for excessive self-dramatization, rather than being more interested in the social researcher as an expert and a person to converse with, who takes a different analytical and conceptional perspective.[8] In fact, managers exhibit quite a broad range of different interview behaviour. Some are very open-minded and self-reflective in weighing different options and positions, carefully argue their own views, display some willingness to give counterarguments thoughtful consideration, and enquire about experiences the interviewers may have made in other companies. Others are more inclined to sweep aside objections, presenting their own position as ultimately the only reasonable stance on an issue. However, such managers, too, are obviously also bound by the tacit norms of discourse: Well-argued interviewer interventions are not perceived mainly as annoying instances of interfering with the process of self-dramatization; rather, it seems as if at times the interviewees virtually hope for objections to be raised, thus providing them with an opportunity to all the more effectively present their own arguments to repudiate them as inadequate, out of touch with reality, or limited in perspective.

Irrespective of the specific behaviour displayed in the interview, the great majority of managers on all accounts gives the impression that it perceives the conversation as an opportunity to indulge its "appetite" for intellectual exchange, reasoning and debating under conditions free from the demands of action; and it seems to be precisely this condition of freedom from the need to act characteristic of the interview situation that whets this "appetite" to begin with. Freedom from the demands of action is also the key difference to the expert discussion, which managers are familiar with from daily experience and which provides a communication structure that they can easily adopt in an interview situation. There is, however, no difference – and this needs to be emphasized – in terms of the fundamental principles of communication that are in effect in asking questions and giving answers, in reasoning and debating.

Interviewee expectations that in this way call for a discursive interview structure require a specific type of interviewing that only to a limited extent corresponds to the standards of qualitative research as regularly stressed in the literature. These standards, as we all know, emphasize that the interviewer takes a neutral and supportive stance in interviewing and under all circumstances abstains from his or her own interventions to not run the risk of interfering with the interviewees developing their own subjective structures of relevance. The contrary holds true when interviewing managers: in light of the above outlined "prior rules of everyday communication" in this specific field of research, an expert interview with managers must by necessity be designed to be conducted in a discursive, argumentative fashion.

The researcher must of course allow interviewees time and sufficient opportunity to give shape to their positions; on the other hand, the interviewer regularly confronts the interviewees with opposing views during the interview. Such a mode of "discursive, argumentative" interviewing does not intend to suggest that such interviews must necessarily be "confrontational." It is a matter of interviewer competence to find the appropriate "dosage" when challenging the interviewee. The purpose of bringing up objections and opposing views is as a matter of course not to get interviewees to modify their positions during an interview; rather, the ultimate objective of such interventions is to encourage interviewees to discursively develop their structures of relevance by establishing a conversation structure that is common to everyday company life beyond the "artificial" interview situation. In line with this intention, the interviewer should explicitly assume the role of an "actor diabolus" when intervening in order to minimize the risk of interviewees implicitly adjusting their responses along supposed lines of social desirability possibly conveyed by the interviewer.

Admittedly, a constructive discursive interview situation presupposes an interviewer commanding a high level of competence, both socially and pertaining to the subject matter in question. As a necessary condition for managers to accept and engage in a discursive, argumentative, and for the research project potentially productive interview situation, the interviewer must be able to give the impression of being sufficiently compatible and on a par with the interviewee. This, just to mention in passing, also frequently has to do with age and status of the researchers. The higher a manager's own level of qualification, formal status, or the greater the area of responsibility, the higher are his or her tacit expectations concerning the formal status of the other. Young researchers who have yet to acquire their doctoral degree hardly stand a chance to be accepted as a competent counterpart in the eyes of managers, irrespective of their actual abilities. In their view, if the university is not going to send a "real professor," the researcher should at least have a PhD.[9]

Irrespective of such status issues, for a discursive, argumentative expert interview with management representatives to achieve its goal, the interviewer is indeed required to be an expert himself: the more an interviewer demonstrates knowledgeability during the interview by giving competent assessments, stating reasons, and raising counterarguments, the more managers in turn will be willing to offer their own knowledge and take a stance on issues, thus disclosing their subjective structures of relevance and patterns of orientation in absence of strategic considerations.

9.6 Interviewing managers about "life-world" issues

In the case just discussed, the interview technique was adjusted within the range of the typical (non-narrative) forms of everyday communication characteristic of the company setting. In management studies aimed more at the lifeworld of managers (as the study on "life arrangements of executives") it is perfectly possible – and depending on the specific research interest it might even be imperative – to use the transition stage of the interview following the opening sequence in order to switch to a narrative form of interviewing by providing a stimulus encouraging the interviewee to engage in a more extensive impromptu narration. This may or may not be successful. In the course of the said project, there regularly were cases (although in total not a large number!) where the interviewees had difficulty in veering away from their professional roles and the respective forms of communication in spite of the fact that the focus of the research project was on life outside of the company. The project team had approached them as managers, thus in their role as persons bearing certain responsibilities, and it proved extremely difficult for them to let go of this role even after a more relaxed atmosphere of conversation had been established. In some cases, the fact that the interviews were conducted in a company environment may have further aggravated the difficulty of freeing oneself from the typical modes of in-house communication. These interviews largely remained locked into the question-answer mode, and the fact that the interview addressed a topic at the interface between company and private life did not provide an opportunity for switching to a discourse "free from the demands of action" either. The respective mode of communication associated with this subject matter in these cases, does not appear to be a part of the repertoire of everyday communication, which the researcher can easily draw upon in conducting the interview.

9.7   Conclusions

In sum, we may state that there is no single ideal recipe for conducting interviews with managers. Rather, here too the general methodological principle applies that the method employed ought to be adequate to the object of research. Research methods, in this case interviews, must be adapted to the specific modes of communication characteristic of the social setting that they seek to address. This is the only way to effectively live up to the methodological demand of qualitative research that the research process respect the existing structures of everyday communication in the field.

The typical question-answer structure characteristic of the interview situation in the opening sequence of expert interviews with managers, as well as the "argumentative, discursive" structure of interviewing in the second stage of the interview, in the first study, and the more narrative form of interviewing, in the other study, all meet this key standard of qualitative research: On the one hand, such an interview strategy avoids violating interviewee expectations of the interview; on the other hand, it allows to align the research process with the prior structures of everyday communication such that the process of developing subjective structures of relevance in the interview as they are operative in everyday life is supported to the best possible extent.

In case of topics revolving around company matters, the "success" of question-answer-based and "argumentative, discursive" interviewing respectively is to no small part due to the fact that the forms of interviewing correspond with the situation managers face in the company when, for instance, the works council or their superiors question their positions and they are required to justify them. For this reason, although the interview situation compared to the everyday situations of company life can be considered to be more "open" and there is in principle less need for "tactical" behaviour, "argumentative, discursive" interviewing in thematically focused expert interviews is the appropriate research method for this setting. The same is true for the more narrative structure characteristic of lifeworld communication and the respectively adjusted mode of interviewing employed in the second case where the interview topic aimed more at life outside the company.

The pronounced methodological and methodical disinterest in expert interviews even among the advocates of the qualitative paradigm, which this method belongs to, was the starting point of these considerations. The disregard shown for the guided interview as a "dirty" method – and this was our initial thesis – is rooted in the qualitative paradigm's fetish that interviewing must involve as little interviewer interference as possible. As demonstrated above, this tenet is an untenable case of generalizing and rendering as absolute rules of everyday communication related to a very specific social context. Resulting insistence that the interviewer deny the self or at least remain reticent has been shown to be methodological and methodical nonsense in certain research settings. Precisely when we take the basic principles of qualitative research seriously – for instance, the rule that Hoffmann-Riem has described as the "key principle" of the interpretive paradigm, which states "that the researcher generally only gains access to data disclosing meaning when entering a communication relationship that respects the research subject's system of communication rules" (Hoffmann-Riem, 1980, p. 346 f., own translation from German) – it is sometimes necessary to take a more active role by structuring the interview and engaging in argument while maintaining an open interview situation. It still holds true that no single best solution in the choice of interview method can be derived from abstract methodological considerations. There is only one appropriate criterion for such choice: adequacy! Adequacy with regard to the research object.

Notes

*This text has a longer history. It is based on a presentation given at a workshop conducted by the *Institut für Arbeitsmarkt- und Berufsforschung* (Institute for Labor Market and Vocational Research – IAB) on "Expert Interviews in Labor Market Research" and was published accordingly in the report on the workshop (Trinczek, 1995). In the meantime, I have gained new insights in a research project on "'Executives' Ways of Life in light of New Challenges in Professional and Private Life," mainly conducted by Cornelia Behnke and Renate Liebold at the Institute of Sociology at the University of Erlangen, Germany, and sponsored by the German Research Foundation (DFG). Today, I have come to take a somewhat different view from my initial position in the mid-1990s. Hence, while major parts of the current article draw on the initial article, certain sections differ considerably.

1. Lamnek (1989) provides an especially instructive example of the ambiguity in classifying guided interviews in terms of the qualitative-quantitative universe (a dichotomy which has frequently been criticized but nevertheless still structures the debate). Concerning the similar focused interview, he writes, "Although the focused interview falls into the category of quali-tative survey methods, it is closer to quantitative methodology than are other qualitative methods" (Lamnek, 1989, p. 80, own translation from German).
2. The "expert interview" is essentially an interview whose specific nature is determined by the fact that the interviewee qualifies as being an "expert." In the strict

sense, the expert interview hence cannot claim to be a method of data collection in its own right, since there are various different ways of interviewing experts. Nevertheless, there exists a kind of "tacit consensus" in the research community that an expert interview is a "guided interview," and I will keep with this consensus: in the following, I will discuss the guided expert interview (for a more general discussion, see also Liebold and Trinczek, 2002).

3. This assessment is deliberately somewhat exaggerated to clearly state the point. Without doubt, there are some very thoughtful articles that deal with various aspects of the guided interview, for instance, by Christel Hopf (1978), Meuser and Nagel (1989, 1994, 1997); they are, however, exceptions from the mainstream. And the debate in the English-speaking world has been dominated by Merton and Kendall's text (1946), which is now more than 50 years old (see also Merton and others, 1956).

4. Numerous interviews with managers – mostly from industry – conducted by the project team "Labor and Industry Research" at the Institute of Sociology in Erlangen and, more recently, by the Chair of Sociology at TU Munich in the context of various projects on issues concerning working hours, problems regarding the modernization of production, on various aspects of exchange relations in companies, as well as issues concerning work-life balance provide the empirical background and data basis for my exposition.

5. This, in my opinion, simplified view of potential communication situations in everyday life can probably only be explained as the result of a gradual, unnoticed process of equating everyday communication with communication in the context of private life associated with the lifeworld. In the discourse of the qualitative research community, the rules of communication identified in such settings have been tacitly generalized as the universal rules of everyday communication as such.

6. Guided expert interviews are also frequently conducted simply to obtain information that might otherwise not be available – for instance, because the research touches upon issues that are thought to be problematic. For most advocates of qualitative research, this type of "information mining" does not represent an application that makes effective use of the strengths of their methods.

7. Welch and others (2002) also state that successful interviews with "company elites" tend to succeed in "encouraging elite interviewees to regard the interview as an intellectual discussion very different in nature to company meetings and briefings."

8. The differences between Kern and others' experiences and my own may also be related to the fact that the interviews involved different levels of company hierarchy. It may be assumed that behaviour as observed by Kern and others is more frequently encountered at the very top of a company hierarchy than among middle management. For interviews with this group of managers see also Thomas 1993.

9. The situation is similar concerning the ascriptive characteristic "age." It is easier for a researcher in his mid-fifties to interview a plant manager of similar age than it would be for a colleague in her early thirties. However, it seems that age, to a certain extent, can be compensated by academic titles and status.

Further readings

Bloom, N., Krabbenhöft, K. and Lamba, N. (2006) *LSE – University of Cambridge – Stanford University – Management Interview Guide*, http://www.stanford.edu/~nbloom/ManagementInterviewGuide.pdf.

Welch, C., Marschan-Piekkari, R., Penttinen, H. and Tahvanainen, M. (2002) "Corporate elites as informants in qualitative international business research" in *International Business Research Review 11*, 611–28.

Thomas Th. R. J. (1993) "Interviewing important people in big companies" in *Journal of Contemporary Ethnography 22*, 80–96.

References

Behnke, C. and Liebold, R. (2000) "Zwischen Fraglosigkeit und Gleichheitsrhetorik – Familie und Partnerschaft aus der Sicht beruflich erfolgreicher Männer" in *Feministische Studien 18*, 64–77.

Cicourel, A.V. (1964) *Method and Measurement in Sociology* (New York: Free Press).

Ellguth, P., Liebold, R. and Trinczek, R. (1998) " 'Double-Squeeze' – Manager zwischen veränderten beruflichen und privaten Herausforderungen" in *Kölner Zeitschrift für Soziologie und Sozialpsychologie 50*, 517–35.

Hoffmann-Riem, C. (1980) "Die Sozialforschung einer interpretativen Soziologie. Der Datengewinn" in *Kölner Zeitschrift für Soziologie und Sozialpsychologie 32*, 339–72.

Hopf, C. (1978) "Die Pseudo-Exploration – Überlegungen zur Technik qualitativer Interviews in der Sozialforschung" in *Zeitschrift für Soziologie 7*, 97–115.

Kern, B., Kern, H. and Schumann, M. (1988) "Industriesoziologie als Katharsis" in *Soziale Welt 39*, 86–96.

Lamnek, S. (1989) *Qualitative Sozialforschung, Bd.2: Methoden und Techniken* (München: Psychologie Verlags Union).

Liebold, R. (2001) *"Meine Frau managt das ganze Leben zu Hause..." Partnerschaft und Familie aus der Sicht männlicher Führungskräfte* (Wiesbaden: Westdeutscher Verlag).

Liebold, R. and Trinczek, R. (2002) "Experteninterview" in Kühl, S. and Strodtholz, P. (eds) *Methoden der Organisationsforschung. Ein Handbuch* (Reinbek: Rowohlt), pp. 33–71.

Merton, R. K., Fiske, M. and Kendall, P. L. (1956) *The Focused Interview: a Manual of Problems and Procedures* (Glencoe, Illinois: The Free Press).

Merton, R. K. and Kendall, P. L. (1946) "The focused interview" in *American Journal of Sociology 51*, 541–57.

Merton, R. K. and Kendall, P. L. (1979) "Das fokussierte Interview" in Hopf, C. and Weingarten, E. (eds) *Qualitative Sozialforschung* (Stuttgart: Klett Cotta), pp. 171–204.

Meuser, M. and Nagel, U. (1989) "Experteninterviews – vielfach erprobt, wenig bedacht. Ein Beitrag zur qualitativen Methodendiskussion." Arbeitspapier Nr. 6 des Sonderforschungsbereichs 186 der Uni Bremen, Statuspassagen und Risikolagen im Lebensverlauf' Bremen.

Meuser, M. and Nagel, U. (1997) "Das ExpertInneninterview – Wissenssoziologische Voraussetzungen und methodische Durchführung" in Friebertshäuser, B. and Prengel, A. (eds) *Handbuch Qualitative Forschungsmethoden in der Erziehungswissenschaft* (Weinheim/München: Juventa), pp. 481–91.

Schütze, F. (1977) *Die Technik des narrativen Interviews in Interaktionsfeldstudien – dargestellt an einem Projekt zur Erforschung von kommunale Machtstrukturen* (Bielefeld: Manuskript der Universität Bielefeld).

Schütze, F., Meinefeld, W., Springer, R. and Weymann, A. (1981) "Grundlagentheoretische Voraussetzungen methodisch kontrollierten Fremdverstehens" in Arbeitsgruppe Bielefelder Soziologen (ed.) *Alltagswissen, Interaktion und gesellschaftliche Wirklichkeit*, 5th edn (Opladen: Leske + Budrich), pp. 433–529.

Thomas, R. J. (1993) "Interviewing important people in big companies" in *Journal of Contemporary Ethnography 22*, 80–96.

Trinczek, R. (1993) *Management und betriebliche Mitbestimmung. Eine Typologie kollektiver Orientierungsmuster* (Erlangen: Habil-Schrift).

Trinczek, R. (1995) "Experteninterviews mit Managern: Methodische und methodologische Hintergründe" in Brinkmann, C., Deeke, A. and Völkel, B. (eds) *Experteninterviews in der Arbeitsmarktforschung*. BeitrAB191 (Nürnberg: IAB), pp. 59–67.

Welch, C., Marschan-Piekkari, R., Penttinen H. and Tahvanainen, M. (2002) "Corporate elites as informants in qualitative international business research" in *International Business Research Review 11*, 611–28.

10
Expert Interviews in Interpretive Organizational Research

Ulrike Froschauer and Manfred Lueger

Reputable and scientifically founded research strategies adhere to certain basic methodological assumptions impressed upon the analysis procedures by the specifics of the actual area of research. In this way, the underlying methodology regulates the entire research process and assumes a reporting function that covers everything from the definition of relevant research issues and the characteristics of any material collected or produced through to the interpretive adaptation of the analysis results. Against this background, this article focuses (first line of argumentation) on how best to view the subject of "the organization" from an interpretive social research methodological perspective to (second line of argumentation) determine the consequences and relevance of different types of expertise and procedural specifics on the characteristics and applicability of expert interviews. In the process, three types of expertise are differentiated, each with its own specific functions in the research process. A case study is then used to address the systematic inclusion of expert interviews in interpretive research design (third line of argumentation).

10.1 Interpretive organisational research

In broad terms, interpretative organizational research is based on two lead perspectives: (1) *constructionism*, which ties knowledge of reality to communication and the way people are anchored in separate collectives (cf. Baecker and others, 1992, Gergen, 1994, Frindte, 1998), and (2) the general understanding of *social reality as a social construct* (Berger and Luckmann, 1981). It also embraces those methodological positions, which focus on the joint construction of reality as a condition for the creation of collective forms of action (see for example Berger and Luckmann, 1981, Gergen, 2000, Lueger, 2001, Luckmann, 2006). Thus, organizations are, at the same time, both condition and consequence of the social world: they might set the parameters for the construction of concepts of reality and thereby structure the way people act in organizations and their relevant

environments, but these actions themselves, in turn, also constitute real
ity as a subject-independent phenomenon. In this respect – as summed up
by Weick's (2003, p.190ff.) notion of *enactment* – organizations do more
that just observe their environments: by acting with regard to them, they
not only develop themselves, they also develop and actively shape their
environments as well.

The collective focus and individual capacity to act developed through
our dealings with a social environment and its particular requirements for
social cooperation. The people involved in the social internalisation pro
cess in a specific organizational environment develop standardized social
interpretation schemes (cf. Fleck, 1981), which establish the context for the
coordination of collectively binding action. The actual interaction, that
is the interplay between the communicative acts in a social setting, helps
shape the experiences gained through interaction into a mutually access
ible worldview for use in the joint management of action requirements.
Collective patterns of meaning are therefore by no means simply attitudes
they are contexts of argumentation regarding mutual action problem.
(Knoblauch, 2005, p. 178f.).

In this way, the inter-individual and interactive construction of reality
organizes the construction of subjective structures of meaning and know
ledge into common organizational practices. Weick (1995) refers consist
ently in this context to a process of *sensemaking* ("Sinngenerierung") in
organizations, which enables people to act by adding coherence to the
world and thus creating both system and expectability. In addition to this
sensemaking on an individual level, the collective also produces interaction
patterns – objective, latent structures of meaning which escape the atten
tion of the individual consciousness and cannot be intentionally accessed
by individuals. From an organizational theory perspective, this develop
ment process not only focuses the collective construction of reality as a
condition for joint action, it is also where this construction of reality is
interpreted as an expression of the context behind the action.

Consequently, interpretive organizational analysis is not based on an
organization's quasi "objective" given "reality," it draws on the condi
tions and substantiation of the inter-subjective construction of the
views of the organization shared by so-called "meaning collectives"
("Deutungsmuster," cf. Fleck, 1981) and analysed in reaction to object
ive problems. Neither events nor actions make sense here as such, they
draw their meaning and relevance from being embedded in the require
ments for action and from the available frameworks of meaning. Since
as Goffmann (1975) also notes, these frameworks determine the analysis
approach used for a specific object and set out the possible contextual
horizon of meaning for the interpretation, the contextual sensemaking
process forms a key component of interpretive organizational analysis.
The core elements here are *communication* as a sensemaking process

meaning as a form of order in experience and action and *structuring* as a production of order (Froschauer, 2006, p. 194f.).

- *Communication*: according to Luhmann (1995, p. 147ff.) communication unifies three selection levels, namely information, utterance and understanding. Information is not simply communicated, it must first be reconstructed from the utterance which made it observable and introduced it into the communication process. This is why the information gathered from an utterance can differ from its original intent. Simply considering the manifest meaning of what is said and done does not suffice to understand what happens in organizations: the context-bound nature of linguistic meaning also requires an analysis of the social embeddedness of messages.
- *Meaning*: to be able to coordinate interaction, meaning is required as a form of order in human experience (Luhmann, 1982, p. 31) endowed in the consciousness as reference parameter (Schütz and Luckmann, 1984, p. 13). However, the intended meaning of the individual actors nonetheless remains inaccessible to research. Consequently, other forms of meaning come to the fore in interpretive analysis: (a) the type of subjective meaning intended by the actors (Weber, 1978), (b) the objective meaning embedded in the phenomenon as structuring principle (Schütz, 1972, p. 31ff., p. 132ff.) and (c) the practical meaning (Bourdieu 1995) expressed through customary practices of interpretation and action in a particular social field, which acts as a bridge between the understanding of the world (subjective meaning) and the world itself (objective meaning).
- *Structuring*: in general, the actors in social systems face the apparently contradictory task of constructing a level of complexity that enables them to both develop and reduce their knowledge of the environment and their capacity to create meaningful order through action. This order is based on the establishment of security in expectations (for example as a result of the generalizability of behavioural expectations) and rules for interpreting observations within a horizon of meaning. Since it is the structures that define how actual subjects or objects are integrated in topological and relational systems (Deleuze, 1992, p. 15f.) and these structures – as possible ways of expressing phenomena – remain invisible, only the actual bearers of expression material can be observed. These, in turn, are based on objective latent structures of meaning as products of unobservable yet formal rule system algorithms, deducible as standard rules from the material forms of expression (Oevermann, 1993, p. 114ff.).

Interpretive organizational analysis therefore adheres to methodological frameworks which link an appropriate understanding of organizations to several considerations: a dialectic (re)production of reality and actuality (as individual and collective notions) constructed on communicative sensemaking processes whose latent structure manifests itself in the actions and views of the actors involved. In this context, the methodological determination of expert knowledge must also consider the communicative basis of organizational dynamics, the specific form of organizational sensemaking and the particular system of structural organizational integration in all their complexity.

10.2   Expert interviews in an interpretive organizational research context

In the interpretive social research context, it quickly becomes clear that the key to understanding organizations lies in understanding how they produce order (and hence meaning). At the core of this issue lie the communicative information creation processes embedded and assembled in lifeworlds and organizational contexts as orderly wholes in the form of knowledge. This means there are two basic components to organizational analysis: (1) familiarity with the knowledge creation process, and (2) the content of the knowledge created, which must be stabilized and made available in some way. Experts can provide a research process with valuable information on both components. However, to enable them to do so, clarification is first needed of where such relevant expertise or skills lie in an interpretive organizational analysis context.

10.2.1   Types of expertise

According to popular definition, *experts* are equipped with explicit specialist knowledge gained through specific training which provides them with an in-depth understanding of a particular topic or field and enables them to provide clarification or resolve specific issues or problems (cf. Hitzler, 1994, see also the Five Stage Model of Skill Acquisition in Dreyfus/Dreyfus, 2005). They are also confronted with a number of expectations regarding their knowledge that legitimize their expert status. For example, their knowledge must be different from everyday knowledge (otherwise it would not be expert knowledge), is not accessible to everyone (otherwise we would have no need for experts), is superior to everyday knowledge (otherwise we could all rely on our own knowledge) and must avail itself of a theoretical perspective (otherwise it would have no explanatory value). Consequently, their expertise is characterized not only by the content of their knowledge but also by a specific system of knowledge representation (cf. De Sombre and Mieg, 2005, p. 59f.). Experts can thus provide assistance in situations of uncertainty (for example in court) or help solve complex problems (for example organizational consultants). To enable them to fulfil these functions, their expert status must be recognized, backed up in generalizable terms by a relevant qualification and communicated convincingly in each individual situation (cf. Honer, 1994, p. 49ff.). Nonetheless, in an interpretive organizational analysis context, such expertise can only contribute to a limited extent towards understanding the way an organization and its members work, because its relationship to the research object operates on a purely knowledge-based level. As a result, the notion of expertise must be expanded further in this context.

Meuser and Nagel (1991, p. 442f.) consider participation in the actual area of expertise a prerequisite for expert status, whereby such status is accorded by the researchers in line with their field of research (relational expert status). Accordingly, an expert is someone "who is responsible in some way or another for the development, implementation or monitoring of a problem or who has privileged access to information about people or decision processes" (Meuser and Nagel, 1991, p. 443, own translation). This results in a twofold definition of expert status, namely through the *according of expertise* by the researchers and the assumption of a *disproportionate distribution of knowledge* seen as the sedimentation, storage and availability of privileged experience.

Furthermore, according to Schütz and Luckmann (1973, p. 99ff.), lifeworld knowledge is bound to the situatedness of a subject's personal history and is used to deal with everyday situations. Bourdieu takes this a step further with his "habitus," which serves as a matrix of perception, interpretation and action and, as such, forms a generative principle of common practice (Bourdieu, 2005, p. 78ff., 1995, p. 55). By this concept, human behaviour can be aligned without direct communication by the homogenizing of human habitus forms as a result of similar life circumstances and conditions. Thus, although individual action is by no means purely subjective, it is not bound exclusively to objective factors either. Instead, it follows the common sense developed from real life experience. Knowledge is incorporated in the habitus as a structured principle and serves generatively as a structure-giving principle. This kind of knowledge is thus always practical and is linked not in the consciousness but through practical activities.

To embrace these standpoints, empirical social sciences research must focus primarily on the knowledge held by the people involved with an organization or its relevant environments. For the interpretive research process, this leads to a distinction between three types of expertise, each with an increasingly abstractive degree of distance to practical knowledge of the research field (subject matter knowledge).

- *Subject matter know-how*: this type of expertise is based primarily on experience drawn from participating in activities in the field of research. Hörning (2001) describes such people as "everyday experts." Their expertise is grounded to a great extent in direct first order observation and generally stored as tacit knowledge in the way they perceive, think and act (Polanyi, 1983, Oevermann, 2001). In the shaping of social practices based on this type of expertise, social differentiation can be seen in different fields of activity and in the interplay between these fields. Consequently, this type of expertise is essential to the development of a deeper understanding of the research object and the creation of new knowledge. This knowledge is extremely heterogeneous because the sedimentation of experience is accompanied at a subjective level by the life-world background and relevance structures.

- *Reflective subject matter expertise*: this kind of expertise rests on more far-reaching primary and secondary experience and encompasses more than "just" procedural knowledge or know-how. It is developed primarily by those actors who depend in structural terms on second order observation (to observe how others observe) and whose interactions systematically cross internal and external field boundaries. Because people with reflective expertise act as organizational hubs, they are usually perforce mindful observers of the organizational context who piece the various partial perspectives together to form a whole. Thus, this type of knowledge is more relational, reflective and abstract than concrete know-how. It can be explicated above all with regard to the organization's official view, but is also subject to multiple thematic restraints.
- *External expertise*: this incorporates sound relevant theoretical knowledge supported by secondary experience and second order observation and can throw light on various aspects of a subject (both intra- and interdisciplinary). It is up to the researchers to integrate such reflective knowledge into their research, where it can contribute to planning activities, provide information on specific contextual assumptions or be used in the testing, classifying or contrasting of results. External experts with systematic, abstract special knowledge can only be accorded marginal relevance in interpretive organizational analysis because they lack practical know-how and/or knowledge gained through experience. This kind of expertise reproduces the knowledge already available and snatches control of the topic away from the research.

Much of the expert knowledge relevant for interpretive organizational analysis is therefore derived from elements of the existing social knowledge base imparted through observation, interaction or as part of the socialization process (Schütz and Luckmann, 1973, p. 111ff.). The experiential knowledge used in organizations is thus socially acquired knowledge, which reflects the internal differences between groups of people whose actions are based on internally comparable yet externally different situations. The corresponding structures of meaning are both the reason for and consequence of internal cooperation relationships and demarcations and represent the actual distribution of knowledge in the organization. The holders of such *subject matter know-how* are not allocated a "lay" status in the research context because it is not their everyday knowledge that is relevant but rather the *specialist knowledge* they require to act successfully in a specific organizational field.

In contrast, the distribution of the primarily scientific knowledge held by *external experts* is based on the institutionalized acquisition of skills encountered in the academic world (that is inter- and intra-disciplinary, by thematic focus, and so on). This incorporates a basic set of skills – textbook knowledge – which represent a relatively homogeneous basis of generally accepted views. The underlying collective of meaning is found in the corresponding discipline or sub-discipline (where accreditation rules are also defined) but only bears a limited relation to the actual organization under analysis. One such particular form of knowledge is *research expertise*, which focuses on the methodology behind the planning, organizing and carrying out of research processes and deals with the systematic process of obtaining contextual knowledge of a research field. It concentrates on second order social sciences (re)construction based on the reconstruction of a social field in which expert knowledge and experts appear as everyday phenomena ("Experts for us"; cf. Aman, 1994, p. 35). This type of expertise is not factored into the subsequent discussion, because it refers to methodological procedures not contextual knowledge generation.

All three types can also be further differentiated according to *specialization*, where the focus lies on the application of specific expertise to a specific problem (cf. Hitzler, 1994, p. 22f.). Since the particular competences involved serve to resolve specific functional issues, this type of knowledge is of limited relevance in understanding the organization under analysis: external specialists rarely have an overview of the entire subject, and their knowledge is thus only of limited use for establishing an overview and contrasting results; while internal specialists can provide important information on specific issues, this usually concerns the manifest content level, not the level of latent sensemaking that is of far greater importance in understanding organizational dynamics. Nonetheless, it may prove pertinent to the research (for example from a specific evaluation or interpretation perspective) to also integrate specialists in the course of the project.

10.2.2   Procedural consequences for expert interviews

Different types of expertise place different requirements on survey and interpretation procedures. The following section examines the relevance of the three types of expertise described above for various interview and evaluation techniques and methods.

- *Subject matter know-how*: this assumes a central position in interpretive organizational analysis. Since this type of knowledge is linked to individuals or groups of individuals, is activated in specific situations and can only be explicated (unconsciously) to a limited extent, it cannot be made topical by means of exact questioning in the interview setting but must instead be largely reconstructed from the form of knowledge representation. Since it is not so much the manifest content but rather the form of expression used to describe organizational practices that is important in interviews of this kind, open, narrative interview forms prove particularly suitable for bringing this kind of expertise to the fore (see for example Schütze, 1977, Glinka, 1998, Froschauer and Lueger, 2003, Holstein and Gubrium, 2003, Küsters, 2006). The freedom afforded by this type of interview technique forces interviewees to structure their information, while this structure, in turn, serves as an expression of organizational dynamics and offers important clues for understanding the organization. Group interviews are also a good method of revealing the dynamics of communication in organizations (Froschauer and Lueger, 2003, p. 55ff.) and generally focus on the day-to-day situation and practices in organizations and their environment. As far as the interpretation of results is concerned, methods suited to the analysis of latent structures of meaning, such as those applied in social sciences related hermeneutics (cf. Hitzle and Honer, 1997, for variations on objective hermeneutics cf. Oevermann and others, 1979, Oevermann, 1984, Lueger, 2000, Froschauer and Lueger 2003) are also suitable here. To avoid receiving one-sided views, consideration must also be given to the organization's social complexity in the selection of appropriate experts.

- *Reflective subject matter expertise*: this follows on seamlessly from the above, with one key difference, namely a shift in emphasis away from the actual work situation towards a stronger focus on the internal relationships between the different organizational units and/or the organization and its environment.

- *External expertise*: contrary to the information found in scientific literature, interviews with this group can focus on the concrete topic of research and thus bring otherwise disjointed background information into the equation. Experts of this kind are not particularly difficult to interview and because it is centred on explicable, explicit knowledge, the information they provide is not difficult to interpret either. A good tactic here is to let their expertise come to the fore of its own accord in the course of the interview and then use targeted questions to obtain greater depth of information and establish any limits. In the analysis phase, the specific issues addressed are then condensed, elaborated and put into a systematic context using appropriate condensing techniques (such as the qualitative content analysis found in Mayring 2003).

To gain access to latent structures of meaning, rigorous interpretive organizational analysis must always consider the way people differentiate the situated practices of action collectives within the actual organization. Researchers cannot rely here on external experts, because their knowledge has already been homogenized in line with generalizable principles and thus, cannot be used to shed appropriate light on specific individual situations. Similarly, the information that can be drawn from an organization' formal structure is also of limited use, since it only represents the surface beneath which different ways of regulating action and cooperation can establish themselves.

To uncover this differentiation in the course of the organizational analysis, research must be carried out in cycles, with each cycle integrating both survey and interpretation phases (Lueger, 2001, p. 363ff., Froschauer and Lueger, 2006, p. 254ff.). In this sense, the progressive insights obtained indicate the path for further surveys. The basic strategy behind this approach echoes two of the principles of *theoretical sampling* (Glaser and Strauss, 1967, p. 45ff.): *maximum structural variation* and *minimization of differences*. Maximum structural variation seeks out extreme cases and possible anomalies to demarcate the internal setting and identify general characteristics pertaining to the research field (scope and generalizability of conclusions), while a minimization of differences compares prior interpretations with similar cases to identify unclarity in the argumentation. Such sampling strategies continue with survey and interpretation activities until the "theoretical saturation" point is reached and the inclusion of additional new data can no longer be expected to contribute further to theory development (Glaser and Strauss, 1967, p. 61f.).

In general, expert interviews of this kind generally require a high degree of flexibility to provoke a level of structuring that takes into consideration a range of different aspects. This flexibility extends across the entire research process: from the selection of content central to the general area of interest (for example to explicate the full breadth of the research area with regard to the specific knowledge interests in the case of external experts) to the choice of interview candidates (for example to uncover everyday working relationships in the case of subject matter experts), the way interviews are started (for example with a clarification of the research topic in the case of external experts, by focusing on activating organizational knowledge and establishing links to concrete lifeworld experience in the case of subject matter experts and by the introduction of an organizational context relevant to all participants in the case of group interviews), the adopting of an open approach to individual interviews (as a general rule) and the sparing use of moderation in group interviews (to reveal relationship dynamics, in particular in the case of subject matter experts). By incorporating interventions into the composition of such expert interviews, organizations reveal their way of dealing with such "disruptions" or demands and thus divulge specific internal *modus operandi* and management principles that are difficult to tap into by other means.

Open interviews encourage interviewees (experts) to talk to outsiders (researchers) about their organizational lifeworld. Researchers define themselves as the "learners" in such settings, explicitly allocate the role of the expert to the interviewee(s) and later orient themselves on the information provided. For the analysis, the interview process embodies the representation strategies used in the organization, strategies which can, however, only be disclosed in an intensive analysis of the dynamics of interaction. These dynamics are more prevalent in group interviews, where expectations and established patterns of behaviour gain relevance and depict (at least in part) the communication structures found in actual organizational relationships.

In all cases, it is always useful to determine and clarify any areas that were not mentioned in the open interviews yet, given the assumed expertise, would also appear to play a role. Subsequent interviews can then focus on such aspects and explore such open issues in greater depth. However, in particular in the case of interviews with experts with subject matter know-how, priority should not be given to the use of guided interviews (thereby pushing the content dimension to the fore): the actual expertise in question is not reflective knowledge but rather practical know-how which can only be explicated to a limited extent. A further risk with guided interviews (in particular in combination with an assessment of the manifest content) is that the information provided will offer a retrospective, rationalized view of organizational phenomena which bears no relation to the interviewee's relevance system and provides only limited insight into the social dynamics of the field of research.

Differences can also be determined with regard to interpretation: the analysis of interviews with external experts focuses primarily on manifest content (confirming the need to cover as many areas of reference and factors of influences as possible), while with subject matter experts it centres on latent meaning content. The expertise attributed to experts with organizational know-how can be seen as a particularly good expression of organizational sensemaking processes.

Since hermeneutic and reconstructive interpretation methods are susceptible to subsumptive interpretation, *quality assurance* strategies that fit both the requirements of the interpretation framework and the actual interpretation method are also required (cf. Lueger, 2001).

- *Interpretation framework requirements*: to avoid researcher know-how affecting results, it is a good idea to keep the interpretation and survey processes separate; team-based interpretation offers a good way of raising the level of the argumentation and wealth of possible readings; the interpretation should not be subject to time or results constraints to give it depth and avoid premature conclusions.
- *Interpretation method*: appropriate strategies here include deconstruction to avoid any premature use of available knowledge, sequential analysis to explicate the generative structure of meaning, comparative constitution of meaning to contrast alternative assumptions, an emphasis on verifying the analytical viability of the interpretation as well as a careful examination of any anomalies.

10.3 Expert interviews and organisational analysis in practice: a case study

The following section demonstrates the practical use of expert interviews in interpretive organizational analysis. The actual case study described (cf. Lueger, 1997) sits at the crossroads between autonomous and contracted research and was deliberately chosen for its ability to illustrate the appropriateness of a research-based approach in interpretive organizational research. The case study is described in accordance with the key research phases applied in expert interviews.

10.3.1 Negotiation of research framework

The knowledge interests behind the study were both theoretical and practical. Firstly, and from a research perspective, it sought to examine the basic theoretical question of the conditions and possibilities of social order in organizations in the context of alternative ways of seeing and doing things. Consequently, it aimed to analyse communication relationships, examine the specific social constructions of reality in an organizational context and study the communication control mechanisms, which create, maintain or change social order in an organization.

During the search for a suitable target (that is organization), meetings were held with the Director of a major manufacturing company with his own very specific interest: his company was – as he saw it – struggling with management-workforce communication problems. The workforce no longer trusted its management, and this situation had led to severe difficulties in communication as well as conflicts and friction. Any attempts to organize information in a better manner and provide more information had only served to aggravate the situation and make the relationship between the management and the workforce even worse. At that time, the company was planning to develop a new communication strategy that would be acceptable to the workforce and could be used to provide information that would be accepted and considered reliable.

This immediately opened up one of the basic problems of interpretive organizational research: accepting the Director's viewpoint would, in turn, mean (a) accepting the problem as defined by management, (b) assuming the "communication problem" to be purely technical, and (c) condoning the proposed solution (an improved communication strategy). This is an unproductive approach from a social sciences perspective because it focuses entirely on external expertise and reveals nothing about the relevance of the "communication problem," the views of the workforce, the reasons why the problem emerged in the first place or indeed why it continued to be a problem. This would be tantamount to a one-sided instrumentalisation of the research by the management (as the client contracting the research). Such an approach would also be of limited benefit to the company as a whole as it contributes nothing towards a long-term understanding or resolution of the already identified problem.

It thus became clear that a joint definition of the commissioned research was required – one which redefined the starting point for the "problem" and granted the research team sufficient leeway to study all aspects of the phenomenon. The joint definition that was subsequently agreed upon redefined the problem in accordance with the interests of both sides (research and organization): the project would seek to uncover the *organizational dynamics behind the actual specifics of internal communication*. In this way, the research was relieved of the political function of delivering and legitimizing a particular solution to a predefined problem. It would "simply" seek to understand why the problem was indeed a problem, who actually saw it as a problem, where the possible causes lay and, thus, identify potential starting points for resolving the situation properly.

Consequently, the study had to have access to those people with knowledge of the subject matter in hand. To do so, the researchers had to be able to interview all members of staff (with their prior agreement) without intervention on the part of management in the way the interviews were organized. From a research perspective, all members of staff are considered equal interview partners regardless of their hierarchical position in the organization and differ only in their specific area(s) of expertise.

Interpretive social research assumes the research results to be dependent not only on the analysed object, but also on the approach taken by the research (cf. Lueger, 2001, p. 272ff.). The positioning of the research in the organization is a particularly delicate point, because it influences the way people see the researchers (for example as emissaries of the Board) and, as a result, can have lasting effects on the research work itself (for example willingness to cooperate, atmosphere in interviews). Consequently, and given the conflict situation between the management and the workforce, the following three positioning elements were used in this particular study.

- A member of the organization was sought to act as coordinator between the research team and the organization. The person chosen should fulfill three requirements: he or she should (a) occupy a position in the organization that had limited links to management (*decoupling of research from management*), (b) have at least a rough overview of the organization and relatively good contacts to as many divisions as possible (*reflective subject matter expertise*), and (c) not be involved in the current lines of conflict (*internal organizational acceptance*). The coordinator chosen acted as a central point of contact for the research team, negotiated research decisions and organized all research activities at an internal level.
- Everyone who participated in the study was given a guarantee that the information they provided would be treated in absolute *confidence* and that the results of the analysis would be based solely on organizational

structures. This guarantee of anonymity was also extended to the organization as a whole (for reasons of competition).

- To increase trust, it was also agreed that all members of staff would be informed of the results (feedback) to both prevent one-sided access and generate *transparency* about the project within the organization.

10.3.2 Selection of experts and stimulation of structuring processes

The *negotiations regarding the scope of the research* served as an *initial source of information*, because the view of the problem and ideas about possible results or problem-solving strategies provided offered important insights into internal organizational processes. These meetings centred on the relationships between the different operations around the world and the internal divisions, with a focus on the development of the company as a whole, its business activities, corporate strategies and the specific problem in hand (reflective subject matter expertise from a management perspective).

The meetings with the *coordinator* (as subject matter expert) served as the *information basis for the implementation of the project*. The first of these meetings fulfilled three functions: (1) to discuss the proposed project in detail, (2) to provide initial orientation regarding the organizational structure, internal differentiations and peculiarities, and (3) to agree on how the actual work would be carried out (selection of possible interview candidates). In the process, a number of other topics were also addressed, such as the issues to look out for and who best to contact to obtain a better understanding of the way things worked in the organization. Reflective subject matter knowledge also played a key role in subsequent meetings with the coordinator although the focus from then on lay on the relationships between the organizational units. The analysis of these meetings served to establish an initial level of understanding and paved the way for the interviews that were to follow.

Based on these analysis results, a procedure and the specific criteria (subject matter know-how and reflective expertise) for selecting participants for the individual *interview groups* were negotiated with the coordinator in line with the current status of analysis. Examples of know-how criteria included contacts in a given field or direct cooperation relationships. To activate reflective subject matter expertise, individual and group interviews were held with people who acted as points of contact either within the organization or to its relevant environments. The intention here was to incorporate internal organizational relationship structures in the make-up of the interview groups. Consequently, and to reconstruct communication relationships in the organization, interviews began with a description of how the individual participants had been chosen for that group.

Pursuant to the theoretical sampling method (Glaser and Strauss, 1967, p. 45ff.), the interviews conducted in the course of the analysis sought to activate the kind of sensitive subject matter knowledge required to provide an understanding of actual organizational dynamics. For example, in the initial research cycle, interviews were held either with members of staff in operations which had only recently joined the group (outsiders), with members of staff in established core corporate areas (company traditions), with members of staff in executive positions (to determine the mood) or with particularly exposed members of the management team (conflict positions). In accordance with the insights gained from reflection on the status of the analysis following the first interview and interpretation phase, a second research cycle was introduced in which interview groups were put together with the primary purpose of expanding the initial differentiation and validating the reliability of the views already collected. Since the interpretation had revealed the central role played by two conflicting corporate philosophies, the interview groups in this cycle all contained representatives of both corporate philosophies. They also included some members of staff who were directly affected by the conflict and others who had kept a neutral distance. As a result of the internal communication barriers between some divisions, all the interviewees had access to highly specialized know-how and reflective knowledge.

Since the analysis had uncovered two areas of context of particular relevance to understanding this case, *external expertise* was also sought: a meeting with an industry expert (to find out more about industry developments) and a meeting with a finance expert (since financial issues also played an enormous part in the conflict).

10.4   Expected results of this procedure

The above discussion underlines the central requirements placed on the carrying out and analysis of expert interviews in an interpretive research-based approach to organizational analysis. These can be summarized as follows:

- If the analysis seriously considers the requirements of interpretive social research, reliance on external expertise is completely inadequate.
- The assumption of a disproportionate distribution of knowledge forms the starting point for differentiating between different types of expertise.
- These types of expertise differ in the knowledge structures they represent with practical subject matter experience providing key input for the research.
- Specific data collection and interpretation procedures and techniques are required to gain access to the different types of expertise.
- The performance capabilities of such expert interviews only develop in the context of an appropriately organized research project.

Expert interviews can be used to address two important areas of knowledge. First and foremost, they provide communicative access to the field of research, whereby descriptions and reasons serve as an expression of the underlying selection mechanisms in the organization. In addition, in their role as subject matter experts, the members of the organization find themselves confronted with specific research settings in which they themselves have to take the initiative. By assuming at least partial responsibility for the organization of the research process, they demonstrate their specific competences as a special form of expertise.

The final remaining step is to clarify which types of knowledge can be accessed by a methodological procedure of this kind. The answer to this question is illustrated below on three levels using the case study described above:

- This study revealed that the *company's original intention* of developing an elaborate information strategy would have started out from a completely wrong point. Since the workforce no longer had any trust in company management, any initiatives automatically took place in an organizational setting which interpreted all attempts by management to improve the flow of information as negative. However, the study was able to show how the lack of trust, which formed the background to the problem had arisen and identify the events and actions that maintained and stabilized this situation (starting points for solving the problem).
- A number of important events occurred on a *scientific level*. For example, the analysis showed that the everyday practical interpretation of events in the company had gathered such a momentum of its own that the people involved could almost no longer control it. The polarization of two different views of the company that had formed in the course of its development and created two contextually different horizons of meaning meant reaching an understanding was almost impossible in some areas. That explained why entire divisions effectively blocked each other in their daily work, although they were each dedicated to contributing to the company's future success. Furthermore, the study clearly demonstrated the blocking effect of long-term success on development. In this context, important insights were gained into organizational learning, revealing a blind spot in similar studies, namely the building of defence strategies as an important protection mechanism on the part of the workforce.
- *Methodological insights* regarding the implementation of such analyses were also gained. For example, the dynamics of the research processes showed that the conditions for access in areas of conflict area changed as the study progressed. At the start of this study, they were characterized by defensive attitudes and reproduced the exclusion strategy common throughout the company. With the development of the first partly trusting relationship, this mistrust suddenly changed into great openness. Two aspects were instrumental in this change: researchers basically work across all borders in the organization and quickly come to know more

(or other things) about certain (predominantly 'cross-border') events in the company than the interviewees themselves. Agreeing to participate in an interview created pressure on the interviewees to be frank, because although they could not know what the researchers already knew or didn't know, they could at least assume that they already had access to a wealth of information.

In general, a key element in the classification of different expertise is the *variation in perspectives*: contrasting various horizons of meaning for organizational knowledge and constructing images of normality for different collectives reveals the interaction between very different strategies of action. A systematic differentiation into various areas of subject matter know-how and reflective expertise provides understanding of the dynamics of mutual coordination. Doing so requires a move away from the traditional view of expertise (and its focus on special cognitive knowledge) towards a stronger focus on perceptive competences and know-how in form of practical expertise. This requires data collection and interpretation methods designed to provide a systematic reconstruction of latent structures of meaning.

Further readings

Holstein, J. A. and Gubrium, J. F. (2003) *Inside Interviewing. New Lenses, New Concerns* (Thousand Oaks: Sage).

Kimberley, D. E. (2005) *Qualitative Organizational Research* (Grennwich: Information Age Publisher).

Riessman, C. K. (2008) *Narrative Methods für the Human Sciences* (Los Angeles: Sage).

References

Amann, K. (1994) "Guck mal, Du Experte. Wissenschaftliche Expertise unter ethnographischer Beobachtung und wissenssoziologischer Rekonstruktion" in Hitzler, R., Honer, A. and Maeder, C. (eds) *Expertenwissen. Die institutionalisierte Kompetenz zur Konstruktion von Wirklichkeit* (Opladen: Westdeutscher Verlag), pp. 32–43.

Baecker, J., Borg-Laufs, M., Duda, L. and Matthies, E. (1992) "Sozialer Konstruktivismus – eine neue Perspektive in der Psychologie" in Schmidt, S. J. (ed.) *Kognition und Gesellschaft. Der Diskurs des Radikalen Konstruktivismus 2* (Frankfurt am Main: Suhrkamp), pp. 116–45.

Berger, P. L. and Luckmann, T. (1981) *The Social Construction of Reality. A Treatise in the Sociology of Knowledge* (Harmondsworth: Penguin Books).

Bourdieu, P. (2005) *Outline of a Theory of Practice*, 19th printing (Cambridge: Cambridge University Press).

Bourdieu, P. (1995) *The Logic of Practice* (Stanford: Stanford University Press).

Deleuze, G. (1992) *Woran erkennt man den Strukturalismus?* (Berlin: Merve-Verlag).

De Sombre, S. and Mieg, H. (2005) "Professionelles Handeln aus der Perspektive einer Kognitiven Professionssoziologie" in Pfadenhauer, M. (ed.) *Professionelles Handeln* 1st edn (Wiesbaden: VS Verlag für Sozialwissenschaften), pp. 55–66.

Dreyfus, H. L. and Dreyfus, S. E. (2005) "Expertise in Real World Contexts" in *Organization Studies 26(5)*, 779–92.

Fleck, L. (1981) *Genesis and Development of a Scientific Fact* (Chicago: University of Chicago Press).

Frindte, W. (1998) *Soziale Konstruktionen. Sozialpsychologische Vorlesungen* (Opladen: Westdeutscher Verlag).

Froschauer, U. (2006) "Veränderungsdynamik in Organisationen" in Tänzler, D., Knoblauch, H. and Soeffner, H. G. (eds) *Zur Kritik der Wissensgesellschaft* (Konstanz: UVK Verlagsgesellschaft), pp. 189–215.

Froschauer, U. and Lueger, M. (2003) *Das qualitative Interview. Zur Praxis interpretativer Analyse sozialer Systeme.* (Wien: WUV-Universitätsverlag).

Froschauer, U. and Lueger, M. (2006) "Qualitative Organisationsdiagnose als Grundlage für Interventionen und als Intervention" in Frank, H. (ed.) *Corporate Entrepreneurship* (Wien: WUV), pp. 233–87.

Gergen, K. J. (1994) *Realities and Relationships: Soundings in Social Construction* (Cambrigde: Harvard University Press).

Gergen, K. J. (2000) *An Invitation to Social Construction* (London: Sage).

Glaser, B. G. and Strauss, A. L. (1967) *The Discovery of Grounded Theory* (New York: de Gruyter).

Glinka, H. -J. (1998) *Das narrative Interview. Eine Einführung für Sozialpädagogen* (Weinheim: Juventa-Verlag).

Goffman, E. (1975) *Frame Analysis: An Essay on the Organization of Experience*, 2nd printing (Cambridge: Harvard University Press).

Hitzler, R. (1994) "Wissen und Wesen des Experten. Ein Annäherungsversuch – zur Einleitung" in Hitzler, R., Honer, A. and Maeder, C. (eds) *Expertenwissen. Die institutionalisierte Kompetenz zur Konstruktion von Wirklichkeit* (Opladen: Westdeutscher Verlag), pp. 13–30.

Hitzler, R. and Honer, A. (eds) (1997) *Sozialwissenschaftliche Hermeneutik. Eine Einführung* (Opladen: Leske & Budrich).

Holstein, J. A. and Gubrium, J. F. (2003) "Active Interviewing" in Holstein, J. A. and Gubrium, J. F. (eds) *Postmodern Interviewing* (London: Sage), pp. 67–80.

Honer, A. (1994) "Die Produktion von Geduld und Vertrauen. Zur audiovisuellen Selbstdarstellung des Fortpflanzungsexperten" in Hitzler, R., Honer, A. and Maeder, C. (eds) *Expertenwissen. Die institutionalisierte Kompetenz zur Konstruktion von Wirklichkeit* (Opladen: Westdeutscher Verlag), pp. 44–61.

Hörning, K. H. (2001) *Experten des Alltags. Die Wiederentdeckung des praktischen Wissens*, 1st edn (Weilerswist: Velbrück Wissenschaft).

Knoblauch, H. (2005) *Wissenssoziologie* (Konstanz: UVK Verlagsgesellschaft).

Küsters, I. (2006) *Narrative Interviews. Grundlagen und Anwendungen*, 1st edn (Wiesbaden: VS Verlag für Sozialwissenschaften).

Luckmann, T. (2006) "Die kommunikative Konstruktion der Wirklichkeit" in Tänzler, D., Knoblauch, H and Soeffner, H. G. (eds) *Neue Perspektiven der Wissenssoziologie* (Konstanz: UVK Verlagsgesellschaft), pp. 15–26.

Lueger, M. (1997) "Unternehmenserfolg als Hindernis. Zur sozialen Logik von Entwicklungsbarrieren" in *Journal für Betriebswirtschaft 47(5)*, 248–65.

Lueger, M. (2000) *Grundlagen qualitativer Feldforschung. Methodologie – Organisierung – Materialanalyse* (Wien: WUV Universitätsverlag).

Lueger, M. (2001) *Auf den Spuren der sozialen Welt. Methodologie und Organisierung interpretativer Sozialforschung* (Frankfurt am Main: Lang).

Luhmann, N. (1982) "Sinn als Grundbegriff der Soziologie" in Habermas, J. and Luhmann, N. (eds) *Theorie der Gesellschaft oder Sozialtechnologie. Was leistet die Systemforschung?* (Frankfurt am Main: Suhrkamp), pp. 25–100.

Luhmann, N. (1995) *Social Systems* (Stanford: Stanford University Press).

Mayring, P. (2003) *Qualitative Inhaltsanalyse. Grundlagen und Techniken*, 8th edn (Weinheim: Beltz).

Meuser, M. and Nagel, U. (1991) "ExpertInneninterviews – vielfach erprobt, wenig bedacht. Ein Beitrag zur qualitativen Methodendiskussion" in Garz, D. and Kraimer, K. (eds) *Qualitativ-empirische Sozialforschung. Konzepte, Methoden, Analysen* (Opladen: Westdeutscher Verlag), pp. 441–71.

Oevermann, U. (1984) "Zur Sache. Die Bedeutung von Adornos methodologischem Selbstverständnis für die Begründung einer materialen soziologischen Strukturanalyse" in Friedeburg, L. von and Habermas, J. (eds) *Adorno-Konferenz 1983* (Frankfurt am Main: Suhrkamp), pp. 234–89.

Oevermann, U. (1993) "Die objektive Hermeneutik als unverzichtbare Größe für die Analyse von Subjektivität. Zugleich eine Kritik der Tiefenhermeneutik" in Jung, T. and Müller-Doohm, S. (eds) *Wirklichkeit" im Deutungsprozess. Verstehen und Methoden in den Kultur- und Sozialwissenschaften*, 1st edn (Frankfurt am Main: Suhrkamp), pp. 106–89.

Oevermann, U. (2001) "Die Struktur sozialer Deutungsmuster" in *sozialersinn. Zeitschrift für hermeneutische Sozialforschung 1*, 35–81.

Oevermann, U., Allert, T., Konau, E. and Krambeck, J. (1979) "Die Methodologie einer 'objektiven Hermeneutik' und ihre allgemeine forschungslogische Bedeutung in den Sozialwissenschaften" in Soeffner, H. G. (ed.) *Interpretative Verfahren in den Sozial- und Textwissenschaften* (Stuttgart: Metzler), pp. 352–434.

Polanyi, M. (1983) *The Tacit Dimension* (Gloucester: Peter Smith).

Schütz, A. (1972) *The Phenomenology of the Social World* (Evanston: Northwestern University Press).

Schütz, A. and Luckmann, T. (1973) *The Structures of the Life-World* (Evanston: Northwestern University Press).

Schütz, A. and Luckmann, T. (1984) *Strukturen der Lebenswelt*, 2nd volume (Frankfurt am Main: Suhrkamp).

Schütze, F. (1977) *Die Technik des narrativen Interviews in Interaktionsfeldstudien – dargestellt an einem Projekt zur Erforschung kommunaler Machtstrukturen* (Bielefeld: manuscript unpublished).

Weber, M. (1978) *Economy and Society: An outline of Interpretative Sociology* (Berkeley: University of California Press).

Weick, K. E. (1995) *Sensemaking in Organizations* (London: Sage).

Weick, K. E. (2003) "Enacting an Environment. The Infrastructure of Organizing" in Westwood, R. I. and Clegg, S. R. (eds) *Debating Organization: Point-Counterpoint in Organization Studies* (Malden: Blackwell), pp. 184–94.

11

Between Scientific Standards and Claims to Efficiency: Expert Interviews in Programme Evaluation

Angela Wroblewski and Andrea Leitner

In the past 20 years evaluation has been established in the German-speaking area as an integral part of social policy, particularly in connection with the development and implementation of social policy programmes. This development was strongly influenced by EU policy, specifically by the "open method of coordination" and the precept to evaluate all programmes co-financed by EU money. In most European countries this resulted in a boost to professionalization, which had already set in decades earlier in the USA[1] In the meantime, in the field of evaluation of social policy programmes a state-of-the-art has developed in the German-speaking area that does receive Anglo-American research but which simultaneously foregrounds participatory and responsive practices as antithesis to quantitatively oriented effect analysis.

Especially in this context expert interviews play an important role for generating information and validating hypotheses. This has several reasons: first, due to a lack of other data sources or for reasons of efficiency certain questions can only be answered by involving experts. Second, interviews with different players make it possible to take differing points of view and perspectives into account and to reveal possible areas of conflict. Third, access to information in the evaluation process is made easier and acceptance of the results is increased. Finally, expert interviews offer the possibility to reflect on experiences with implementation, thus contributing to the further development of programmes.

Even though practically no evaluation can make do without expert interviews, the question arises to what extent generally valid rules for their performance and analysis can be drawn up for this method (Flick, 2006, Deeke, 1995). These doubts in a "methodology" of expert interviews in the practice of programme evaluation result, among other things, from the variety of different approaches to and methods of evaluation. This variety developed due to the increased use of evaluations in the private as well as the public domain, in which expert interviews carry different respective weight. It would therefore be amiss to present one particular approach or a limited spectre of approaches as the "ideal way" in evaluation practice in general and thus for expert interviews in evaluation research. At the same time abiding by certain standards of acquiring information seems essential to put evaluations, which are usually located in the vicinity of political consulting, on a methodological basis that makes scientific practice intersubjectively verifiable and thus easier to control.

Despite the variety in approaches to evaluation, expert interviews in evaluations generally display special characteristics which are of lesser significance in other research contexts: the experts usually are also participants in the intervention to be evaluated, so-called *stakeholders*[2]; from this they have a special interest in the results of the investigation. This causes a specific interaction process in which the evaluators are often perceived as controlling bodies. This may not only lead to distortions in response behaviour – certain aspects are made out to be more positive or negative than they actually are – but may in particular compromise the willingness to provide information. On the other hand, evaluations mostly are commissioned projects, in which the clients not only (co)determine the subject matter of the evaluation content-wise by formulating the questions and the objective of the evaluation. Clients also influence the choice of method(s) through their interest in fast results and the resources that are made available for the evaluation.

Based on our experiences with evaluation studies in the areas of labour market and education[3], this paper discusses the challenges and applicability of expert interviews that result from the "stakeholder" problem and the claim to efficiency. The first part illustrates the spectre of different scientific approaches in evaluation; the approach we use, which is mostly oriented at the model of responsive evaluation, is embedded. Subsequently we show which value expert interviews have for certain evaluation steps and questions. The second part of the paper presents our approach to expert interviews and how we try to cope with the stakeholder-question.

11.1   Methodological variety in evaluation practice and significance of expert interviews

11.1.1   The development of approaches to evaluation

Evaluation research has emerged in various disciplines (Rossi and others 2004, Beywl, 1988, Shadish and others, 1991), constantly keeps developing, has adopted more or less uniform and standardized procedures depending on topics and organizational frame conditions, but is still far from a generally accepted methodology and terminology (Stufflebeam and others, 2000, Lassnigg and others, 2000). This is, among other things, due to the fact that evaluation as applied field of research has developed from a variety of scientific areas, which have all introduced "their" methods. Williams (1989) attempts to reduce this theoretical variety of conceptions on the basis of meta-theoretical analyses of the "classics" of evaluation research. He ultimately distinguishes between two dimensions:

- the *methodological dimension* alternates between qualitative and quantitative approaches with the extreme positions interpretative and descriptive versus scaled and causal.
- depending on orientation and inclusion of user or client interests the *application-oriented dimension* alternates between the extreme positions of orientation on general audience versus specific end users.

Based on these two dimensions, a map of evaluation practice may be drawn which also renders the basic developmental tendency of evaluation research visible. According to Lassnigg (1997), the approaches to evaluation by no means develop in a linear manner. Rather, he illustrates multiplication and diversification with the image of a balloon which has air blown into it and which slowly expands without the previous approaches losing in importance. For a long time the highly quantitatively-oriented experimental method, in which the use of resources and the achieved outputs are compared while the processes of the programme remain in the "blackbox."[4] This was considered the ideal approach to effect analysis. Over time, however, not only effects were of interest also questions regarding the underlying effect mechanisms and conditions became more relevant. This development led to an increasing application of qualitative methods in evaluation research. In addition, the perception increasingly spread that evaluation should support the further development of programmes. Hence, special emphasis was placed on the clients' interests and evaluation became more like political consulting.

In general, however, the "balloon effect" described above suggests to (potential) users of evaluations that the evaluation methods are arbitrary and barely comprehensible. The impression is created that it is possible to "prove anything" at will; that evaluation is primarily used to legitimize unpleasant decisions or as a substitute to appease those who are dissatisfied or to postpone decisions.[5] This, however, is where evaluation practice begins its efforts to develop uniform and binding evaluation standards. Most developed are the *Standards of the Joint Committee* in the USA, which – based on evaluation in the education sector – define terms of reference for programme evaluations (Sanders 1999) and which have also strongly influenced the development of evaluation standards in the German-speaking area.[6] These standards explicitly attempt to take the competing demands on evaluation from clients and science into account. Clients expect to be provided with evaluation results that have a useful format, meet the requirements and are on schedule and inexpensive, whereas for science adhering to criteria of scientific quality and high methodological standards are foregrounded.

The *Standards of the Joint Committee*, however, focus on practical aspects of research (applicability and preparation of the results, performance of the evaluation and propriety of the approach), whereas methodological questions are only touched upon briefly and the prevailing standards in the various disciplines referred to.[7]

One approach in evaluation that explicitly takes user and client interests into consideration, sets clear standards for evaluation and is characterized by increased application of qualitative methods is the model of "responsive evaluation" (Beywl, 1988). Beywl defines a number of central principles of responsive evaluation which show a rather close affinity to the general principles of qualitative methodology (for example Lamnek, 1995, p. 21ff). Initially the evaluators are to react flexibly to the concrete events of the object of investigation, that is to resolve preconceptions, prejudices and implicit paradigms to the extent possible (principle of stimulus reception from the field of enquiry). Neither the object of investigation itself nor its context is to be regarded as fixed or limited from the start. Either area may change in the course of the evaluation; here the problems perceived by the participants play a central role (principle of openness). Depending on the encountered conditions, flexibility and openness are also required with regard to the methods used. The object is to be approached from all angles, with several methods, ideally by different researchers and from different perspectives (triangulation[8]). Even in case of a clear preference for qualitative methods, this principle includes the use of quantitative methods.

11.1.2   Relevance of expert interviews for certain steps in the evaluation and sets of questions

Using expert interviews is not equally suitable for all evaluation models. To show the significance and function of expert interviews for specific sets of questions we first describe an evaluation scheme oriented at the model of responsive evaluation originally developed for programmes of active labour market policy (Lassnigg and others, 2000). The individual evaluation steps and related sets of questions are described in broad strokes and the relevance of expert interviews is discussed for each.

In the responsive evaluation model expert interviews play an important role. Various possibilities and approaches are utilized in order to acquire expert opinions in the evaluation: classical one-on-one interviews and repeated conversations with the same experts[9] or group discussions (possibly to supplement one-on-one interviews). In addition written methods may also be used (for example the Delphi method) or oral and written interviews combined.

In principle we distinguish between four evaluation steps: policy analysis, analysis implementation, effect analysis and cost-benefit analysis. Which steps are actually performed in a particular evaluation depends on the respective question(s) and objective(s) of the evaluation. In a comprehensive evaluation of a programme these steps build on and refer to one another.

In a *policy evaluation* the objective(s) of the programme, its labour market context and the target group's characteristics are put in relation to one another. Concretely, the main concern is to grasp the programme in its essential parameters and to subject it to a general examination of its internal consistency and its appropriateness regarding the context (economic development, labour market situation) and the target group. Usually this evaluation step is based on document analysis (planning document, funding applications, and so on). Against the background of the labour market situation, the concept is analysed in general as well as for the respective target group; for this labour market statistics are usually used. The key questions of the policy evaluation, such as for example those about the motivation, expectations and assumed effects the programme is based on, can only be answered on the basis of interviews with decision-makers and the people involved in programme development, for they are hardly ever stated explicitly in concepts or planning documents. In addition, experts are important when a programme that has been targeted at a particular group is to be assessed with regard to its appropriateness for the group's needs This especially when the programme is targeted at problematic groups about whose life situation or needs the evaluators are not sufficiently informed (for example handicapped, former addicts, homeless people or migrants).

The *implementation evaluation* focuses on the implementation and realization of the programme. Organizational aspects are taken into account, as are contents and the composition of participants. The realization of the programme is analysed against the background of the respective objective, that is feedback is given to the conception of the programme in order to be able to identify problem areas (for example difficulties with reaching the target group, acceptance problems, or regional disparities) and to develop suggestions for improvement. Methodologically the analysis is – to the extent available – based on monitoring data (information on number of participants and their characteristics, length of participation, premature dropouts and so on). Depending on the main question of the evaluation and available resources, field research (such as for example participant surveys) may also be performed. For complex programmes, for example if several institutions are involved in the implementation, the analysis of the intersection points between the players or institutions becomes a key question. The questions are the design of the points of intersection, the type of cooperation between the involved parties, information flows and possible problem areas (for example ill-defined assignment of competences, duplication of work or differing ideas about objective and implementation of the programme). In this regard personal interviews often are the only feasible way of acquiring information, since the mechanisms forming the basis of certain developments can hardly be uncovered in any other way. If it becomes apparent in the implementation evaluation, for example, that the target group could not be reached or certain subgroups among participants are underrepresented (such as for example older women or people with only compulsory schooling), the access paths to the programme should be analysed. Typically several players are involved in the selection process, such as for example the advisors of the Public Employment Service (*AMS*) branch offices, who suggest a programme to the unemployed, the realizing institutions, which select particular participants, and finally the unemployed themselves, who decide whether or not they consider participating. Each of these players has a certain range of freedom in decision-making and acts according to individual values, norms and motives, which ultimately determine specific participant selection. The interplay of these factors can only be shown through expert interviews.

Through *effect analysis* all effects caused by the programme (intended as well as unintended) are to be assessed. The analysis aims at filtering out those effects that can be traced to the intervention.[10] The methods selected for effect analysis are primarily quantitative; in recent years significant progress has been made in this respect (for example Schmid and others, 1996, Shadish and others, 2001). Apart from determining particular effects (output), however, the underlying effect mechanisms are to be analysed as well. These can usually not be measured quantitatively, but are for example based on experts' subjective assessment of macroeconomic or social changes.

Expert opinions also play a role in the *cost-benefit analysis*, which may seem surprising at first glance since this is the monetary appraisal of a programme's costs and benefits. Quantifying benefit components, however, is often connected with information problems, if for example factors such as transfer payment or administrative expense savings or cost efficiency due to reduced alcohol or drug consumption are to be included on the benefit side. In the cost-benefit analysis, assumptions about these factors are to be made and explicated, for which – in addition to experiences from other studies – expert opinions are frequently taken into account as well.

11.2   Practical aspects of preparing, conducting and analysing expert interviews

The key objective of expert interviews in the context of evaluations is to efficiently supplement the information derived from documents and data with the various perspectives of experts in order to obtain a well-rounded picture of the programme to be evaluated. At the core of the following remarks is the "classical" conversation with experts. We particularly address the characteristics resulting from the evaluation situation, especially the "stakeholder problem" and the related interaction process.

The "stakeholder problem" emerges already when selecting the interview partners, since the experts mainly come from those institutions that are substantially involved in the development or implementation of the programme. The "stakeholders" frequently associate an evaluation with controlling functions, even if the evaluation primarily is to fulfil insight-generating functions and changes or questions regarding the continuation of programmes and programmes are not directly linked to the results. The social situation at the interview can thus be regarded as an oral examination, in which arguments justifying one's behaviour are provided to and the real problems are concealed from the evaluators. Such self-portrayal and information control strategies are of course not only found in expert interviews in the context of evaluations, but also affect other forms of data collection and social interactions in general (Leitner, 1994, Steinert, 1984, Goffmann, 1967). Based on the interviewees' occupational position, however, it can be assumed that they present themselves more frequently and in front of different audiences with this topic and consider certain precautionary measures or strategies already before the interview in order to perform as well as possible in the "exam situation." Due to the co-occurrence of these two factors (evaluation situation and the specific competences of the experts), distortion effects such as refusal to answer, interviewer effects, position effects, presence effects or client effects are to be expected at higher levels than with classical interviews or expert interviews with lower interest in the results.[11]

In the following, a possible approach to expert interviews is described which has resulted from practice and being confronted with problems and which continues to be developed further. Here the specific interaction process in evaluations is explicitly taken into account, and the involved parties are specifically included in phrasing the questions and designing the enquiry. In this way response distortions are reduced. As a consequence acceptance of the evaluation increases and thus the quality of the results improves. A number of key points arising in connection with preparing, conducting and analysing expert interviews in evaluation research are addressed.

11.2.1 Preparing the interviews

Before conducting the interviews it must be clarified who is to be included as an expert and which topic areas are to be focused on in the conversations with the experts. When choosing the experts special consideration must be given to including all levels of players to the extent possible. In practice it can be difficult when choosing the interview partners to reach all relevant players (due to lack of information, but also for reasons of availability, such as for example former "key players" changing jobs, scheduling problems) or to induce the important people to participate in the evaluation. It has proven useful initially to make only a preliminary selection since additional key players, who are for example mentioned in several interviews and who were originally not known to the evaluators, may still emerge during the project.

As stated above, the experts are part of the programme in various form or functions. They are involved in conception and planning, implementa tion and realization as well as in changes to and further developments o the programme. In addition it is often helpful to confront their perspective with those of users or players from the environment of the programme (similar or complementary programmes). Expert status is therefore based or function and includes both decision-makers as well as implementers with out decision-making authority. Experts with decision-making authority are mostly selected on the basis of the position they occupy in the hierarchy of the institution involved in the programme. By contrast, for the selection of experts from the implementation level, evaluators frequently depend or additional information (which they for example receive from other expert or gather from documents).

In a further step, the intended topic areas of the interviews are estab lished on the basis of the evaluation question. In an implementation evalu ation, for example, which is to give information on the implementation o a programme, show problem areas and starting points for changes, the key topic areas will be the practical experiences gained when realizing the pro gramme, the perception of problem areas, opportunities for improvemen in the experts' view, the appraisal of individual aspects of the programme a well as the assessment of its effects.

From these topic areas a "rough guideline" (catalogue of topics) is devel oped which defines the framework for the expert interviews. The design o the guideline is based on theoretical assumptions about influencing fac tors, problem areas or effects resulting from already available informatior about the programme (for example documents, media coverage, or previ ous studies) and experiences with the evaluation of similar programmes Starting from this catalogue of topics, however, the focus of each individua conversation varies depending on the position of the experts. Interview with trainers, for example, will focus on the immediate contact to the par ticipants, whereas with Public Employment Service representatives the exe cution of the programme and the cooperation within other institution involved in the programme will be of central interest.

Individual preparation is therefore necessary for each interview. The spe cific questions for the individual topics are developed, which are orientec at the function or position of the respective experts and which take the current state of information in the project into account. In the process o the evaluation the underlying guideline is continuously revised, if individ ual topic areas turn out to be irrelevant or if no new information arises fo certain topics (that is the topic is considered "saturated").[12] Each individ ual expert interview is prepared taking the respective expert's occupationa positions into consideration by formulating hypotheses that are presentec to the experts during the interview. This facilitates thematizing and dis cussing diverging interests between the groups of players or resulting rolé conflicts without calling the expert status of the interview partners into question. Simultaneously, the interviewers demonstrate their knowledge of correlations and effects, thus strengthening their competence and position in the interview.

It is tried and tested practice not to conduct the interviews en bloc, but to distribute them over the duration of the project. At the start of the evaluation, interviews with the heads of the institutions involved prove helpful since these frequently have a good overview of the programme, its organization, content and changes that may already have been made as well as special characteristics compared to other programmes. In combination with the analysis of programme-related documents (for example concept, annual reports), this information provides a solid basis for the further evaluation steps. Since frequently several people from the participating institutions are interviewed as experts (for example in addition to senior staff also employees from the planning department), it has proven useful to conduct one interview each in the initial phase and towards the end of the project, because often additional questions appear during the duration of the project or surprising results (positive as well as negative) emerge which can be discussed with the experts. For this reason, the expert interviews should be held parallel to the other steps of the enquiry, such as for example analysing the administrative data or conducting a participant survey, in order to be able to react flexibly to the results of the respective work stages.

11.2.2 Conducting the interviews

Due to the specific interaction process in the expert interview and the evaluation situation it is frequently not easy in the interviews to persevere with the topic of the interview or gain access to experts and identify such distortions in the analysis. Vogel (1995, p. 78ff.) paraphrases the problems occurring in expert interviews with iceberg, paternalism, feedback and catharsis effects. "Iceberg effect" refers to an interview situation that is characterized by obvious mistrust or disinterest on the expert's part. "Paternalisation effects" emerge when experts attempt to take charge of the interview and challenge the interviewers' competence. The phenomenon of interviewees repeatedly attempting to reverse the question-answer situation in the interview and to obtain information from the interviewers is referred to as "feedback effects." Another situation, in which the topic of the interview can hardly be maintained is constituted by the experts using the interview as an opportunity to vent their day-to-day professional frustration and annoyance or to primarily showcase themselves ("catharsis effects"). To avoid such problems it is important to regard the interview as a social interaction that is characterized by the roles of the conversation partners and the expectations of these roles as well as a stimulus-response pattern.

A brief outline of the evaluation design (key questions and methodological approach) and the current project status provides a suitable introduction to the interview. In the process the interviewers' status is also clarified, the respective expert interview is placed in the context of the overall project, and the topics and sets of questions to be prioritized with a particular expert are defined. This approach facilitates eliminating possible objections from the interviewees – they have nothing to say to the programme or have not been involved in the programme for a long time already – in advance.[13] Simultaneously, also the distribution of roles in the interview is established and possible assumptions about it are corrected. It is attempted from the start to avoid potential iceberg effects by emphasizing the cooperative nature of the interview and underlining the significance of the expert's knowledge for the evaluation. In this context it should, as a matter of principle, also be made clear how information obtained in the interview will be handled (for example anonymity of the interview partners' statements, release of interview transcripts). This may also contribute to increasing the interviewee's willingness to cooperate since fears of undesirable consequences are reduced.

In practice the introductory phase proves essential for the success of the interview and the amount of work involved in its utilization. This pertains not only to gaining access to the interview partners by creating a pleasant environment for the conversation, but also to setting the course regarding content. Here it is important to demonstrate the interviewers' knowledge and competences by inserting quotes from key documents for example about official positions of the institution on the topic. With regard to topics such as for example gender mainstreaming, for which almost all institutions have written commitments by now – which are however heavily based on unchallenged hollow phrases – this can facilitate that the time of the interview is not devoted to clarifying "official" definitions, but that the contents of specific interest can be reached quickly.

The "stakeholder problem" was also apparent in conversations with trainers of training programmes, since they are in a control situation and self-presentation and information control form a part of their teaching contents and competences. In a programme to support women returning to their careers after a longer absence from work (back-to-work programme), for example, the selected participants differed significantly from the target group. This "creaming – effect" (that is selecting the best among the applicants) was linked to trainer behaviour in the programme: the trainers are assessed on the basis of achieving certain targets, especially their placement rate (Leitner and Wroblewski, 2001). In the interviews with the trainers it was nearly impossible to obtain specific information on the problem of participant selection, because the interview partners – experts in rhetoric, communication and self-presentation – were not willing to discuss this sensitive topic. Consequently, hypotheses about participant selection were introduced in the interviews, and on this basis the effects of the criteria by which the participating institutions are assessed were addressed and their usefulness discussed. In addition, further sources of information (for example administrative data, interviews with other players) were included to analyse the selection processes.

An essential aid for sticking to the point and returning to questions that have remained open in the course of the conversation is the use of the guideline to monitor the questions that have been answered. Two interviewers who cooperate can more easily avoid an "exam situation" and create a "relaxed" conversational atmosphere, for it is easier to follow the "natural" course of the conversation without constantly returning to the guideline – the second interviewer is mindful of still open questions and can introduce these into the conversation. Using two interviewers makes conducting the interviews easier because they support each other, avoid "lows" in the conversation and are able to react more quickly to unexpected information. For this it is necessary however to "distribute the roles": one interviewer primarily takes over the "question part," the other is responsible for follow-up or additional questions. The interviews are recorded on tape – with the interview partners' consent. If such a consent is refused or if important information emerges only after the tape has been switched off, which may for example be the case when evaluating a problematic programme (in the sense of conflict-laden or controversial in public or within the participating institutions), the second interviewer is also responsible for keeping a written record.

Conducting the interviews is also made significantly easier if the pertinent terminology is used. For one thing, the experts are more likely to accept the interview partners as equal conversation partners, because they have certain prior knowledge and can therefore be expected to be able to grasp also the respective relevant context. Furthermore, the interviews may thus become much shorter, since considerably fewer additional questions are necessary. Simultaneously – as is the case also in other research areas – the interviewers must take care not to accept unchallenged certain assumptions that have turned out to be relevant in similar contexts.

For the end of the interview it has proven useful to ask an open question about possibly unaddressed points that are in the expert's opinion important with regard to the programme. Thus the interview partners are given the opportunity to introduce points that are important to them (or also to vent their frustration; see "catharsis effects" above) in a rather informal context (since this is after the end of the interview).

11.2.3 Analysing the results and feedback

In the analysis of expert interviews the "stakeholder problem" must explicitly be taken into account. Besides, here the tension between the demanded adherence to scientific quality criteria and efficiency criteria becomes most obvious. How is it possible within the specified time and with scarce resources to meet the standards demanded by science? This becomes even more of a challenge as expert interviews are frequently characterized by subjective interpretation or strategic disclosure of information, but due to limited resources a more detailed textual analysis is hardly possible. Our approach – and this should have become clear from the previous chapters – consists in preparing and conducting the interviews with a clear eye to their analysis. Due to the topic-centred questions and the iterative process of developing the guideline and obtaining the information, which also includes other sources apart from the expert interviews, the process of analysis is in part anticipated already in the previous steps. Intensive preparation and well-attuned teamwork in conducting the interviews make the analysis significantly easier. The analysis will be focused on the main topics mentioned in the interviews. The transcripts of the interviews form the basis for the analysis. For resource reasons frequently only key passages are transcribed verbatim; the remaining parts of the interview are paraphrased and summarized if necessary. In practice additional parts of the interview may also turn out to be vital at a later project stage and are transcribed verbatim afterwards.

Gathering the interview partners' different opinions and positions regarding the topic or problem areas specified in the guideline is emphasized in the analysis. Here the respective interests are to be pointed out and juxtaposed. Contrasting the various positions and interests also facilitates a plausibility check of the results. All information is to be summarized, categorized and interpreted thus that ultimately the overall structure of the programme becomes graspable. Conflict-free as well as current or potential problem areas are to be taken into account. In the already mentioned evaluation of the back-to-work programme, for example, it became apparent that the involved parties were hardly aware of any conflict areas within the programme. Among other reasons, however, this is also due to the fact that the programme was implemented highly successfully, that is different ideas about the objectives and target group of the programme were not relevant. Nevertheless those were possible areas of conflict.

The most significant step in the analysis consists in disengaging from the interview level and coming to the programme level. This is achieved by juxtaposing the individual interviews against the background of further information on the programme and its context. Thus diverging interests, contradictory requirements for individual players, inefficient processes but also "best practices" can be pointed out and included in the analysis. Through this approach the expert interviews attain central significance within the evaluation project, since precise knowledge of the frame conditions as well as the processes in the programme is a prerequisite for interpreting the results.

The involved parties (stakeholder) are informed of the results either in feedback rounds, which are an integral part of responsive evaluation, or through the final presentation and reporting. In the report particular attention is paid to possible deviations of the implementation from the original conception as well as to possibilities of further developing the programme. These aspects generally obtain greater acceptance if the main stakeholders, who are in most cases also the addressees of the evaluation results, have contributed to the evaluation as experts. Through this feedback of results the experts have the possibility to see their situation in the context of the overall programme "in a new light" so to speak, which increases understanding for the situation of the other players and improves the basis for cooperation. This does not only grant greater importance to the principle of objectivity, it is also evident that expert interviews – and in particular methods which require the different players' immediate reaction to one another – have yet another function: they increase the players' self-reflection and stimulate the communication process between the different players.

11.3   Conclusions

As has been shown in this contribution, expert interviews are an important but methodologically little noticed information-gathering instrument in evaluation research, which is characterized by a specific type of social interaction resulting from the "stakeholder problem." These characteristics increase the need for methodological reflection in practice and for the further development of standards for the use of expert interviews in evaluation research.

It seems necessary, however, not only to continue to develop the methodology but also to raise the significance of expert interviews in relation to quantitative approaches. This is a matter of putting the results of quantitative and qualitative approaches side by side at equal weight and to regard them as mutual complements. Quantitative results, so-called "hard facts," are frequently emphasized in the evaluations, because they are easier to exploit politically or as effective publicity and enable comparison with other programmes. On the basis of quantitative results alone, however, the really exciting questions of evaluation, such as for example "How do these results come about?" or "How can undesirable effects be avoided?," cannot be answered. To determine connections between effects or factors influencing the results, expert interviews are a scientifically suitable method which additionally also meets the claims to efficiency demanded in commissioned research.

Notes

1. For example, in the USA the first textbooks and professional journals were published in the 1970s, the American Evaluation Association was founded in the early 1980s. In Europe a comparable professionalization process set in about 20 years

later (for example the *European Evaluation Society* was founded in 1994, th German *Evaluation Society – Deutsche Gesellschaft für Evaluation –* in 1997). Se also Steiner and others 2008.

2. According to Weiss (1983), "stakeholders" are "those whose lives are affected b the program and its evaluation" (Weiss, C. H. 1983: "The stakeholder approac to evaluation" in Bryk, A. S. (ed.) *Stakeholder-based evaluation*, San Francisco; cite from Shadish and others 1991: 179ff.).

3. For example Leitner and Wagner (2008); Leitner (2007); Wroblewski and other (2007a, b); Wroblewski and Vogtenhuber (2006); Lutz and others (2005); Leitne and Wroblewski (2001); Lassnigg and others (2000); Lassnigg and others (1999)

4. The roots of evaluation research are located in the USA in the 1960s. It primaril aimed at ascertaining the effects of governmental programmes in order to b able to assess and improve the interventions. Experimental methods are com parative group approaches in which participants in a programme are compare to an as-identical-as-possible group of non-participants in order thus to be abl to filter out the effects of participation. Ideally participants are assigned to th two groups randomly (Shadish and others 1991, 2001).

5. This problem was clearly expressed by two very well-known evaluatio researchers: "...if you advocate a particular policy reform or innovation, do nc press to have it tested" (Burtless and Haveman [1984]: Policy Lessons From Thre Labor Market Experiments, Ottawa; cited from OECD 1991: 49), or more astutel yet by Wilensky's law: "the more evaluation, the less program development, th more demonstration projects, the less follow-through" (Wilensky 1985: 9).

6. See for this the standards of the *German Evaluation Society (Gesellschaft fí Evaluation*, or DGEval; www.degeval.de) or those of the *Swiss Evaluation Societ (Schweizerische Evaluationsgesellschaft*, or SEVAL; www.seval.ch).

7. The Joint Committee (Sanders 1999) divides the total of 30 standards into fou groups (utility, feasibility, propriety, accuracy), which are called "standards c excellence" by Patton (1997, p. 15ff). Utility standards are to ensure that a evaluation is oriented at the information requirements of the designated evalu ation users. Feasibility standards are to ensure that an evaluation is performe realistically, well thought out, diplomatically and cost-consciously. Propriet standards are to ensure that an evaluation is legally and ethically proper an the rights of those included in the evaluation and/or affected by its results ar preserved. Accuracy standards are to ensure that an evaluation concerning th quality and/or the applicability of the evaluated programme generates and con veys adequate subject-specific information.

8. Method triangulation is referred to by Vogel (1995, p. 74) as "cross-examination. To us this term seems too narrow, since the concern here is not only to chec individual enquiries through other methods. Rather, an enquiry into differer aspects of the evaluation through a division of labour also seems useful.

9. Vogel (1995, p. 77) refers to expert interviews "en passant" or to experts a "sources."

10. It is customary to work with quasi-experimental approaches (comparative grou designs) to answer this question (Heckman and Smith, 1996, or Shadish an others, 2001).

11. Distortion effect overviews can be found for example in Steinert (1984) o Reinecke (1991). Systematic response distortions, such as socially desirabl response behaviour or agreement tendencies, which have comparatively lowe significance in expert interviews, were analysed for example by Reinecke (1991 or Esser (1986).

12. Voelzkow (1995) refers to interviews that are based on a similar approach as "iterative expert interviews."
13. These objections may arise if evaluation is primarily understood as the gathering and analysis of the effects of a programme, that is if a wide-spread but nevertheless too narrow notion of evaluation is used.

Further readings

Gubrium, J. and Holstein J. (eds) (2002) *Handbook of Interview Research: Context and Methodology* (Thousand Oaks, CA: Sage Publications).
Patton, M. Q. (2002) *Qualitative Research & Evaluation Methods*, 3rd edn (Thousand Oaks, CA: Sage Publications).
Yin, R. K. (2003) *Case Study Research. Design and Methods*, 3rd edn (Thousand Oaks, CA: Sage Publications).

References

Beywl, W. (1988) *Zur Weiterentwicklung der Evaluationsmethodologie. Grundlegung, Konzeption und Anwendung eines Modells der responsiven Evaluation* (Frankfurt am Main, Bern and New York: Verlag Peter Lang).
Brinkmann, C., Deeke, A. and Völkel, B. (eds) (1995) "ExpertInneninterviews in der Arbeitsmarktforschung" in *Beiträge zur Arbeitsmarkt- und Berufsforschung 191* (Nürnberg: Institut für Arbeitsmarkt- und Berufsforschung).
Deeke, A. (1995) "Experteninterviews – ein methodologisches und forschungspraktisches Problem" in Brinkmann, C., Deeke, A. and Völkel, B. (eds) *Experteninterviews in der Arbeitsmarktforschung. Diskussionsbeiträge zu methodischen Fragen und praktischen Erfahrungen. Beiträge zur Arbeitsmarkt- und Berufsforschung Nr. 191* (Nürnberg: Bundesanstalt für Arbeit), pp. 7–22.
Esser, H. (1986) "Können Befragte lügen? Zum Konzept des 'wahren Wertes' im Rahmen der handlungstheoretischen Erklärung von Situationseinflüssen bei der Befragung" in *Kölner Zeitschrift für Soziologie und Sozialpsychologie 38/2*, 314–36.
Flick, U. (2006) "Interviews in der qualitativen Evaluationsforschung" in Flick, U. (ed.) *Qualitative Evaluationsforschung. Konzepte, Methoden, Umsetzungen* (Reinbek bei Hamburg: Rowohlt Taschenbuch Verlag), pp. 214–32.
Goffman, E. (1967) *Interaction Ritual* (Chicago: Aldine Publishing Company).
Heckman, J. J. and Smith, J. A. (1996) "Experimental and Nonexperimental Evaluation" in Schmid, G., O'Reilly, J. and Schömann, K. (eds) *International Handbook of Labour Market Policy and Evaluation* (Cheltenham: Edward Elgar), pp. 37–88.
Lamnek, S. (1995) *Qualitative Sozialforschung, Bd. 1: Methodologie*, 3rd edn (Weinheim: Beltz).
Lassnigg, L. (1997) "Evaluation: Aufdecken, Zudecken, oder was sonst..." in Zilian, H. G. and Flecker, J. (eds) *Pathologien und Paradoxien der Arbeitswelt* (Vienna: Forum Sozialforschung), 227–62.
Lassnigg, L., Leitner, A., Steiner, P. M. and Wroblewski, A. (1999) *Unterstützung beim Wiedereinstieg, Möglichkeiten und Wirkungen frauenspezifischer Maßnahmen* (Vienna: AMS Österreich).
Lassnigg, L., Leitner, A., Unger, M. and Wroblewski, A. (2000) *Zukunftsmodell Qualifizierungsverbund – Evaluierung des Qualifizierungsverbundes Triestingtal* (Vienna: AMS Österreich).

Lassnigg, L., Leitner, A., Wroblewski, A., Steiner, M., Steiner, P. M., Mayer, K., Schmid, G. and Schömann, K. (2000) *Evaluationsschema für Maßnahmen der aktiven Arbeitsmarktpolitik in Wien* (Vienna: Institute for Advanced Studies).

Leitner, A. (1994) "Rationalität im Alltagshandeln. Über den Erklärungswert der Rational Choice-Theorie für systematische Antwortverzerrungen im Interview" in *Sociological Series No. 5* (Vienna: Institute for Advanced Studies).

Leitner, A. (2007) *Frauenförderung im Wandel. Gender Mainstreaming in der österreichischen Arbeitsmarktpolitik* (Frankfurt am Main: Campus Verlag).

Leitner, A. and Wagner, E. (2008) *Evaluation der Implacementstiftung Pflegeberufe* (Vienna: Institute for Advanced Studies).

Leitner, A. and Wroblewski, A. (2001) *Aktive Arbeitsmarktpolitik im Brennpunkt V: Chancen für Wiedereinsteigerinnen mit längeren Berufsunterbrechungen* (Vienna: AMS Österreich).

Lutz, H., Mahringer, H. and Pöschl, A. (2005) *Evaluierung Europäischer Sozialfonds 2000–2006. Ziel 3. Österreich* (Vienna: WIFO).

OECD (1991) *Evaluating Labour Market and Social Programmes: The State of a Complex Art* (Paris: OECD).

Patton, M. Q. (1997) *Utilization-Focused Evaluation*, 3rd edn (Thousand Oaks, London and New Delhi: SAGE Publications).

Reinecke, J. (1991) *Interviewer- und Befragtenverhalten: Theoretische Ansätze und methodische Konzepte* (Opladen: Westdeutscher Verlag).

Rossi, P. H., Freeman, H. E. and Lipsey, M. W. (2004) *Evaluation: A Systematic Approach*, 6th edn (Thousand Oaks, London and New Delhi: SAGE Publications).

Sanders, J. R. (ed.) (1999) *Handbuch der Evaluationsstandards. Die Standards des "Joint Committee on Standards for Educational Evaluation"* (Wiesbaden: Verlag für Sozialwissenschaften).

Schmid, G., O'Reilly, J. and Schömann, K. (eds) (1996) *International Handbook of Labour Market Policy and Evaluation* (Cheltenham and Brookfield: Edward Elgar Publishing Company).

Shadish, W. R., Cook, T. D. and Campbell, D. T. (2001) *Experimental and Quasi-Experimental Designs for Generalized Causal Interference* (Boston and New York: Houghton Mifflin Company).

Shadish, W. R., Cook, T. D. and Levition, L. (1991) *Foundations of Program Evaluation. Theories of Practice* (Newbury Park, London and New Delhi: SAGE Publications).

Steiner, P. M., Wroblewski, A. and Cook, T. D. (2009) "Randomized Experiments and Quasi-Experimental Designs in Educational Research" in Ryan, K. and Cousins, B. (eds) *International Handbook of Educational Evaluation* (Thousand Oaks, London and New Delhi: SAGE Publications), pp. 75–95.

Steinert, H. (1984) "Das Interview als soziale Interaktion" in Meulemann, H. and Reuband, K. H. (eds) *Soziale Realität im Interview. Empirische Analysen methodischer Probleme* (Frankfurt am Main: Campus Verlag), pp. 17–59.

Stufflebeam, D. L., Madaus, G. F. and Kellaghan, T. (2000) *Evaluation models. Viewpoints on Educational and Human Services Evaluation*, 2nd edn (Bosten, Dordrecht and London: Kluwer Academic Publishers).

Voelzkow, H. (1995) "'Iterative Experteninterviews': Forschungspraktische Erfahrungen mit einem Erhebungsinstrument" in Brinkmann, C., Deeke, A. and Völkel, B. (eds) *Experteninterviews in der Arbeitsmarktforschung. Diskussionsbeiträge zu methodischen Fragen und praktischen Erfahrungen. Beiträge zur Arbeitsmarkt- und Berufsforschung Nr. 191* (Nürnberg: Bundesanstalt für Arbeit), pp. 51–8.

Vogel, B. (1995) "'Wenn der Eisberg zu schmelzen beginnt ...' – Einige Reflexionen über den Stellenwert und die Probleme des Experteninterviews in der Praxis der empirischen Sozialforschung" in Brinkmann, C., Deeke, A. and Völkel, B. (eds) *Experteninterviews in der Arbeitsmarktforschung. Diskussionsbeiträge zu methodischen Fragen und praktischen Erfahrungen. Beiträge zur Arbeitsmarkt- und Berufsforschung Nr. 191* (Nürnberg: Bundesanstalt für Arbeit), pp. 73–84.

Wilensky, H. L. (1985) "Nothing Fails Like Success: the Evaluation-Research Industry and Labour Market Policy" in *Industrial Relations 24/1*, 1–19.

Williams, J. (1989) "A numerically developed taxonomy of evaluation theory and practice" in *Evaluation Review 13/1*, 18–31.

Wroblewski, A., Leitner, A., Gindl, M., Pellert, A. and Woitech, B. (2007) "Wirkungsanalyse frauenfördernder Maßnahmen des bm:bwk" in BMBWK (ed.) *Materialien zur Förderung von Frauen in der Wissenschaft*, 21 (Vienna: Verlag Österreich).

Wroblewski, A., Leitner, A. and Osterhaus, I. (2007) *IBEA – Integrative Berufsorientierung: Evaluation der Maßnahmen und Ergebnisse des Moduls 3* (Vienna: Karl-Kummer-Institut).

Wroblewski, A., Vogtenhuber, S. (2006) *Studienbedingungen an Wiener Universitäten* (Vienna: Austrian Chamber for Employees), http://www.equi.at/dateien/studienbedingungen.pdf, date accessed 8 June 2008.

12

The Delphi Method: Eliciting Experts' Knowledge in Technology Foresight

Georg Aichholzer

12.1 Abstract

The Delphi method is basically a highly structured group process through which experts assess issues on which knowledge is uncertain and imperfect by nature. The Expert Delphi has in the meantime acquired a fixed position as part of the technology foresight projects that are becoming of increasing importance around the world. This paper presents the methodological principles, sets out specific advantages and critical aspects and illustrates the evolution and application in the context of foresight with examples at international level. Design decisions, innovative elements and exploitation context are presented in the light of the Austrian Technology Delphi (including the problem-oriented approach, the application in the form of a "Decision Delphi," the broader definition of the expert and special measures to motivate participation). This is followed by an investigation of more recent methodological modifications: the combination with a cross-impact analysis on future European transport systems; a Finnish approach based on a balance between consensus and diversity objectives; and the use of the Expert Delphi with internet support.

12.2 The Delphi method

12.2.1 Basic features

As a rule, the Delphi method is carried out as an anonymous enquiry put to a group of experts in two, rarely more, rounds, the questionnaire for the second round feeding back the results of the first round mostly in the form of values for the median or arithmetic mean and the distribution parameters. Basic characteristics are anonymity, iteration, controlled feedback and statistical aggregation to create a group response (Rowe and Wright, 1999, p. 354). Anonymity and the feedback of the results are intended to allow a virtual debate permitting an approximation to consensus uninfluenced by distorting influences (status, group pressure, rhetoric etc). In this sense, the Delphi method is seen as an efficient and effective group process that allows many of the psychological distracting factors in conventional group discussions to be eliminated. The use of the pragmatic knowledge of experts organized by a monitor group ultimately leads to future-related statements on issues on which knowledge is only uncertain or incomplete. The method promises "to obtain the most reliable consensus of opinion of a group of experts...by a series of intensive questionnaires interspersed with controlled feedback" (Dalkey and Helmer, 1963, p. 458).

A major justification for the validity of the Delphi method derives from the "theory of errors," according to which the aggregated group responses can be expected to represent a statement that is superior to the majority of the individual experts' ones (Parentè and Anderson-Parentè, 1987, p. 140ff.). A further argument for its use in the field of technology foresight is the fundamental possibility of identifying new development tendencies and trend shifts and of making the circle of persons any size whatsoever. The latter is of importance particularly for the desired stimuli for longer term thinking, knowledge transfer and indirect coordination amongst the actors in national innovation systems.

At the same time, many aspects of the Delphi method are fundamentally regarded as problematic, such as a tendency towards conformity instead of genuine consensus, feedback at the risk of manipulation, negative responses on the basis of anonymity, formulation of suitable statements as objects of assessment, unclear criteria in the selection of participants, expert biases, low response rates in final rounds, proof of reliability and validity, time and effort required (cf. Landeta 2006, Keeney and others, 2001). Strategies for improving internal and external validity concentrate inter alia on the consideration of multiple perspectives in the research process, and attempt to increase the credibility and applicability of the results by a combination of the Delphi method with other investigations (cf. Engels and Powell Kennedy, 2007).

12.2.2 Evaluation results

The at times controversial discussion about the scientific value of the Delphi method has in the meantime led to a number of efforts to evaluate the Delphi approach. Overall, the positive aspects prevail. Although the assessment uses a wide variety of criteria, the focus is mostly on validity, reliability, accuracy of prediction and achievement of consensus.

A systematic meta-analysis conducted by Rowe and Wright (1999) in the form of the analysis of 27 papers on the evaluation of the Delphi method showed the following: overall, accuracy proved to be superior as against statistical groups and as against groups interacting normally. In comparison with other structured group methods such as the Nominal Group

Technique, however, the results were not consistently better. The phenomenon of consensus increase is to be found practically everywhere, while the precise cause remains unsolved. In conclusion, the authors argue for a shift from method comparative studies to process studies on Delphi, and an increased consideration of the phenomenon of assessment change and the role of feedback.[1]

In Germany, Michael and Sabine Häder in particular have contributed further analyses on the essential design aspects and the evaluation of the Delphi method. Their conclusion, like that of Rowe and Wright, is that the "possibilities and limits have still not been investigated satisfactorily," and that an important task is to "describe more accurately the preconditions for the successful use of the method" (Häder and Häder, 2000, p. 27ff., own translation from German), with cognitive psychological contributions being of considerable importance in the theoretical justification of the effectiveness of Delphi.

Landeta (2006) sums up his evaluation by emphasizing that despite the manifold weaknesses and points of criticism the Delphi method is superior to using expert knowledge through statistical groups and classic direct interaction groups. A growing application of this technique over decades together with an enormous extension of the subject domains is clearly evidenced by research and published articles. An important field for the use of the Delphi method is *Technology Foresight*. As one of the best-known prognostic methods, the Delphi method is particularly appreciated in this field both because of the advantages that result from its basic characteristics and thanks to the fact that it has proved its value relatively well.

12.3   Technology foresight as a field of application

12.3.1   Objectives and development trends

Technology foresight has developed into an important instrument worldwide,[2] and recently for instance was also tried in China (Rongping and others, 2008). In technology policies today, it is regarded as a "source of strategic intelligence" and a "strategic core competence" (Major and others, 2001). Foresight studies aim at a methodologically controlled assessment of scientific and technical development trends promising high benefits for society. A common definition characterises foresight as a "systematic attempt to look into the long-term future of science, technology, economy and society"...with the aim "to identify the areas of strategic research and the emergence of generic technologies likely to yield the greatest economic and social benefits" (Irvine and Martin, 1984).

Foresight is thus the attempt to apply suitable methods to use the knowledge of experts to reduce uncertainty and as it were to rationalize the future, although still loaded with tensions and certain restrictions (Rappert, 1999)

At the same time, foresight projects are also attributed an important function in communication and mediation between social interests.[3] Martin and Johnson (1999) emphasize above all the role of the networking of activities in different social subsystems and see this as a central contribution to strengthening the national innovation systems.

Since the 1990s, there has been a huge growth in foresight activities and national foresight programmes (cf. Grupp and Linstone, 1999, Blind and others 1999, Cagnin and others, 2008). The more recent generation of technology foresight distinguishes itself from the term forecasting, not regarding itself as a deterministic prognosis but rather emphasizing the probability character of its statements, attempting to take account of the interdependence of technological and social factors and seeing its function not restricted to mere content-related *results*. At least equally important is the foresight *process* by which the central elements of the *"five Cs"* – "communication, concentration on the longer term, co-ordination, consensus and commitment" (Martin, 1995, p. 144) all have an effect above all in promoting networking, coordination and implementation. In this way, the focus is on the communication processes, the consultative components and the feedback to technology policy actors as elements of the desired self-learning system.

Over the last 15 years, a considerable differentiation of the field in both conceptual and thematic respects can be observed, as reflected in the variety of alternatives such as "Adaptive Foresight" (Eriksson and Weber, 2008), "Regulatory Foresight" (Blind, 2008), or "Sustainability Foresight" (Truffer and others, 2008).

12.3.2 The role of Delphi

All foresight activities rely on the estimates of experts. In the light of the open definition of the term expert, a variety of degrees of factual knowledge is mostly distinguished, operationalized correspondingly in various grades and investigated empirically. The methodological approaches to obtaining informative statements about long-term technology trends and the opportunities they can be expected to offer as a result at national level vary. The most important methods include Delphi surveys, scenario analyses, committees of experts, trend analyses, relevance tree analyses and morphological approaches (Johnston, 2001, p. 718). Mention should also be made of lists of critical technologies and workshops. Frequent application is made firstly of mostly broadly designed Delphi surveys amongst experts and secondly analyses by expert committees. More recent studies combine elements of both approaches or apply Delphi together with other methods such as Cross Impact Analysis (Scapolo and Miles, 2006) or Technology Roadmapping (Kanama and others, 2008). Other attempts such as using the potential of social online networks for the fundamental objectives of foresight – the opening up of creativity, expertise and collective intelligence – are still at a rather explorative stage (Cachia and others, 2007).

In a number of applied studies in the field of technology foresight, Delphi methods have hitherto achieved an acceptable accuracy level in the assessment of technological developments (Grupp, 1995, p. 53, Ono and Wedemeyer, 1994). Delphi appears to be particularly appropriate as a result of the fact that the variety of important factors and corresponding knowledge requirements (technical, commercial, political, social and so on) in this field can only be partially covered by individual experts and the latter therefore profit from the simulated reciprocal communication. The field of application of technology foresight itself is moreover, irrespective of the methods used and despite the observable advances, not free from criticism: objections are raised inter alia to a fixation on the supply of technologies, the continued influence of technological determinism and the ignoring of progress in more recent social science technology research (Knie, 1997, p. 227). Other objections concern the questionable transfer of the approach and issues of Japanese technology foresight, the domination of the centralized instead of decentralized determination of the points of focus and the technical "expertocracy" that results, as well as the neglect of steps to ensure a greater focus on demand and needs (Tichy, 1997, p. 198f.). Accordingly, attempts are continually being made to achieve methodological and conceptual adaptations and improvements.

The following intends to show the design and implementation of an Expert Delphi in the light of an example. Technology Delphi Austria represents an innovative autonomous alternative form of technology foresight that attempts to take account of more recent progress in theory and to combine the need situation specific to the country with political relevance.

12.4　Technology Delphi Austria: an application example

12.4.1　Objectives and project design

Technology Delphi Austria was a central element of the first technology foresight project carried out at national level in Austria. The main objective was to explore global technology trends with regard to relevance and opportunities for Austria and to determine niches with future potentials. This meant identifying innovation opportunities through which Austria could achieve topic leadership in the long-run, meet with economic demand and respond to the need to solve societal problems. At the same time the foresight process should stimulate the actors of and those affected by innovation projects to deal with different future developments the realization of which would be essentially shaped by their own decisions. This should contribute to the self organization of the national innovation system. Hence it was imperative to develop an approach tailored to Austria's situation which concentrated on some key areas, taking account of demand side aspects, including a parallel exploration of societal trends and providing a decided bottom-up generated, implementation-relevant input to a more long-term oriented technology policy.

The Institute of Technology Assessment (ITA) of the Austrian Academy of Sciences was entrusted with the execution of the Technology Delphi and developed a foresight design with some innovative elements. These were in particular a decided problem-, demand- and implementation-oriented approach, a conception as "decision Delphi," an emphasis on bottom-up generated input and the combination with a Society and Culture Delphi. The approach also included a combination of methods and, being a pilot project for Austria, it deliberately concentrated on a number of selected areas. Thus the Technology Delphi consisted of a whole set of Delphi projects in seven subject fields involving a broad range of experts. The Delphi method was employed as a form of interviewing these experts in a basic round and two main rounds: the basic round consisted of expert panels of two dozen persons at most per subject area, whereas the two main rounds comprised a considerably larger circle of experts of up to 300 participants per subject area.[4] The overall organization of the expert Delphi is shown in Table 12.1.

Table 12.1 The Austrian Technology Delphi: organization, roles and tasks

Sponsor	Organizer/Monitor group	Experts
Ministry of Science and Transport commissions foresight project "Delphi Austria"	Institute of Technology Assessment (ITA)	Expert panels in seven subject fields: 1. Sustainable buildings 2. Lifelong learning 3. Medical technology/ self-help 4. Sustainable production 5. Organic food 6. Physical mobility 7. Quality defined materials
Establishment of steering committee	Project preparation: preparatory studies and basic project design (for example review of major technology Delphi studies, scenarios of global technology trends, strength/ weakness analysis of the Austrian R&D system, exploratory expert survey for identification of priorities and co-nomination of experts, citizen survey on attitudes towards technology); selection of seven subject fields; establishment and briefing of expert panels for each field; concept for Delphi surveys	

Continued

Table 12.1   Continued

Sponsor	Organizer/Monitor group	Experts
	Organization of expert panels for Delphi basic round; development of Delphi questionnaires for each subject field; organization of pre-tests	Basic round of expert Delphi: Expert panels in each subject field develop theses for subsequent Delphi main rounds
Organization of regular meetings; discussion of interim reports by ITA; co-ordination of two combined Delphi processes (Technology Delphi together with Society and Culture Delphi)	Organization of expert Delphi in two main rounds (expert data base, technical design, printing, mailing, collection of completed files) Statistical analysis for feedback in second main round	Two main rounds of expert Delphi survey among extended expert circle (in each subject field)
	Statistical analysis of final results and elaboration of draft reports	Discussion of draft reports among expert panels and comments on results in each subject field
Use of results as decision basis for (technology) policy programmes; implementation measures	Final reports with results of expert Delphi; public presentation; publication and dissemination activities	Individual follow-up activities in some expert panels

The Ministry of Science and Transport as the sponsor of Delphi Austria established a steering committee, which also cared for the integration of the overall project carried out by three independent teams, ITA being responsible for the Technology Delphi. Strictly speaking, this was not one Technology Delphi but a set of seven Delphi projects carried out in seven subject areas in parallel. (In addition, one other research team was responsible for a similar structure of Delphi projects as part of the Society and Culture Delphi). The methodological decision in favour of broadly conceived Delphi surveys was taken very early mainly for two reasons: strengthening the cooperation between business, government and science was seen as imperative and expert committees alone were considered to be less suitable because of the danger of dominance by single experts (Tichy, 1997, p. 201). The determination of subject areas deliberately aimed at a problem-oriented rather than a pure technology-oriented conception and built on a number of preparatory studies. Based on these and a set of priority criteria seven problem-oriented subject areas were finally selected for the Technology Delphi (ITA, 1998, vol 1, p. 30ff.).

12.4.2   Organization as decision Delphi

The three generic types of Delphi introduced by Rauch (1979) – *classical, policy,* and *decision Delphi* – suggested the design of the Austrian Technology Delphi towards a decision Delphi (Tichy, 2001). The classical Delphi is a means for achieving a group opinion based on anonymous, multiple-level group interaction on a principally factual basis. A precondition for allowing assessments according to the pattern of a conditional scientific prognosis is that these can essentially build on some underlying laws and regularities. A policy Delphi, in contrast, is a tool for revealing the views of lobbyists on political issues. It is a matter of ideas and concepts, and not of future data and facts or of decision mechanisms.

A *decision Delphi*, finally, is an instrument which allows the preparation and influencing of decisions and hence processes in society where developments are not governed by whatever kind of regularity or law but evolve out of countless small, decentralized and uncoordinated actions: "In a decision Delphi reality is not predicted or described; it is made. ... Decision Delphi, however, has to be seen as much more than a simple self-fulfilling prophecy. Its main social function could be to coordinate and structure the general lines of thinking in a diffuse and unexplored field of social relations, and to transfer the future development of such an area from mere accident to carefully considered decisions. ... The Delphi feedback serves as a major source of information in this process. Some elements of brainstorming are in this way taken over by Delphi" (Rauch, 1979, p. 163ff.).

Given these characteristics of the decision Delphi it seemed to be predestined for the Austrian Technology Delphi: after all this foresight project was a matter of developments which are shaped by a multitude of individual decisions by actors of the innovation system in a wide variety of segments of society. What was of key interest was the foresight *process*, particularly its contribution to facilitating coordination and consensus finding among decision-makers.

This was supported in several ways: on the one hand, through opinion forming among the respondents of the two main rounds of the expert Delphi survey (1,638 in round 1 and 1,127 in round 2), many of the participants being decision-makers at various levels. Here the main mechanism allowing for virtual exchange and individual adjustment of assessments was the feedback of group response on each innovation statement and suggested measure from round 1 in round 2 of the Delphi survey. On the other hand, exchange and coordination of views occurred through the (only partially anonymous)[5] interaction in the much smaller expert panels of the basic round (14 – 23 persons per subject area, in total 128). These panels consisted

primarily of decision-makers who not only defined the innovation state‐
ments for the Delphi questionnaires but also later on commented on the
final results and drafted recommendations. Debating the replies of the
extended group of experts on questions formulated by the smaller panel
in the basic round meant a further cause for exchange and coordination o‐
opinions. This set-up was deliberately aimed so that the experts who nor‐
mally take numerous and largely uncoordinated small decisions in their
professional roles were each confronted with the different views of their
peers. All this should help the Technology Delphi acquire a dynamic char‐
acter in the sense of a feedback loop on the decisions of the participants i‐
the expert panels and Delphi surveys and contribute "to create the future i‐
reality rather than just predicting it" (Rauch, 1979, p. 159).

12.4.3   Selection of experts

The selection of the "right" experts is regarded as one of the main meth‐
odological problems (Häder and Häder, 2000, p. 18f.). This revolves abov‐
all around the appropriate subject knowledge, motivation and influence o‐
the practical implementation of the results and the composition and size o‐
the group. Technology Delphi thus involves a twofold selection: firstly th‐
experts in the basic round who develop the content for the Delphi surve‐
carried out using standardized questionnaires in two further rounds, an‐
secondly the much larger group of experts included as respondents in thes‐
two main rounds.

The aim was to achieve a high level of *competence* for the assessment of th‐
prospects, opportunities and consequences of a wide variety of (technica‐
and organizational) innovations and at the same time to eliminate as far a‐
possible the problems of interest-related points of view and the narrowin‐
of perspectives that results from specialisation. The risk of faulty progno‐
ses resulting from "déformation professionelle" has long been identified‐
"We find a curious ahistoricity in the outlook of most scientists and tech‐
nologists, together with a tendency for inbreeding" (Linstone, 1978, p. 298)‐
There is also evidence of a tendency towards an optimism bias amongs‐
experts (Tichy, 2004).

For this reason, the Technology Delphi by no means only involved scien‐
tific and technical experts but also experts from business, the state admin‐
istration, the social and economic sciences, professional interest groups‐
social movements, NGOs, and user representatives in the broadest sense‐
The assessment of the chances of implementation and the social desirabilit‐
of individual innovation projects were also investigated and taken appro‐
priately into account in the overall assessment. It was precisely because th‐
objective of Delphi Austria was to regard subject areas under investigatio‐
more as problem fields than as purely technology fields that account wa‐
taken of correspondingly more broad-ranging competencies in the defin‐
ition of the expert group. In addition to expertise in the core technologica‐

field, the aim was to include the knowledge necessary to assess problem-solving capacities, and to explore opportunities for topic leadership as well as the institutional preconditions.

Given this objective, the circle of experts to be surveyed in every specialist field extends into a large number of different areas of competence that are applied in the individual stages of the innovation cycle – from familiarity with area-specific problems and needs through scientific and technical expertise to market-side and socio-economic know-how. The questionnaires were adjusted to the involvement of a deliberately heterogeneous skills base inter alia by allowing each question to be answered or omitted according to the degree of the individual person's subject knowledge. For the subsequent analysis, only responses with at least average subject knowledge were taken into account.

The main *selection principle* was to specifically include and take account of the *diversity* of the fields of competence of relevance for the identification, development and use or exploitation of technical and organizational innovations. This principle was operationally implemented by determining corresponding target areas or institutional contexts as the basis for the choice of experts. These were grouped into the following three basic categories:

- *scientific research* (universities and non-university research institutions, broken down according to natural science / technical and social science disciplines);
- *business* (broken down according to industry, production and services);
- *administration and federations* (public administration and research promotion institutions, interest, consumer and user representatives, and NGOs).

Persons with subject knowledge were selected for the expert survey for the seven Delphi fields in a way that as far as possible achieved a balanced distribution over the three basic categories. Within the fields, the concrete competence areas and institutions attributable to the general categories of technology/science, social science, industry, services, public administration and user representation needed to be identified: in the field of (technologies for) lifelong learning, for instance, these were in the category business (producers and service providers), further education and distance learning institutions, personnel consulting companies, persons responsible for in-company training in major enterprises, the Austrian employment service, evening schools, publishing houses, the producers of educational software, postal and telecommunications facilities, network operators and providers of internet services, computer companies, the ORF broadcasting company, educational journalists and similar units. The field-specific characteristics were identified analogously in the other categories and taken as the basis for the selection.

Table 12.2   Size of the two main Expert Delphi rounds

Field	Round 1		Round 2	
	Experts	Return rate %	Experts	Return rate %
Sustainable buildings	219	43,2	142	66,7
Lifelong learning	309	52,2	219	73,0
Medical technology / self-help	191	41,2	139	73,5
Sustainable production	313	41,6	211	70,6
Organic food	183	43,0	126	71,6
Physical mobility	300	50,3	200	69,9
Quality defined materials	123	50,0	90	75,0
Total	1638	45,7	1127	71,2

Source: ITA (1998, vol. 1), pp. 72–73.

With respect to the *optimum size* of Delphi groups, recommendations vary considerably (cf. Häder and Häder, 2000, p. 18ff.). In the opinion of Parentè and Anderson-Parentè (1987, p. 149ff.), there is in fact no fixed upper limit; however, at least ten is recommended as the lower limit, after deduction of possible dropouts. For this reason, a size suitable for group discussions was aimed at for the working groups in the (less strongly structured) basic round. In expectation of a drop-out rate of up to 50 per cent for each field, around two dozen experts were invited; the effective group size was ultimately between 14 and 23 per field. For the considerably larger circle of experts in the two main Delphi rounds, the target size was based more on the number of cases that would be sufficient for statistical analysis, the average expected return rates and the dropout rate, which depends inter alia on the degree of specialization or the heterogeneity of the area. The operational selection criteria at individual level were a number of indicators for maximum subject competence and high professional reputation such as nominations by peers, relevant management functions or a professorial chair, membership in leading bodies, receipt of subsidies and subject-related awards. The effective participation in the two main rounds of the Expert Delphi is shown in Table 12.2.

12.4.4   Development of Delphi statements and questionnaires

In the same way as the selection of the experts, the selection of meaningful and intelligible scenarios – in the foresight context the terms statements and theses are also used – are also among the key questions of a Delphi application. Both creativity and methodological experience are required. According to the recommendations by Parentè and Anderson-Parentè (1987, p. 149f.), a Delphi statement should not be longer than 20 words, should be easy to verify or specific and should not exceed a total of 25 statements for one expert group.

In the Technology Delphi, the theses describe specific innovations and their future development states. They were developed by the expert panels in the basic round. For each of the seven fields of investigation, this was done in the form of chaired workshops led by two members of the ITA team and assisted by communication via email. Following an introduction to the objectives and methods, the participants were given information material and secondary analysis results on international technology trends and familiarized with their *task*. This consisted essentially in identifying the technical and organizational innovations that are most likely to achieve Austrian topic leadership over the next 15 years in each of the seven areas. These high-opportunity innovations were to be formulated, in the form of *theses*, as a description of the development stage to be expected in 15 years, the hypothetical state being expressed as a gradation from development up to general dissemination. An *example* of such an innovation thesis from the field of medical technology and self-help for older people read for instance as follows:

> Biosensors (antibody sensors) are being developed that detect specific allergens in the surroundings (air, water) and for instance permit asthma warnings.

On the basis of the theses on innovations and measures developed by the expert working groups in the basic round, the ITA team designed a separate *questionnaire* with the following basic structure for each of the seven fields. This was posted to a much broader circle of experts for an assessment in the above-mentioned two main Delphi rounds for each field.

The following *questions* were put for each thesis:

- level of subject knowledge of the respondent,
- degree of innovation,
- importance,
- probability of implementation in Austria within the next 15 years,
- the chances of topic leadership for Austria with respect to (a) research and development, (b) organizational and social implementation and (c) commercial exploitation,
- desirability of the development.

The first four questions were assessed using a five stage *assessment scale* based on the Austrian school grading system (1 = very high or positive, 5 = very low or negative), the others concerned agreement/disagreement; multiple responses were permitted for the "chances."

In addition, a list of *measures* proposed by the experts in the basic round was checked for its ability to increase the Austrian chances of success for promising innovations. However, this was not done for each individual innovation thesis but for groups. These were concrete individual measures in the following seven categories: research-related, technological, commercial, regulatory, cooperation-related, training and further training related and society-related. A proposed measure in the technical category in the field of "lifelong learning" was for instance:

> Offering information about certification issues (requirements, certification offices, organisational process) using information and communication technology.

Measures proposed were also subjected to the five-level assessment scale. For each thesis and list of measures there was in addition a corresponding space for comments. Since the range of possibilities for innovations and support measures suggested by the experts in the basic round was not to be regarded as absolutely complete, the respondents were also asked in an open question to propose any further innovations as well as measures with which Austria might have even better chances.

Finally, the questionnaires on all the subject fields ended with a standard list of 17 statements on "megatrends" enquiring firstly about basic tendencies in the field in question and secondly the assessment of trends in social, commercial, political and ecological conditions. In this way, the innovations and developments raised in individual fields were placed in the greater context of the surrounding influences and at the same time it was possible to investigate the range of interpretation patterns, perspectives and subjective world images amongst the Delphi experts. However, this framing with assessing megatrends was only implemented in the first main round (for more details see Aichholzer, 2000, p. 81f.).

Overall, the Technology Delphi thus comprised 30 to 42 innovation theses to be assessed in each of the seven fields of investigation (hence a total of 271), as well as 10 to 24 measures theses and questions on 17 megatrends in each theme block.

12.4.5   Encouragement of the motivation to participate

Achieving the maximum participation across all the rounds of the Delphi process and in each of the thematic fields constitutes a particular challenge for a national Technology Delphi. In order to secure a sufficient number of respondents with a high subject knowledge including at the level of the individual theses (or innovations) in the light of the wide variety of special expertises required, the Delphi groups must be relatively large and in particular efforts must be made to secure a maximum return rate. Finally, there is also the problem of *motivating experts* to participate in the Delphi. In the foresight sector, a number of incentives can be identified whose application can be differentiated depending on the methods used and the stakeholder category (Salo, 2001, p. 698f.): exercising influence, using learning opportunities, developing contacts, demonstrating loyalty, receiving compensation. With the Delphi method, the main stimuli are seen to be in the learning and influence possibilities. Both were appropriately raised in the invitation to the experts, above all by emphasizing the intention of implementing the results at the highest level of technology policy, namely that of the minister.

In securing motivation, the Technology Delphi largely relied on a procedure that had been successfully carried out in postal survey research, the *Total Design Method* (TDM) introduced by Dillman (1970). The basic idea is to design each element of the survey and to coordinate the individual aspects in such a way that maximizes the quality and quantity of the responses (Hippler, 1988, p. 246). Two of the *basic principles* applied in implementation are:

- minimizing the costs of participation and the answering of the questions for the respondent, while at the same time maximizing the visible advantages;
- creating a relationship of trust between the researcher and the respondent.

Accordingly the aim was to design each stage of the survey in such a way that it satisfied these conditions as far as possible:

One essential measure was that the *design of the questionnaires* involved a reduction of the often extremely large scope in other foresight studies. While for instance the German (Cuhls and others 1998) and British Delphi studies (Loveridge and others, 1995) involved the assessment of over 100 theses according to more than a dozen criteria in a large number of areas, the scope per field of the Austrian Technology Delphi was limited to around 30 to 40 theses that were only to be assessed according to six criteria (plus a list of measures with up to two dozen items per list but which were only assessed according to one criterion, the degree of suitability).

This type of proposed measures is, as compared with the forms previously used in technology forecasting, a further innovation, characterized by a considerably larger extent of specificity, that was also intended to have a positive effect on motivation. Instead of "commercial and political measures," a typical proposed measure in the field of "environmental production and sustainability" was for instance "granting specific subsidies to small and medium-sized enterprises."

Other specific TDM recommendations implemented in the design of the questionnaires concerned the technically uniform design and structure, the ease of completion by means of a single scale (based on the Austrian school grading system), the avoidance of filters and response coding, the invitation to personal comments, an attractive graphic design, printed in brochure form and on good quality paper.

The *implementation* of the survey as a central design item of the TDM concept followed a series of special preparatory measures: a personal letter to the potential expert respondents by the director of the institute organizing the Technology Delphi (personal address in the letterhead accompanying text with the explanation of the importance, the expected benefits, reward through early receipt of the results; personal signature) official letter from the Minister for Science with a request for participation in the Delphi survey; guarantee of confidentiality through the possibility of anonymous responses; enclosed envelope for post-paid return; mid-week mailing; a polite reminder card after three weeks; telephone follow-up in the fifth week (in the second round, two waves of telephone follow-up in the fourth and fifth weeks), if necessary with a repeat mailing of the questionnaire; joint letter of thanks by the institute carrying out the study and the Ministry for Science.

This approach made a major contribution to the higher degree of acceptance and willingness to co-operate amongst the experts addressed. A number of indicators can also be cited as *criteria for quality*:

- The good response level was expressed not only in the return ratio of 46 per cent in the first and 71 per cent in the second round, which were above average for the field of a Technology Delphi.
- The high level of willingness to comment and the quality of the contents of the comments on the individual innovations and proposed measures (resulting for each field in several dozen pages of comments) is a further indication.
- The rate of item non-response, even taking into account the responses not considered for lack of sufficient subject knowledge, is relatively low at an average of less than 25 per cent (even the lowest number of valid responses, to a highly specialized innovation in the field of materials, still amounted to 33).
- The response rates across the questionnaires are relatively constant in all fields and do not show any clear decline towards the end.
- Explicit refusals, finally, only amounted to a marginal percentage of the dropout rate.

12.4.6   Feedback and analysis

If account is taken of the basic round with its lower degree of structure, its face-to-face approach and considerably smaller size, but nevertheless of central importance for the generation of the Delphi content (cf. Rowe and Wright, 1999, p. 354), the Austrian Technology Delphi was conducted in a total of three stages. The first stage, referred to as the basic round, is clearly distinguishable from the following two main rounds in terms of function and form. The Delphi survey proper with standardized questionnaires was carried out with a considerably larger number of participants in the two main rounds over a period of roughly four months. The first round was carried out in June and July, and the statistical interim analysis for the feedback for the second round was made in August, the second round extending over September into October. Together with the questionnaire for the second round, the respondents were given feedback in the form of the mean values (arithmetic mean) from the individual questions of the first round, with the result that these group responses could be taken into consideration by the experts in their second assessments. With an average return rate of 71.2 per cent and a total of 1,127 remaining participants in the second and final round, panel dropout remained very much within limits. The restriction to two rounds took account firstly of the experience that major changes to the experts' decisions are limited to the initial rounds (Rowe and Wright, 1999, p. 372), and secondly of the expectation that motivation would decline considerably with each further round.

The final results were analysed in two stages: an initial overall analysis resulted in a Technology Delphi Volume 1 (objectives, investigation approach, and overall results). In the second stage, the results were analysed in detail according to the seven investigation areas. The results, summarized in a draft report, were discussed with the experts of the basic round in the concluding workshop and then set out in Technology Delphi Volume 2. A further technology Delphi Volume 3, finally, contains the tables with statistical data in the form of frequency counts on all questions.

These results of the Technology Delphi summarized in the three report volumes (ITA 1998) took account of the variable "subject knowledge" in the following form: the analysis only included the responses of experts who stated that they had an "average," "rather high" or "very high" subject knowledge of the question concerned. Conversely, this meant that the responses by respondents who stated that their subject knowledge was only "rather small" or "very small" was excluded. This approach appeared appropriate, since it has been shown that a restriction to the highest expertise level does not necessarily lead to more valid results (Parentè and Anderson-Parentè, 1987, p. 137), while at the same time a minimum level of information about the topic in question is essential.

12.4.7 Results and implementation

The *results* of this example application are only set out briefly as illustrations here: alongside the wealth of concrete innovation opportunities (for example high-tech steels and lightweight materials or the low noise railway project), a number of broader insights can be highlighted, such as the good opportunities for Austria's topic leadership in particular in the application of high – although not always highest – technology in fields of medium technology penetration and on Austria's lead markets (for example environment technology, organic food). At the same time, deficits became apparent, such as too short innovation horizons and the ambivalent attitude to organizational innovations.

The objective of providing implementation-relevant results for technology policy at national level was achieved. This is demonstrated for instance by the *implementation measures* observable after completion of the Technology Delphi. These included systematic focus and stimulus programmes in subsidy policies such as an "Austrian Program on Technologies for Sustainable Development", with the subprograms "Building of Tomorrow," "Energy Systems of Tomorrow" and "Factory of Tomorrow."

Three results can be ascribed to the use of the Delphi method in the Austrian Technology Delphi: the experience of a social process that is of value, acts as a focus, promotes information transfer and contributes to the networking of the national innovation system, the generation of relevant results and the achievement of practical political effects.

12.5   Delphi and method innovation

The following shall first illustrate the use of the Expert Delphi as described in combination with other methods in the light of two international examples. The second part examines fundamental methodological innovations based on the internet.

12.5.1   Combinations of methods

An interesting combination of *Expert Delphi* and *Cross-Impact Analysis* (SMIC, a French acronym for interactive systems and matrices) that also includes a comparison of methods is provided by a study analysed by Scapolo and Miles (2006) about future transport systems and the role of advanced transport telematics in European cities. This project used both methods as quantitative approaches to identify the knowledge of the same expert base, namely to verify and improve the validity of the Delphi results. In particular, the SMIC method, by identifying interdependency, was intended to compensate for a weakness in the Delphi technique, namely the possibility of events that mutually amplify or exclude each other, or the generation of an "artificial" consensus. SMIC served not as an instrument to refine probability assessments but rather to clarify complex causal relationships that ultimately led to a fundamental progression of possible scenarios, thereby offering additional information to decision makers in the assessment of a problem.

The cornerstones of the study design were as follows: from a pool of 300 international experts, three subgroups were formed with the aim of having one available for the two-round Delphi, one for the SMIC method and one to reply to both instruments, and, after conclusion of the investigations, to complete an evaluation questionnaire. The assessment criteria for the individual Delphi statements focused on the extent of use of transport telematics over the next 20 years, their effects on transport volume and environment and the influence of economic, social, legal and political factors. The number of individual questions for the relatively flexible Delphi method was ultimately set as a list of 19 statements, while the SMIC approach is generally limited to a maximum of six events. A typical SMIC statement reads:

> "51–70 per cent of European medium size cities use automated systems to monitor traffic in real-time which are able to provide real-time on-board journey information, as well as congestion level and incidents warnings." (Scapolo and Miles, 2006, p. 694)

While in the first stage the probability of an event was to be assessed individually, in the second stage the task was to consider them in pairs in a matrix and to assess conditional probabilities. Further details of the operationalization of the Delphi and SMIC methods are summarized in the article together with reflections on design decisions.

The main result of a combination of methods and their evaluation is as follows: as far as concerns usefulness, the assessment is overall positive, and the experts regard the process as a valuable means of communication for the exchange of opinion, in particular the Delphi method with the informative feedback of group opinion. However, not all the respondents appreciated one of the characteristics of the Delphi method, specifically the several rounds of the survey, and regard this as a pressure towards the convergence of opinions. The failure to take account of possible interdependencies between the individual statement contents is also seen as a deficiency. The SMIC method is generally experienced as being more difficult; its main advantage, the assessment of interdependencies, is regarded as complex and time-consuming. On the other hand, its accuracy is seen as a considerable advantage. Overall, the implementation of the two methods raises many similar questions to which as yet insufficient attention has been paid and which emphasize the need for practical methodological guidelines.

The consensus pressure in the Delphi method also gave rise to a search for a complementary methodological reinforcement of the aspect of diversity. A Finnish research group developed a foresight method that combines consensual elements for the setting of priorities, networking and the development of visions with complementary elements such as controversial ideas to increase diversity and to encourage innovation. The *RPM Screening*[6] method is based on an invitation to experts to generate innovation ideas and was used in a foresight project in Finland by the Minister for Trade and Industry (Könnölä and others, 2007). In the pilot project, around 50 experts from each of five stakeholder groups (industry, government, research, trade and NGOs, technology enterprises and investors) were invited to jointly generate, revise and evaluate specific innovation ideas on three topic areas – nutrigenomics, health and social services, and services for personal experiences. This was done via internet-assisted instruments based on RPM screening in conjunction with a workshop meeting. Sixty postgraduate students on a decision analysis course were also included. The selection decision was based so as to ensure diversity in three carefully differentiated dimensions: variety, balance and difference. The RPM screening method relates above all to the analysis of the innovation ideas collected, the screening being based on the systematic linking and mathematical modelling of a consensus-based and a dissent-based approach (for further details see 8ff.). The pilot project generated 166 innovation ideas, some of which were used in the Delphi process of a regional foresight project.

12.5.2   Online and Real-Time Delphi

The first approaches using the Delphi method with computer systems and networked communication can, according to Gordon (2008, p. 160), be dated back to 1970, when Murray Turoff organized a computer conference on the basis of the ARPA network and the term *"collaborative intelligence"* was already being used in conjunction with Delphi-like methods. Efforts to use the new possibilities of the internet for a modified and more efficient Delphi technique finally led to a form that in certain respects can be regarded as method innovation, above all because the feature of consecutive/iterative survey rounds is eliminated.

This internet supported "round-free" approach developed by Theodore Gordon and Adam Pease is called *Real Time* or *RT Delphi* (Gordon and Pease 2006). "Real time" refers to the fact that the state of responses to the Delphi questions is updated and accessible online practically in real time. The RT Delphi is regarded as being particularly suitable for synchronous participation, a small number of participants and the need for rapid completion; it can, however, as a matter of principle also be used for asynchronous participation if the number of participants is larger and more time is available. If a participant joins an ongoing RT Delphi with numeric response codes, the following information is shown on the screen for each question: the average or median of the group answers so far plus any distribution parameters; the number of previous responses; a button that opens a window to show the justifications for the other participants' responses; another button that opens a window for entering the respondent's own justification for his responses; and finally a space for the respondent's own assessments on the individual questions. This alternative does not involve an explicit second round, and instead the process is restricted to one round. The organizer of the process can select the time limit and invite participants to make repeated visits. Participants can return to their current responses at any time and amend or retain them in the light of information about the other participants' responses. Anonymity and feedback are guaranteed. The type of questions can relate both to individual features of future developments and to matrix-like question formats such as for benefits matrices or cross-impact matrices. Basic alternatives of the RT Delphi are firstly its use with persons present simultaneously in a conference room setting and secondly a group of participants linked via an internet platform and distributed at random geographically. The authors also briefly present a number of available systems for an online Delphi.

The principal strengths of the RT Delphi are apparently its efficiency and suitability for standard question formats and for matrix formats, its main weakness is that it has only been subject to rudimentary trials and hence there are still outstanding questions concerning quality assurance. The use of an RT Delphi on global energy scenarios (Gordon, 2007) is regarded as having succeeded in that the number of responses it produced was comparable to that from conventional alternatives.

Further light is shed by a similar comparison between two online versions of the Delphi method (Zipfinger, 2007), one with a conventional series of rounds and an RT Delphi with a single round. This produced a lower panel dropout rate in the round-based Delphi, while the number of responses and comments was greater in the RT Delphi. Furthermore, there was a greater tendency to amend responses in the round-based Delphi, while the degree of consensus in the RT Delphi was higher. The future will show whether the author of this comparative test is right to predict that the round-based Delphi will prove to be more workable in practice.

Notes

1. See also the comments by Ayton and others (1999) addressing additional aspects and inter alia emphasizing the urgent need to include insights from social psychology and cognitive psychology.
2. For an overview, see for instance Georghiou and others (2008) or the *International Journal of Technology Management* (2001) Vol. 21, issue 7/8, Special Issue on Technology Foresight.
3. "Foresight is part of the ever-present need to establish a 'social contract' between researchers, government, and the public" (Rappert, 1999, p. 544). Similarly, Grupp and Linstone: "Foresight...(brings in) elements to moderate or negotiate between the social interest groups. Foresight results provide the code to communicate between social actors in science, technology, and society" (1999, p. 89).
4. Detailed documentation on the Technology Delphi is provided in a research report comprising three volumes (ITA 1998). On the overall design of Delphi Austria and the combination of the Technology Delphi with a Society and Culture Delphi see Aichholzer (2001).
5. Proposals for Delphi statements were developed in expert workshops moderated by ITA's team in writing on small cards without visible individual origin and partially amended via electronic communication.
6. Based on *Robust Portfolio Modelling*.

Further readings

Gupta, U. G. and Clarke, R. E. (1996) "Theory and Applications of the Delphi Technique: A Bibliography (1975–1994)" in *Technological Forecasting and Social Change 53(2)*, 185–211.

Rask, M. (2008) "Foresight – balancing between increasing variety and productiv« convergence" in *Technological Forecasting and Social Change 75(8)*, 1157–75.
Rowe, G. and Wright, G. (2001) "Expert Opinions in Forecasting: The role of th« Delphi Technique" in Armstrong, J. S. (ed.) *Principles of Forecasting: A Handbook fo Researchers and Practitioners* (Berlin, New York: Springer), pp. 125–44.

References

Aichholzer, G. (2000) "Innovative Elemente des österreichischen Technologie-Delphi in Häder, M. and Häder, S. (eds) *Die Delphi-Technik in den Sozialwissenschaften Methodische Forschungen und innovative Anwendungen* (Wiesbaden: Westdeutsche Verlag), pp. 67–93.
Aichholzer, G. (2001) "The Austrian foresight program: organization and exper profile" in *International Journal of Technology Management 21(7/8)*, 739–55.
Ayton, P., Ferrell, W. R and Stewart, T. R. (1999) Commentaries on "The Delph technique as a forecasting tool: issues ad analysis" by Rowe and Wright i» *International Journal of Forecasting 15(4)*, 377–79.
Blind, K. (2008) "Regulatory foresight: Methodologies and selected applications" i» *Technological Forecasting and Social Change 75(4)*, 496–516.
Blind, K., Cuhls, K. and Grupp, H. (1999) "Current foresight activities in Centra Europe" in *Technological Forecasting and Social Change 60(1)*, 15–35.
Cachia, R., Compañó, R. and Da Costa, O. (2007) "Grasping the potential of onlin social networks for foresight" in *Technological Forecasting and Social Change 74(8)* 1179–203.
Cagnin, C., Keenan, M., Johnston, R., Scapolo, F. and Barré, R. (eds) (2008 *Future-Oriented Technology Analysis: Strategic Intelligence for an Innovative Econom* (Berlin, Heidelberg, New York: Springer).
Cuhls, K., Blind, K. And Grupp, H. (1998) *Delphi '98 Umfrage. Studie zur globale« Entwicklung von Wissenschaft und Technik* (Karlsruhe: Fraunhofer Institut fü Systemtechnik und Innovationsforschung, unpubl).
Dalkey, N. C. and Helmer, O. (1963) "An experimental application of the Delph method to the use of experts" *in Management Science 9(3)*, 458–67.
Dillman, D. (1978) *Mail and Telephone Surveys: The Total Design Method* (New York Wiley).
Engels, T. C. E. and Powell Kennedy, H. (2007) "Enhancing a Delphi study on family focused prevention" *in Technological Forecasting and Social Change 74(4)*, 433–51.
Eriksson, E. A. and Weber, K. M. (2008) "Adaptive Foresight: Navigating the comple« landscape of policy strategies" in *Technological Forecasting and Social Change 75(4)* 462–82.
Georghiou, L., Harper, J. C., Keenan, M., Miles, I. and Popper, R. (eds) (2008) *Th« Handbook of Technology Foresight: Concepts and Practice* (Cheltenham, UK: Edwar« Elgar Publishing).
Gordon, T. J. (2007) "Energy forecasts using a 'Roundless' approach to running ä Delphi study" in *Foresight 9(2)*, 27–35.
Gordon, T. (2008) "Book Review: Sabine Zipfinger, Computer-aided Delphi: A» experimental study of comparing round-based with real-time implementatio» of the method. Johannes Kepler University, Linz, Austria (2007)" in *Technologica Forecasting and Social Change 75(1)*, 160–64.
Gordon, T. and Pease, A. (2006) "RT Delphi: An efficient, 'round-less' almost rea time Delphi method" in *Technological Forecasting and Social Change 73(4)*, 321–33.

Grupp, H. (1995) *Der Delphi-Report – Innovationen für unsere Zukunft* (Stuttgart: Deutsche Verlags-Anstalt).

Grupp, H. and Linstone, H. A. (1999) "National technology foresight activities around the globe: resurrection and new paradigms" in *Technological Forecasting and Social Change 60(1)*, 85–94.

Häder, M. and Häder, S. (2000) "Die Delphi-Methode als Gegenstand methodischer Forschungen" in Häder, M. and Häder, S. (eds) *Die Delphi-Technik in den Sozialwissenschaften. Methodische Forschungen und innovative Anwendungen* (Wiesbaden: Westdeutscher Verlag), pp. 11–31.

Hippler, H. J. (1988) "Methodische Aspekte schriftlicher Befragungen. Probleme und Forschungsperspektiven" in *planung und analyse 6*, 244–48.

Irvine, J. and Martin, B. (1984) *Foresight in Science: Picking the Winners* (London: Pinter).

ITA Institut für Technikfolgen-Abschätzung (1998) "Technologie Delphi" (3 Bände). In Bundesministerium für Wissenschaft und Verkehr (ed.) *Delphi Report Austria 1–3* (Wien: Bundesministerium für Verkehr, Innovation und Technologie).

Johnston, R. (2001) "Foresight – refining the process" in *International Journal of Technology Management 21(7/8)*, 711–25.

Kanama, D., Kondo, A. and Yokoo, Y. (2008) "Development of technology foresight: integration of technology roadmapping and the Delphi method" in *International Journal of Technology Intelligence and Planning 4(2)*, 184–200.

Keeney, S., Hasson, F. and Mc Kenna, H. P. (2001) "A critical review of the Delphi technique as a research methodology for nursing" in *International Journal of Nursing Studies 38*, 195–200.

Knie, A. (1997) "Technik als gesellschaftliche Konstruktion. Institutionen als soziale Maschinen" in Dierkes, M. (ed.) *Technikgenese* (Berlin: edition sigma), pp. 225–43.

Könnölä, T., Brummer, V. and Salo, A. (2007) "Diversity in foresight: Insights from the fostering of innovation ideas" in *Technological Forecasting and Social Change 74(5)*, 608–26.

Landeta, J. (2006) "Current validity of the Delphi method in social sciences" in *Technological Forecasting and Social Change 73(5)*, 467–82.

Linstone, H. A. (1978) "The Delphi Technique" in Fowles, J. (ed.) *Handbook of Futures Research* (Westport: Greenwood Press).

Loveridge, D., Georghiou, L. and Nedeva, M. (1995) *United Kingdom Technology Foresight Programme: Delphi Survey* (Manchester: Policy Research in Engineering, Science and Technology, PREST, The University of Manchester, unpubl.).

Major, E., Asch, D. and Cordey-Hayes, M. (2001) "Foresight as a core competence" in *Futures 33(2)*, 91–107.

Martin, B. R. (1995) "Foresight in Science and Technology" in *Technology Analysis & Strategic Management*, 7(2), 139–68.

Martin, B. and Johnston, R. (1999) "Technology foresight for wiring up the national innovation system" in *Technological Forecasting and Social Change 60(1)*, 37–54.

Ono, R. and Wedemeyer, D. J. (1994) "Assessing the validity of the Delphi Technique" in *Futures*, April, 289–304.

Parentè, F.J. and Anderson-Parentè, J.K. (1987) "Delphi inquiry systems" in Wright, G. and Ayton, P. (eds) *Judgemental forecasting* (Chichester: John Wiley), pp. 129–56.

Rappert, B. (1999) "Rationalising the future? Foresight in science and technology policy co-ordination" in *Futures 31(6)*, 527–45.

Rauch, W. (1979) "The Decision Delphi" in *Technological Forecasting and Social Change*, 15(2), 159–69.

Rongping, M., Zhongbao, R., Sida, Y. and Yan, Q. (2008) "Technology foresight towards 2020 in China: the practice and its impacts" in *Technology Analysis & Strategic Management 20(3)*, 287–307.

Rowe, G. and Wright, G. (1999) "The Delphi technique as a forecasting tool: issues and analysis" in *International Journal of Forecasting 15(4)*, 353–75.

Salo, A. A. (2001) "Incentives in technology foresight" in *International Journal of Technology Management 21(7/8)*, 694–710.

Scapolo, F. and Miles, I. (2006) "Eliciting experts' knowledge: A comparison of two methods" in *Technological Forecasting and Social Change 73(6)*, 679–704.

Tichy, G. (1997) "Technologieprognosen und Technologiepolitik" in *Wirtschaft und Gesellschaft 23(2)*, 193–209.

Tichy, G. (2001) "The decision Delphi as a tool of technology policy – the Austrian experience" in *International Journal of Technology Management 21(7/8)*, 756–66.

Tichy, G. (2004) "The over-optimism among experts in assessment and foresight" in *Technological Forecasting and Social Change 71(4)*, 341–63.

Truffer, B., Voß, J. P. and Konrad, K. (2008) "Mapping expectations for system transformations: Lessons from Sustainability Foresight in German utility sectors" in *Technological Forecasting and Social Change 75(9)*, 1360–72.

Zipfinger, S. (2007) *Computer Aided-Delphi. An Experimental Study of Comparing Round-Based with Real-Time Implementation of the Method* (Linz: Trauner).

Index